D0873273

The Politics of Pensions

Ann Shola Orloff

The Politics of Pensions

A Comparative Analysis of Britain,
Canada, and the United States,
1880–1940

The University of Wisconsin Press

The University of Wisconsin Press
114 North Murray Street
Madison, Wisconsin 53715 ,

3 Henrietta Street
London WC2E 8LU, England

Library of Congress Cataloging-in-Publication Data
Orloff, Ann Shola.
    The politics of pensions: a comparative analysis of Britain, Canada, and the United States,
    1880–1940 / Ann Shola Orloff.
    396 pp.   cm.
    Includes bibliographical references and index.
    ISBN 0-299-13220-X   ISBN 0-299-13224-2 (pbk.)
    1. Old age pensions—Great Britain—History.   2. Old age pensions—Canada—History.
3. Old age pensions—United States—History.   I. Title.
HD7105.3.075   1992
331.25'2—dc20   92-50256

Contents

Figures and Tables

Figures

Tables

Acknowledgments

In the course of working on this book, I've spent a good deal of time trying to understand the conditions under which production (of books or anything else) can take place. Certainly, social provision contributes to people's capacities to be productive. But, as feminists make clear, public social provision is only part of the story; daily, unpaid, "private" domestic and caring work are also critical to creating the conditions for production. Having read many a book acknowledgment, I'd like to do at the outset what many save only for the end—acknowledge who and what made possible my productive efforts and simultaneously ensured the care and support of my family. My daughter Joanna was five when I started writing the dissertation that eventually, after considerable addition and revision, became this book. I could not have written this book without two things. First, there is the love and support Joanna and my husband, Paul, always gave me—in the cheery little notes Jo wrote ("Mom, don't get an ulcer!"), and the countless pep talks Paul gave, and through their combined help in many other ways.

But of course there's more. While housework could wait, Paul and I, both working, needed some sort of arrangements for Joanna's care. Unfortunately, the American welfare state does not step in to provide services for the households of working parents, nor do our employers. This of course makes it difficult to combine work and parenthood for anyone who wants to take both seriously. We were fortunate when I was in graduate school. The tail end of Great Society welfare programs in the form of a Title XX child care scholarship allowed us to give Jo great, full-time day care at the University-NOW Day Nursery. Once we moved to Madison and Joanna entered grade school, we were faced with the need for after-school care. My husband, Paul, gave his time to take care of Jo so that I could work the evenings and weekends that an academic career demands. When she was little, Joanna thought I was trying get "ten-year"— that the job security my friends and I longed for and worked for would come after we'd put in ten years of work (as it did, more or less, if you count grad school). After I did get tenure, she decided as a joke to give her father a "ten-year certificate" of his own, for the approximately ten years he "put in" while I was trying to get tenure and working on the book (simultaneous tasks). Her letter says best what providing care is about: "It is called the ten-year award because that is as long as you have taken good care of me. The things you did to earn this award include: pancake-making at 7:00 A.M. almost every morning, and if not pancakes, then French toast, tuna melts, etc.; doing Mom's and my laundry; been home after school at precisely 3:00 P.M.; not been a 'watch-looker' Dad; you have always been around (so has Mom, but this is your award) when I was in the dumps. . . ." He took care of me, too. To Joanna and Paul, this book is dedicated.

Many friends and professional colleagues also helped me in various ways, and I am very happy to have the chance to offer my thanks here. (And, of course, none of them is to be held responsible for any errors and shortcomings that remain.) The members of my dissertation committee—Theda Skocpol, Bob Wuthnow and Bob Liebman—gave me excellent advice, some of which did not find its way into the thesis, but is, I hope, reflected this time around. Theda has continued to be the kind of mentor that young academics hope for, and her influence on this work will be readily apparent. At the University of Wisconsin Sociology Department, where I have spent the last seven years, a number of individuals have epitomized the senior faculty's collective commitment to helping their junior colleagues: Cora Marrett, Sara McLanahan, Hal Winsborough, Franklin Wilson, Steve Bunker (who asked me some great questions, which, when answered, improved the introduction considerably), and Chas Camic, who read the entire manuscript and made extremely helpful suggestions for revisions. Jill Quadagno, John Myles, Michael Katz, and Pat Thane all took the time to read the manuscript and offer extensive and insightful comments. I did not always take their advice, particularly on matters of theoretical emphasis, but I profited from it nonetheless. In the course of tracking down information about three countries over a long time span, I found I needed to call upon the expertise of a number of colleagues, all of whom offered it kindly: John Sutton, Ed Amenta, Bruce Carruthers, James Struthers, Brian Gratton, Carol Haber, Susan Houston, Reg Whitaker, H. V. Nelles, Bryan Palmer, Mildred Schwartz, Betty Havens, Neena Chappell, Kenneth Bryden. Bill Skocpol drew the first version of what eventually became figure 4.1. I am also indebted to a number of friends for more general discussions of the state and welfare: Julia Adams, George Steinmetz, Larry Bobo, Sara McLanahan, Irv Garfinkel, Margy Weir, Lis Clemens, John Sutton, Ed Amenta, Bruce Carruthers, Julia O'Connor, Sheila Shaver, Linda Gordon, and Jens Alber. With Eric Parker, a graduate student at Wisconsin, I have written on business, agrarian interests and social policy in North America; I am indebted to him for his help in carrying out the research and in framing the arguments. A number of graduate students at Madison engaged me in stimulating arguments about the state, class, gender and social provision: Lisa Brush, Kris Barker, Renee Monson, Leslie McCall, Mire Koikari, Karen Booth, Karen Shire, Marc Schneiberg and Lane Kenworthy. They helped to make Madison an excellent place to write this book.

Resourceful and competent research assistance was provided at variouus times by Lisa Brush, Eric Parker, Robert Biggert, Joy Maciejewski, Leslie McCall, and Heather Hartley. Extremely helpful were the librarians at the Public Archives of Canada, particularly John Smart and Gabrielle Blais, the libraries of the University of Toronto and the City of Toronto, the Wisconsin State Historical Society, and the University of Wisconsin Memorial Library, particularly the Inter-Library Loan Department. The staff at the University of Wisconsin Press, Raphael Kadushin, Carol Olsen, and, especially Barbara Hanrahan, graciously and cheerfully got the book through the various phases of production. Funding that allowed me to travel, and gave me the time to conduct research and to write, came from a series of Canadian Studies Faculty Research Grants and from a grant from the University of Wisconsin Graduate School Research Committee.

I have presented the ideas in the book in a number of forums at which I received useful feedback. Of particular help were the talk arranged by John Myles at the Carleton University Department of Sociology and meetings at the University of Toronto with Victor Marshall, Jane Synge, Robert Brym and Julia O'Connor. I also learned a tremendous amount that was relevant to this book from the discussions at the series of conferences on the "Politics of Social Policy in the United States," held at the University of Chicago with the support of Alan Pifer and Forrest Chisman. My co-editors for the volume (of the same name) that came out of those conferences, Margaret Weir and Theda Skocpol, helped me to shape my arguments about U.S. social provision.

A whole host of people offered friendship, first and foremost among them the FAPS—Nora Schaeffer, Judy Seltzer and Sara McLanahan. Also at Wisconsin, later FAP additions Cindy Truelove, Emily Kane, Karen Barkey and Laurie Edelman provided support as did Larry Bobo, Larry Wu, Denis O'Hearn, Richard Lachmann, Sam Cohn, Adam Gamoran, Jeff Gilbert, Pam Oliver, and Chas Camic. Bert Adams and Gerry Marwell provided diverting discussions of baseball. Other friends in more distant places also helped me get through the years of work on the book: Margy Weir (who shared my goal of not going down the tubes), Theda Skocpol, Lis Clemens, Ed Amenta, Bruce Carruthers, Julia Adams, George Steinmetz, John Sutton, Bob Wuthnow, Bob Liebman, Harriet Friedmann (who also put me up when I was doing research in Toronto), Nancy Fraser, Barbara Hobson, Eileen McDonagh, and Ron Aminzade.

Members of my family—my mother, Kay Orloff, my brothers Alvin and Bo, their significant others, Tony Vaguely and Tory Jenner—were all wonderful, full of the compassion and ironic understanding of life that I cherish. Gert and Morris Moskowitz were model in-laws. My father, Ed Orloff, died just as I was starting to do the research that is discussed in this book, but, as a newspaper editor who brought his love for his work home with him, he is responsible for most of what I know about writing prose and for my commitment to trying to get the facts straight.

Friends outside academia are a must surviving within it, I think. Nancy Mann regularly reminded me of New Jersey and the ironies of radical politics and culture in America. Michael Collins, Cindy Hansen, Charlotte Shimura, Jamie Kitman, and the late Jeff Slaight helped me to keep my spirits up whenever I was home; Leonard Cirino, Joe Smith, Teresa Whitehill, Isabel and Kendrick Petty put me and my family up when we needed a place to stay and talk poetry, baseball and politics in Elk, Albion, and Caspar. And I don't think I could have made it through the years of work without baseball; I especially appreciated the play of Rich Reuschel, Will Clark, Dave Henderson, Dave Stewart, Carney Lansford and Walter Weiss (all of whom display a quality of determination that I like to think authors show as well, even if we're much less well paid). Thanks also to Cafe Europa for lattes, which I sipped happily while reading over the endless revisions, to the Big Ten Pub, where I went to watch baseball and escape the endless revisions, and to Peet's Coffee, without which I couldn't have written a word (since I needed it to wake up).

Finally, I want to acknowledge the social scientists of the era this book covers. The work of men such as Isaac Rubinow and Charles Hendersen is well-known and I am not alone in admiring them; there are also lesser-known women like Mabel Nassau and Margaret Gould. I very much respect the commitment of so many of them to solving the "social question." I would like to think that this book contributes to carrying on their work.

Part 1
Introduction

1
The Problem of Old Age and Modern Social Provision

In the last years of the nineteenth century and the first years of the twentieth, social reformers, labor leaders, and political elites across Europe, North America, and the Antipodes were actively debating the "social question." This term referred to a range of issues, all of which in some way touched on the question of how increasingly well-organized and politically mobilized industrial working classes were to be integrated into the polity. A key aspect of the social question concerned the character of the provision that should be made available by the state for the relief or prevention of problems of economic insecurity and poverty. Some of these problems—such as sickness and old age—had existed before capitalist industrialization, while others—unemployment and industrial accidents—were largely its creations. But all were exacerbated by the changes that transformed families that were largely self-sufficient in rural, agricultural regions into families supported by wage earners in urban-industrial areas. Wage earning created a new form of vulnerability; when people lost their jobs, or depended economically on someone who did, their options were quite limited and unpleasant. The first line of defense for those without income from wage-work was their families. In the poorer classes of society, families were often severely impoverished themselves and unable to offer aid; moreover, especially with the great geographic mobility and high mortality rates of the period, it was not unlikely that people could reach the ends of their lives without ties to any nearby kin. This left public poor relief or private charity—given not as a right of citizenship, but as a degrading alternative to it (Marshall 1950, p. 24).

In a political context that was changing as dramatically as the economy and social structure were, the concerns of wage earning families were brought to the fore. Not surprisingly, poor relief was a policy that became increasingly out of favor as those who worked for wages developed political strength. Many Americans, Britons, and Canadians argued that pensions were a fairer alternative than poor relief or institutionalization for the aged "soldiers of labor" who had built up their societies but could work no longer. They, like others in many parts of the world, recognized that the new social and political conditions created by capitalist industrialization and urbanization had fundamentally changed the situation of the aged. Thus, in 1908 a Canadian observer of social politics, M. A. Mackenzie, noted that "public orators, with both eyes on the next election, may talk in a large way about the soldiers of the industrial army who have been crippled or worn out in the competitive strife of our civilization, and we will all agree that such a man should have some claim upon society for the support of his old age" (1908, p. 260). Indeed, Mackenzie touched on a theme which has received consistent attention in analyses of pension politics, the electoral incentive for pensions provided by the expansion of the working-class electorate in the late nineteenth and early twentieth centuries.

Political, intellectual and reform elites were preoccupied with how to respond to the political challenges of popular discontent and potential electoral advantage, as well as to the practical problems of administering public social provision. Their questions centered on whether social policies based on the principles of deterrent poor relief should be replaced (at least for some groups in the population) with contributory social insurance or noncontributory pension programs, which would offer protection against the risk of destitution faced by wage earning families due to interruption of income associated with unemployment, sickness, industrial accident, death of the family breadwinner, and old age. Men of these elite groups allied with (predominantly male) working-class organizations in a cross-class coalition, which in all three countries was the proximate force behind the introduction of pensions. Yet the emergence of a cross-class coalition was not simply the result of the growth of the working-class electorate. In their response to the social question, elites made use of and helped to stimulate momentous changes occurring in political institutions: the growth in size of the state administration, the development of state capacities to penetrate civil society, the extension of the franchise to all adults, the reorientation of political parties, and the emergence of new forms of political organization and action.

Poor relief was, indeed, replaced by social insurance and pensions. In the decades between 1900 and 1940, Canada, Great Britain, and the United States first debated, then adopted, old age pension and insurance legislation. Indeed, the period from Germany's pioneering institution of social insurance programs in the 1880s through the First World War has been called the classic introductory phase of the welfare state (Flora and Alber 1981, p. 54), as various social insurance and income maintenance programs were adopted in a wide range of industrializing capitalist nations in Europe and Latin America (Rimlinger 1971; Mesa-Lago 1978). The term *welfare state* has come to refer to the whole set of modern social programs offering income maintenance in cases of unemployment, industrial accident, illness, forced retirement, loss of a family breadwinner, or extreme economic deprivation, as well as various sorts of educational, preventive, and regulatory programs (see Flora and Heidenheimer 1981). Although scholars now routinely discuss the "origins of the welfare state" in the pre–World War I period, the term *welfare state* did not actually emerge until World War II. Prior to that time, contributory insurance and pension programs were usually called workingmen's insurance or social insurance, which meant both contributory and noncontributory programs. To avoid the anachronistic usage of the term *welfare state* for the period before World War II, when I refer to the programs in question collectively, I will use the terms *modern social provision, social benefits, modern welfare programs, or social insurance.*

This book offers an explanation of when, how, and why poor relief was replaced by modern social insurance and pensions for the elderly in Britain, Canada, and the United States and accounts for the characteristics of that modern social provision. Old age pension and insurance systems represent an especially important component of the welfare state—one well worth examining—for several reasons. First, popular pressure for new state welfare activity commonly originated in demands for provision for the dependent aged outside the traditional poor law framework, under which assistance for the poor was limited to relief in semipenal workhouses ("indoor relief") or inadequate, unpredictable cash or in-kind grants ("outdoor relief"). In fact, for most countries, income maintenance programs for the aged represented the first break with long-standing deterrent policies for dealing with the indigent (Flora and Alber 1981, pp. 51–52). Second, mass support for the new welfare programs for the aged, which were, at least initially, the most popular of the modern welfare and social insurance measures (Gilbert 1966, p. 160), often provided a crucial momentum toward other, less immediately popular programs such as unemployment and health insurance. This was indeed the case in Canada, Great Britain, and the United States. Third, old age pensions are a key aspect of what some feminist analysts call "the paternalist welfare state," that is, those sets of programs that bolster the position of wage-earning male breadwinners (see, e.g., Skocpol forthcoming). Pensions contributed to elderly men's ability to maintain independent households and alleviated the burden on working-aged men who often were called upon to support widowed aged mothers or mothers-in-law. The provisions of contributory old age insurance more directly bolstered the male breadwinner–female homemaker family through making women's benefits dependent upon their husbands' taxes. Fourth, even labor officials and organizations that focused their efforts on improving wages and viewed state social insurance with some suspicion, as did many in the labor movement in the United States, Canada, and Great Britain, considered noncontributory old. age pensions acceptable and, indeed, necessary, given the enormity of the task of saving for old age even for the best-paid wage earners (Castles 1985, pp.

86–87; Reed 1930, pp. 117; American Federation of Labor 1919, pp. 303–4). Pensions complemented rather than contradicted their vision of the gender and class orders, in which "independent" working-class men would support their families either through wage-earning activities or honorable pensions. Thus pensions were a policy around which a wide range of interests—including those often seen as liberal or voluntaristic—could rally. Finally, public provision of support for the elderly, either through pensions or insurance, has come to be the largest single social undertaking of most national governments in the West, both in the numbers of people involved and the amount of money spent (Heclo 1974, p. 13).

One might wonder about the relevance of a study of the origins and early development of public social provision while, throughout the advanced capitalist world, "welfare states" have fallen on political hard times. Politicians and scholars alike are rethinking the welfare state, yet the impact of recent restructuring and indeed whether or not this restructuring is experienced politically as a "crisis," has differed cross-nationally (Alber 1987). It has differed because the ways in which international trends affect particular systems of state social provision are shaped by historically specific institutional structures and capacities, policy legacies, intellectual, discursive, and ideological orientations, and political coalitions (see, e.g., Esping-Andersen 1985, 1990; Weir, Orloff, and Skocpol 1988; Castles 1985; Heclo 1974). Francis Castles offers a cogent justification for historical investigation in social policy research:

> Once reform initiatives are framed as policies and once historic compromises are effected among conflicting interests, what follows is a bureaucratisation and institutionalisation of social choice. This is not so much a question of the determination of such particularities as levels of spending and the specific programmes offered, but of *the basic shape of the system and its trade-off priorities*. Policy change, thereafter, tends to develop in a predetermined way, not infrequently on a growth path, but usually in such a way as not to disturb the established policy implementation modes and the balance of incorporated interests. . . . if we are to seek explanations for the adoption of divergent strategic options and policy trade-offs, we must examine the *historical evolution of policy formulation,* going back to the point where reforms were the live substance of political conflict rather than the dead routines of administrative agencies or the taken for granted orthodoxies of contemporary public opinion. (1985, p. 75, my emphases)

Certainly, if we want to understand the possibilities and constraints that face us now, we will need to examine the particular paths along which our national systems of social provision have developed.

Poor Relief or Social Insurance?

In Britain, Canada, and the United States, as across Europe and in Australia and New Zealand, a number of social policy reforms, including old age pensions, workers' compensation, mothers' pensions, and health and unemployment insurance, were proposed and enacted in the years between the turn of the century and World War II. The common impulse behind all of the innovations in public social provision was to help groups considered to be "worthy" with relief given outside the poor law and private charity, and to remove the worthy poor, especially children and the elderly, from public poor relief institutions. Poor relief was based upon two central tenets: "less eligibility," the principle that the position of any pauper (anyone receiving public poor relief) should be no better ("less eligible") than that of the poorest laborer; and the "workhouse test," the principle that no assistance should be offered to able-bodied adults outside of the semipenal workhouse, on the assumption that only the "truly" needy would accept help under such deliberately dreadful conditions. Moreover, paupers forfeited the rights of citizenship. In theory, the elderly could be aided in their own homes; this practice was called outdoor relief. In North America, and in England by the 1870s, outdoor relief would not be offered until any possible support from relatives was extracted, and recipients often might be required to pay back their doles out of any estates they might leave after their deaths. Toward the end of the nineteenth century, institutionalization within public poor relief institutions—so-called indoor relief—became more and more common for the aged poor, particularly for those who had no kin or whose relatives could not be coerced into supporting them by poor law authorities (Haber 1983; Thomson 1983, 1984a; Anderson 1977).

What was poor relief like? Many draw images from the mid-nineteenth-century descriptions in novels such as Charles Dickens' *Oliver Twist*. I offer the sketch contained in a rather ordinary speech, given in 1898 by the Honorable John Keller, the head of the New York City Department of Public Charities, to the annual meeting of the National Conference of Charities and Correction:

> The other day, going to the island [the location of the city's poorhouse], there was a sleety rain falling; and down from the city hospital came two men bearing a stretcher, on which was an old woman. The icy rain fell on her face; and they put her down on the pier, and left her lying there, exposed to the storm, while the prisoners in stripes were carrying bags of potatoes under shelter. They would have left her there till the whole cargo had been put on the boat if I had not happened to see her, and ordered her brought under cover. (Keller 1899, p. 217)

Indifference, much more than deliberate cruelty, was characteristic of poor relief everywhere, as was forced work, meager provisions, and the separation of spouses in sex-segregated wards. These harsh poor relief practices were based on the premise that the "worthy poor" were to be helped by private charities, which were expected to be more generous. Receiving aid from private charity did not entail loss of citizenship. In practice, however, private charity never had sufficient funds to meet the needs of all those deemed worthy, and like public poor relief, private charity was quite intrusive in the lives of clients (demanding support from relatives, checks of "character," and so on). Thus, many were forced to depend upon the overseers of the poor for erratic, puny doles, to be separated from spouse or family in the prisonlike workhouse, or to endure great hardships in avoiding public or private charity.

During the nineteenth century, poor relief came under attack from a number of sources. Popular sentiment had probably never been favorable to deterrent poor relief, but popular movements aimed at changing the character of public social provision gained strength—as did the weight of popular opinion—as the franchise was extended and working-class and women's organizations and other groups emerged as important political actors. Moreover, members of various elites—social scientists, social reformers, and politicians—developed new views about poor relief. Pioneering social scientific surveys and the work of some charity workers revealed that large numbers from among "worthy" groups, especially the aged, widowed mothers, and children, in fact had to rely on inadequate, demeaning poor relief and were often forced into institutions, which led to the breakup of families "for poverty alone." Others uncovered some of the societal forces that led to poverty, undermining individualist explanations and the rationale for a deterrent poor relief policy. Modern pension and insurance programs were suggested as alternatives to poor relief for those who were poor through no fault of their own.

Most older people in Canada, Great Britain, or the United States around the turn of the century did not end up in poorhouses; indeed, in none of these countries were more than ten percent of the aged population institutionalized between the 1880s and 1910s. Yet the risk of such a fate faced far larger numbers of the population, and it was in this context that the poorhouse became such a potent symbol for those who wanted to reform public social provision. Charles Henderson, professor of sociology and founder of the Terre Haute, Indiana, Charity Organization Society, wrote in 1899, "When we consider the anxiety, the terror with which the average thoughtful wage earner regards the problems of accidents, sickness, and the infirmities of old age, and when we take into account the grave social unrest which springs from the solicitude about the future, we may well give a large place in our social studies to the modern inventions for distributing the burdens of provision for the emergencies of the workman's life" (cited in Tishler 1971, p. 75).

Such a risk was politically constructed, as well as being the result of socioeconomic trends such as the rise of waged work. For example, Keller observed that the inhumane treatment of New York's wards and the dilapidated, unsafe physical plant over which he presided reflected the fact that previous administrations "seem to have thought that because the Department of Public Charities has to care for paupers, the department itself ought to be pauperized" (1899, p. 212). Keller was on a crusade to increase public appropriations for poor relief, which would reverse the cutoff of funds for public relief which had occurred about two decades earlier. Indeed, in the 1870s, under the banner of a "crusade against outrelief," charity officials and reformers across Britain, the United States, and Canada had deliberately made the administration of poor relief far harsher than it had been even as Dickens composed *Oliver Twist*. A key aspect of this policy movement was to institutionalize those elderly people who had no kin or whose families could not or would not support them. The improvement of treatment within the poor relief framework that Keller championed was also paralleled in other U.S. cities, Britain, and Canada around the turn of the century. Although these reforms of poor relief had some successes, they were ultimately inadequate to stem growing popular and elite disgust with the poor law. Indeed, we cannot understand the politics of pensions except as a reaction against the poor law policy legacy.

The most important alternative to the poor law was what was then called workingmen's insurance or social insurance, which in common usage implied noncontributory pensions as well as contributory benefit schemes. This was "a complete and connected system of insurance for workingmen . . . against all the contingencies where support from wages is lost or interrupted by any cause other than voluntary cessation of labor" (Frankel and Dawson 1910, p. 395). Social insurance was based on the idea of sharing risks embodied in commercial insurance, but social insurance by definition could not live up to the "exacting laws of actuarial science" (Rubinow 1913, p. 11). The class of workers whose need for insurance was greatest—as they faced the greatest risks and hazards—was "unable to meet the true cost of insurance conducted as a business" (Rubinow 1913, p. 10). Thus, argued social insurance advocates, the state must take on the burden of providing protection to its citizens. "Social insurance, when properly developed, is nothing if not the well-defined effort of the organized state to come to the assistance of the wage earner and furnish him something he is individually quite unable to obtain for himself," which was precisely an income to maintain an independent household, as American social scientist and reformer Isaac Max Rubinow wrote in his 1913 book, *Social Insurance* (p. 9).

Recent feminist analyses have focused on the gendered character of these early initiatives (see Pedersen 1989; Skocpol and Ritter 1991; Skocpol forthcoming; Jenson 1986; Gordon 1990; Hernes 1987; Shaver 1990). "Workingmen's insurance" was indeed aimed at bolstering the position of male breadwinners when they were unable to support their families financially due to loss of jobs or wage-earning capacities. In the late nineteenth and early twentieth centuries, across most countries in the industrializing West, alliances of overwhelmingly male working-class movements and male intellectual, political, and reform elites upheld the sexual division of labor within the family and believed that families were, and ought to be, constituted of male breadwinners with their economically dependent wives, children, and (sometimes) elderly kin. Pensions, unemployment and sickness insurance, and workmen's compensation all would go to clienteles of working-class men to allow them to maintain their position as breadwinners even when they were unable to continue wage-earning activities. Thus, some analysts have referred to these systems as "paternalist" welfare states. Meanwhile, this period was also marked by the attempts of feminists and women reformers to valorize caring work and motherhood as bases for claims to honorable citizenship benefits. Feminist scholars are rediscovering a crucial, "maternalist" strand of early welfare politics that proposed to provide state support to women in their role as mothers, through various programs of infant and maternal welfare (see Michel and Koven 1990; Skocpol forthcoming; Gordon 1990). By focusing on old age benefits, I will be concentrating on the paternalist side of social provision, although it is important to note that pensions—more so than unemployment and sickness insurance— were understood as potentially benefiting women as well as men, even if the political concerns of those who led in the campaigns to introduce them centered on the "aged veterans of labor."

Our task is to understand the significance and the causes of the policy shift from poor relief to old age pensions and insurance. Traditional and modern assistance schemes reflected quite different conceptions of the rights of citizens and of the proper role of the state in such provision. "Modern" social programs offer assistance as a right of citizenship, rather than as an alternative to it, as was the case with poor relief (Marshall 1950, p. 24). Their benefits are distributed to universally defined categories of citizens, while poor relief offered aid on the basis of the particularistic judgments of local overseers of the poor or charity organization functionaries. For elites, an important element of this policy shift was the professionalization of public provision, as they looked to build and staff agencies that were created and re-created in the course of the development of public social provision. Thus, social policy reform encompassed conflicts over administrative procedures within the state as well as over the reach of the state into civil society. The struggles over the character and control of these agencies, themselves shaped by distinctive national institutional structures and political practices, importantly shaped the politics of pensions and policy outcomes in each country. This shift in policy was certainly an epochal one which characterized the entire industrialized West. Still, there are significant cross-national differences in the timing of the shift, in the character of the programs which came to replace poor relief, and in the configuration of causal factors which combined to produce policy change. Even in countries with many structural, political, and cultural similarities such as the United States, Canada, and Britain, one sees notable policy differences.

The Sociological Significance of the Welfare State

Social benefits are consequential for the standard of living and life-chances of various social groups and as such are worthy of social scientific attention. We may also link the varying features of modern social provision to broader sociological issues of power and to changing macropolitical and social processes and structures. As Gøsta Esping-Andersen and others have pointed out, the questions which guide current debates about the welfare state are "the legacy of classical political economy" and concern the relationship between capitalism and welfare: "Can the welfare state fundamentally transform capitalist society?" (Esping-Andersen 1989, p. 11). Feminists might add, "Can social policies transform systems of male dominance?" (see Pascall 1986; Hernes 1987; Piven 1985), while other analysts might ask about the possible effects on relations based on racial, ethnic, or religious inequalities. The question might well be rephrased to be inclusive: To what extent can the state transform social structures and relations? Which groups are empowered by modern welfare programs? Whose interests are furthered by specific social policies? To address the relationships of policy, power, and interests, we need to look closely at the provisions of social programs, which set benefit levels, eligibility requirements, and so on. Another issue concerns the mutual effects of social policy developments and state-building: In what ways does modern social provision reflect and promote changes in the character and capacity of the state? Here, in addition to looking at the provisions of programs, we can examine the timing of policy innovations, as these tap the capacity of states to intervene in civil society. Finally, given the significance of modern social provision, the causal factors behind its emergence have been explored extensively. A particularly important current controversy focuses on the extent to which state officials act autonomously—independent of both dominant and popular forces.

The Welfare State, Power, and Interests

The programs that make up the modern welfare state differentially advantage and disadvantage various social groups. In addition, asking which groups are empowered by public social provision is another way of looking at the debate about the functionality of modern social provision. Old-style functionalists saw the welfare state as stabilizing society as a whole; radical functionalists assume that modern welfare provision, by promoting "accumulation" and "legitimation," is primarily a tool of dominant classes to maintain exploitative regimes.

Others operate on the premise that benefits based on citizenship rather than on market criteria have the potential to be an important resource to subordinate groups, helping to offset their weaknesses vis-à-vis dominant groups in the market, in the family, and in other social spheres. To the extent that policies address need (even if inadequately) rather than market value as the basis for allocation of resources, they are at odds with—and may even undermine— the capitalist logic of the market.[1] Similarly, social programs may offer resources to subordinate groups which give them greater leverage within other relationships based on unequal power, such as marriage (see Okin 1989). Some examples of programmatic variation may illustrate the variability of interests embodied in different schemes of social provision. Some retirement programs offer a universal benefit to all aged citizens; others, a means-tested, somewhat discretionary benefit. In addition, some programs structure entitlement so that men and women qualify simply by virtue of being a certain age, and sometimes of having a certain income level, while others base entitlement on financial contributions, thus limiting coverage to wage earners. In the latter type of program, women typically qualify for benefits based on their status as economic dependents. Finally, programs may offer coverage only to people in certain occupations, effectively excluding certain ethnic or racial groups who disproportionately work outside these jobs. In short, modern welfare programs embody the interests and demands of conflicting groups. The potential for social policies to work against markets and to offer independent resources outside of family relationships is variable, and this variability is significant. When characteristics and expenditure levels of social policies are determined by political mechanisms in a democratic polity, politics can indeed offset the effects of market and family. Thus, in all advanced capitalist democracies, questions concerning the initiation and character of such programs have assumed central political importance.

The Welfare State and the Expansion of State Capacities and Power

During the nineteenth and twentieth centuries, the development of modern social provision has been associated with three key political transformations: the expansion of state administrative and fiscal capacities, as the government assumed important functions in redistributing resources and structuring social and economic relationships; the increasing centralization of state power and activities; and the emergence of mass politics, with an expanded franchise and

1. Even the deterrent, repressive poor law embodied a "right to exist" that might not be guaranteed under a purely laissez-faire capitalist regime such as the one prescribed by political economist Thomas Malthus, who argued for the complete abolition of poor relief (Himmelfarb 1983, p. 112, chap. 4). Yet the conditions under which one has a "right to exist" are far less harsh under modern social provision than they were under the poor law.

increased popular political mobilization. Basically, we see the growing penetration of civil society by the state—an increase in the "infrastructural power" of the state, to use Michael Mann's terminology (1988)—and the growing ability of new political forces to affect the state. Poor relief reflected the characteristics of the nineteenth century society and polity: it was locally administered and financed, reflected elite political dominance, and did not require extensive administrative capacities. The initiation of modern social provision reflects changes in state administrative capacities and practices and furthers such changes. Thus, scholars are interested in the "welfare state" as a distinctive type of state and as an institutional embodiment of the new facets of twentieth-century politics. In addition to examining these general processes of change in political institutions, institutionalist analyses have begun to demonstrate how variation in the timing and character of social programs is conditioned by distinctive state-building patterns.

Modern Social Provision for the Elderly in Canada, Great Britain, and the United States

We are interested in two aspects of policy outcomes in the three countries under investigation. First, when did the countries break with poor relief approaches to the needs of the elderly and initiate modern social provision—pensions or contributory old age insurance? Second, what was the form of the programs enacted? The timing and programmatic provisions of new policies reflect the characteristic relationship in a given country between the state and markets and households and also embody principles of rights and stratification. Analysts have called this constellation of characteristics the social policy regime (see Esping-Andersen 1990; Shaver 1990).

Great Britain adopted old age pension legislation in 1908 and other major social insurance programs within a few years. A contributory pension program was added in 1925. By contrast, the United States and Canada, as is often pointed out, were "laggards" in the institution of modern welfare programs relative to the European countries and others of European origin; the majority of their social legislation was passed in the post–World War I period when other countries were already expanding upon previously established programmatic frameworks (Kudrle and Marmor 1981, pp. 81–84). Only in 1927 did Canada enact federal or provincial pension legislation. The United States did not establish a nationwide program of old age insurance until the Social Security Act of 1935, although a few states enacted very limited pension legislation beginning in the 1920s. Subnational legislation that made these national laws fully nationwide in operation was not completed until 1936 in Canada and 1938 in the United States (Bryden 1974, p. 92; Amenta and Carruthers 1988, p. 664). Table 1.1 presents the dates of adoption of modern provision for the elderly

Table 1.1. Dates of adoption of modern provision for the elderly

Adoption of old age insurance laws		Adoption of old age assistance laws	
Year	Countries	Year	Countries
1889	Germany	1891	Denmark
1906	Austria (1)	1898	New Zealand
1907	Yugoslavia (1)	1905	France
1910	France	1906	Australia, Great Britain,
1911	Luxembourg		Irish Free State
1912	Rumania	1909	Iceland
1913	Netherlands, Sweden	1911	Newfoundland
1919	Italy, Portugal, Spain	1919	Uruguay
1922	Greece, Soviet Union,	1923	Norway
	Yugoslavia (2)	1926	Greenland
1924	Belgium, Bulgaria, Chile,	1927	Canada
	Czechoslovakia, Yugoslavia (3)	1926	South Africa
1925	Great Britain	1935	United States
1927	Austria (2)		
1926	Hungary		
1933	Poland		
1935	United States		

in Canada, Great Britain, and the United States, along with the countries of Europe, Latin America, and the British Commonwealth that introduced pensions or insurance during the period 1880–1938.

The relatively late establishment of modern social provision in Canada and the United States occurred in spite of the fact that, in both countries, the issue of new state policies for the aged poor had been debated since before 1900 (Lubove 1968; Tishler 1971; Guest 1980, pp. 18–63). In fact, American and Canadian reformers and politicians were part of the same community of policy discourse as were their counterparts in Britain, Europe, and British Commonwealth nations such as New Zealand and Australia, where legislative action on behalf of the aged poor was taken in the earlier period. In the United States and Canada, as well as in Britain, pensions were supported on the grounds that they represented a measure of social justice and communal responsibility for members of society who had contributed their labor and had thereby earned the right to nonstigmatized public support, rather than poor relief, when old age prevented their working any longer (see L. T. Hobhouse, quoted in Freeden 1978, p. 205; Wisconsin Industrial Commission 1915; Nassau 1915; Squier 1912, p. 320; Henderson 1909, p. 308; National Conference of Charities and Correction Committee on Standards of Living and Labor 1912; J. J. Kelso, quoted in Canadian House of Commons 1912, pp. 13–17; Mackenzie 1908). Indeed, reform during the classic introductory phase was not unsuccessful across the board in either Canada or the United States; the majority of states and provinces did pass workers' compensation and mothers' pension legislation prior to 1920 (Leff 1973; Strong-Boag 1979; Guest 1980, pp. 39–61; Van Doren 1918). In addition, and somewhat surprisingly given America's present reputation as a welfare laggard, at the turn of the century the United States had the functional equivalent of an old age and disability pension system for some one million of its elderly citizens (albeit predominantly male, white, and native-born) through its Civil War pension program. This remarkable system was allowed to pass out of existence with the dying of the Civil War cohort, although several Progressive Era reformers and labor leaders explicitly called for its extension into a modern pension program (Rubinow 1913, pp. 404–9; Fischer 1978, p. 171; Massachusetts Commission on Old Age Pensions 1910, pp. 333–39).

In addition to timing, we are also interested in the form chosen for these social programs. Form involves a number of dimensions. *Financing:* Which parties—employers, workers, the government—had to contribute revenues, and in what proportion? A particularly important distinction was between noncontributory programs, or "pensions," and contributory, or "insurance" programs. The latter could be voluntary or compulsory. What sorts of taxes and revenue sources were involved in the program—earmarked contributions, income taxes, or some other source? *Coverage and eligibility:* Coverage is determined by the conditions of eligibility; we want to know who was covered, who was excluded from coverage, and how. Especially significant distinctions here are between means-tested and non–means-tested programs and between universal and targeted or categorical programs. How did eligibility requirements affect different social groups—men and women, racial or ethnic minorities and majorities, or different classes and occupational groups? How tightly did requirements bind potential beneficiaries to work or to specific family roles? *Benefits:* What were the benefit levels, relative to average wages, poverty levels, poor relief, and the benefits of other programs? Were benefits the same for all, or was variation allowed on the basis of income, occupation, marital status, sex, or some other criterion? *Administrative arrangements:* Which level of government enacted legislation? How were different levels of government—national, local, and (in the North American cases) subnational—involved in administration and financing? In all three cases, initiation of the new programs involved a renegotiation of intergovernmental relationships. What was the relationship of the new programs to poor relief and to other modern welfare programs? What were the administrative practices required? In the United States, where patronage practices lingered in many states, serious struggles occurred over civil service (merit) requirements in the 1930s. These provisions of old age policy in Great Britain, Canada, and the United States are summarized in table 1.2.

In Great Britain, the Old Age Pension Act, passed in 1908, established means-tested, noncontributory pensions for British subjects aged seventy and above (information on the British pension program is based on Gilbert 1966,

Table 1.2. Policy outcomes in Great Britain, Canada, and the United States, 1900–1940

	1910s	1920s	1930s
Great Britain	Old Age Pension Act passed in 1908 establishing means-tested, noncontributory pensions for citizens age seventy or older.	—	—
Canada Federal	Several old age pension bills introduced beginning in 1906, but none are successful. Voluntary old age annuities program initiated in 1908. Two parliamentary committees study pensions.	The Old Age Pensions Act is passed in 1927, giving a 50 percent financial subsidy to provinces that establish pension programs paying noncontributory, means-tested benefits to British subjects age seventy and older.	Reimbursements to provinces increased to 75 percent. Contributory old age insurance program passed but declared invalid by Privy Council.
Provincial	Nova Scotia enacts law for miners in 1908, but it never becomes operational.	Five provinces pass enabling legislation by 1929.	Remaining provinces pass legislation by 1936.
United States Federal	Several old age pension bills introduced, beginning in 1909, but none are successful.	Several bills introduced, but none are successful.	Social Security Act passed in 1935, establishing a purely national, contributory old age program for retired persons age sixty-five and over and 50 percent financial subsidies to qualifying state-level old age assistance programs.
State	Several bills introduced and investigatory commissions established, but no laws are passed prior to World War I. Massachusetts (1907) and Wisconsin (1911) establish voluntary old age annuities.	Legislation introduced in most states and adopted in twelve by 1930.	Twenty-eight states have laws by the beginning of 1935; all pass enabling legislation by 1938.

pp. 221–27; Ritter 1986, pp. 181, 191; Phelps Brown and Hopkins 1981, pp. 194–95; Heclo 1974, pp. 173–78). Receipt of benefits required a character test, and recipients must have been "habitually employed" and residents of Britain for twenty or more years. Unlike poor relief, pensions entailed no loss of civil rights or privileges. These pensions were funded entirely by the central government and were financed through direct taxes—an income tax and duties on some consumer goods. In 1910 about 45 percent of people over seventy in England received the pension; in Scotland, the figure was 54 percent, in Ireland, 99 percent. The maximum pension benefit of five shillings, received by 95 percent of pensioners, was the equivalent of about 22 percent of average earnings in 1910. Men and women received the same pension amount, and both members of married couples received an independent pension. Pensions were paid through local post offices and administered by local pension committees appointed by county, borough, or district councils. Nationally, pension administration was the responsibility of pension officers appointed by the Treasury.

In contrast, old age pension legislation was introduced in the U.S. Congress from 1909 on, but it was unsuccessful (Commons and Andrews 1927, p. 471; Brandeis 1935, p. 611). Several American states, including Massachusetts, Wisconsin, Ohio, California, and Pennsylvania, appointed commissions to investigate the feasibility of establishing old age pension programs at the state level, but only a minority recommended pension legislation. In 1915 the territory of Alaska initiated a pension program, and Arizona passed a pension law that was declared unconstitutional soon after; no other state passed pension legislation until after World War I. Massachusetts and Wisconsin established voluntary annuities programs in 1907 and 1911, respectively (Fischer 1978, p. 165). In Canada, old age pension legislation was introduced into the House of Commons from 1906 on, but it was unsuccessful prior to World War I. Special committees were established in the House of Commons in the 1911–12 and 1912–13 sessions to investigate the feasibility of enacting an old age pension system at the federal level, but no formal recommendation was made (Bryden 1974, pp. 46–52). In 1908 a federal voluntary annuities program was established. The province of Nova Scotia enacted a law establishing public pensions for miners in 1908, but it was never operational.

A special committee was established in the Canadian House of Commons in the 1923–24 session to investigate the feasibility of enacting an old age pension system at the federal level, and this committee formally recommended pension legislation (see Bryden 1974, chaps. 4–5; Leacy 1983, ser. E44). The Old Age Pension Act was passed in 1927, providing a federal financial subsidy of 50 percent for provincial pension systems; pensions were paid out of federal and provincial general revenues. The federal Department of Labour was responsible for the administration of the pension program. Provincial programs gave noncontributory benefits to all British subjects aged seventy and above (including both members of married couples) who had lived in Canada for at least twenty years and in the province responsible for their pension for five years. The pension, uniform across provinces, was set at twenty dollars per month, about 24 percent of the average production worker's wage in 1928. The pension was reduced by any amount by which outside income exceeded $125 per year, resulting in a maximum income from all sources of $365 (about 36 percent of average wages). British Columbia, Alberta, Saskatchewan, Manitoba, and Ontario passed enabling legislation by 1929 and began to pay out pensions. Provincial legislatures in Quebec and the Maritimes failed to pass enabling legislation.

In the United States in the 1920s, several pension bills were introduced into the U.S. Congress, but none were favorably acted upon (see U.S. Social Security Board 1937, pp. 156–67; U.S. Bureau of the Census 1960, pp. 94–95). More policy activity occurred in the American states, as several states appointed commissions to investigate the feasibility of establishing old age pension programs at the state level. All recommended pension legislation. Old age pension legislation was introduced in twenty-one state legislatures, and six pension systems were actually in operation before the onset of the Depression in 1929, a year in which four more laws were passed. These laws initiated "county-optional" systems, which left counties with the option to give pensions as well as the responsibility for their administration and financing (except in Wisconsin, where the state paid one-third of costs for participating counties). All were means-tested, required long periods of state and county residence and citizenship, and included a number of behavioral standards. Prior to the Depression, very few pensions were actually paid out; in 1928, only about one thousand elderly people were actually collecting pensions. These averaged $17.37, about 15 percent of average earnings of full-time workers. Administrative arrangements differed widely across the states.

The remaining Canadian provinces passed enabling legislation for old age pensions by 1936. The federal government increased reimbursement levels to provinces from 50 percent to 75 percent in 1931, and at the same time federal oversight powers were enhanced (see Bryden 1974, chaps. 4–5). In 1935 federal administration was transferred to the Department of Finance. In the same year, the Dominion Parliament passed legislation establishing a contributory old age insurance program, but it was declared *ultra vires* in 1937, and no further changes in public old age provision were made until after World War II.

Policy activity in the United States regarding old age provision was especially intense during the 1930s (see U.S. Social Security Board 1937, pp. 156–67; U.S. Bureau of the Census 1960, pp. 94–95; Achenbaum 1978, p. 136; U.S. Social Security Board 1940, p. 201). Many more states appointed investigatory commissions, and all recommended establishing old age pension programs at the state level. Twenty-eight states and two territories had established some form of old age provision, including "county-optional" as well as mandatory statewide programs, by January 1935. Benefit levels varied across states and counties; the average payment per month (for all states with programs) in 1934 was $14.68, about 18 percent of average earnings of production workers. A large number of pension bills were introduced in the U.S. Congress and received favorable action in committee. The Roosevelt administration set up the Committee on Economic Security in 1934 to investigate social insurance and pensions and to draft a comprehensive social security bill. The administration-backed Social Security Act was passed in August 1935. The Social Security Act had three titles relating to programs for the elderly. Title I established a federal subsidy (of 50 percent of costs) for state-level pension programs, to be paid from general revenues, which gave noncontributory benefits to people aged sixty-five or more, subject to federal standards. This made programs mandatory statewide but did not mandate uniform benefit levels across states nor even levels that would ensure the "health and decency" of recipients. All states enacted enabling legislation under the Social Security Act by 1938; in 1938–39, the median pension payment for all states was eighteen dollars (about 18 percent of average wages); state medians ranged from six dollars in Arkansas to forty dollars in California. Title II established a purely federal program of contributory retirement benefits for retired people aged sixty-five or more who had been wage earners—thus excluding most women—outside agriculture and domestic service, an exclusion which resulted in a majority of blacks being ineligible. Title VIII provided for payroll taxes on workers and employers, which financed the benefits; the government made no contribution from general revenues. Taxes began to be collected in 1937, and the first payment went out in 1940. In 1939 the Social Security Act was amended; key changes included the addition of survivors' and dependents' benefits to old age insurance, thus bringing many more women into the system, and a shift in financing arrangements from a "full reserves system" to a modified "pay-as-you-go" system.

The Social Policy Regime

The concept of a social policy regime offers a useful way to think about the qualitative variation across national systems of social provision, including the timing and the characteristics of programs of public social provision. Here, a basic distinction is between "residual" and "institutional" welfare states, that is, between states whose action is taken only as a reaction to market or family failures and is limited to marginal social groups, and states which institutionalize a commitment to the welfare needs of all strata of the population (Titmuss 1958). Esping-Andersen (1989, 1990) has recently extended this notion and developed a new typology of what he calls welfare state regimes, based on principles of rights and stratification and the relationship of state policy action to the market, households and families, and other social structures; he identifies liberal, statist-corporatist and social democratic regime types. Moreover, a number of scholars have noted that distinctive patterns of policy development and characteristic clusters of programmatic features can be distinguished in the formative period of modern social provision. Esping-Andersen (1990, pp. 24–25) sketches two kinds of early social provision: a liberal, means-tested social assistance model, and a conservative, status-differentiating social insurance model (see also Flora and Alber 1981).

In most typologies, the contemporary United States, Canada, and Britain fit into the category of liberal or residual welfare states. In countries with a liberal social policy regime, the state has tended to assume a reactive rather than a proactive stance vis-à-vis social problems such as old age poverty; in other words, the state tends to act to respond to societal "failures," rather than intervening in civil society to prevent such problems from occurring. While social democratic regimes work proactively to change market outcomes in an egalitarian direction and conservative regimes work to preserve status differentiation, programs in liberal policy regimes tend to avoid undercutting market functioning and outcomes. Finally, in liberal regimes, the initiation of modern social programs occurred relatively late in historical time and at relatively higher levels of industrialization and urbanization (Flora and Alber 1981; Esping-Andersen 1990, chap. 1). Britain, Canada, and the United States acted later than did most states in which "corporatist-statist" or "social democratic" policy regimes emerged, thus indicating a less-developed capacity for proactive policy, but it was not so clear from the beginning that the three would converge on the residual, liberal regimes of today. Liberal elements were, arguably, predominant in all three countries' programmatic initiatives; the first modern public programs of old age provision were means-tested, noncontributory pensions, and the initial contributory old age insurance programs established in the interwar years by the United States and Britain (and attempted by Canada) were earnings-related schemes with rather limited redistributive potential. There were also other potentials, however, as Esping-Andersen notes, using as illustrations the "social democratic" aspects of the early New Deal and the universalist initiatives made by Britain and Canada in the immediate post–World War II years (1990, pp. 25–26, 28). Certainly, we must be careful not to read today's outcomes back into history. It will be important to determine the character of early programs as well as to compare the conjuncture of causal factors leading to the initiation of modern social provision in the three countries.

As I have stressed above, the timing and character of policy initiatives varied across Canada, Great Britain, and the United States. Clearly, the range of times of adoption across national and subnational governments in the three countries shows diverse levels of proactive state capacities, even if all were "tardy" relative to continental Europe: Britain preceded her daughter countries in legislating old age pensions in the years just prior to the outbreak of World War I, as comparable pension proposals failed in Canada and the United States. After the war, some U.S. states, such as Wisconsin, were comparable to the Canadian federal government in timing, while some Canadian provinces, like Quebec, compared with lagging American states. The old age assistance legislation passed by Britain, Canada, and many U.S. states was relatively nonintrusive into the workings of the market and households, providing a small income to those too poor to survive without recourse to poor relief. In no sense were these benefits a "retirement wage," and the elderly still tended to live with their families if they had kin; what had changed was the burden they represented to those families. Noncontributory pensions did not function to clear the market of elderly workers but to offer nonstigmatized support to those who could no longer work full-time or at all (Myles 1984). Old age pension legislation in the United States allowed substantial scope for state control over eligibility, which in part reflected the power of southern politicians to protect racially based systems of economic domination in their region from federal interference and the ability of all state-level officials to protect their prerogatives to set many of the terms of public provision (Orloff 1988; Quadagno 1988a, b).

In contrast with the old age assistance legislation of all three countries, the old age insurance portions of the U.S. Social Security Act showed a "premature" concern with regulating the labor market through the establishment of the retirement test, which British and other European contributory old age programs did not include in the 1930s (Myles 1984; Graebner 1980). Likewise, amendments to this legislation passed a few years later institutionalized a particular household form, the "housewife-maintaining family," to use Barbara Bergmann's term (1986, p. 258), through rules about wage earners' and dependents' benefits. This was similar to Britain's contributory program for the elderly, established in 1925 to supplement old age pensions (and to the program Canada's leaders attempted to establish in the mid-1930s), and contrasted sharply with men's and women's equal access to equivalent, though low, benefits under old age assistance programs. Old age assistance tended to go to the neediest elderly people, but racial discrimination in most southern states prevented many blacks from receiving pensions at levels equal to those paid to whites (Quadagno 1988a); eligibility provisions in old age insurance excluded most blacks altogether, again reinforcing unequal racial relations.

The Determinants of Policy Developments

The emergence of modern social provision signifies a pivotal transformation of state activities, and the varying features of its programmatic components are extremely consequential for the life-chances and power of different social groups. Thus, social scientists and historians have engaged in lively debates about the origins, development, and consequences of those features. Industrialization and its social and political concomitants are usually invoked in explanations of the social policy developments leading to the emergence of modern welfare states. The logic of industrialization model suggests that social policies are state responses to the functional requirements for the reproduction of a changing socioeconomic system (see Wilensky 1975; Cutright 1965; Jackman 1975; Banting 1982, pp. 31–34). Concern with the effects of the welfare state on the interests and power of social groups has encouraged scholars to focus on the factors which affect the strength of political actors who have so much at stake in policy, and which therefore can be expected to affect the timing of policy enactment and to shape the character of social programs.

There are a range of interpretations of the interests served by social policy and of the key actors in the introduction of such policies. A neo-Marxist approach focuses on the ways in which social policies bolster capitalist interests and economic principles. A functionalist corporate liberalism model—so far limited to the North American cases—suggests that social policies are initiated at the behest of far-sighted monopoly capitalists who believe concessions will ensure the long-term stability of the system and long-term rates of profit (Berkowitz and McQuaid 1980; Finkel 1977; Jenkins and Brents 1989; Quadagno 1984; for commentary, see Skocpol and Amenta 1985; Esping-Andersen 1989; Orloff and Parker 1990). The working-class strength model (also referred to as the power resources or social democratic model) suggests that social policies are initiated in response to working-class demands when the capacity of workers to advance their interests compels the state to set aside the objections of capitalists (Hewitt 1977; Korpi 1978; Myles 1984; Schneider 1982; Stephens 1979; Shalev 1983b). Another variant of the class politics approach sees social policies as fundamentally helpful to popular rather than capitalist interests but stresses the policy effects of right party weakness as opposed to labor or left party strength (Castles 1982).

Some scholars have suggested modifications of both the logic of industrialism and the class politics approaches by including the effect of ideology, which, depending on its character, might encourage early initiation of programs or delay their introduction (see Rimlinger 1971). Interest in the issues of state autonomy and capacity, and dissatisfaction with explanatory accounts that neglect the role of state (and other) institutions, have inspired investigations into the role of elected and appointed state officials, their relationships with powerful actors in civil society, and the institutional context that is an important legacy of state-building. Indeed, one of the most contentious issues within the literature concerns the role of state institutions and officials in explaining the timing and character of policy developments. This reflects the larger debate within social science and history around societal, especially class, versus state dynamics in explaining sociopolitical events and processes. For all of these approaches, the key question is whether they will hold up to comparative analysis.

The Welfare State and State Autonomy

In the most recent discussions of the welfare state, analysts have begun to explore the extent to which state officials act autonomously in developing policy and the ways in which the character of state and political institutions shape policy developments. In other words, scholars have begun to move beyond purely "society-centered" explanations. At first, this debate was dominated by neo-Marxist scholars who examined social policies primarily as a way to adjudicate between competing "theories of the state." Basically, they questioned whether state officials could act independent of the economically dominant capitalist class. Although assuming that state autonomy must be relative (that is, limited), they differed over how much maneuvering room was available to state officials, how direct would be the influence of dominant class interests (the debate between so-called instrumentalists versus structuralists; see Carnoy 1984), and the extent to which nondominant class interests might be embodied in social policy. In the last decade, this debate has been joined by so-called state-centered or institutionalist analysts (among whom I count myself), who have argued that states are potentially autonomous. Investigations of state policy, including social provision, offer illustrations of independent initiatives on the part of state officials (as well as instances of nonautonomy, to be sure). Moreover, in-depth examinations of policy-making reveal that the character, structures, and capacities of states and political organizations—as well as socioeconomic factors—are important to understanding outcomes. My aim is to contribute toward the resolution of the questions raised in debates over the determinants of the timing and character of policy developments—particularly the role of state officials and the effects of state and political institutions—and to properly assess the character of social programs.

Methodological Strategies for Explaining the Emergence of the Modern Social Provision

Comparative research on the development of modern social provision, of which old age pension and insurance schemes are an important part, has proliferated in the last two decades.[2] Analytic approaches have changed a good deal—for

---

2. Cross-national research on social policy was carried out as early as the 1890s, but until after the Second World War, research was almost exclusively descriptive, often highlighting programs that the authors wanted to see enacted in their own countries.

the better—since scholars first turned their attention to the modern welfare state. Initial studies attempted to explain cross-national variation in the level and growth of public welfare expenditures in the post–World War II period as an outcome of universal developmental processes in which causal factors had a linear effect on policy. More recent analytic efforts have generated new comparative strategies for understanding historically specific national policy trajectories, addressing the complexity of both the objects of explanation—policy outcomes—and the combination of causal factors which determine them. Generally, we see more focused studies that attempt to develop time- and space-limited generalizations about policy developments. The conception and design of this study reflects these intellectual trends. I hope to offer a compelling sociological and historical explanation for the emergence of a particularly important set of programs, provisions for the aged, as well as for the variations in the timing and character of these programs, in three countries with many economic, political, social, and cultural similarities: Canada, Great Britain, and the United States.

A Case-Oriented, Historical Approach

In early cross-national studies, analysts tended to consider the welfare state as an undifferentiated whole and typically used social expenditures as a proportion of GNP to represent a given state's "welfare effort." Yet it is now clear that such measures alone do not reveal the full sociological significance of the welfare state. At the very least, analysts must look at expenditure levels for different programs separately, for their determinants and effects are distinctive (see Steinmetz 1987; O'Connor 1989; Castles 1982; Kohl 1981; Cameron 1986). In a recent article, Gøsta Esping-Andersen offered a cogent critique of the way the early research operationalized the dependent variable, the welfare state, with expenditure levels:

> Their focus on spending may be irrelevant, or, at best, misleading. Expenditures are epiphenomenal to the theoretical substance of welfare states. Moreover, the linear scoring approach (more or less power, democracy, or spending) contradicts the sociological notion that power, democracy, or welfare are relational and structured phenomena. By scoring welfare states on spending, we assume that all spending counts equally. . . . some nations spend enormous sums on fiscal welfare in the form of tax privileges to private insurance plans that mainly benefit the middle class. But these tax expenditures do not show up on expenditure accounts. In Britain, total social expenditure has grown during the Thatcher period; yet, this is almost exclusively a function of very high unemployment. Low expenditures may signify a welfare state more seriously committed to full employment. (Esping-Andersen 1989, p. 19)

I would argue more strongly that to address the relational issues of power, state autonomy, and capacity and to unravel the complex causality behind the multifaceted character of social provision, scholars must look at much more than even disaggregated expenditure data. Many quantitative studies have made unjustified assumptions of linear causation and have used overly simplistic— but easily quantified—measures to get at complicated notions of state autonomy or ideology. Thus, for example, the insights of the institutionalist or state-centered model have been represented in some studies with measures such as government share of GNP or the sheer number of bureaucrats. Can a measure such as "bureaucrats per capita" or the absolute number of state bureaucrats fully capture the qualitatively different effects of the patronage-dominated administration, set in a mass-democratic polity, of turn-of-the-century America as opposed to the reformed and meritocratic administration, set in the political context of expanding suffrage and increasing electoral competition of turn-of-the-century Britain? As you might guess, I think not. To take another example, ideological concerns often enter quantitative analyses only through the measure of party in power, yet we know that significant shifts in the character of liberal ideology were instrumental in gaining elite support for new social spending, although the label *Liberal* did not change.

The character of the object of explanation, conditions of causal complexity, and the qualitatively varying character of the causal factors in which I am particularly interested—state and political institutions—encouraged me to take a holistic, historical, and case-oriented approach, rather than to conduct a variable-oriented quantitative analysis. My motivation to use qualitative and historical analysis flows from the character of the problems I wanted to solve: What was the contribution of reformers and state officials to policy developments, and how did this compare with that of the leaders of business or working-class organizations and other groups? Was there evidence of autonomously generated interests and independent action on the part of state officials and politicians? How did differing state and political structures and institutions affect the meanings and methods of all political actors involved in social policy debates? How did socioeconomic and state or political factors combine to produce the different policy outcomes seen in Britain, Canada, and the United States? To answer these sorts of questions, we need an accurate picture of the "dependent variable," the qualitatively varying features of social programs— eligibility requirements, financing, coverage, administrative arrangements, the timing of their enactment, and so on—and of the character of the whole ensemble of programs—the "social policy regimes"—that is, the relationship of the state to markets and households, the characteristic modes of state action, and the impact of different regimes on particular social groups. We also need to take account of the full range of causal factors, and of their interactions, involved in producing these outcomes over time.

Research has established that the configurations of causal factors leading to the emergence of modern social provision differed across the major regime types of the countries of the industrializing West (Flora and Alber 1981), between early and late industrializers (Collier and Messick 1975), and across different programs (see Amenta and Carruthers 1988; Orloff and Parker 1990; Steinmetz 1987). The causal factors important to policy outcomes (as is the case with other macrolevel social and political phenomena) operate not in linear fashion, but in complex interaction with each other. Combinations or configurations of conditions produce change. Further complicating our task are the possibilities that different combinations of conditions may produce similar outcomes—a situation of "multiple causation"—and that the effect of specific conditions may vary depending on the overall context (Ragin 1987, pp. 24–27). Moreover, we need to take a historical approach to understanding policy outcomes, for there is no standard developmental sequence of policy-making, but rather a variety of paths to qualitatively varying policy regimes (see Skocpol 1984; Tilly 1984). The temporal sequence in which determinative processes take place makes a difference for outcomes. Some causal factors, such as the political "feedback effects" of the policy legacy, can only be observed over time, and other factors, such as popular unrest, though fluctuating in "level," have irreversible effects on policy developments through the emergence of a discourse about the "social question" (on irreversibility, see Lieberson 1985, chap. 4). Political choices are never fully determined, and choices made at one point in time influence later options. In short, we need an approach that can examine the interplay of actions and structural contexts and that situates the explanation for policy developments in time and space.

Even had I been willing to focus on a quantitatively varying outcome—the timing of initiation or some specific set of expenditures, for example—there are serious problems for a quantitative analysis of the sort necessary to examine a range of cases and generalize broadly about the issues outlined above, assuming one could find ways to overcome problems of nonlinearity. All the cases of industrialized countries initiating modern social provision over the period 1880–1940 would still yield too small a number for a quantitative analysis including the number of potential causal factors and, most crucially, interaction terms identified as important in the literature.[3]

---

3. As Charles Ragin notes of the statistical method, "It is difficult to use this method to address questions concerning the consequences of different combinations of conditions (that is, to investigate situations as wholes). To investigate combinations of conditions, the user of the statistical method must examine statistical interactions. The examination of a large number of statistical interactions in variable-oriented studies is complicated by collinearity and by problems with scarce degrees of freedom, especially in comparative research where the number of relevant cases is often small. An exhaustive examination of different combinations of seven preconditions, for example, would require a statistical analysis of the effects of more than one hundred different interaction terms" (1987, p. 15).

Moreover, the independence of cases of national policy development is dubious at best. Policymakers and reformers shared information across borders, and the experiences of other countries significantly influenced political actors (examples will be given in chaps. 5–10; on the problem of contamination, see Lieberson 1985, chap. 3). The close observation inherent in the case-oriented comparative approach minimizes the chances that "Galton's problem" will undermine the results without the investigator's knowledge; more important, the analysis of macropolitical processes that has been the hallmark of the state-centered or institutional approach allows for diffusion to be incorporated into the explanation of policy developments (see Heclo 1974).

At this point in our collective effort to understand the combinations of forces underlying the development and variation of modern social provision, we will better be able to resolve issues of power, state autonomy, and capacity through direct examinations of the policy-making process, which allow us to observe causal linkages and mechanisms of influence. As recent commentaries have pointed out, the comparative analysis of a few cases—three or four at most—forces the analyst to become familiar with the context of the outcomes of interest and allows for the direct examination of wholes in a way not possible when one is examining the relationships among variables for a large number of cases (Ragin 1987, chaps. 1–3; Tilly 1984, pp. 76–77; for an earlier statement of the advantages of the comparative approach vis-à-vis the statistical, see Lijphart 1975). At present, while analysts have conducted scores of quantitative studies of a range of countries—with somewhat inconclusive results (Esping-Andersen 1989)—we still have only a handful of genuinely historical case-oriented and analytic comparative studies of the welfare state or modern social programs (see Esping-Andersen 1985; Ruggie 1984; Heclo 1974; Jenson 1986; Orloff and Skocpol 1984; Amenta et al. 1987; Weir and Skocpol 1985; Baldwin 1990). While single-case studies allow for perhaps the most thorough observation of policy-making processes, one gives up a great deal of explanatory power (through, for example, the loss of any controls) by confining the analysis to a single case. If one is interested in generalization while still addressing historical specificity, allowing for the direct examination of cases, and assessing the influence of qualitatively varying factors, the ideal design is a comparison of a few carefully selected cases. Case-oriented comparison is an excellent method for generating new hypotheses, which may later be evaluated and modified in new arenas, sometimes with the use of quantitative techniques.

A Comparative Strategy

Comparative research focusing on macrosocial processes and structures is undoubtedly enjoying a renaissance in sociology. In the last few years, scholars engaged in this type of research have become more self-consciously analytic about comparative methodology and the variety of strategies present in contemporary research (see Tilly 1984; Skocpol 1984; Ragin 1987). Most (but not all) contemporary comparative research deals with "big structures, large processes, and huge comparisons," borrowing Charles Tilly's words. Research on modern social provision certainly falls into this category. Both Charles Tilly (1984) and Theda Skocpol (1984) have recently offered typologies of what Skocpol calls recurrent strategies in comparative research (see also Skocpol and Somers 1980). A common approach involves using comparison as a way of "highlighting difference" (Skocpol 1984, pp. 368–74). Tilly notes that "individualizing comparisons" use the contrast between cases to highlight the specific features of each case and often take an interpretive approach (Tilly 1984, chap. 5). Their contribution is "to establish exactly what is particular about a particular historical experience" (Tilly 1984, p. 88). That is no mean feat, whether done by historian or social scientist. As both Tilly and Skocpol point out, this strategy is not "a bungled attempt at generalization" (Tilly 1984, p. 88), for it deliberately eschews generalizing, yet for precisely this reason it is not likely to be satisfying for those interested in establishing causal regularities that could be applied to more than one case. Thus, those concerned with developing generalizations have turned to other strategies of comparison, applying theory to history or analyzing causal regularities (Skocpol 1984), which may be broken down into "universalizing" and "variation-finding comparisons" (Tilly 1984).

Analysts sometimes apply a general model, deductively derived, to a range of cases to illustrate that the theory "fits" history. Here, the problem is that facts might be arbitrarily chosen to "prove" the theorists' points. To guard against this potential pitfall, some analysts argue that one must apply the model to all known instances of the phenomenon in question: "Universalizing comparison . . . aims to establish that every instance of a phenomenon follows essentially the same rule" (Tilly 1984, p. 82). Yet the presence of many such instances may well push the analyst away from the direct involvement with the cases which is so important for untangling the complex causality inherent in macrolevel social and political processes and structures and remaining sensitive to the specific context needed to sort through many of the relevant causal issues (Skocpol 1984, p. 366). Skocpol thus recommends a third strategy: "analyzing causal regularities." It is this strategy that I pursue in my analysis of policy developments in the United States, Canada, and Great Britain.

The strategy of analyzing causal regularities emerges from the attempt to account for important historical patterns within specific and significant sets of cases, developing middle-range theory. It combines inductive and deductive work: existing theory and alternative hypotheses are used to guide the examination of empirical materials, but modified or new generalizations are developed inductively from the "conversation" between evidence and theory. Single-case studies may be used in this way, principally to reject certain explanations and to develop tentative hypotheses that may be evaluated fully in comparative analyses. Analyzing several cases, however, is preferable for developing positive explanatory accounts.

In analyzing causal regularities, investigators make use of John Stuart Mill's logical methods of agreement and of difference (Mill 1950). Charles Ragin states that "the method of agreement is a search for patterns of invariance. . . . the investigator attempts to determine which of the possible causal variables is a constant across all instances," even though there may be variation along other dimensions (1987, p. 37). With the method of difference, Theda Skocpol notes, the analyst "can contrast cases in which the phenomenon to be explained and the hypothesized causes are present to other ('negative') cases, in which the phenomenon and the causes are absent, even though those negative cases are as similar as possible to the 'positive' cases in other respects" (1984, p. 378). The method of agreement alone cannot establish necessary links between cause and effect and may identify spurious relationships; this disadvantage, of course, is by no means unique to this method. Direct examination of causal processes and mechanisms (to the extent this is possible with historical materials) can minimize this possibility, and an examination of negative cases can best bolster findings based on the analysis of the positive cases. Of course, "the examination of negative cases presupposes a theory [or set of alternative theories] allowing the investigator to identify the set of observations that embraces *possible* instances of the phenomenon of interest" (Ragin 1987, p. 41). Thus, the search for generalization must be guided by the existing body of literature on the phenomenon in question. Both Ragin and Skocpol agree that a combination of the two methods is likely to be the most powerful explanatory strategy.

Although combining the methods of agreement and difference in a case-oriented comparative design is potentially quite powerful, there are difficulties in applying both logical methods, as Charles Ragin has discussed in his recent book on comparative methodology (1987). Of particular importance are the far-from-atypical situations in which multiple and/or conjunctural causation exists. Ragin defines multiple causation as the situation in which "several different combinations of conditions produce the same outcome" (1987, p. xii); he defines conjunctural causation as outcomes resulting from the "intersection of a set of conditions in time and space" (1987, p. 25). He argues, persuasively, that these are common situations, so common, in fact, that they constitute one of the principal arguments for preferring the holistic, case-oriented strategy to variable-oriented analysis for many sorts of inquiry. Yet a formal application of the methods of agreement and/or difference to comparative cases may be "immobilized" by these situations. How does this happen? To begin, let's recap Ragin's sketch of how the typical analyst carries out a dual application of the methods of agreement and difference (the preferred strategy by most accounts). First, the investigator identifies instances of the phenomenon of interest (positive cases) to see if they agree in displaying a particular causal factor. If they do, the investigator carries out a second phase of analysis, in which the instances of the absence of the phenomenon of interest (negative cases) are examined to see if they agree in displaying the absence of that causal factor. In effect, the presence and absence of the outcome is cross-tabulated against the presence and absence of the causal factor. If all cases fall into the presence/presence or absence/absence cells of the 2×2 matrix, then the argument that this particular factor is the cause of the outcome is supported.[4] Ideally, the second set of cases—the negative cases—should also provide a basis for rejecting competing hypotheses, a third phase of the investigation. Typically, this is carried out through paired comparisons of the form: "Even though it appears that X (causal factor) is the cause of Y (outcome) in country A, it is not, because country B has X, but lacks Y" (Ragin 1987, pp. 39–41).

Multiple causation could create difficulties at the second stage. If there are two causal factors, X_1 and X_2, that independently cause Y, the outcome of interest, then there would be cases in which absence of X_1 would be associated with Y as well as cases in which absence of X_2 would be found along with Y, leading to the independent rejection of both variables (Ragin 1987, p. 40). For example, "early and indigenous state initiatives on unemployment insurance in the 1930s [in the United States] required an alliance between reformers *or* organized labor *or* both and a cohesive political organization that could engineer a majority in the legislature," Edwin Amenta and his colleagues conclude in their comparative analysis of five U.S. states (1987, p. 177; my emphasis). The "cohesive political organization" could be either a unified, popularly oriented political party, such as New York's Democrats, or a government body, such as Wisconsin's Industrial Commission. I have emphasized the points at which the authors show that there are multiple paths to a common outcome— the initiation of unemployment compensation. They also demonstrate that the different paths were associated with somewhat different types of programs. The mechanical application of the methods of agreement and difference, however, would have led to the rejection of both combinations of causal factors, since unemployment insurance can be initiated in the *absence* of either an alliance of reformers and labor with a state organization or such an alliance and a cohesive political party.

Conjunctural causation makes for difficulties in the third phase. Say Y happens only when there is a conjunction of X_1 and X_2 and that all instances of X_1 are instances of X_2, but not the reverse. The analyst thinks that X_1 alone is the cause, and the data appear to support this conclusion, for all instances of X_1 would also be instances of Y, and all absences of X_1 would agree in showing the

---

4. Ragin cautions us not to consider this as a statistical technique, for the interest is not in probabilistic relationships, but in patterns of invariance (1987, p. 40).

absence of Y. Further, in the third phase, one would reject X_2 as a cause of Y because some instances of the absence of Y display X_2 without X_1. Yet actually the combination of the two causal factors is critical (Ragin 1987, p. 41). This appears to me to be an underlying problem in a number of studies, limited to Western European states, which have argued that politically strong labor movements were responsible for the development of modern social benefit programs but which never consider the extent to which these outcomes reflect the combination of such labor movements and well-developed state administrative capacities, patronage-free and programmatic politics, and concomitant statist political cultures.

A final difficulty concerns the identification of appropriate negative cases in order to be able to apply the method of difference. The method of difference depends on the use of negative cases, but there are situations in which "the set of negative cases is ill-defined."[5] This would rule out using the method of difference and force the analyst to rely exclusively on the method of agreement. Such an approach may be acceptable if investigators are "interested in unusual or extreme outcomes" (Ragin 1987, p. 42). In this case, all (or almost all) cases—the universe—of the phenomenon in question may be examined. What should one do if the outcome in question is not an unusual or extreme outcome, but the negative cases are still hard to define or "borderline at best"? This, of course, describes the situation in regard to social policy outcomes, and the holistic, case-oriented strategy—selected in deference to causal complexity— runs into methodological complications. Obviously, systems of modern social provision are not rare phenomena, and one cannot hope to examine the entire universe of cases using anything but quantitative methods (in any event, this has already been done quite extensively). Furthermore, since all industrialized countries eventually enacted at least some programs of modern social provision, it is at least arguable that no such country is a "true" negative case.

Luckily for comparative investigators, there are ways of coping with multiple and conjunctural causation and with problems in defining negative cases.

5. Ragin uses the example of Theda Skocpol's *States and Social Revolutions* (1979). Skocpol herself says that she uses both the method of agreement to assess common causes of revolution across China, France, and Russia, the positive cases, and the method of difference to show that her key causal factors were absent in England, Prussia, and Japan, the negative cases. Ragin, however, argues that her negative cases are "borderline at best" and that "it would be difficult to define the set that includes all negative instances of social revolution" (1987, p. 42). Thus, he agrees with Tilly's characterization of Skocpol's work as utilizing a "universalizing comparison," that is, as limited to the method of agreement by searching for patterns of invariance in positive cases of a phenomenon. Tilly claims that the negative cases "occupied a distinctly minor position" in an analysis that in his view relentlessly stressed the common features of revolutions in France, Russia, and China (1984, p. 108, chap. 6). We need not adjudicate between Skocpol and Tilly and Ragin in order to appreciate that the identification of negative cases for any given phenomenon is hardly uncontentious.

In cases of conjunctural causation in which the analyst initially finds the hypothesized causal conditions in both positive and negative cases, he or she may then search for further condition(s) which have to occur in conjunction with the first set for the outcome to ensue. This is the methodological strategy that Theda Skocpol and I pursued in our article comparing policy outcomes in turn-of-the-century Britain and America, "Why Not Equal Protection?" (Orloff and Skocpol 1984). The causal factors commonly hypothesized as significant in the emergence of modern social provision—ideological change, demographic pressure, rising labor movements—existed in both cases, but only in Britain were programs of public social protection enacted. We looked for additional causal factors that could differentiate between the two cases and found that variation in the character and capacity of state and political institutions was associated with the different policy outcomes. We then offered a modification of explanatory accounts of the emergence of modern social provision, which, while immediately applicable to the two cases we investigated, could potentially—with modifications—be evaluated in other contexts.

In situations of multiple causation, the method of agreement may show no common cause or set of causes. Rather than conclude that there are no invariant relationships, the investigator may suspect that there are actually different *types* of the outcome in question and that different sets of causes are relevant to each type. "Multiple causation is addressed by reconceptualizing the phenomenon of interest so that types can be distinguished. . . . the investigator may be able to link distinctive causal configurations with sub-types of the phenomenon in question" (Ragin 1987, pp. 43–44). This strategy may also be used when negative cases are difficult to define. "The indirect method of difference can then be applied to types because instances of other types also provide negative cases whenever the conditions relevant to a certain type are assessed" (Ragin 1987, p. 44). Likewise, Tilly recommends that if one examines positive cases of a phenomenon using the method of agreement to find the common explanatory factors but has difficulty in identifying suitable negative cases, then one should also look at variation among and within positive cases. To undertake what Tilly calls variation-finding comparison is to "establish a principle of variation in the character or intensity of a phenomenon having more than one form by examining systematic differences among instances" (1984, p. 116).

Comparing the United States, Canada, and Great Britain

I came to this project initially with an interest in making sense of the U.S. case and an attraction to then-new state-centered analytic approaches. In my view, no satisfactory explanation existed for the unusual character of American public social provision, despite many attempts to provide one. I was not convinced by the common arguments that liberal ideology and working-class weakness were to blame. Liberal ideology had been put in service of a good many reforms in the Progressive Era and the New Deal, and the work of U.S. labor historians had convinced me that American labor was not exceptionally weak around the time that social policy reforms were first being considered. I was becoming familiar with the work of Theda Skocpol and other political sociologists that highlighted the importance of state capacity, autonomy, and structure in explaining political outcomes and with the research of scholars such as Martin Shefter and Stephen Skowronek that focused on the particular characteristics of American state-building. I suspected that state and political institutions, organizations, and processes were likely to hold the key to understanding America's cross-nationally unusual path of policy development. Thus, a complete understanding of the U.S. welfare state would require an analysis that combined these state-centered or political-institutional factors with the so-called society-centered factors more commonly invoked in the literature— demography, ideology, and the power resources of political actors.

My purposes in developing a comparative design were twofold; I wanted to make sense of the U.S. case and to highlight the causal contribution of state and political factors in producing policy outcomes—the timing and character of initial modern programs of old age protection. Thus, I decided against using cases such as Germany or Sweden, which, while very different from the United States in state capacities and structures, provided no controls for ideology or labor strength. (Such a selection of cases might well make sense if my goal had been to highlight difference; as Ragin notes of Reinhard Bendix, everybody's favorite exemplar of "individualizing comparison," "differences between the cases he selects overwhelm their similarities" [1987, p. 35]). In short, there was too much variation between these potential cases and the United States to allow me to specify the causal role of any particular factor or set of factors, much less to highlight the role of state factors specifically. Conversely, a "most-similar nations" strategy, in which one minimizes variation among control or background variables while maximizing variation along potentially explanatory dimensions, seemed ideal for my purposes (Lijphart 1971, 1975). The United States, Canada, and Great Britain share substantial similarities along dimensions which are commonly invoked to explain cross-national differences in social welfare policy. The most important of these factors are their common liberal cultural and ideological heritage and democratic political systems. Moreover, politically active innovators from all three nations participated in transnational policy reform circles, and North Americans were particularly attuned to each other and to the British example. Against the background of similarity in culture and ideology, political democracy, and reform activity, significant differences exist in state and political institutions and processes, rooted in the distinctive state-building experience of the three countries.[6]

---

6. Of course, there are differences along some socioeconomic dimensions as well, but these are not sufficient to explain policy variation among the three.

Theda Skocpol and I compared the United States with Britain for the pre–World War I period in which pensions and other social insurances were initially considered in both countries but were adopted only in Britain (Orloff and Skocpol 1984). Of all the European countries adopting modern pensions or insurance in the "formative period" of the welfare state, Britain had the greatest degree of similarity to the United States in ideology and culture and working-class strength (however measured), thus allowing the evaluation of the impact of variation in state and political factors. While Britain differed on some demographic and economic factors with the United States as a whole, some American states—we used Massachusetts—were quite similar to Britain along these dimensions. The comparison between Massachusetts and Britain revealed the insufficiency of explanations based solely on level of industrialization, urbanization, or population aging, echoing the findings of a substantial body of cross-national comparative research. We were able to show that differences in state capacity, the character of political institutions, and policy legacies were important contributors to the differing policy outcomes in the two countries. In this book I have expanded the initial investigation of pre–World War I Britain and America and have augmented it with an analysis of the factors leading to the adoption of modern old age protection in the United States in the 1930s and an analysis of Canadian policy developments over the period 1900–1935.

Canada provided an excellent comparative case for further evaluating the initial findings about policy developments. Canada is even more similar to the United States than is Britain, sharing with the United States a common cultural and ideological commitment to liberalism and individualism, democratic and federal political institutions, a craft-oriented trade union movement, immigration, ethnic conflict, and an absence of a feudal heritage. Alongside important common socioeconomic characteristics, the Canadian and American experiences of state-building varied. The two North American countries share some elements of the state-building experience, in particular, a relatively protected geopolitical position, the early development of democracy, and relatively delayed bureaucratization. Canada's position in the world economy, however, contributed to a greater development of state administrative capacities and intervention in the economy than was the case in the United States. In this way Canada resembled some of the world's "late followers" (Laxer 1989; Orloff and Parker 1990). Like the United States, Canada considered pensions in the years before World War I but did not adopt them. Thus, for the prewar period, a comparison of the Canadian and U.S. cases could provide a check on the findings about the factors responsible for the failure of the United States to adopt pensions. In the interwar decades, both the United States and Canada initiated nationwide schemes of public old age protection, but these occurred under very different circumstances and at different historic moments. Canada adopted pensions in the 1920s, in a period of relative political calm, while the

United States adopted social security in the midst of the turbulent Depression years. The character of the programs enacted differed considerably as well, with Canada opting for a federalized version of an old age pension program very similar to the British plan of 1908 and the United States initiating both a federal old age assistance plan and a purely national contributory insurance scheme. Here we have two distinctive types of policy, and these outcomes may be linked to the different combinations of factors which led to their enactment. A close comparison of the two cases highlights the political and state factors important for the different timing of the two cases and the different configuration of causal factors implicated in the break with poor relief in each.

The analysis involves conceptualizing the American and Canadian experiences in the form of three "cases," covering the pre–World War I period of failure to adopt modern old age coverage; the 1920s, when Canada adopted a federal pension law but the United States did not; and the 1930s, when the United States adopted nationwide programs for the elderly, including a contributory old age insurance scheme, while Canadians did not succeed in enacting contributory insurance. This follows Lijphart's definition of a case as not synonomous with any given entity, but as "an entity on which only one basic observation is made and in which the independent and dependent variables do not change during the period of observation—which may cover a long time, even several years" (1975, p. 160). For the period from the 1880s through the end of World War I, I will examine all three countries to develop an explanation of the differing policy outcomes: the debate over and eventual enactment of old age pension legislation in 1908 in Britain, and the similar debates over pensions but subsequent failure to enact pension legislation in the United States and Canada. Canada passed the federal Old Age Pension Act in 1927, while the United States failed to pass federal pension legislation during the 1920s, although several American states did enact limited pension schemes. In the 1930s the U.S. federal government passed the Social Security Act, but the Canadians failed to enact contributory old age insurance. For all three periods, I use the method of difference to pinpoint the crucial difference(s) between the positive and negative cases. In the first period Britain is the positive case, and the United States and Canada serve as negative contrasts. In the 1920s Canada is the positive case of enactment, while the United States again serves as a negative case. Finally, in the 1930s the success of the United States in enacting nationwide systems of contributory and noncontributory old age protections is contrasted with the policy deadlock surrounding extensions of old age assistance into a contributory scheme in Canada. A second set of comparisons using the method of difference involves longitudinal comparisons for both the United States and Canada, in which, within each country, the prewar failure to enact modern social spending programs for the elderly is contrasted with the later successes in enacting such policies.

This particular strategy is unusual in the welfare literature in that it permits an explicit juxtaposition of the actual institution of income maintenance programs for the elderly in Britain with the simultaneous failure of potential parallel developments in the United States and Canada in the pre–World War I era, the success of Canada against the failure of the United States in the 1920s, and the "role reversal" of the two North American countries in the 1930s. Thus, the information gained from examining the "failures" as well as the successes can be applied to pinpointing the necessary and sufficient conditions for the adoption of these welfare state programs. Generally, comparative analyses of modern social provision have examined only positive instances of program enactment. As I noted above, however, there are potential objections to almost any way of identifying negative cases. Arguably, Canada and the United States in the pre–World War I period are "borderline at best" negative cases, given the fact that both countries did go on to enact old age protections. I think one can make a good case for "finding variation," that is, conceptualizing the three countries as having different types of policy for the elderly, which would include the timing of enactment as well as the differing dimensions of policy content. Thinking about the cases in this way allows for the method of difference to be applied to types "because instances of other types also provide negative cases whenever the conditions relevant to a certain type are assessed" (Ragin 1987, p. 44). The method of difference may still be used for highlighting the specific factors leading to different political outcomes in each period. In the end, I use the method of agreement to develop a summary model of the necessary and sufficient causal factors for policy innovation in these three liberal countries, by examining all the positive cases to see if there are any common configurations of causal factors—both presences and absences of conditions—involved in all three cases.

In the design just sketched, I am reversing the usual ordering of applications of the methods of agreement and difference. Nevertheless, if research is seen as the collective enterprise it undoubtedly is, then this book can be seen as following from a wide range of studies—both case- and variable-oriented—which have attempted to find a common causal factor (such as working-class mobilization or industrialization) responsible for all cases of the enactment of modern social benefits schemes but have faltered in the face of multiple and conjunctural causation. Indeed, problems in the search for universal causal relationships have led a number of scholars to conclude that policy outcomes are more likely to be the result of a combination of conditions and, moreover, that there is no common set of factors behind all instances of the break with poor relief. There are some preliminary typologies of systems of modern social provision—Esping-Andersen's or Flora and Alber's come to mind. Both differentiate between liberal-democratic countries and others, and this adds justification to the selection of these three liberal countries. My research will show what factors are similar across the three largest liberal countries and which conditions differ among them that led to distinctive policies even within a generally liberal policy orientation. I hope that this offers to the collective research enterprise a new set of claims to be investigated through comparisons across and within regime types.[7]

Even once we agree that a most-similar nations strategy is warranted, the problem remains of how directly to compare federal states like Canada and the United States with a unitary state like Britain. This is addressed by including as a part of the policy outcomes to be explained events occurring across the subnational units (states and provinces) of the United States and Canada. This research strategy is justified by the fact that North American reformers consciously adopted a political strategy of pressing for uniform legislation simultaneously across states and provinces in order to achieve the results their counterparts in unitary polities could gain through national legislation.

The federal structure of the American and Canadian states was important in several ways to the policy outcomes of the early twentieth century, particularly in shaping the strategies of political actors working for change, although federalism per se cannot be blamed for the failure of the new social welfare spending initiatives in this early period—as both the success of other forms of social legislation in that same time period and the eventual success of national legislation incorporating the necessary "concessions" to federated structure would attest. But federal structure and constitutional requirements imposed certain exigencies on reformers and politicians interested in the passage of social legislation and afforded a different structure of political opportunity than did the unitary polity of Great Britain.

The British North American Act, which established the Canadian state, and the U.S. Constitution were interpreted as mandating that social welfare activities and legislation fall within the sphere of subnational responsibility (Birch 1955, chaps. 2, 6, 7). Moreover, the national capitalist economy made the subnational units themselves part of the "economics of competition" in the market

---

7. Another way to understand the methodology and case-selection of this study is through the language of case-control analysis (Schlesselman 1982). Case-control studies proceed, as my investigation does, from effect or outcome to cause, in an attempt to "identify antecedents that led to the . . . condition of study. . . . the case-control method uses a comparison group (controls) to support or refute an inference of a causal role for any particular factor" (Schlesselman 1982, p. 25). Thus, they are retrospective, or historical, and comparative. In the analysis undertaken here, each case is contrasted with the others, which are matched on certain conditions but differ on others. First, we try to understand why old age pension legislation passed in Britain, but not in Canada and the United States. Then we attempt to understand the differences between the two North American cases for the 1920s and 1930s. Because the three cases are matched on a range of socioeconomic and cultural dimensions—liberal ideological heritages, industrial-capitalist economies, democratic institutions, and so on—we can focus on the potentially causal factors that differ, such as state capacities, policy feedback, state structure, party orientations, and other aspects of the institutional context.

(Graebner 1977, p. 332). Historian William Graebner describes the situation in the United States, but the problem applied to federal Canada as well (see Guest 1980, p. 123). "Key business groups, largely from highly competitive industries with interstate markets, opposed most state social legislation on the grounds that it would place their firms at a competitive disadvantage in relation to firms operating in states with less advanced, and therefore less costly, programs" (Graebner 1977, p. 332). In the face of this problem and the constitutional obstacles, reformers hit upon the strategy of "uniform legislation." Reformers across the states attempted to coordinate their legislative activity, often using a "model bill" provided by a national organization—the American Association for Labor Legislation (AALL) was the main such group in the field of labor and social insurance legislation—and the simultaneous introduction of the bill in many state legislatures (Graebner 1977; Lubove 1968). The Social Service Council of Canada played a similar role in Canada (Social Service Council 1914; Guest 1980, p. 217), and the National Conference of Charities and Correction, with which the members of the AALL worked, was important in diffusing ideas for legislative action throughout North America (Splane 1973, pp. 17–19; Bruno 1957).

Sources of Evidence

Like most investigations using comparative-historical methods, this one depends principally on the analysis of secondary sources, although I have supplemented secondary sources with primary sources where needed. As in any investigation of a number of cases over a considerable period of time, here I found it would be prohibitively time-consuming to carry out primary research on each case. Moreover, historians and area specialists have produced many excellent studies covering the development of modern social policy in each of the three countries I examine as well as the various factors—working-class organization, state-building, and the like—which constitute potential causes of policy outcomes. I compiled basic information from a thorough survey of the available historical and sociological literature, asking the same questions about each case in order to assure comparability and to fully evaluate alternative interpretations of the forces leading to the initiation of modern old age benefits. Thus, secondary material is used to make explicit cross-national comparisons which are usually omitted from the literature on a particular country. (For example, in single-case studies of U.S. policy developments, researchers often assume that the observed liberalism of political culture is unusually strong—without any explicit comparison with other countries.) Of course, historians do not universally oblige the comparative researcher; not every issue I wanted to evaluate was present in the literature for each country. In these cases, I turned to primary sources of evidence to augment the basic information provided in secondary sources; this also allowed me to familiarize myself with the evidentiary bases of historians' conclusions. Among the primary sources I used were government statistics, documents, and reports, periodical publications, and the writings of important figures involved in the development, administration, and reform of social policy. Particularly important sources of primary data were the journals published by social and labor reform organizations; the unpublished papers of a range of Canadian social reformers, whose activities have been less extensively documented than those of their British and American counterparts; and the reports of various special government commissions which worked in all three countries (and many U.S. states) to investigate the conditions of the aged and existing modes of support and policy, particularly the operation of poor relief, and to recommend policy changes.

Historians are trained to observe the kinds of biases inherent in the primary sources they use; they note what documents are likely to be preserved and what sorts are more likely to be lost, as well as the biases incorporated in the documents themselves (Schafer 1974; Bailey 1978). Historical sociologists are now learning these skills, as well as how to interpret the writings of the historians on whose analyses of primary sources they rely (see Tilly 1981; Skocpol 1984, pp. 382–83). One cannot simply assume that the "facts speak" from the pages of books and articles by historians, any more than one can make such assumptions about the documents themselves. One needs to be aware of changing intellectual trends in analytic orientation and subject focus among historians and to use this information in interpreting the findings of these scholars for new purposes.[8]

The comparative analysis focuses on events—the enactment of modern income maintenance programs for the aged—rather than on trends, such as time-series of welfare expenditures. Therefore, the information needed to evaluate the role of various causal conditions is for the most part qualitatively, rather than quantitatively, varying, and measurements of "independent variables" are categorical or ordinal rather than continuous. Nevertheless, where possible and appropriate, I use statistical information to document the level of hypothesized causal factors such as trade union organization, proportion of the population over age sixty-five, or industrialization at crucial moments of transformation in policies for the aged.

Plan of the Book

Next, I present a review of the literature on welfare states as it is relevant to the emergence of public old age provision in the United States, Canada, and

---

8. This is quite comparable to the work of a survey researcher reanalyzing the data of earlier scholars, who has to be aware of the biases built in to the wording of questions, selection of samples, and so on.

Britain. After these introductory materials, the book is divided into two parts: a section on the emergence of the social question as it pertained to the aged and a section focusing on the ways it was answered across the three countries. In Part 2 I discuss several aspects of the development of the social question: in chapters 3 and 4, the demographic, economic, and policy "baseline" which provided the conditions for the problem of old age poverty to become politicized, and in chapter 5, the cultural, ideological, and political processes which constituted old age poverty as an issue for public resolution. Here, I focus on the different responses of elites to forming cross-class alliances for public social spending across the three countries and to the social question over time, arguing that this represents a significant factor differentiating instances of policy success and failure. The task of Part 3 is to understand the institutional underpinnings of these different political outcomes through focusing on the state-building processes, which critically affected both the timing and character of policy developments, and on the policy legacy. There are separate chapters on Britain and Canada, explaining how relevant causal conditions combined to produce the different historical outcomes for old age pensions, for the period 1880–1910 in Britain and 1880–1940 for Canada. I have two chapters on the United States, one for the 1880–1920 period and another for the 1920–40 period. In a final chapter, I sketch out the common features in the emergence of initial modern social spending programs in these liberal countries and offer some suggestions for future research.

2
Explaining the Emergence of Modern Social Provision

The literature on welfare states offers resources for explaining the timing and character of the initial programs for public old age protection in Canada, Great Britain, and the United States in the first half of this century. This field has thrived within the social sciences and history, and a range of analytic perspectives has developed to explain various aspects of social policy outcomes. There are five principal approaches to the explanation of variation in the timing and character of modern social provision. The first four focus respectively on the logic of industrialism, cultural values, political conflict (in a large number of variants), and state capacities. The fifth, the institutional perspective, encompasses many of the factors highlighted by the other approaches and emphasizes state and political institutions. I will first review the claims of each analytic perspective and the empirical evidence relevant to it, and then I will suggest what aspects of the perspective we want to retain and what to discard. The standard of judgment is whether any given perspective can hold up to comparative historical analysis. Can it explain the variation in the timing and character of modern social provision for the aged in Britain, Canada, and the United States? While each analytic approach yields some helpful insights about the process of policy development, only the institutional approach can fully explain why and when the three countries initiated old age pensions and insurance and why these policy initiatives took the forms they did.

In the past I used the term *state-centered* to describe my analytic perspective. I now prefer the term *institutional* to *state-centered* for several reasons; most important, the earlier term tended to give readers the impression that factors outside the state were unimportant to the explanation. In fact, demographic, economic, ideological, and social factors are indeed significant for the shape of the policies in any given country, as are the character, structure, and capacity of the state and other political institutions, particularly parties. The term *institutional analysis* also signals my belief that we must consider the ways in which institutions shape and constrain the choices of actors; context-free analyses of "rational" actors will not explain historically and institutionally specific policy outcomes.

The Logic of Industrialism

One of the earliest perspectives on the emergence of modern social provision for the aged focused on the "logic of industrialism." This approach highlights the "social needs" (broadly defined) produced by universal developmental processes such as industrialization, urbanization, and population aging. Analysts working with this perspective have typically been indifferent to variation in the character of policy, preferring to focus on the commonalities of social provision across industrialized or capitalist countries. Yet they are interested in differences in the timing of initiation of modern social programs, proposing that these resulted from cross-national demographic and socioeconomic differences.

Explanations of the development of the modern welfare state based on the logic of industrialism emerged from the convergence theory of industrial society. Many analysts found in cross-sectional, quantitative studies of social security expenditures of large numbers of nations that social spending is associated with economic development (Cutright 1965; Pryor 1968; Jackman 1975; Wilensky 1975). Despite their ahistorical research designs, logic of industrialism studies have put forward extrapolations about the causes of the *origins* of the welfare state (Wilensky 1975, p. 27; Wilensky and Lebeaux 1965, p. 230; Kerr et al. 1964, pp. 14–29). The basic argument about the emergence of modern social policies is as follows: Industrialization causes the rise of a labor force dependent on wages for its livelihood and increasingly bereft of the traditional social "safety nets" of kin networks, especially the extended family, and land ownership. Thus new needs are created for public spending to protect the unemployed, the sick and disabled, dependent widows and children, and older workers no longer able to remain in the labor force. At the same time, industrialization creates the new wealth to make collective social provision possible and the new organizational means through which social benefits can be demanded and delivered. Urbanization and population aging exacerbate these trends. In response to the new needs and strains on traditional, and increasingly inadequate, social assistance systems such as poor relief, the state expands through the adoption of modern welfare programs. As Harold Wilensky puts it, inferring from his cross-sectional data to historical patterns, "With economic growth, the percentage of the aged goes up, which makes for an early start and swift spread of social security programs" (1975, p. 27). Approaches based on the logic of industrialism thus would predict that policy breakthroughs should come whenever nations experience new needs or strains on existing programs through changes in demographic or economic conditions.

Industrialism and the Initiation of New Social Programs

Many analysts have investigated the association between industrialization and the initiation of modern welfare programs, namely that shifts in the economic and social situations of populations are responsible for policy shifts. Analysts highlight the creation of new economic insecurities through the spread of waged work and argue that governments will respond to these new needs through the creation of social programs. The line of reasoning stressing the logic of industrialism would lead one to predict that the earliest industrializers, which experienced the earliest incidence of problems associated with industrialization, should have been the first to adopt social insurance and pension programs. Let's examine the historical evidence about the level of industrialism and emergence of the welfare state.

It is tempting to attribute the earlier initiation of old age pensions in Britain relative to that in the United States and Canada to the higher levels of industrialization and urbanization which existed there in the pre–World War I period. Yet a range of studies belie the claim that the initiation of modern social provision is determined by levels of industrialization and urbanization. One must also keep in mind that, compared with other European nations which also initiated modern social welfare programs in the pre-1920 "formative period of welfare state development," Britain had the highest observed levels of industrialization and urbanization at the time of program initiation. Moreover, British levels of industrialization and urbanization in the 1910s were higher than those which existed in Canada and the United States in the 1920s and 1930s, when the North American countries did initiate old age pension and insurance programs. This can be seen from an examination of the data in figures 2.1 and 2.2, which give the proportions of the labor force engaged in mining, manufacturing, and construction and in agriculture, in Canada, Great Britain, the United States, France, and Germany, along with dates of adoption of modern social protection for the elderly.

Pryor (1968, p. 474) failed to find a relationship between any of the various economic development indicators and the existence of social insurance programs in 1913 in Europe, the United States, Canada, New Zealand, and Australia. Collier and Messick (1975) addressed the hypotheses that welfare states have emerged as a by-product of economic development or socioeconomic modernization. Working with data on fifty-nine nations that "had formal political autonomy with regard to domestic policy at the time of first adoption," these researchers found no support for the level of economic modernization (measured by work force in agriculture, work force in industry, or real income per capita) as a necessary and sufficient condition for the initiation of social security programs and only very slack support for the idea of economic modernization as a necessary threshold, since the "least modernized nations" in

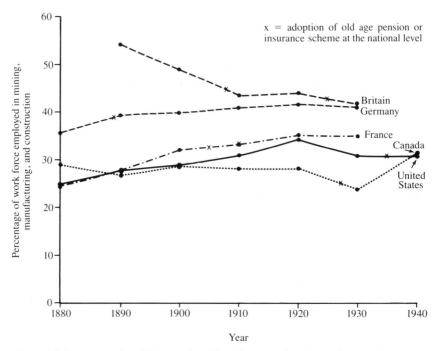

Figure 2.1. Percentage of work force employed in mining, manufacturing, and construction. *Source:* U.S. Bureau of the Census, 1966, p. 103.

their sample initiated social security with less than 5 percent of the work force in industry, over 80 percent in agriculture, and a per capita income of less than fifty-one dollars (in 1961 U.S. dollars) (Collier and Messick 1975, p. 1299). According to Collier and Messick, processes of international diffusion of social security programs from more to less developed nations account for overall world patterns in which later-adopting nations, especially those adopting since 1922, initiate social security at much lower levels of economic development than earlier adopters. They attribute the ease of such diffusion to the "larger role of the state in later-developing countries" (p. 1313). Regardless of social needs or demands, Collier and Messick suggest (1975, p. 1310), political authorities in later-developing countries may realize that social security policies represent easy ways to tax citizens and to co-opt labor movements (for evidence on the latter point, see Rimlinger 1968). By disaggregating their data, Collier and Messick noted a sharply reverse pattern of international "diffusion up the hierarchy" of economic development among the earliest adopters of social security.

Some researchers, such as Walker (1969) and Gray (1973), have shown

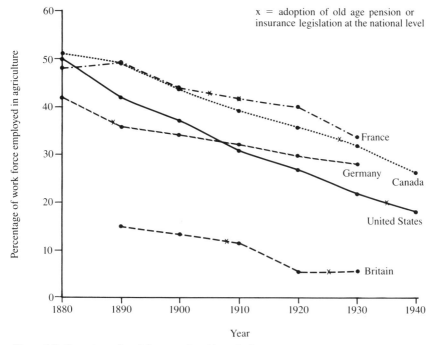

Figure 2.2. Percentage of work force employed in agriculture.
Source: U.S. Bureau of the Census, 1966, p. 103.

that factors such as industrialization help to explain variation in the timing of the adoption of a wide range of policy innovations (including some in the area of social policy and many outside it) across the American states. Yet until recently researchers had not investigated the impact of such variables on the adoption of modern social programs within the group of industrialized states. A study by Amenta and Carruthers (1988) found that within the sample of industrialized American states, industrialization had no effect on the timing of adoption of old age pension or unemployment insurance legislation.

In another important study, Flora and Alber (1981) explored patterns of legislative innovation among European nations using more nuanced measures of welfare legislation and "modernization" than those applied by Collier and Messick. Their study examines the timing of seventy-four social insurance laws in twelve European nations. These laws established the "institutional core" of four basic insurance systems: industrial accident insurance, old age insurance or pensions, health insurance, and unemployment insurance. Overall, Flora and Alber confirm Collier and Messick's descriptive findings, showing that successive European nations "established their systems at a slightly higher level of socioeconomic development" (measured as the product of industrialization and urbanization) and "generally at a much higher level of political mobilization" (measured by the electoral participation of the working class) (Flora and Alber 1981, pp. 61–63). Economic level, which Flora and Alber see as creating specific, objective welfare and security problems in the population, cannot predict the timing of the emergence of new social insurance or pension programs. Moreover, developmental thresholds of socioeconomic change are found to have "weak explanatory power" in accounting for the timing of welfare breakthroughs: "The variation in developmental levels is too great to allow any generalizations about thresholds" of industrialization (1981, p. 65). They argue that the level of economic development will not produce new programs unless needs not only are felt but also are registered in politically effective demands. They caution, however, that this does not "suggest that governments simply act in response to pressures; they may not act at all or they may anticipate some of the problems and act to prevent their full realization" (1981, p. 43).

Flora and Alber's study suggests that we need to look more carefully at the politics of public social provision; we cannot simply assume that the emergence of needs will lead to policy change. The importance of politics is also suggested by the by now well-known cross-sectional assessments of the effect of economic development on social expenditures. While one finds a positive relationship between the level of economic development and the level of social security spending when examining the entire range of developed and less developed nations, among the twelve to eighteen wealthiest, most industrialized countries that relationship breaks down. In the smaller group of more developed countries, political factors, such as the degree of governmental centralization, the strength of social democratic or labor parties, or the extent of corporatist political bargaining, must be invoked to explain the level of social expenditures (Wilensky 1975, 1976, 1981; Castles and McKinlay 1979a, b; Stephens 1979; Cameron 1978; Shalev 1983a, b).

The Aged and the Welfare State

Harold Wilensky (1975) has suggested one route through which the social changes concomitant with industrialization might lead to a changed politics of social policy. In his cross-sectional analysis of sixty nations, he finds economic development (GNP per capita) and social security effort (social security spending as a percentage of GNP) to be strongly correlated. He further specifies in path analysis that this relationship is mediated by the proportion of the population over age sixty-five and the age of the social security system. Wilensky concludes that "over the long pull, economic development is the root cause of welfare state development, but its effects are felt chiefly through the demographic changes of the past century and the momentum of the programs themselves, once established" (1975, p. 47). The impact of the increasing population proportion of the aged, Wilensky argues, came both from their objective need and through the political force of both the aged themselves and those who would be forced to support them in lieu of new welfare programs (1975, pp. 26–27).

There is an appealing logic to the notion that the increase in the number of aged persons, newly dependent due to the changes in social structure wrought by industrialization, is responsible for the development of the welfare state and certainly for that portion of it that addresses the particular needs of the elderly. Is this the case? Many analysts have looked to the evidence about the proportion of the aged in the population to assess the weight of the burden represented by the elderly, but for our three cases, the comparative picture does not suggest that a straightforward relationship between population aging and the initiation of new forms of social provision exists. The proportion of people over sixty-five did not increase over the last half of the nineteenth century in England, while it did in the two North American countries; thus, in the country in which pensions were enacted earliest, this "burden" had not risen at all, and the rising "burden" in Canada and the United States did not lead immediately to new social provisions. Quadagno (1982) shows that in Britain, old age pensions were instituted prior to an appreciable increase in the proportion of the aged, which went from 4.6 percent in 1850 to only 4.7 percent in 1900, just before pension legislation was enacted in 1908 (see also Heclo 1974, p. 21). On the other hand, those aged sixty-five and older were increasing as a percentage of the Canadian and U.S. populations for several decades before the institution of modern programs of income support for the aged in 1927 and 1935, respectively (Achenbaum 1978, p. 60; Bryden 1974, p. 30).[1] This point is made graphically in figure 2.3, which presents the proportion of the population aged sixty-five and over and the dates of initiation of new public programs for the aged. In one of the few statistical analyses to address the impact of the proportion of the population over age sixty-five on public welfare provision in the formative period of the welfare state, Pryor (1968, p. 474) found no statistically significant relationship between a nation's age distribution and the existence of social insurance programs in 1913 in the sample of nations made up of independent European nations and the developed nations of North America and the British Commonwealth.

An even more serious problem, however, results from using measures of population aging as measures of an increasing "burden" that ought to lead to

---

1. Indeed, several Progressive Era American state investigatory commissions noted the increasing numbers of elderly, but no action was then taken (see Wisconsin Industrial Commission 1915, pp. 3–4).

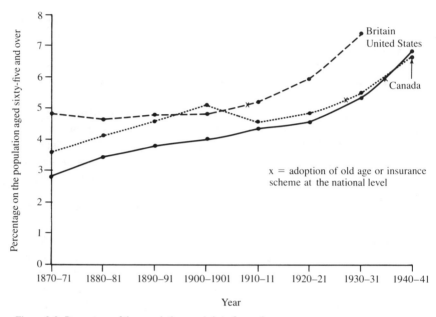

Figure 2.3. Percentage of the population aged sixty-five and over.
Sources: Data used to construct this figure were drawn from Achenbaum 1978, p. 60 (U.S.); Bryden 1974, p. 30 (Canada); Mitchell and Deane 1962, pp. 12–13 (Britain).

demands for new social protections. Inferring need simply from the proportion of the population over sixty-five assumes the dependency of the elderly, extrapolating from late twentieth-century conditions, particularly near-universal, formal retirement after age sixty-five. In fact, most elderly people in the late nineteenth and early twentieth centuries were householders and worked, men in the paid work force, women in the home (Gratton 1986; Gratton and Haber forthcoming; Myles 1984; Smith 1979; Quadagno 1982). Without widespread formal retirement, one cannot assume that all, or even most, of the aged population constituted an economic burden to younger adults. Nor is there evidence that the non–self-supporting elderly were neglected by their kin. Most of those who did become economically dependent were cared for in the homes of their relations (Smith 1979; Quadagno 1982). No more than a small fraction of the elderly in the late nineteenth and early twentieth centuries lived alone or in the poorhouse, and these were overwhelmingly the single, widowed, and childless, not people who had been abandoned by their relatives (Thomson 1983; Anderson 1977; Gratton 1986).

It is quite right to stress that dependence on wagework—the result of capitalist industrialization and capitalist penetration of the agricultural sector—created a new form of economic vulnerability that did not affect the self-employed or landowners. With dependence on wages, a range of factors beyond the control of individuals can result in the deprivation of economic livelihood—for the elderly, forced retirement. There was considerable stability, however, in the work and household arrangements of elderly people during the period before the consideration of pensions. Although some changes occurred in the character of work, the available evidence suggests that most elderly men continued to be economically active, and most older women were supported financially by working spouses. At most, there was a very small increase in the proportion of younger adults who might have to take in an elderly relative. Thus, the initial problem of social provision for the elderly focused on the nonworking minority and was not aimed at establishing a retirement wage for all of the aged (Myles 1984, pp. 11–16).

The problem of supporting the dependent minority of older people was not in fact new to industrial society, although the transition to wagework associated with capitalist industrialization did exacerbate that problem. The aged who were working and householders were not a burden on their kin or others. But to the extent that the aged were economically dependent and unable to maintain an independent residence, they represented—at least potentially—a burden on those who had to support and care for them. In some cases where the elderly were householders, they might rely somewhat on the income provided by working children. Whether these people would be a burden depended at least partially on systems of public and private social provision, the character of which was largely a function of politics. These forms of provision—principally poor relief, but in the United States also military pensions—could affect whether or not the elderly could maintain their independence or contribute to the family economy if they were living with kin. In contrast with the relative stability in work and household arrangements over the late nineteenth and early twentieth centuries, there was important variation in the forms of social provision over this period. In the late nineteenth century British and some U.S. officials instituted a policy shift which cut back on the availability of poor relief (the "campaign against outrelief"). This undermined the ability of the elderly to maintain their own households or to augment the family economies of their kin when they were unable to work. Later the decline of U.S. military pensions also contributed to a worsening of the situation of the elderly. Moreover, in Canada, Great Britain, and the United States, there were disadvantages to poor relief (to put it mildly) as a system of public social provision. As popular classes gained in political strength, they were able to demand changes. These are political issues, rather than a result of the logic of industrialism alone.

The importance of politics in mediating the effect of population aging is also suggested in Pampel and Williamson's study (1985) of the determinants of pension expenditures and of their relative generosity in forty-eight nations at all levels of development, for the period 1960–75. They find that in the industrial democracies, the proportion of the population over age sixty-five positively affects relative pensions, though age structure does not have this effect in less democratic countries. This lends support to the notion that the aged, given encouraging political conditions, can be an important political force for pension expansion above and beyond what would be expected from sheer demographic increases (Pampel and Williamson 1985, p. 791). Once a categorical program of public provision for the aged is in place, an increase in the number eligible will lead to increased social expenditures; indeed, just such a phenomenon explains a large portion of the increase in welfare spending in the post–World War II era found in so many studies. Pampel and Williamson's study documents the "entitlement effect" of the percentage of aged on pension expenditures in all but "low-democracy" countries (1985, pp. 791, 794).

Aging in a Social and Political Context

It is clear from this review of the empirical findings bearing on the hypotheses based on the logic of industrialism that the tempos of social policy innovation do not simply mirror those of economic development and urbanization and that, by themselves, economic and demographic factors cannot explain the timing of introduction of welfare programs for the aged. Both in Europe and in our three cases, the evidence reveals that the level of industrialization does not predict the timing of the initiation of new social programs. Different countries launched modern social programs at different phases of economic development; generally, the liberal countries were at relatively high levels of industrialization and urbanization when they initiated pensions and social insurance, although this is more true of Britain and the United States than of Canada (Banting 1982, pp. 32–34). In addition, scholars are finding that the configuration of causal factors leading to the break with poor relief and the initiation of modern social provision differs across regime types (Flora and Alber 1981; Esping-Andersen 1989). Like developmental models in other areas of political sociology (e.g., state-building; Tilly 1975), the logic of industrialism approach to the emergence and growth of the welfare state has fallen out of favor as analysts have turned to more historically and politically contingent perspectives that are sensitive to variations in the relationship between economic change and social policy.

The changes associated with capitalist industrialization did set the stage for the development of new approaches to the problems of economic need and insecurity, for most of the problems addressed by the new programs of workingmen's insurance either did not exist prior to large-scale capitalist industrialization or, as in the case of sickness or old age, were exacerbated by it. Thus, social insurance is an invention of an age marked by a capitalist and industrial economy; it was in this sense a "response to [capitalist] industrialism." The effect of socioeconomic and demographic transformations, however, was mediated by existing systems of social provision—the policy legacy—and cannot be understood apart from that politically created context. Furthermore, social insurance was also created in response to the political problems and opportunities that emerged from state-building and electoral democratization as much as from processes of capitalist industrialization. The invention of social insurance reflects intellectual and ideological trends, as well as reactions to existing systems of public social provision. Wilensky is not wrong to suggest that the elderly and their kin may be a political force for pensions, but his point must be amended to take note of the way in which this potential is mediated by politics and policy. We must turn to specifically ideological, political, and state-structural factors to understand how the potential was realized in any given case. In short, we must move beyond investigations of systemic "needs" and economic demands to more nuanced explorations of the situations of relevant political actors, particularly how they were affected by existing systems of social provision, and the political-institutional context within which they act. The questions then become: Under what conditions are the needs of the aged created and translated into politically effective demands, how, and by whom?

Cultural Values

Some of the first attempts to amend accounts based on the logic of industrialism highlighted the effects of differing national cultural values in producing variation in the timing and character of policy innovations; I call this the cultural values approach. In this account, the cultural predispositions of the populace shape social policy developments. The cultural values approach represents what we may consider an anthropological perspective on culture; that is, cultural systems constitute society and, by implication, are homogeneous across groups within the society. Case studies of social policy in Britain, Canada, and the United States often claim that liberal ideology and cultural values are responsible for the residual character of their social policy and the tardiness of the three—relative to continental Europe—in initiating modern social programs (see Guest 1980; Bryden 1974; Rimlinger 1971). Many cross-national studies of social expenditures appeal to the liberal and individualist culture of the United States in an ad hoc way to explain the outlier status of the U.S. case. How do these analysts conceptualize the effect of cultural values? Popular cultural values define for the electorate what state actions are legitimate or acceptable, determine voters' preferences among parties with distinctive approaches to social policy,[2] and affect the probability of individuals' engaging in

2. The welfare policy of the successful party is thus assumed to reflect the preferences of the majority. This presents some difficulties of interpretation if parties do not supply distinctive programs, but most analysts assume that parties—like governments—will supply what the voters demand. The absence of programmatic diversity among parties then reflects consensus on the part of the electorate.

voluntary group activity, as well as the type and policy orientation of the organizations they join. Aggregate social demand determines what governments can do in the field of social policy. Elite cultural values give leaders policy preferences which are acted on through the development of political party programs, bureaucratic initiatives, and the demands of voluntary organizations, although elites are constrained by popular beliefs.

The cultural values perspective highlights the strength of liberalism in determining the timing of policy initiatives in Europe and North America. In the constitutional monarchies of Europe which were the first to initiate modern social programs, liberalism was fairly weak, and political actors had access to paternalist and collectivist understandings of state-citizen relations with which to justify new public welfare initiatives. In contrast, in the liberal democracies, an ideological reorientation was a prerequisite to overcoming or at least neutralizing individualist and voluntarist arguments against welfare provision outside the punitive poor law. Differences in the relative strength of traditional liberalism have been invoked to explain variation in the timing of new welfare programs among Britain, Canada, and the United States. Rimlinger contends that "in the United States the commitment to individualism—to individual achievement and self-help—was much stronger than . . . in England. . . . The survival of the liberal tradition, therefore, was . . . stronger and the resistance to social protection more tenacious" (Rimlinger 1971, p. 62). Only in the wake of the Depression could Americans break with traditional liberalism to support social security (Rimlinger 1971 pp. 193–97; Grønbjerg, Street, and Suttles 1978, pp. 45–46; Williamson et al. 1982, pp. 149–50, 156–60). The Canadian case has been argued both ways. Some maintain that liberalism held back welfare development in Canada much as it did in the United States (Wallace 1950a). Others hold that a "Tory touch" made social policy debates less acrimonious and the acceptance of new state welfare activities less difficult than in the United States (Horowitz 1968, pp. 19–23; Kudrle and Marmor 1981, p. 92). Canada's late start on modern social programs is then merely a result of generally later development.

It was actually in Britain, not the United States or Canada, that the most spectacular instance of popular, voluntarist resistance to the coming of modern welfare programs occurred. Opposition from the predominantly working-class British friendly societies helped to delay the passage of public old age pensions for over two decades (Treble 1970). At the turn of the century, more than half of the adult men in Britain were enrolled in the friendlies (outnumbering the trade unions threefold), and they came from those strata of the working class most likely to be enfranchised. In politics, they were Gladstonian Liberals, favorable to voluntary self-help rather than public welfare protection (Gilbert 1966, p. 165; Yeo 1979). In contrast with the individualist views held by middle- and upper-class members of the classically liberal Charity Organization Society, friendly society members' views tended to identify low wages rather than immorality as the cause of old age poverty; rather than support public old age pensions, they called for increased wages to allow for self-help and personal responsibility (Treble 1970, p. 277). They especially opposed any form of state contributory social insurance for old age or sickness, since this would have meant direct government competition for their members' limited funds in the areas their benefits covered. Yet they also resisted noncontributory pensions for many years, and although some of the societies withdrew into cautious acquiescence by the early 1900s, none ever became active champions of pensions (Gilbert 1966, p. 198).[3]

In contrast with the voluntarist resistance of large sections of the organized British working class, U.S. voluntary benefit societies, which may have enrolled up to one-third of the voting population (i.e., adult males minus most southern blacks; Stevens 1966, p. 116), were for the most part neutral toward new public welfare initiatives. Canadian societies, too, remained neutral in the debates over pensions and social insurance from the turn of the century through the passage of both the 1908 Government Annuities Act and the 1927 pension act, even as they issued life insurance and carefully guarded their organizational independence in the federal and provincial parliaments (Schmidt 1980, pp. 59–61; Canadian Fraternal Association 1907, 1908, 1909, 1919).

But perhaps the most telling contrast with the received image of American popular views on the welfare state comes from the support given various public welfare initiatives by the Fraternal Order of Eagles, a mainstream voluntary benefit association with a white, predominantly native-born, working-class membership of five hundred thousand in 1924. The Eagles, founded by trade unionists in Seattle in 1898, carried out a remarkable series of campaigns in favor of mothers' pensions, the eight-hour day, workers' compensation, and old age pensions in the early 1900s (O'Reilly 1904, pp. 12–17; Fraternal Order of Eagles 1929; Preuss 1966; personal communication with Lawrence Leahy, former national leader of the Eagles). Although, like the British friendly soci-

---

3. It would appear that public old age pensions would have helped the societies. Although designed to give only sickness and funeral benefits, the friendlies by the 1880s were paying a large and increasing number of de facto pensions in the guise of sickness benefits to members (who were living longer than the societies had calculated) no longer able to work due to the infirmities of old age and who would otherwise be forced to undergo the degradation of applying for poor relief (Gilbert 1966, p. 177; Treble 1970, pp. 278–79). In the 1890s the financial burden of the de facto pensions caused the bankruptcy and collapse of many local lodges. Several leaders recognized the problem as due to "pressure of claims made for sickness which were in fact due to the infirmities of old age," yet no reform of the societies' financing was undertaken, largely because of increasing competition for new members who were unlikely to be willing to pay the higher premiums necessary for such reform (J. L. Stead of the Foresters, quoted in Treble 1970, p. 279). Public pensions would have provided a solution to their financial problems, but as Gilbert put it, "in effect they preferred insolvency to immorality," at least for a while (1966, p. 180).

eties, the Eagles sold life insurance to their membership and gave sickness and funeral benefits, they did not object to public activity in these fields (Fraternal Order of Eagles 1929). Juvenile court judges who were members of the Eagles were among the initiators of the mothers' pension movement, and Frank Hering, a Grand Worthy president during the Progressive Era and the influential editor of *Eagle Magazine* for many years afterward, mobilized the organization to lead state-level campaigns for old age pensions during the 1920s and 1930s, in cooperation with labor unions, other fraternal groups, and middle-class reform groups such as the American Association for Labor Legislation (*Eagle Magazine* 1920–35; Fraternal Order of Eagles 1929; Lubove 1968, pp. 136–43; Quadagno 1988a).

Voting results also undermine the conventional view that Americans were unalterably hostile to new welfare departures in the pre–New Deal era and that British voters clearly endorsed such initiatives. In the presidential election of 1912, the Progressive party, led by former president Theodore Roosevelt, garnered the second-highest vote total (four million to Wilson's six million; U.S. Bureau of the Census 1960, p. 682) with a platform which endorsed "the protection of home life against the hazards of sickness, irregular employment, and old age through the adoption of a system of social insurance adapted to American use" (Porter and Johnson 1970, p. 177). In Massachusetts, referenda on old age pensions were held in eight cities in 1915–16, and they were approved by a more than four-to-one margin (Massachusetts Special Commission on Social Insurance 1917, p. 57). Meanwhile, in Britain, although pension proposals had been on the national political agenda for many years, the Liberals were not officially committed to enacting pensions or social insurance when they won in the 1906 landslide which ushered in the administration responsible for passing old age pensions and other significant welfare and labor reforms (Russell 1973, p. 65; Rogers 1973, p. 261). Nor, for that matter, were the Conservatives (Gilbert 1966, p. 197). Moreover, support for socialist parties was comparable: the Socialist party in the United States and the Labour party in Britain, both committed to new old age protections, received 6 percent and 7.6 percent of the vote, respectively, in 1912 and 1910 (Butler and Freeman 1969, p. 141; Weinstein 1974, pp. 314–15). In Canada, pensions and social insurance did not become electoral issues prior to World War I, but a number of M.P.'s supported pension initiatives (Bryden 1974, chap. 3).

Trade union federations in both Britain and Canada were among the earliest proponents of old age pensions, with endorsements of universal pensions coming in 1899 and 1905, respectively (Heclo 1974, p. 168; Bryden 1974, p. 48). Their support, however, was based not on a socialist viewpoint, but on a new liberal understanding in some ways similar to that espoused by middle- and upper-class reformers. In contrast with the situation in Britain and, to a lesser extent, in Canada, in the United States a number of analysts have highlighted the unusually strong commitment to liberalism of the working class as the critical factor underlying the failure to institutionalize the new social protections in the Progressive Era: "The struggle for the establishment of modern social rights had no chance to succeed unless it had the full support of organized labor. Unfortunately, unlike the British trade unions, which paid at least lip service to the idea of social security in the early days, American unions were mostly hostile" (Rimlinger 1971, p. 80).

The picture usually drawn of hostile American labor unions, however, is partial at best. To be sure, Samuel Gompers and some members of the national leadership of the American Federation of Labor spoke out against contributory social insurance, which would tax workers, and they certainly glorified voluntary union activity as the best way to improve the economic situation of U.S. workers (Rimlinger 1971, pp. 80–82; Horowitz 1978, chaps. 1–2; Gompers 1916).[4] But even Gompers favored noncontributory old age pensions, stating in 1916 that pensions "carry with them the conviction of their self-evident necessity and justice," and the AFL passed resolutions in favor of pensions in 1908, 1911, 1912, and 1913 (Reed 1930, pp. 117; American Federation of Labor 1919, pp. 303–4; Witte 1961, p. 244). The first pension proposal introduced in the U.S. Congress came from former United Mine Workers leader William B. Wilson in 1909 and was soon endorsed by the AFL, along with many state and local labor leaders (Fischer 1978, p. 171). Moreover, most legislative activity on labor and welfare matters occurred at the state and local levels in the pre–New Deal era (Graebner 1977). Here, too, organized labor was most favorable to both pensions and social insurance (Fink 1973, pp. 161–83). State labor federations endorsed a number of social insurance and pension measures in the important industrial states of Massachusetts, New York, California, Ohio, New Jersey, Pennsylvania, and Missouri, both in the Progressive Era and in the 1920s (Nelson 1969, pp. 18, 70–71; Gratton 1983, pp. 404, 412; Tishler 1971, p. 173; Numbers 1978, p. 79; Starr 1982, p. 250; The Survey 1918; Linford 1949, pp. 6–59; Pennsylvania Commission on Old Age Assistance 1925, p. 83).

The evidence suggests that pensions had popular backing in all three countries. What of elites? Liberalism was in many ways even more hegemonic in nineteenth-century Great Britain than it was in Canada or the United States, yet a wide range of new social welfare programs—including old age pensions

---

4. The British experience in welfare development also shows that it was not necessary for the unions or any working-class group to demand social insurance for these programs to be instituted. Indeed, in Britain the contributory social insurances were the product of initiatives by reformers turned ministers and civil servants, who from positions in the Liberal administration and the Board of Trade developed health and unemployment insurance and persuaded reluctant friendly society, trade union, and other interst group leaders to accept them (Heclo 1974, pp. 78–90; Gilbert 1966, chaps. 5–7; Mowat 1969, pp. 90–91).

and health and unemployment insurance—was enacted into law in the years between 1906 and 1911 under a Liberal administration. The programs were intellectually and politically justified by appeals to the "new liberalism," an intellectual reworking of traditional liberalism that was making headway in all the English-speaking democracies (Allen 1973; Bremner 1956a; Clarke 1974; Collini 1979; Fine 1956). The new liberals in and out of government argued that in modern industrial society, government becomes a necessary support for individual dignity, providing security and regulating competition so as to undergird responsible individual initiatives (Freeden 1978; Hobson 1909; Hobhouse 1911; Addison 1983; Evans 1978, pp. 215–20; Hay 1978, pp. 72–73). If British liberals could use such ideas to legitimate social policy innovations in the early years of the twentieth century, why couldn't Canadians and Americans? In fact, they did.

By the early years of this century, elite opinion in the United States and Canada was also shifting toward a new liberalism that provided ideological resources with which to defend and justify state intervention within a liberal framework. These arguments were used by both labor leaders and middle-class reformers in connection with proposals for workers' compensation and mothers' pensions, which were successful, as well as with old age pension proposals, which were not. (On the U.S., see Skocpol forthcoming; Orloff 1991; Addams 1964; Henderson 1909; Seager 1910; Squier 1912; Rubinow 1913; *American Labor Legislation Review* 1911–20; the Progressive party platform of 1912 in Porter and Johnson 1970, pp. 175–82, the social policy planks of which were written by reformist liberals and social workers. For Canada, see Social Service Council 1914; Simpson 1914, p. 40; Bryden 1974, chaps. 3–4; Guest 1980, chap. 3; Allen 1973, chaps. 1–2; King 1918, pp. 347–48.)

The new or progressive liberals were not uncontested in any of the three countries in the pre–World War I period. The charity organization societies, especially, vociferously opposed all the proposed new social protections, arguing on old liberal grounds. Yet they were unable to halt old age pensions in Britain or mothers' pensions in Canada and the United States (Mowat 1961, chap. 7; Katz 1983, p. 192; Leff 1973, pp. 402–5; Bruno 1957, pp. 81–83; Tishler 1971, chaps. 2, 3, 7; Guest 1980, pp. 51–53). In all of the successful social legislation of this period, in Britain as well as in Canada and the United States, concessions had to be made to established views and practices directed against the "undeserving" poor (Gilbert 1966, chap. 4; Mowat 1961, p. 158; Leff 1973, pp. 412–13; Strong-Boag 1979, pp. 26–28; Guest 1980, pp. 55–63). The point is simply that, by the early twentieth century, new liberal understandings of the uses of state action to support the dignity of individual citizens were sufficiently well developed in all three nations to allow new public welfare departures to be discussed and justified within a cultural framework that emphasized liberalism and individualism. The shift to new liberalism may well have been necessary for the adoption of new public welfare measures, but alone it was not sufficient to cause policy change. Thus, the relative strength of ideological liberalism cannot be invoked to explain the failure of the North American democracies to establish public protections for their aged citizens. In the United States and Canada, as in Britain, elites and the broader political public had ways to justify such programs within a liberal framework, and substantial popular support was available for their initiation.

Furthermore, as had been the case in Britain, when old age pension legislation was finally adopted in Canada and the United States, it was discussed and justified in liberal, rather than paternalist or collectivist, terms. Old age pensions were advocated along with a full range of labor and social legislation in the Canadian Liberal party's 1919 program and were eventually passed under the auspices of W. L. Mackenzie King's Liberal administration, with prodding from the Left. In the United States, the administration of Franklin Roosevelt argued for new social legislation in liberal terms (Holt 1975). The Social Security Act, although it represented an important departure in policy, is widely acknowledged to have been justified in liberal, and even individualist, terms (Leff 1983, p. 373; Lubove 1968, chap. 8; Rimlinger 1971, pp. 213–15, 226; Brown 1956). As Edwin Witte, chief architect of the Social Security Act, explained in 1938, the old age insurance program did "not relieve the individual of primary responsibility for his own support and that of his dependents" because of its contributory character (quoted in Horowitz 1978, p. 153). The individualist basis of the program was allegedly guaranteed in the technically unnecessary individual accounting and was reinforced through the use of contractual and private insurance imagery which underlined workers' earned right—through contributions rather than "service"—to benefits (Cates 1983, chaps. 2–3).

Culture, Ideology, and Political Action

Clearly, the historical evidence on popular policy orientations and elite discourse about new social protection is at odds with explanations based on national cultural values. Popular views about public social protection and ideological and intellectual resources for justifying such programs were far more comparable across the three countries than is suggested in conventional accounts. There was resistance to policy innovation among elites and the public in all three, to be sure. Significant segments of elites, however, had embraced new liberal arguments for an active state role in guaranteeing individual opportunity and economic security, which had much popular support. Thus, cultural values cannot alone explain the specifics of policy preferences or ultimate policy outcomes, both of which differed across the three liberal countries. As Keith Banting has noted, cultural values arguments tend to be circular, asserting "that a country has a limited social policy because the inhabitants of that

country wanted a limited social policy" (1982, p. 37), and have lacked preci-
sion and analytic rigor. Other potential determinants of policy outcomes, such
as the strength of competing political actors or the extent of state administrative
capacity, were not "held constant." In the few quantitative studies that have
examined ideology along with other factors, ideology cannot explain policy
variations (Wilensky 1975, pp. 48–49; Coughlin 1979). Finally, the cultural
values approach assumes too much uniformity of policy-relevant preferences
across social groups. It is apparent even from our brief review of popular and
elite orientations toward social provision that a great deal of disagreement and
conflict of interest existed. In short, the anthropological conception of cultural values, however well- or ill-suited it may be for less stratified societies, is
inadequate for understanding the role of ideas and preferences in highly stratified, heterogeneous capitalist industrial countries. I do not want to argue that
culture and the ideas and preferences of political actors play no role in policy
developments, however. Let me sketch how they do.

First, we need to supplement the notion of culture with the concept of ideology. These two concepts are often used interchangeably. They are certainly
related, but I find it useful to distinguish them. Ideologies are sets of ideas and
symbols that "express or dramatize something about the moral order . . . [which
may be understood as] definitions of the manner in which social relations
should be constructed" (Wuthnow 1987, p. 145). Moreover, "ideologies inevitably include claims about power" (Wuthnow 1987, p. 149) and "are developed
and deployed by particular groups or alliances engaged in temporally-specific
political conflicts or attempts to justify the use of state power" (Skocpol 1985a,
p. 91). Cultures, by contrast, are not tied to specific groups and times. National
cultures provide common vocabularies, symbolic elements, and assumptions
from which political actors develop ideological arguments for particular purposes (see Wuthnow 1987; Skocpol 1985a). Thus, for example, Lipset (1970)
argues that a range of different interest groups—labor, business, and so on—in
the United States have a common set of liberal vocabularies and symbols which
are used as the groups carry on debates, although their interests and goals differ.

Cultural systems and the ideologies derived from them are implicated in
the mobilization of political actors. As Robert Wuthnow (1987) has suggested,
ideology offers a way of dramatizing and maintaining the solidarity of groups
mobilizing politically and identifies the sources of problems and solutions, sug-
gesting a strategy for reform, although we do not wish to consider ideology
simply a blueprint for action. Lynn Hunt (1984, 1989) and other practitioners of
what she calls the new cultural history have highlighted the importance of elements of popular culture—colors, clothing styles, and other symbols—to the
politicization of popular groups. We shall return to this point in our discussion
of the role of political, intellectual, and reform elites in policy developments.

The common cultural frameworks of Britain, Canada, and the United

States can help—along with other elements—to explain these three countries' policy similarities, although here our ability to draw conclusions is hampered by the lack of variation across the three countries. The range of preferences, idioms, and other symbolic elements available within a given cultural system may structure ideological arguments and political debates in partially unintended ways, as is the case for any structure (Wuthnow 1987; Sewell 1985; Skocpol 1985a). Certainly ideologies drawn from those cultural systems affect the scope and character of transformations attempted by political actors. Yet we cannot presume that ideologies operate in unmediated fashion to shape policy choices. To get a proper understanding of the role of cultural frameworks and ideologies in policy developments specifically, we must put the production and effects of ideologies into political and social context. Recently, analysts such as Jane Jenson (1986) have utilized the terms *policy discourse* and *universe of political discourse* to denote the dialogues and debates around specific sets of policies. These reflect ideological orientations, and the cultural idioms and symbols upon which they draw, as these are developed by political actors in reactions to existing policy, political coalitions and enmities, and political and administrative institutions.

Political Conflict

In the 1970s and 1980s the predominant approaches within the literature on the welfare state and social policy have looked to political conflicts surrounding social policy and to the relative strength of competing actors to explain differing outcomes. As we noted in discussing the logic of industrialism perspective, a range of political factors have been found to affect the timing and variation of policy developments. Generally, analysts have focused on class-based political actors, seeing the "balance of class forces" as the principal determinant of the character of modern social provision and the timing of its initiation. Indeed, the problems of industrial wage earners have been at the heart of social policy concerns, so it seems reasonable to inquire about the political role of this group and its antagonists in determining the course of policy development.

There are a range of variations on the theme of political conflict. First, there is a neo-Marxist functionalist variant, stressing the predominance of capitalist interests in policy. Another perspective focuses on popular disruption as the causal factor behind the emergence or expansion of state social provision, which is used by elites as a method of social control. Most widely accepted is the so-called social democratic or power resources approach, which stresses the "strength" of the working class, usually measured by the extent of labor unionization and working-class political party predominance, in bringing extensive development of social programs. After discussing the general findings of this perspective, we will examine both areas of working-class power in the

United States, Canada, and Britain specifically. A variation of the power resources model focuses on the weakness of the Right, rather than the strength of the Left, in explaining the initiation and expansion of the welfare state and argues that the key policy split tends to be between center and right-wing parties. At first glance this approach seems especially useful for North America, where labor parties have been weaker than in Europe and the main political contest is between center and right-wing parties (Castles 1982; Borg and Castles 1981). In the last few years, power resource scholars such as Gøsta Esping-Andersen and Walter Korpi have given greater analytic emphasis to cross-class alliances, an element of their earlier work that had received less attention that "working-class strength" (see Esping-Andersen and Korpi 1987; Esping-Andersen 1989, 1990). I consider this an especially promising development and incorporate an amended version of these insights in my own analytic model.

Neo-Marxist Approaches

Some neo-Marxist scholars, most prominently James O'Connor (1973) and Claus Offe (1984), have argued deductively that the process of capitalist accumulation and the nature of the capitalist state impose certain exigencies on state managers and the policy they make. Managers must act to ensure that the conditions for capitalist accumulation are sustained and that the system maintains "legitimacy" among the masses. The political conflict in this perspective is only latent; these analysts assume that if not for the "legitimation" activities of the state, workers would rebel. Thus, according to the influential radical (and I would say functionalist) analysis of James O'Connor,

> although social security contributes to social and political stability by conservatizing unemployed and retired workers, the primary purpose of the system is to create a sense of economic security within the ranks of employed workers . . . and thereby raise morale and reinforce discipline. This contributes to harmonious management-labor relations which are indispensable to capital accumulation and the growth of production. Thus the fundamental intent and effect of social security is to expand productivity, production, and profits. *Seen in this way, social insurance is not primarily insurance for workers, but a kind of insurance for capitalists and corporations.* (1973, p. 138)

Offe (1984) has further argued that the state must develop policies which will complete and sustain the process of proletarianization (stripping workers of the means of production and forcing them to sell their labor power) and maintain "catchment areas" for the unemployable (such as the aged), and the unemployable alone. This perspective shares a great deal with the logic of industrialism account. Although the language of neo-Marxists differs somewhat from that of mainstream functionalists, both groups argue that policies promote the investment in human capital and reproduction of the labor force required by the capitalist economy and, through the offer of benefits, prevent or defuse social unrest while enhancing worker loyalty and social and labor control required in capitalist political and social systems (see Myles 1983; Mishra 1984; and Esping-Andersen 1989 for similar observations).

There are two issues to be dealt with in neo-Marxist accounts—the compatibility of modern social policy and capitalist economic principles, and the extent to which policies reflect the preferences and interests of the dominant capitalist economic class. It is true that modern social policies are compatible with the free labor market required for capitalism to function in a way that the old poor laws, with their barriers to labor mobility, were not. Again, this is similar to the points raised by the logic of industrialism analysis and does not get us very far in probing the causes of the important variation in the social policies of capitalist countries, which in various ways may bolster the position of groups outside the dominant economic class. I would simply argue that policy variation within capitalist countries is consequential for the lives of many people and worth understanding. Neo-Marxist analyses such as Offe's give us no way to understand policy variation, since they are pitched at the analytic level of the "mode of production" and are not easily subjected to empirical evaluation.

Neo-Marxist analysts contend that variation in the secondary aspects of social policy can be explained by differences in the interests of dominant economic classes or the needs of the capitalist economy—the specific character of labor markets, relationship to world markets, and so on. This claim is closer in spirit to analyses of policy stressing the role of the "balance of class forces" in determining policy outcomes, since it is possible to conceptualize capitalists as one set of political actors among the contenders, even if the most powerful (although of course the presumption of political unity is problematic; see Useem 1986). It differs from other class politics approaches in stressing the procapitalist, rather than the pro-working-class, aspects of social policies. Capitalists are politically powerful, but there is a good deal of evidence against the proposition that they are able to determine the character and timing of social benefits programs, at least in its strongest form. To take only one set of examples, the social democratic analysts have demonstrated in numerous studies of social policy in the post–World War II period that labor's political strength, particularly where social democrats have had long tenure, has led to more generous social provision for the aged and less reliance on market mechanisms (see Shalev 1983b; Myles 1984; Esping-Andersen 1990). Moreover, there are a range of other actors—particularly agrarian classes—who had and continue to have some influence over the policy-making process (see Quadagno 1988b for a similar point). Institutional factors also constrain policy choices.

The notion that the specific characteristics of the economy determine the features of social provision has not been subjected to much empirical assessment. In his study of urban unemployment policy in German cities during the Second Empire (1871–1914), Steinmetz (1987) did find that employers of skilled labor were more willing to accept unemployment insurance than those whose labor needs were more easily met. Still he argues that it was a specifically political logic—including an important role for Socialist party strength—which led to political elites initiating such schemes. Myles (1984, pp. 93–95) examined the effects of two factors invoked by some neo-Marxists, the centralization and concentration of capital and the size of the "surplus" population, on pension quality in a number of advanced capitalist countries; neither factor explained variation in this policy outcome. One might consider the fact that despite widely varying positions in the world economy, levels of industrialization, and other economic characteristics, New Zealand, Australia, Britain, France, and Denmark all initiated flat-rate, means-tested old age pensions in the years between 1890 and the onset of World War I. It strikes me as being very difficult to argue that these remarkably similar policies resulted from the widely divergent economic interests of dominant economic classes in these countries. It may well be useful to consider economic situations as informing the policy preferences of economically based groups, but that is certainly not the only source of their preferences. We should not forget interests based on gender, race, ethnicity, religion, and so on, nor about the potential for existing policies to influence the formation of policy preferences among all groups.

American scholars are particularly prominent in arguing that a group of "corporate liberals"—far-sighted capitalists and, to a lesser extent, social scientists in their employ—laid the foundations for modern social policy in their private welfare plans and shaped public programs to their interests (see Jenkins and Brents 1989; Quadagno 1984; Ferguson 1984). Analyses underscoring the role of corporate liberals are almost wholly limited to the twentieth-century United States, as this approach has not been given much credence in the literature on European welfare states, nor has it been in evidence in explanations of the initiation of old age pensions in Great Britain or in Canada, with the exception of the work of Alvin Finkel (1977, 1979). A number of analysts have shown that although modern social programs have turned out to be useful for capitalists in a number of ways, the majority of businessmen did not support these programs initially (see Skocpol and Amenta 1985; Esping-Andersen 1989; Orloff and Parker 1990; Pal 1988). Moreover, as I have argued elsewhere (Orloff and Parker 1990), the failure of analyses of corporate liberalism to consider comparative evidence about the policy role of business undermines their case considerably. Although I think it is fundamentally in error on the basis of the historical record (and surely betrays an ethnocentric bias), the stress on the role of allegedly enlightened employers in the literature on the American welfare state is so persistent that the specific historical claims made by this group of analysts must be addressed.

Like those relying on the causal efficacy of the logic of industrialism, those stressing capitalist logic and the seemingly inevitable triumph of capitalist interests have ignored political struggle over policy and the range of factors— variable across capitalist countries—that affect the course of policy developments. This perspective is not a particularly promising one.

Social Disruption and the Origins of the Welfare State

The "social disruption" model associated with the work of Frances Piven and Richard Cloward (1971, 1979), conceptualizes pensions and other forms of social provision as concessions by elites to popular disruption and as a crucial method of social control. Thus, this analysis is in some ways comparable to the neo-Marxist approaches in assuming that elites can come up with needed policies to co-opt the (disorderly) masses, although its proponents focus much more on actual instances of popular disruption and highlight the importance of relatively unorganized popular groups rather than the organized working class.[5] The Piven and Cloward thesis is quite popular in the United States as an explanation for welfare reform, particularly in the 1960s, since organized working-class activity was much less in evidence than in Britain and Europe (Shalev 1983b; Quadagno 1984, pp. 638–40). For the expansion of welfare in the United States in the 1960s, there is mixed evidence on the role of racial insurgency (see Skocpol and Amenta 1986, pp. 138–39). More relevant for our purposes, during the 1930s in the United States, there was a rough coincidence of social unrest, electoral realignment, and social reform. According to this interpretation, noninstitutional political action—mass movements, strikes, demonstrations, and the like—by members of the working classes or other nonelites, if it is sufficiently threatening to continued capitalist control of the economy and the government, prompts the elites to restore order. Whether they turn to repression or co-optation—as through enacting social legislation— depends on electoral conditions. Only if the "calculus of electoral instability favors protestors" (i.e., political leaders need popular support due to shifts in voting alignments) will concessions be made (Piven and Cloward 1979, pp. 16– 18, 32). In the U.S. case, social legislation is seen as having been introduced in Bismarckian fashion, with the explicit commitment to the reform and salvation of capitalism on the part of President Roosevelt and other members of his administration invoked to prove this point (Conkin 1967, pp. 71–75; Bernstein 1968, pp. 267, 273–74; Williamson et al. 1982, pp. 158–59; Olson 1982, pp.

5. Piven's recent work (1985) stresses the potentially empowering effects of welfare-state policies.

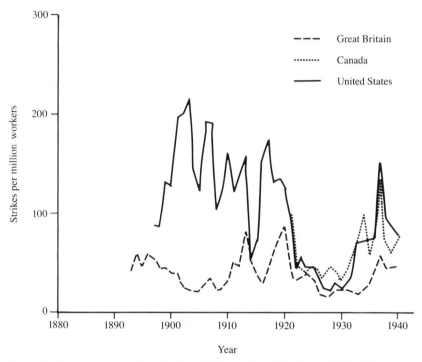

Figure 2.4. Strike frequency in Canada, Great Britain, and the United States, 1880–1940.
  Sources: Data used to construct this figure were drawn from Leacy 1983, ser. E190; Bain and
    Price 1980, pp. 39, 88, 107; Great Britain, Department of Employment and Productivity
    1971, p. 396; U.S. Bureau of the Census 1975, p. 179; Griffin 1939, p. 38.

44–47). Evidence from Canada and Britain tends to undermine the notion that
disruption, or noninstitutionalized politics, "produces" reform directly. Social
unrest and disruption are not usually invoked as an immediate cause of the enactment of welfare legislation in the cases of the British Liberal welfare reforms
and of the Canadian pension law; the timing is too clearly off.

  While strikes are only one kind of popular insurgency, they are often seen
as particularly important to the initiation of reforms by state officials. Figure 2.4
shows time series of strike statistics for the United States, Canada, and Britain.
Strike levels were not at a peak in the years immediately preceding the passage
of old age pension legislation in Canada and Britain. In Britain, levels during
the first decade of the twentieth century—when a range of welfare reforms
passed in Parliament—were lower than they had been in the preceding decade,
and the peak of strike activity followed the introduction of welfare reforms.
Canadian strike statistics show a pattern similar to the British: levels of activity
were higher prior to World War I, when reforms failed, than in the 1920s, when

old age pensions were enacted. Indeed, in the Canadian case, strike levels were on a decline in the 1920s after the immediate postwar peak of 1920.

The U.S. case does seem to be different from the pattern in the other countries. Strike levels increased during the Progressive Era and in the 1930s, although peak strike activity came after 1935. Bjorn (1979) found in a comparative-historical analysis of Australia, Norway, Sweden, Great Britain, and the United States over the years 1920–70 that "government vertical redistribution of income"[6] was more likely to occur under prolabor governments in "class-cohesive" party systems, but in other types of party systems—most notably that of the United States—such programs might be initiated in response to popular insurgency. Although strike activity is associated with the initiation of social spending in the 1930s, it was not so linked in the Progressive Era. This fact casts doubt on the sufficiency of the factor for the introduction of modern social benefits programs. Moreover, a closer look at the U.S. case shows that the social disruption approach is mistaken on some key points in the account of the 1930s. For now, let me note only that Roosevelt and his advisers were committed to social insurance long before the Depression and that disruption and the mobilization of mass movements in favor of social spending had a rather paradoxical effect on the character of policy, from the point of view of these analysts. It tended to reinforce the conservatism of administration policymakers, although it did help to weaken congressional opposition to any social spending initiatives.

These differences among Britain, Canada, and the United States should alert us to the fact that popular insurgency alone will not adequately explain social welfare innovations. Clearly, other factors must explain why in the United States social disruption was necessary to overcome congressional opposition to social welfare reform and why the temporal pattern of events appears to be different—with a disjuncture between periods of disruption and periods of social welfare innovation—in Canada and Great Britain. What sets the U.S. political system apart from others cannot be specified by the various class politics or social disruption approaches. We will need to know more about state and political institutions and the political transformations of the past century. But first we will deal with the arguments of and evidence for the predominant variant of the political conflict perspective—the power resources approach. Unlike the neo-Marxist "logic of capitalism" accounts, this perspective has been subjected to a great deal of empirical assessment. Unlike the empirical assessments carried out for the social disruption approach, those testing the propositions of the power resources perspective have been comparative, and some have been historical as well.

6. Bjorn defines this as public assistance expenditure as a percentage of GNP, corrected for demand.

The Power Resources Approach

The power resources, or social democratic, perspective sees the conflict between workers and capitalists as central in the politics of capitalist countries
and, further, sees social policy as a critical arena for the deployment and enhancement of power resources. Proponents argue that the working class has
variable capacities to affect social policy in a direction which is advantageous
to its interests and to build up further its resources (Korpi 1978, 1983). They
identify two types of power resources: market-based resources, inherently un-
equally distributed under capitalism, and the right to vote and organize for
collective action in the political arena, presumed to be more equally distributed in a democracy (Korpi 1989). Capitalists have greater resources within the
market, while workers—because of their numbers—have greater resources in
the polity. Wage earners, they argue, will be interested in using political resources to modify market processes and to extend citizenship rights to social
benefits. In short, politics can be used against markets (to borrow from the title
of Esping-Andersen's 1985 book). According to social democratic analysts, a
fully developed welfare state is a product of "a highly centralized trade union
movement with a class-wide membership base, operating in close coordination
with a unified reformist-socialist party which, primarily on the basis of massive
working class support, is able to achieve hegemonic status in the party system.
To the extent that these criteria are met, it is hypothesized that the welfare state
will emerge earlier, grow faster, and be structured in ways which systematically
favor the interests of labor over those of capital" (Shalev 1983b, p. 321).

   This perspective has been fairly successful in explaining policy variations
in the post–World War II years, when labor or socialist parties have held power
and increases in "working-class strength" through increased unionization or
electoral mobilization have led directly to enhanced power for these political
parties. Thus, both overall levels of social expenditures and the relative generosity of benefits such as pensions have been shown by power resources analysts
to be related to working-class organizational and political power (see Myles
1984; Korpi 1978, 1983, 1989; Stephens 1979; Bjorn 1979; Castles 1978;
Esping-Andersen 1985; for an excellent summary, see Shalev 1983b). Castles
(1982) has shown that the relative weakness of the Right is also involved—to an
even greater degree than the strength of the Left—in the level of social expenditures. Based on these impressive findings of support for the power resources
perspective in the contemporary period, some analysts have extrapolated back
in time and argued that similar increases in working-class strength led to the
initiation of pensions and social insurances (Stephens 1979).

Trade Unions and Social Benefit Programs
Analyses of British social politics in the early twentieth century highlight the
demands of rapidly growing unions for social protections, especially old age

pensions, outside the restrictions of the new poor law (Gilbert 1966, pp. 196, 211; Fraser 1973, p. 129; Stephens 1979, p. 145; Quadagno 1982, pp. 181–82, 187–88, 190). In 1899 trade union leaders helped to launch a campaign through the National Committee of Organized Labour on Old Age Pensions (NCOL), calling for noncontributory public pensions to cover all British citizens over sixty-five years of age. Later that same year the Trade Union Congress (TUC) endorsed universal pensions for all citizens at age sixty (Gilbert 1966, p. 196). By 1908 the British government partially satisfied this extraparliamentary campaign by legislating pensions. In contrast, many students of social policy in early-twentieth-century North America—even when they do not make the common mistake of assuming that U.S. trade unions invariably opposed new public protections—portray unions as too weak, defensive, and politically unimportant to gain legislative success for pensions or other new social programs proposed in the early years of the twentieth century. (For the United States, see Rimlinger 1971, pp. 80–84; Nelson 1969, chap. 4; Horowitz 1978, chaps. 1–2; Stephens 1979, pp. 149–56. For Canada, see Finkel 1977, p. 346; Lipton 1967, chaps. 6–7.) Following this frame of reference, changes in the distribution of power between capital and labor in North American civil society after World War I must have occurred to permit the success of new public programs of income support for the aged in the 1920s and 1930s (Stephens 1979, pp. 150–51).

A closer look at the evidence, however, shows that matters were more complex than conventional portraits of British versus North American unions suggest. Let's start with a look at trends in union density, the proportion of the labor force unionized (see figure 2.5). Although Canadian data is unavailable for the years prior to 1911 and from 1912 to 1920 (Bain and Price 1980, pp. 103–8), we can assume from the 1911 figure and the rest of the available statistical data that unionization there mirrored U.S. trends, though at a slightly lower level.

While unionization was higher in Britain than in the United States during the pre–World War I period, the percentages of the labor force unionized were comparable—from 9 to 16 percent—during each country's period of greatest reform ferment, between 1900 and 1910 in Britain and between 1906 and 1920 in the United States. Moreover, the first years of the twentieth century saw explosive growth for North American unions: The number of Canadians who were union members more than tripled (going from 50,000 to 175,800) between 1900 and 1913 (Lipton 1967, p. 99; see also Logan 1928, p. 123; Jamieson 1973, p. 18). In the United States, membership grew sixfold between 1898 and 1904, then almost doubled by 1914 (Greenstone 1969, p. 24). American unionization exceeded Canadian throughout the twenties, when pension legislation, supported by both U.S. and Canadian unions, succeeded in Canada but not in the United States at the national level. In fact, the proportion of the labor force in Canada's unions was declining during the period when the pen-

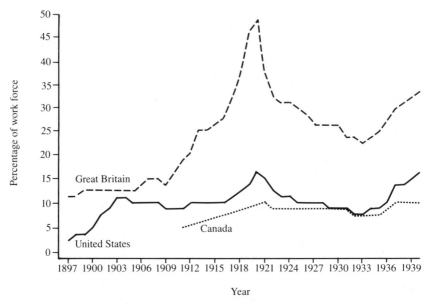

Figure 2.5. Union density in Canada, Great Britain, and the United States, 1880–1940.
Source: Data used to construct this figure were drawn from Bain and Price 1980, pp. 39, 88, 107.

sion law was being debated (Jamieson 1973, pp. 18–19, 21). Finally, American unionization levels were actually lower in the early thirties—just before the New Deal's social security legislation—than they had been in the Progressive Era when pensions first came onto the political agenda.[7]

In comparing Britain with the North American cases, it is also important to take into account state- and province-level variation in unionization. Based on the social democratic model, one might expect policy breakthroughs at the subnational, if not the national, level in the years before World War I. The most industrialized American states must have been much more similar to Britain in the prewar years in their levels of unionization than was the United States as a whole.[8] For example, imperfect data available for the state of Massachusetts

7. In the United States and Britain, large gains in unionization actually occurred after the initiation of the new social welfare programs, at least partially in response to the governments' prolabor policies, which included prounion as well as welfare legislation.

8. Bain and Price (1980, pp. 82, 92) show that unionization varied between 4 percent, for South Carolina, and 41.7 percent, for West Virginia, in 1939, the first year for which there are reliable estimates of union density on a state-by-state basis. Similarly, in 1941—the first year for which reliable statistics on union density exist for the Canadian provinces—unionization varied between 13 percent, for Ontario, and 22.4 percent, for British Columbia (Bain and Price 1980, pp. 104–5, 110).

show that unionization there more closely paralleled the British trends than did U.S. trends overall (Orloff and Skocpol 1984, p. 736). Not only was unionized American labor more weighty in the more industrialized states, but organized labor also exercised most of its political influence at local and state levels, and at the subnational level, unions more consistently supported old age pensions (Taft 1964, p. 233; Rogin 1962, pp. 534–35; Fink 1973, pp. 161–82; Anglim and Gratton 1987). Canadian industrialization and unionization were also concentrated in certain areas of the country, leading to provincial disparities in organization (Babcock 1974, pp. 38–39, 52, 156; Logan 1928, p. 124). The unions had more influence at the local and constituency level of Canadian politics than on a national scale (Lipton 1967, p. 121; Babcock 1974, chap. 5), but they were not able to build successful political alliances for pensions until after the war. In the United States, variation in unionization levels across the states was not associated with the differential success of pension legislation in the 1920s, when such laws were first enacted. Pensions succeeded in ten states in the 1920s: Montana in 1923, Nevada and Wisconsin in 1925, Kentucky in 1926, Maryland and Colorado in 1927, and Minnesota, Utah, Wyoming, and California in 1929 (U.S. Social Security Board 1937, pp. 160–61). With the exception of California and Wisconsin, these were not states with strong labor movements, and noticeably absent were the relatively well-organized states of America's industrial heartland (Taft 1968; Nash 1960; Ozanne 1984).

In all three countries, therefore, the proportion of the labor force organized was not on the rise in the years preceding each country's legislative breakthrough in old age protection—1908 for Britain, 1927 for Canada, and 1935 for the United States. Rather, the levels were relatively stable, even slightly declining. Nor were the trade unions' memberships growing in absolute terms (Bain and Price 1980, pp. 39, 88, 107). These facts are seriously at odds with the expectation of some analysts that an increasingly organized labor movement, either acting directly as a pressure group or indirectly as a potential disrupter of social order, was responsible for welfare breakthroughs.

The Working Class in Electoral Politics
Working-class pressures for public social protections may have been registered not simply or primarily through trade unions, but more broadly through the processes of democratic electoral politics. As the British, Canadian, and U.S. cases reveal, however, modern social programs do not come as automatic by-products of electoral democratization, although many have assumed that a deterrent poor relief system would be made an obsolete policy option under conditions of universal suffrage. The American electorate was fully democratized for white males by 1840 (Williamson 1960), the Canadian by the 1890s (Ward 1950, p. 223). The key phases of British working-class enfranchisement occurred well before the 1908 passage of the Old Age Pension Act, when better-off workers got the vote through the Reform Acts of 1867 and 1884, and

later, when everyone except women under thirty received the franchise in 1918 (Clarke 1972; Blewett 1965).

Yet far from stressing the sheer fact of working-class enfranchisement, many proponents of the working-class strength perspective argue that modern welfare programs arise from the combined efforts of trade unions and a political party based in the industrial working class and programmatically oriented to furthering its interests. From this perspective, the slow arrival of modern social protections for the aged and others in the United States and Canada is attributed to the absence of a working-class-based socialist or labor party. The British Labour party, along with some of the trade unions, is given the credit for developing old age pensions and other British welfare programs (Stephens 1979, pp. 140–59; Quadagno 1982, chap. 7; Lipton 1967, chaps. 6–7).

Obviously, this argument falls short in explaining why the democratic U.S. polity of the late nineteenth century extended social benefits to many working-class and middle-class Americans under the reworked rubric of the Civil War pension system. It is also misleading about the origins of the British welfare programs for the aged and others and cannot explain the later breakthroughs in North America. As for the British case, by the end of World War I the Labour party overtook the Liberals and became thereafter the chief defender and extender of public social benefits in Britain (Gilbert 1970; Marwick 1967). But the original legislative breakthrough of 1908 and the associated programs of the next few years were not the direct achievement of the fledgling Labour Representation Committee (LRC), founded in 1900 to elect worker representatives to Parliament. It was a Liberal—not a Labour—government, newly invigorated in 1908 by a strong progressive faction under Prime Minister Herbert Asquith, that proposed and put through social insurance and pensions (Morgan 1971, pp. 41–45).

At the juncture in question, the still-tiny LRC, though increasingly successful in elections and by-elections, remained dependent for its electoral and parliamentary prospects on an alliance with the much stronger, established Liberal party (Cole 1941, p. 202; Bealey 1956). Indeed, although many have emphasized the impact of the election in 1906, many of the twenty-nine Labour M.P.'s pledged to the enactment of old age pensions owed their seats to the secret electoral truce between the LRC and the Liberals, which prevented three-cornered races the Tories might win because of a split in the progressive vote between Labour and Liberal (Bealey 1956). The Liberals won in a landslide and did not depend on this electoral truce (Russell 1973). Meanwhile, the progressives within the Liberal party were looking for ways to appeal to working-class voters (Clarke 1974). British voter turnout was increasing in the early twentieth century, and the Liberals were pressed by competition from the Conservatives (Butler and Freeman 1969, p. 141; Morgan 1971, p. 43). Between the 1906 and 1910 elections, the Liberals lost significant ground to the Tories. For progressively minded Liberals, social benefits and pro–trade union measures, besides being morally desirable according to new liberal values, kept working-class voters loyal to their party, with its free trade priorities, and prevented Conservatives from wooing voters with a combination of tariffs and social spending (Freeden 1978, pp. 142–43; Addison 1983, pp. 49–50).

Just as the electoral strength of labor is overplayed as a causal factor in Britain, the political strength that U.S. workers had in the pre–World War I period is often underplayed. American workers in the Progressive Era were not only unionizing; some of them were also voting for the newly organized Socialist party. Indeed, this party's 6 percent share of the vote in the 1912 presidential election was comparable to the 7.6 percent received by the British Labour party in 1910 (Butler and Freeman 1969, p. 141; Weinstein 1974, pp. 314–15). The fact that the New Deal breakthroughs in old age pensions and insurance came in spite of the fact that the United States still had no labor party (Stephens 1979, p. 151) raises serious questions about the necessity of independent working-class political organization to the initiation of new social welfare programs. In any event, it certainly was not clear in the prewar years that a labor party would not become a major actor in the U.S. polity. The electoral success of the Socialist party in 1912 was still fresh in many minds. Competition between Democrats and Republicans and between progressives and stalwarts within both parties increased during the period between Theodore Roosevelt's presidency and the entry of the United States into World War I, although it never reached the levels of the late nineteenth century (Skowronek 1982, p. 167). Thus, during the Progressive Era, working-class voters were important to politicians as a constituency that had to be kept loyal. The extensive reforms enacted during this period, although they did not include programs of social spending, testify to the impact of working-class voters and other popular constituencies, particularly women—newly enfranchised or about to become so—about which elites were concerned (Skocpol forthcoming; Baker 1982; Lemons 1973).

An explanation of the Canadian case along the lines laid out by the working-class strength analysis conceivably could be made on the basis of the role of James Woodsworth and A. A. Heaps, Labour M.P.'s from Winnipeg, who forced consideration of old age pensions in 1925, after many years of trade union agitation in favor of pensions. Such an analysis, however, would be only superficially correct. The Labour M.P.'s did wield their influence in favor of pensions, but their extraordinary ability to affect policy outcomes was the result of holding the balance of power in a nearly evenly split Parliament, not because a powerful, politically organized labor movement was able to dictate its agenda to the government. Competition between Liberals and Conservatives gave working-class—and farmers'—votes and demands increased importance. The ruling Liberal party was willing to enter into an alliance with the Labour party in order to stay in power. The Liberals later worked with

Labour and Progressive candidates against the Conservatives in the election of 1926, much as their British counterparts had done with the LRC in the 1906 election. Social spending would become a key part of the electoral, cross-class alliance between labor, farmers, and liberals in Canada as it had been in Britain earlier. The conditions which made such balance-of-power politics possible are related to the characteristics of the Canadian political structure.

Weakness of the Right

What of Castles' thesis about the role of the weakness of the Right? In the United States, the weakness of the Republicans during the Depression did facilitate the acceptance of the Social Security Act,[9] but neither the Democrats nor the GOP supported pensions in the Progressive Era. British Conservatives vied with the Liberals to be seen as the champions of pension legislation in the first years of the twentieth century (each trying to tie new social protections to their program vis-à-vis tariffs), even as both had opposed such programs in the later years of the nineteenth (Orloff and Skocpol 1984). Canada's right-wing party, the Conservative, was not responsible for the initial rejection of pensions, and after the passage of the 1927 pension law, the Conservatives extended the program and enacted a contributory old age insurance program during the 1930–35 Bennett administration, although the latter was declared *ultra vires* and invalidated (Bryden 1974, chaps. 3–4; McConnell 1969). Like the social democratic perspective, Castles' rightist-weakness model seems to work best in the period after World War II, when modern policies had already been established and the issues centered on their character and cost. Larger political and social trends seem to have influenced whether elites accepted the necessity of social insurance and pensions.

Cross-Class Coalitions and the Initiation of Pensions

Recently, a number of power resources analysts have criticized certain emphases of the earlier work done from this perspective, in particular the failure to consider political forces beyond the working class and capital, the unjustified assumption of a linear relationship between "working-class power" and policy outcomes, and the tendency to assume that causal processes involved in policy-making are constant across countries and over time. (On this latter point, the early power resources perspective has been faulted for its "Swedocentrism," that is, relying too heavily on the atypical, but strongly social democratic, experience of the Swedes in developing a supposedly general model of policy

---

9. Indeed, forces within the Democratic party—the southern Democrats—posed the greatest legislative obstacles to the enactment of the Social Security Act (Witte 1962).

determinants; see Esping-Andersen 1990, chap. 1; Skocpol and Amenta 1986, pp. 141–43). Indeed, Esping-Andersen and Korpi (1987) have argued that an approach investigating cross-class coalitions to explain policy variation works better than a focus on the working class alone.

In his work on the "worlds of welfare capitalism," Esping-Andersen (1990) has argued that we find the key to distinctive welfare state regimes in alternative class coalitions, rather than in the strength of the working class alone (after all, he points out, the working class has only rarely been a numerical majority in the electorate). Such coalitions are affected by varying levels of working-class mobilization and political capacity, but also by the situation of other classes, most notably farmers and the new middle classes, and their orientation toward the welfare state.[10] In short, Esping-Andersen directs our attention from a focus on the mobilization of workers alone to the entire history of political class coalitions, building on the work of Barrington Moore (1966) and more recent analysts. In the years before World War II, farmers were the key to welfare politics—except in England, where rural groups had disappeared from the political stage by the turn of the century. Red-green alliances in Sweden and Norway in the interwar years led to policy innovations favorable to workers and popular interests more generally—a "social democratic" policy regime. In continental Europe, farmer alliances with capital and other elites excluded workers politically and reinforced the original, conservative characteristics of "statist-corporativist" regimes that offered social protections in a manner that reinforced status distinctions and reliance on the market. In the Anglo-American countries, versions of red-green or worker–middle class alliances ushered in modest, but relatively universalistic systems of social provision in the 1930s and 1940s. In the post–World War II period, it is the orientation of the new middle classes that has been decisive for the character of policy regimes (Esping-Andersen 1990, pp. 31–32). To oversimplify the schema, in Scandinavia, the new middle classes were incorporated into generous and universalistic welfare states, and the conservative welfare states of continental Europe institutionalized a middle-class loyalty to the preservation of (earlier-established) occupationally segregated social insurance programs, but in the liberal regimes, public provision was not upgraded to meet the demands of the expanding new middle class, which therefore tends to rely on the market for many welfare services. This has left much of public provision to the poor and working classes; however, there are some important exceptions, such as Canadian health insurance or the U.S. social security system for the retired

10. Jill Quadagno's (1988a,b) work on the American welfare state and James Struthers' (1983) research on Canadian unemployment insurance are also exemplary in considering some of the ways agrarian groups and agricultural economies have affected policy developments in the North American countries.

elderly, which politically incorporates the middle and working classes, even those who are able to supplement their social security with private pensions (Weir, Orloff, and Skocpol 1988, chap. 11).

Contemporary welfare states in Canada, the United States, and Britain do tend to fit a liberal profile. Esping-Andersen contends, however, that both Canada and Britain "achieved" their current liberal status via a somewhat different route than did the United States. In the United States, a red-green alliance under Democratic party auspices was responsible for the initiation of New Deal social programs; in Canada, a grouping similar in its class composition, the coalition among the Liberal, Labour, and Progressive parties, backed pensions in the mid-1920s while the Canadian Commonwealth Federation (an alliance of worker and farmer groups, the forerunner of today's New Democratic party) supported unemployment insurance and other social reforms in the 1930s and 1940s. In Britain, working-class and some middle-class groups under the auspices of the Labour party backed the expansion of the welfare state represented in the Beveridge Plan.[11] The United States remained liberal by virtue of the New Deal coalition's failure fully to promote universalism, foundering on the racial politics of the South. In contrast, Britain and Canada had moved from liberal policy provision to a universalistic strategy (in the 1940s) that only later (in the 1950s, 1960s, and 1970s) degenerated into residualism as better-off workers and others turned to private benefits as the flat-rate benefits declined relative to growing incomes in the postwar years.[12] These distinctive paths of policy development may be related to differences in the conjuncture of causal factors which caused the initiation of modern social provision for the aged and

11. Baldwin (1990, pp. 115–34) discusses the cross-class alliance around universalism in 1940s Britain more fully than does Esping-Andersen and, while also emphasizing the role of the middle classes, does so from a rather different analytic perspective.

12. Castles and Mitchell (1991) offer an interesting interpretation of policy developments in Britain and Canada in the aftermath of World War II, which they describe as moves toward universalism—away from initially liberal characteristics—in social provision. They argue that these changes amount to a shift from a "liberal" to a "radical" regime type, a grouping which also includes the policy regimes of New Zealand and Australia (which took radical shape from their origins). Thus, they maintain that there are four, rather than three, "worlds of welfare capitalism," adding the radical regime type to Esping-Andersen's initial group of three. Radical regimes, like social democratic ones, they say, reflect the policy activity of a strongly mobilized working class but differ from the Scandinavian systems in the character of policy instruments chosen to carry out socialist or labor goals. This seems to me to be a fascinating line of analysis to pursue in understanding post–World War II policy developments. I would note that one of the striking differences between social democratic and radical groupings, which could help to explain the choice of policy instruments, is in their respective experiences of state formation and state building and subsequent administrative capacities, factors as yet unexplored by any of the analysts investigating cross-class coalitions and regime types. Likewise, it is possible that differences among the group of initially liberal regimes in these same factors may help to account for their later policy divergence.

in the character of that provision. One of the key goals of the present analysis is, of course, accounting for this variation among the three countries.

Elites, Class Coalitions, and Ideology

The evidence reviewed suggests that although the political emergence of the working class is implicated in the development of modern social policy, the effect of working-class political action on social policy in the formative period of modern social provision was not direct, linear, or immediate. Thus, we will want to retain from the power resources approaches the point that working-class support for pensions is a necessary factor in the success of pensions in the liberal countries, but we will need to amend other aspects of these accounts. The focus on cross-class coalitions and regime types does seem to be an especially promising way to begin to understand the role of working-class organizations and electorates, yet here, too, amendments will be necessary to fully meet the comparative test.

Most of the political conflict approaches, including the power resources perspective, may be faulted for ignoring significant social bases for the formation of political interests, identities, and ideologies other than those based on class. In particular, recent feminist research has highlighted the gendered character of state social provision and social politics (Pedersen 1989; Skocpol and Ritter 1991; Skocpol forthcoming; Jenson 1986; Gordon 1990; Hernes 1987; Shaver 1990). It is not inaccurate to maintain that cross-class alliances have been important forces in the initiation and development of social programs. We must become more attentive, however, to the ways in which these alliances reflected the gender (as well as class) interests of the men who led and populated their constituent organizations and who voted in the electorates which helped to bring about policy innovations. Likewise, we should pay attention to the roles of race, age, religion, and region in shaping social politics.

The class-coalition approach works well enough for the period when working-class political organizations were in a position to form governments and negotiate with other parties, beginning in the 1930s, but primarily after World War II (although I would suggest that certain important institutional preconditions are not sufficiently noted). But there are difficulties with this perspective for the "formative period of the welfare state," the years between the 1880s and World War I when modern social policy first emerged. Basically, the class-coalition approach investigates the possibilities for workers being a part of a governing coalition with farmers or new middle classes. Certainly, the orientation of farmers in North America and emerging new middle classes in all three countries played a part in the initiation of new social provision for the aged. But in this early era it is impossible to ignore the initiatives and political orientations of elites—authoritarian bureaucrats, liberal politicians, social reformers, and social scientists—in particular, their willingness to form coalitions with emerging nonelite political forces to enact programs directed at popular needs (Heclo 1974; Flora and Alber 1981; Orloff and Skocpol 1984; Steinmetz 1987).

Unfortunately, there has been a tendency within the class politics tradition to ignore political, reform, and intellectual elites. Indeed, I believe that a key difference between power resources and institutionalist analyses is found in their respective understandings of the role of these elites. While in many power resource analyses, the role of elites is simply disregarded, in the United States it has been all too common for scholars to misspecify the character of elites active in policy-making, considering political, reform, and intellectual elites as simply "capitalist lackeys" (see Jenkins and Brents 1989; Ferguson 1984; Conkin 1967). In fact, the activities of party officials, elected leaders, state bureaucrats, social scientists, charity workers, and social reformers were largely separate from those of businessmen. In his study of modern social politics in Britain and Sweden, Heclo (1974) found that reform-oriented "middle-men" operating at the interface of states, parties, and social groups and civil servants familiar with administrative problems and possibilities were the critical actors in shaping the character of policy innovations. He emphasizes the distinctive sources of their ideas in learning about existing policy ("political learning") as well as through international diffusion of experiences and models. The majority of businessmen were not politically active around social policy, and of those who were, most took part in debates and struggles as members of business groups, such as the boards of trade in Canada and Britain or the chambers of commerce in the United States, rather than in other organizations (Orloff and Parker 1990). Of course, a few members of business elites did participate in reform, intellectual, and political circles, but their positions were determined ideologically and politically as well as economically, as was the case with other elites.

I refer to those active in policy debates and struggles and occupying positions of leadership in political, charity, and social reform organizations or academia as political, reform, and intellectual elites. They were distinct both from the middle-class public to whom they provided political leadership as well as from the handful of capitalists with whom they sometimes worked in fashioning policy. The identity of these elites and the patterns of their political interactions with popular forces, however, differed across regime types.

Elites' responses to the expansion of the suffrage were of particular importance. In their study of the initiation of core social insurance and pension legislation in a number of European countries, Flora and Alber note that "in parliamentary democracies, the extension of the suffrage clearly increased the propensity to introduce social insurance schemes" but did not have an effect in constitutional-dualist monarchies. Regardless of suffrage levels, constitutional-dualist monarchies such as Germany and Austria "tended to introduce social insurance schemes earlier (in chronological and developmental time) than the parliamentary democracies" (1981, pp. 70, 72). In initiating social insurance systems, authoritarian elites practiced "anticipatory political incorporation" of the working classes (Skocpol and Ikenberry 1983, p. 90), simultaneously attempting to secure working-class loyalty to the government and head off the socialist challenge. Moreover, through programmatic provisions which re-inforced occupational and status differences, these leaders tried to undermine class solidarity. In these countries, there was not a cross-class alliance in which labor was an active party; rather, national-level policy coalitions excluded working-class organizations.[13]

In the three liberal democratic countries, the pattern of elite-popular inter-action around the introduction of modern social provision was different than that in the constitutional-dualist regimes. In Britain, the Liberals, while still working to incorporate working-class voters in their own ranks, responded to the cross-class campaign for pensions of the National Committee of Orga-nized Labour and concluded an electoral alliance in 1906 with the still-tiny Labour Representation Committee prior to passing pension legislation in 1908. In Canada, the Liberal party worked with Labour M.P.'s, as well as with the agrarian Progressives, to pass the Old Age Pension Act in 1927. In the United States, working-class voters (particularly those of immigrant back-ground) shifted massively into the Democratic party in the 1932 election that brought Franklin Roosevelt into office; FDR pursued coalition politics with unions, farmers' groups, and other popular organizations through the 1930s as he took a number of social policy initiatives, including the Social Security Act of 1935.

To summarize, liberal elites in the democratic regimes of the United States, Canada, and Britain entered into explicit alliances with working-class parties (the British and Canadian cases) and/or competed for working-class and popular support for their own parties partially through social policy ini-tiatives (all three cases). In all three countries, the initiation of modern social provision for the aged was the work of cross-class coalitions of new middle-class, farm, and working-class groups, led by liberal political entrepreneurs, operating within and outside of legislatures. Thus, it was premised on the entry into electoral politics of the working class and their political mobilization, as well as on the ideological reorientation of liberal reform, political, and intel-

13. Interestingly, while this is the case at least on the national level, recent research on the local state and social policy in Germany by George Steinmetz (1987) suggests that patterns of social policy-making in cities were quite different from national patterns and, further, that local welfare initiatives in the area of public works and unemployment insurance were the product of cooperation between liberal and social democratic representatives.

lectual elites through the development of "new liberalism." It is important to note that cross-class coalitions favorable to new social spending, not working-class support, were the critical factor lacking in Canada and the United States when pensions first emerged on the policy agenda but failed in provincial, state, and federal legislatures. Labor was not the senior partner in the alliance in any of the three cases, and to that extent, these alliances may be considered a type of "incorporation from above" and are thus different from cross-class alliances in the post–War II era. Yet in contrast with the "anticipatory incorporation" practiced by authoritarian elites, elites in Canada and the United States were working in a political context in which working-class voters and organizations were formally their equals, and this was increasingly the case in Britain; as noted above, the expansion of the suffrage helped to prompt social policy initiatives, as did partisan competition.[14] Moreover, in all three cases state paternalism had less legitimacy than it did on the Continent.

At times, arguments about the effect of working-class pressure on elite policy initiatives have rested on a rather simplistic view of elites as capable of a near-perfect strategic rationality. There are people in the streets or workers joining socialist or labor organizations, and within a short period, there's legislation on the table, along with a (seemingly cynical) legitimation for the changes to boot. To the extent ideology is invoked, it is characterized as a simple reflection of elites' economic and political interests. Essentially, it is argued that working-class (or popular) organization and mobilization *force* elites to accept such initiatives out of concern for social order and economic productivity. There is no question that these were the concerns of a broad range of elites and of the middle-class public in the periods during which social insurance and pensions came under consideration, but other factors certainly motivated them as well. The concern of elites about social disorder, both actual and potential, I would argue, must be put into a longer time frame and seen as mediated by ideology. Strikes and other forms of popular protest had a long-term impact on elites' political thinking; these forms of mass activity contributed to the conceptualization of a "social question" that demanded an answer. In this sense, popular protest should be conceptualized as an "irreversible" causal factor, to use Lieberson's terminology (1985). The actual levels of strike activity at the time new reforms are enacted are probably less important causal factors than the way levels over time have affected elite thinking, accentuating the need to incorporate workers into the polity.

14. It is worth mentioning that numerous studies of contemporary politics find that various measures of partisan competition have a positive impact on social spending and program adoption in the American states and cross-nationally under conditions of a democratic franchise (see Pampel and Williamson 1985; Jennings 1979; Schneider 1982; Myles 1984; Scharansky and Hofferbert 1969; Amenta and Carruthers 1988), although some research has found a negligible association (Dye 1966; Tucker and Herzik 1986).

Rather than considering those involved in politics as simply rational actors, it is fruitful to consider them as acting on the basis of ideologies which embody views about moral obligations and the moral order, although those ideologies certainly are rooted in the material circumstances of their proponents. The elites in question were liberals, committed to ideals of individual integrity and opportunity as well as to the market.[15] The situation of the working classes, highlighted by new social scientific investigations, presented a challenge to these ideals even as it posed political difficulties. Thus, elites searched for ways, within a liberal framework, to deal with the social question. New liberalism was the answer. The old and new versions of liberalism embodied different views of the moral obligations of citizens and states. In classic liberalism, people are responsible for their own fate, and the (local) state has an obligation toward them only insofar as it should prevent outright starvation; this vision found institutional embodiment in the poor law. In the new liberalism, people are regarded as interdependent, and the fate of individuals is recognized as being affected by events—national in scope—beyond their control. Consequently, the state has an obligation to step in to provide the basis for individual responsibility and competition with measures such as social insurance that offer protection against income interruption and destitution caused by societal forces—unemployment, forced retirement, and so on.

Social insurance was one strategy for solving the social question. It was developed, during the nineteenth century and into the early twentieth, in contention with other approaches, in reaction to existing policies, and with a good deal of international diffusion. No doubt, this vision assumed a capitalist order, but it is worth keeping in mind that there are a range of possible ways to defend capitalist relationships and uphold work incentives, some more in keeping with popular needs than others. The initiation of social policy reform was affected by long-term ideological shifts as well as by short-term political opportunity or threat.

Yet we are interested in understanding the specific content of the policy preferences of various political actors as well as the character of policy outcomes. The ideological orientations of political actors do have an impact on the sorts of policy initiatives they suggest, but ideology cannot alone explain the specifics of policy preferences or ultimate outcomes, both of which differed across the three liberal countries. In the years before World War I, British elites were more receptive to social spending initiatives than their North Ameri-

15. In addition, although one does not want to adopt a "Whig" view of history, the impulses of some reformers toward social insurance stemmed from genuine commitment to improving the conditions of the laboring population, often born of the intimate knowledge of those conditions gained through settlement house or charity work or social scientific research. Those of us who today study the contemporary welfare state from a critical perspective should not consider ourselves the only members of the professional middle classes who have ever been capable of empathy.

can counterparts, despite common commitments to new liberalism. Likewise, Canadian and U.S. elites did not have exactly the same orientations to social spending in the 1920s and 1930s. To understand these differing policy orientations as well as the character of policy finally selected, one must go beyond considerations of ideology and cross-class political alliances to investigate the effects of existing policy on policy debates, political coalitions, and administrative capacities, as well as the overall institutional context.

However one amends models of elites' views of and strategies toward popular groups, there remains a critical component left out of most so-called society-centered explanations of social policy developments: elites' interests and political orientations can never be reduced solely to their position vis-à-vis nonelites in civil society, for they have an irreducible institutional component. Once one accepts a more differentiated view of elites—as comprising business, intellectual, reform, and political segments—it is clear that their struggles for power and authority will be important for policy developments (see Shefter 1977, 1978; Skowronek 1982; Lindblom 1978; Skocpol 1979, 1985a; Lachmann 1989). In this struggle, the positions of various elites within existing institutions constrain them differently and produce distinctive incentives and opportunities for engaging in popular mobilization and "issue entrepreneurship." They also call upon different institutional—including state—capacities in doing so.

State Capacities

A key trend within social science and history has been the revival of interest in the state (Evans, Rueschemeyer, and Skocpol 1985). A range of scholars has recognized that the internal character of the state is relevant to explaining the "output" of the state, that is, its policy. The administrative state—the bureaucracy—has been singled out as being of particular importance. A number of analysts have argued that state capacities—specific organizational structures needed for carrying out given tasks—affect the timing and character of policy innovations such as old age pensions. Generally, it is assumed that countries with more developed state capacities will initiate modern social spending programs before those with less developed capacities. Still others have reasoned that "strong" states, the ones that expand spending most easily, are centralized rather than federated and have tried to link these state features to spending (DeViney 1983; Wilensky 1976, 1981). Many of these scholars also argue that the autonomy of states is important to policy developments and assume that capacities and autonomy are linked, so that more of the former leads to more of the latter (see Nordlinger 1981).

The empirical evidence relevant to the state capacities perspective is generally positive, but not completely unmixed. For example, Flora and Alber note that the earlier initiation of modern social provision in the constitutional-dualist monarchies (relative to the liberal parliamentary democracies) may result from the fact that these countries "had already developed stronger state bureaucracies capable of administering [social insurance] systems" (Flora and Alber 1981, p. 70). Malloy (1979) offers a similar explanation of Brazilian policy developments. Two recent studies of the enactment of old age pensions and unemployment insurance in the American states found that measures of fiscal and administrative capacity were associated with the early adoption of such legislation (Amenta and Carruthers 1988; Amenta et al. 1987). While Steinmetz (1987, p. 236) finds that the size of city bureaucracies had little effect on their social spending in Wilhelmine Germany, he does find that the functional complexity of municipal bureaucracies is associated with the incidence of unemployment insurance. DeViney (1983) finds in his time-series study of social expenditures in twenty advanced industrial countries that bureaucratic resources are sometimes associated with later growth in social expenditures, but this does not hold up universally. On the basis of their time-series analysis of social expenditures in Britain, Germany, France, and Italy, Hage and Hanneman (1980) suggest that centralization of the state may either promote or retard such spending. Finally, a number of analysts have pointed out that state autonomy and state capacities do not necessarily covary (see Mann 1988; Esping-Andersen 1990; Skocpol 1985b).

What might account for the difficulties some analysts have encountered in applying the notion of state capacities? All too often, analysts have attributed to the state bureaucracy a "putatively inherent tendency . . . to expand social expenditures" (Skocpol and Amenta 1986, p. 148), arguing that bureaucrats want as large a budget as they can possibly get, for their pay, power, and prestige are all linked to the size of the budget (Niskanen 1971). These assertions are associated with both a naive Weberianism and the politically conservative public choice school. The argument is often made about all public expenditures, but it has obvious relevance for the social expenditures of the welfare state; by this logic, bureaucrats, particularly in those state agencies responsible for social programs, would be especially interested in initiating new programs of social provision that would expand their fields of action (see Borcherding 1977; Mueller 1979). Even analysts outside the strongly antigovernment public choice school seem to have accepted this view of bureaucracies, seeing "internal pressures within the bureaucracy for expansion" (DeViney 1983, p. 167). By this line of reasoning, the larger the bureaucracy, the greater the likelihood that such programs would in fact be initiated and subsequently expanded.

The rather blinkered vision of bureaucratic politics just described simply assumes that state bureaucrats will have an interest in expanding social expenditures, based on extrapolating from mid-to-late twentieth-century conditions in the advanced capitalist democracies in which Keynesian principles predominated in government. Thus, this perspective actually admits of no political and ideological variation on the part of state officials, to say nothing of differences in the institutional and structural constraints that they face over time and across national contexts. To take a particularly telling example, one might consider the politics of Britain's national poor law officials in the nineteenth century. Rather than looking for ways to expand spending on the programs under their direction, they worked consistently to cut back on social spending for poor relief (Thomson 1990; Rose 1972). Toward the end of the century, as numerous reformers called for the initiation of new forms of social provision, the Local Government Board, which oversaw poor relief administration, remained "a hostile citadel of poor law orthodoxy" (Heclo 1974, p. 173). In the early 1900s these bureaucrats refused to cooperate with Liberal government initiatives in planning pension and unemployment insurance programs (Heclo 1974, chaps. 3–4). In short, in rediscovering the institutional determinants of policy, specifically state administrative capacities (and it should be kept in mind that there are other important institutional factors), we don't want to lose sight of the political and ideological forces which also direct the process of policy-making. Given political incentives for spending, capacities make a difference, but the incentive to use them, and the goals to which they are put, must still be understood.

Another source of the negative findings about state capacities is to be found in the dubious validity of some of the measures used to define state capacities. For example, analysts have operationalized state capacities as simply the government's share of the GNP or the sheer number of bureaucrats; the public choice theorists deduce their hypothesized budget effects simply from the size of the bureaucracy. When more nuanced, and valid, measures are used, analyses are more useful and findings are more supportive of an emphasis on the state. Steinmetz's analysis (1987) of the unemployment policies of almost one hundred pre–World War I German cities offers a nice illustration of this point. A measure of the number of bureaucrats in each city was nonsignificant, but a measure of the functional complexity of a city's government was quite important in explaining the variation in cities' policy. Moreover, Steinmetz found an important interaction between state capacities, more reasonably operationalized, and the political strength of the Social Democrats: "A higher level of administrative complexity enhanced the effect of Socialist municipal councilors on the probability of a city introducing the Ghent system," a system of unemployment insurance favored by the trade unions (Steinmetz 1987, p. 280).

Clearly, the emphasis on state capacities has led to important insights about the determinants of policy developments, but we need a far more nuanced conception of the ways in which states and wider political systems affect policy than that offered by a simple-minded focus on "bureaucratic resources" alone. Here, the amendments to simple state-centered" approaches are so extensive that I will develop them in the following section, on the institutional perspective.

The Determinants of Policy Outcomes in the Liberal Democracies: The Institutional Approach

The distinctive feature of the institutional perspective is a focus on state and political institutions and state-society relationships. This viewpoint does not involve a rejection of the causal importance of factors such as capitalist industrialization and concomitant social-structural changes for the initiation of modern social policy, but rather contends that political institutions and social factors in combination set the conditions for policy change. Specifically, institutionalists argue that state capacity (or readily creatable capacity) to plan, administer, and extract resources is a precondition for the emergence of modern social programs such as pensions and social insurance, and that the institutional context—the character, capacity, and structure of the state and political institutions—affects elite and popular political organization, capacities and orientations, and the formation of cross-class political coalitions. Economic and demographic changes, ideological shifts, and popular political pressures have an impact on the break with poor relief and the initiation of modern social provision, but their effect occurs within specific political and institutional frameworks. Furthermore, institutionalists offer an explanation for the content of policy initiatives that goes beyond ideology and interest: processes of policy feedback—the ways in which the legacy of existing policy informs policy debates, the formation of policy interests and coalitions, and the development of specific administrative capacities—shape the character of policy innovations.

Before sketching the institutionalist explanatory "model," let me stress that this was not generated through deductive methods alone. Instead, the process looked very much like the "conversation" between hypotheses and evidence discussed in the last chapter. I started with a number of working hypotheses drawn from the literature, evaluated them in the course of comparative analysis, and modified them in the light of that evidence. The "model" I am about to describe, then, is the product of the analysis which follows in the remainder of the book. I hope this ordering makes that analysis easier for you, the reader, to follow, but please bear in mind how it was developed.

Let me begin by discussing the elements of the state and larger political-institutional context which are needed to explain variation in the timing and character of modern social provision for the aged in Britain, Canada, and the United States. There are three main elements: state autonomy and capacity, the institutional context, and policy feedback. Once these state and political factors are adequately constructed (or reconstructed, in the case of state capacities), we will have a new basis for understanding the way elements suggested by other perspectives help to produce policy outcomes.

State Autonomy and Capacity

I start from the premise that states are potentially autonomous sets of coercive, extractive, judicial, and administrative organizations controlling territories and the populations within them (see Mann 1988; Skocpol 1985b; Tilly 1975, 1985). In the cases of Britain, Canada, and the United States, these core organizations are embedded within constitutional-representative systems of parliamentary decision-making. Both the autonomous initiatives of state officials and the different structures and capacities of states critically affect the timing and character of social policy developments. Michael Mann (1988) has usefully elaborated on the concepts of state autonomy and capacity in a recent discussion of the "power of the state" (see also Skocpol 1985b). What many refer to as the autonomy of the state Mann terms "the despotic power of the state elite," defined as "the range of actions which the elite is empowered to undertake without routine, institutionalized negotiation with civil society groups" (1988, p. 5). Mann argues that this power is based on the inability of forces within civil society to control state functions. Another influential discussion of state autonomy and capacity by Theda Skocpol (1985b) emphasizes the distinctive sources of state elites' goals, regardless of the relationship of those elites to groups in civil society; thus, even when the state's despotic or autonomous power is circumscribed, the generation of distinctive state elites' interests is not, although the elites' power to achieve those goals may be. Mann describes state capacities as the "infrastructural power" of the state, "the capacity . . . to actually penetrate civil society, and to implement logistically political decisions throughout the realm." He notes that this is an analytically autonomous dimension of power from the "despotic" power of states (Mann 1988, p. 5). Indeed, this type of power "allows the possibility that the state itself is a mere instrument of forces within civil society, i.e., that it has no despotic power at all" (Mann 1988, p. 7).[16]

Insisting on the causal importance of state autonomy and capacities, both rooted largely (although not exclusively) in the dynamics of state-building within an international states system, is not the same thing as asserting that states always and everywhere are fully autonomous from social forces. In fact, state officials are sensitive to a variety of social and economic influences, as are

---

16. This reason undoubtedly has led various society-centered analysts to be much more willing to accept that state capacities may affect policy outcomes than to acknowledge any autonomous generation of goals and interests on the part of state officials.

the leaders of any organization. I would simply argue that the logics of state-building and the international states system are not reducible to an economic or class logic. In that sense, they are "independent" factors. There is no expectation that in "the lonely hour of the last instance" (to use E. P. Thompson's phrase [1978]), the character of state organizations and policies are necessarily limited by class structure and relations. Nor is there any assumption of an inherent tendency to expansionism or progressivism in policies. Investigations of state formation and participation in the international states system help us to understand how changes in the extent of autonomy, structure, capacity, and character of states contribute to the development of social policy in any given country, for most scholars working in this tradition acknowledge that capacities and autonomy may expand and contract and do not always covary.

The potential for state officials, both elected and appointed, to formulate and pursue their own goals is rooted in the distinctive position and functions of states. There may be overlap at times between the interests and policy preferences of elected or appointed state officials and those of the dominant economic class, yet it is critical to understand their different sources. States carry out specific functions, two of which are particularly important for the formation of distinctive interests on the part of state elites and for stimulating their pursuit of policies separate from those of important social groups (Skocpol 1985b, p. 9; Mann 1988, pp. 13–14). These are maintaining internal order, and maintaining (or "improving," perhaps through aggression) the position of the state within the international states system. The basis of state power resides in state elites' control of the administrative and coercive institutions which carry out these tasks and in their ability to take advantage of "balancing possibilities" or "manoeuvering space" (Mann 1988, p. 15). The latter refers to the ways that state elites may be able to play off different social groups against each other to create their own power (see Marx's *Eighteenth Brumaire of Louis Bonaparte* for a classic statement of this source of autonomous state action). Mann points out that through the involvement of state elites in many domestic and institutional tasks, they are able to create even more such room to maneuver. Skocpol (1985b, 1979) has argued that involvement with international affairs has been critical to state elites' attempts to decrease dependence on domestic groups. Autonomous state action is most likely when there are "organizationally coherent collectivities of state officials, especially collectivities of career officials relatively insulated from ties to currently dominant socioeconomic interests"; where there is less autonomy, collectivities of officials may still build upon existing state policies (the policy legacy) in distinctive ways (Skocpol 1985b, p. 9). Thus, it will be important to investigate the character of state officialdom— their training, organization, and ties to various social groups. The existence of patronage or civil service systems is also critical.

Beyond sovereignty and the stable control of territory, state capacities are based on financial and administrative resources; stable access to plentiful finances and a loyal and skilled body of officials facilitate state initiatives. These resources typically are "rooted in institutional relationships that are slow to change and relatively impervious to short-term manipulations" (Skocpol 1985b, p. 16). We will be interested in the sources and amounts of available financial resources and the degree of flexibility in their collection and deployment. Capacities may be, and usually are, uneven across areas of state activity and levels of government (Skocpol 1985b, p. 17; see also Krasner 1978; Evans, Rueschemeyer, and Skocpol 1985; Tilly 1985; Weir and Skocpol 1985; Stepan 1985). In this study, we will be most concerned with the relative development of capacities to carry out the administration of social spending programs, especially a sufficient resource base and officials with social scientific and actuarial expertise. Underlying these specific capacities must be some development of bureaucratic practices and the concomitant freedom from patronage practices.

The Institutional Context and State Formation

It is of course clear that the impact of the state on policy developments is not limited to the qualities of state officials or sheer fiscal and administrative capacities. Also critical are the operating modes and capacities of the very political organizations—parties and state administrative organs—through which public social policies can be collectively formulated and socially supported; the organizational structures of the state and parties affect the meanings and methods of politics for all groups. I use the term *institutional context* to denote the ensemble of political and state organizations in each country. I suggest that processes of state formation and state building decisively shape the institutional context. Thus, I would argue that social policy developments must be understood in the context of the particular political histories of countries and would emphasize that *political* involves interstate as well as domestic power relations. State formation in a given territory is itself affected by several factors, two relating to the international order, three primarily to domestic arrangements: geopolitical position, especially the extent to which a given state is subject to threats of war within the international states system; position within the world economy; the character and sequence of democratization and bureaucratization (that is, the transformation of administrative practices from patronage to civil service); the relative interests and capacities of elites and popular groups in resisting or creating democracy, in keeping social order, and in particular institutional arrangements; and the extent of the economy's commercialization, which affects the difficulty of the extraction of resources for war-making and other activities, and thus the "bulkiness" of the state apparatus.

A state's position within the international states system is a critical determinant of the state-building experience. "War is the mother of states" sums up the reason. Preparation for war has been the key stimulant of state-building in the West since the 1500s (Tilly 1975, 1985, 1990; Mann 1988). The liberal countries as a group, but especially the United States and Canada, have been relatively insulated from threats of war, endemic on the European continent, although the colonies which later became Canada did face a somewhat milder military threat from an expansionist United States in the 1700s and early to mid-1800s. In addition to military pressures, economic competition has encouraged state-building efforts. In this respect, Canada faced greater incentives for the extension of state activities than did Britain, which was the world's first industrializer, or the United States, with its immense internal markets (Laxer 1989). The heating up of international military and economic competition in the 1800s further encouraged state-building efforts, manifest in movements to make state administrations more efficient and effective through bureaucratization and professionalization. Where international military and economic pressures were greatest, greater development of state administrative and extractive capacity and an earlier reform of the civil administration occurred. The initiation of modern social insurance and assistance was earliest in the Continental monarchies, as political leaders like Chancellor Bismarck used existing bureaucratic capacities to initiate the programs they hoped would co-opt popular support and undercut socialist organizing. The liberal countries did not initiate such programs until after the (at least partial) bureaucratization of their state administrations, which occurred later than in the monarchies because of less exposure to military pressures as well as greater development of democracy.

Tilly has argued that the extent of commercialization of the economy was an important determinant of "how much state apparatus emerged" out of war-making and other state activities (1990, p. 94). In Britain, Canada, and the United States, economies were commercialized, making the task of resource extraction relatively less difficult than in economies, such as Russia's, which were not extensively commercialized. This factor, too, led to less pressure for the bureaucratization of the state in the three countries than in some countries of continental Europe.

The character of and balance of power between elite and popular social forces directly affected the pattern and outcome of state formation and mediated the impact of international pressures. Of particular importance was the resolution of intraelite conflicts over the centralization of power in the national state, from which Britain emerged with a centralized state, the United States with a radically decentralized state and fragmented sovereignty, and Canada with a unified federal state set against rival provincial governments (Murrin 1980; Stewart 1986). After the basic institutional pattern of the state was set, the sequence in which bureaucratization and electoral democratization occurred was critical in shaping the capacity of the state administration and the character of party organizations (Shefter 1977). In most European monarchies, the bureaucratization of the state preceded the democratization of the electorate, and a "constituency for bureaucratic autonomy" developed to safeguard state positions from partisan or factional use. When the franchise was extended and parties emerged and sought popular support, the "spoils of office" were unavailable as an inducement to voters and party activists, for jobs in the civil administration were controlled by established bureaucratic elites. Thus, parties had to rely upon programmatic appeals, while state officials could rationalize and professionalize their operations without concern for partisan political considerations. This was significant for the development of social policy, for, as noted earlier, bureaucratic capacities in these states were relatively well developed at the time the working class began to mobilize politically, and state officials could make use of such capacities in attempting to co-opt labor through social policy initiatives. In contrast, in countries where electoral democracy—however limited—preceded state bureaucratization, as it did in Canada, Great Britain, and the United States, the civil administration was not protected from factional or partisan use. This encouraged parties and factions to utilize government jobs and resources—patronage—to mobilize their personal clienteles and constituencies and to reward activists. Electorates and party politicians developed interests in preserving patronage, and the electoral calculus of party politicians dominated the operations of state organizations, rendering them ill-suited to plan and carry out the sorts of state activities required for social insurance and other social spending programs.

Industrialization, urbanization, and international economic and military competition encouraged the development of civil service movements in the 1800s. In those countries where patronage still held sway over state administrations, a "progressive constituency for bureaucratic autonomy" (to use Shefter's term) emerged and struggled against the "political corruption" of patronage in order to create a nonpartisan, predictable, and expert civil service. Britain, Canada, and the United States experienced in common a struggle by civil service reformers to overcome democratized patronage. The character and outcome of these struggles differed in the three countries, based upon the extent of democratization—the capacity of popular groups to make effective claims on the state and to secure a permanent, institutionalized place in decision-making, which in turn depended on the resources and level of solidarity available to both popular and elite groups, and elite-popular relationships.

When pressures for administrative reform emerged, Britain was the least democratic, with extensive restrictions on the franchise based on property and other factors (Blewett 1965). Civil service reform succeeded before full democratization, and as more people were granted the franchise, political parties were encouraged to eschew patronage and to adopt programmatic appeals and constituency-based organization. State administration could then be changed in ways that enhanced its capacity for intervention in civil society, and politicians and reformers were encouraged to think of ways to use or extend that capacity. In North America, patronage was established in an almost fully democratic polity and as a consequence was quite hard to uproot afterward. Mass electorates, and the party politicians appealing to them, had continuing interests in using government as a source of patronage, and civil service reformers had to wage difficult, eventually only partially successful, struggles to overcome democratized "political corruption" in government and party politics. Thus, the delay in civil service reform resulted both from stronger pressures against administrative change because of mass patronage democracy and weaker pressures for civil service reform because of the North American countries' geopolitical position. Yet within this common situation, the United States and Canada differed in some important respects. Essentially, Canada was subject to greater economic competition than was the United States, while its political system was less democratic. This was associated with a larger state role and more complete, less contested civil service reform. Moreover, in part because of the threat of absorption by the larger United States, Canada maintained a strong link to Britain, which led to tighter integration into the world states system. These factors together were important in shaping the character of policy reform in Canada and the United States in the 1920s and 1930s.

Policy Feedback

Institutionalist perspectives also offer an explanation for the content of policy initiatives. Ideological perspectives and cultural frameworks to some extent limit the "universe of policy discourse," but this is influenced as well by the specific features of existing policies and administrative organizations. Policy debates were (and are) informed by the way that existing policy—the policy legacy—shapes the political understanding of problems, the framing of political interests, and the institutional capacities for further action. The policy legacy is the starting point for debates about what should replace it, and such debates are informed by ideas about how best to correct the perceived imperfections of past policy, rather than simply how best to respond to social conditions (Heclo 1974). This means that the goals and demands of politically active groups cannot be inferred from their current social positions or from ideological and value preferences alone, as political learning—reactions to existing policy—colors the interests and goals that groups or politicians define for themselves in public policy struggles (Heclo 1974). Policymakers orient themselves to the legacies of prior state actions: "What is normally considered the dependent variable (policy output) is also an independent variable. . . . Policy invariably builds on policy, either in moving forward what has been inherited, or amending it, or repudiating it" (Heclo 1974, p. 315).

Of course, the impact of existing policy is not limited to the realm of ideas.

Reactions to policies are not the same across all social and political groups: some are disadvantaged, others helped, by particular policies. Existing policies, such as poor relief and military pensions in the United States, mediated the effects of changing economic structures (the transition to wagework, and from agriculture to industry) on the elderly and their families, giving them specific sorts of interests in new forms of social provision at particular times. Indeed, the pattern of policy interests helps to shape political coalitions and enmities (see Weir, Orloff, and Skocpol 1988; Esping-Andersen 1985). Furthermore, policies can create (or dismantle) specific sorts of state capacities, influencing what can be done next. The effects of the policy inheritance on ideas, coalitions, and administrative capacities constitute policy feedback. It was in reaction to the administrative and fiscal difficulties and the cruelties of poor relief as it was administered in the late nineteenth century that European and North American politicians, reformers, and labor leaders proposed social insurance and pensions to provide protection for "respectable" members of the working classes. Consequently, crisis, or at least difficulties, in existing policy provided a necessary condition for policy reform and innovation.

The argument about the role of political learning may also fruitfully be extended to the ways in which groups react to existing state structures in formulating demands, and in the overall development of political orientations. The evaluations of proposed policy reforms are affected by political actors' more general reactions to the administrative characteristics and personnel of the state. Definitions of what is feasible or desirable in politics depend in part on the capacities and qualities that various groups attribute to state organizations and the officials and politicians who run them. Indeed, this is the most straightforward explanation for the varying degrees of "statism" in the political cultures of different countries. Likewise, the appeal of any given policy may depend not only on ideological proclivities but also on how well people think it could be officially implemented or how it might affect the fortunes of specific political organizations. Especially in periods when the very structure of the state is at issue and in transformation—such as the late nineteenth and early twentieth centuries in Britain, Canada, and the United States—particular policies may be advocated or opposed for reasons other than their perceived relevance to socioeconomic interests or cultural ideals. The rationalization and professionalization of state organizations were particularly important for professionalizing elites, the leading force within the "progressive constituency for bureaucratic autonomy." For this group, shifting away from patronage and toward meritocratic state administrative practices reflected an ideological commitment to utility, meritocracy, and universalism and provided a strategy for gaining and maintaining access to positions within the civil administration— a question of political power. Because of the tendency for policy preferences to reflect more general political learning about the state, the extent to which the reform of the civil service had been accomplished at the time social policy debates occurred was important for reform elites' willingness to form cross-class alliances with popular forces demanding new social spending programs such as old age pensions and insurance.

Summary

How, then, can we combine the elements of state autonomy and capacity, the institutional context, and policy feedback with the other causal factors to develop an explanation for the emergence of modern social provision that will meet the comparative test of our three cases?

We have identified three long-term social transformations as significant. First, capitalist industrialization created the basis for the issue of income protection to emerge, as it put people at a new form of social risk by creating mass dependence on wages. It is important to note that the impact of capitalist industrialization on the elderly and their families was mediated by the character of existing public social provision and that demographic changes were significant as well. Second, cultural and ideological shifts toward "new liberal" understandings of moral obligations among groups and between the state and the populace offered political actors justifications for new state activities. Third, the expansion and transformation of state administrative capacities and the concomitant reorientation of political parties over the nineteenth and early twentieth centuries created the institutional and political basis for the development of modern social programs. This involved the development of administrative, planning, and financial capacities and the reorientation of political parties. Socioeconomic, political, and ideological transformations created new bases and forms of political action. In this respect, particularly noteworthy are the growth of working-class and other popular-democratic political forces and the emergence of new middle-class groups, especially intellectuals oriented to social science and state officials. New needs did not simply emerge and receive attention; shifts occurred in the balance of social forces, in the incentives of elected and appointed officials to respond to popular issues, and in the understanding of political actors.

In the shorter term, we can single out two key factors in the shift to modern social provision as well: a policy crisis created through policy feedback and the emergence of a cross-class coalition. *Policy crisis* denotes a situation in which existing policies are no longer working fiscally, administratively, and/or politically, and mechanisms exist for making elites and other groups aware of the problems. Deterrent poor relief was never favored by the working population and was increasingly deemed illegitimate by elites as the "principles of 1834" [17]

---

17. England's Poor Law Amendment Act of 1834 established the so-called new poor law. The new law required that no assistance be offered able-bodied adults outside a workhouse and that the situation of any pauper must be no better than that of the poorest self-supporting laborer. Both

were more stringently applied in the 1870s and 1880s in the United States and Britain (Thomson 1984a; Quadagno 1982; Katz 1986) and social scientific investigations in all three countries highlighted the structural factors underlying poverty and the impact of poor relief on the "worthy" working classes. The development of administrative capacity and centralization in the late nineteenth century had made possible the more thorough implementation of poor relief policy principles, which resulted in assistance becoming less accessible. This added pressure to the aged and the families who took in their needy elderly kin, fueling popular disgruntlement with poor relief. As more people were enfranchised and parties changed in character, the dissatisfaction with poor relief emerged as a political issue. In addition, the local administration and financing of poor relief was increasingly unwieldy from the perspective of national political and bureaucratic elites. When the crisis of poor relief was resolved politically depended in the long run on there being sufficient state capacities to administer new programs and in the short run on political incentives to elites to form cross-class coalitions. How it was resolved depended on the institutional context and the specific character of the policy legacy.

The final step in the break with poor relief and the initiation of modern social provision came in the coalescence of a cross-class coalition of workers, farmers, and middle classes under the political leadership of political and reform elites. The specific form of the coalition depended on the character of the political system. In the United States, it occurred within the Democratic party, as FDR built an electoral coalition of working- and middle-class people, and in some organizations such as the Townsend clubs. In the parliamentary systems of Britain and Canada, the Liberal parties depended on a cross-class electoral base but also concluded agreements with labor and (in Canada) agrarian parties. In Britain, the extraparliamentary National Committee of Organized Labour on Old Age Pensions also had a cross-class character. The support of elites and middle classes for social spending depended in the short run on electoral incentives or a threat to social order—a fact often cited by proponents of popular disruption or working-class strength perspectives. It is important to remember, however, that in the longer term, elite support for social spending was conditioned on the development of administrative capacity, itself the product of successful bureaucratization and uprooting of patronage practices, and the emergence of new liberal ideologies.

Canada and the United States adopted these policy principles in their own poor relief systems, although neither had national poor law legislation as did Britain.

Part 2
The Making of the Social Question

Historically, insurance systems have often developed as protests against relief, against its insufficiency . . . , against its degrading character, and against its social injustice.
—Isaac Max Rubinow, *Social Insurance* (1913)

3

The Problem of Aged Dependency

Work and Family Arrangements of the Elderly

The shifts from agriculture to industry and from self-employment to wagework made the elderly more vulnerable economically; yet these economic changes did not directly lead to the "need" for new forms of state social protection. Changes in the character and organization of work affected people as members of particular types of households. They faced these changes with access to specific forms and amounts of outside assistance (governmental and private), with distinctive understandings, or ideologies, about the obligations of states, families, and employers to citizens, kin, and employees, and with access to particular forms and levels of political power. Demographic changes along with the economic shifts increased the proportion of younger adults called upon to support elderly kin. Also critical were policy shifts which intensified the economic vulnerability of the elderly and led to the politicization of the problem of old age dependency. Thus, we must look at the interrelated effects of all these factors as creating important preconditions for the politicization of the needs of the elderly and the emergence on the political agenda of the poverty and dependency of the aged. First, however, we must deal with some common preconceptions about the way that the elderly became more of a burden over the late nineteenth and early twentieth centuries.

Explanations that presume rising burdens of dependency from increases in the proportion of the aged in the population erroneously assume that the past was very much like today; they presume that a retired elderly population constituted an economic burden on younger, working-aged people and that the elderly would be perceived as a burden, so that an increasing number of aged people would automatically lead to demands for increased state provision. Another set of misconceptions assumes that the past was culturally completely unlike the present and idealizes the treatment of the elderly in "traditional" times. Much of the work of Peter Laslett (see Laslett 1976) has been focused at debunking these "quasi-theoretical assumptions" which abound about the family in the "traditional" past, that "world we have lost." In the mythical past, a majority of households were extended, and the elderly found an honored position within the family, even if they could no longer contribute to the family economically. As "modernization" progressed, the values of the population changed for the worse, causing the elderly to be unceremoniously rejected by employers and callously abandoned by their families to abject but "independent" poverty or the poorhouse. The decline in co-residence rates (rates of aged parents living with their adult children) observed over the course of this century is sometimes invoked as evidence for this view. As Laslett and a host of historical demographers have argued, this is wrong in many ways about both the character of the past and the transformations wrought by "modernization" or, less grandly, capitalist industrialization, urbanization, and assorted other social, economic, and cultural changes of the last century or two.

In the period preceding industrialization in Britain, the United States, and Canada, most old people worked and headed their own households. They could control the pace and amount of work and thus could choose when and to what extent they would retire. Families often took in the minority of elderly people who could not support themselves—principally very elderly widows—or state social provision in the form of extensive outdoor relief allowed the "impotent" (i.e., non–able-bodied) elderly to live on their own. A great deal of work on the history of the family has shown that the notion of a large extended family of three generations being typical in the European past is only a product of "Western nostalgia" (William J. Goode, quoted in Hareven 1976, p. 194). Instead, research on Western Europe and the United States indicates that a nuclear rather than an extended household structure has continuously predominated over the last two hundred years (Hareven 1976, p. 194; Cherlin 1983, pp. 52–53). In preindustrial societies, the extended family with co-residing elderly parents and married adult offspring was possible principally in that limited phase of the life cycle when the parents wanted to retire or when one was widowed, and to the extent that control of property (usually land) gave the elderly the power to require support—often spelled out in detailed retirement contracts—in exchange for giving over control of their estate to their children (Quadagno 1982, p. 14; Berkner 1972). But even in this context, most households contained only two generations. The demographic characteristics of the populations of the three countries (high fertility and mortality and a late average age of marriage, a key aspect of the Western European marriage system; Hajnal 1965) precluded the formation of large numbers of three-generation families (Laslett 1976; Ruggles 1987; Levy 1965).[1] Only a small minority of families—around 10 percent—

---

1. There is disagreement over the extent to which cultural preference also contributed to the paucity of extended families. Most recently, Steven Ruggles (1987) has rejected Laslett's contention that English people in preindustrial times did not live in extended families because of cultural

were extended (Ruggles 1987), and very few young and middle-aged adults were called upon to provide support to the elderly. Historical demographers have also shown that in the industrial era most elderly people continued to head their own households and that families continued to take in their elderly kin who could no longer support themselves. The aged who were institutionalized were disproportionately those who were widowed or single and childless. This is a picture of overall continuity, but clearly, some things changed to bring the situation of the elderly to the status of a social problem.

Opportunities for self-support by the elderly declined slightly, while the proportion of families who had to offer support to the nonworking elderly increased somewhat. It seems quite clear that the willingness of families to support their aged kin did not decline, as best we can judge from data on the living arrangements of the elderly. They certainly were not turned out by their kin when in need. It is possible, however, that even though adult children and other kin continued to offer support, they would have preferred alternative arrangements, such as state social provision. If that were the case, even if one presumes that the level of support from adult children and other kin for the elderly increased only slightly (in fact, even if it remained stable), there was a potential for politicizing the issue of the elderly's support.

Declining Employment Opportunities for the Elderly

Throughout the nineteenth century and the first half of the twentieth, work was by far the most important source of support for the elderly; the majority of men over sixty-five worked and supported their wives economically. Time-series data on labor force participation among the elderly in Britain, Canada, and the United States, however, as displayed in table 3.1, shows that, compared with the rates of younger cohorts, which remained stable and very high, the labor force participation rates of older males were somewhat lower and declined gradually throughout the late nineteenth and early twentieth centuries in Britain and the United States (data is unavailable for Canada before 1921, but trends there tended to track those of the United States). Rates for women were much lower and showed less of a trend, reflecting the severe restrictions on women's employment opportunities. The modal experience for women of all

---

preferences rather than demographic exigencies. Ruggles comes closer to Lutz Berkner's view (1972) that the extended family (in stem form—parent[s], married adult child[ren], and at least one child) was both an ideal and an important phase in the life cycle in preindustrial times. He suggests that demographic conditions prevented its realization in more than a handful of households at any given point in time. This is consonant with the Cambridge Group's consistent finding of quite small proportions of extended (and multiple) households in preindustrial England. Ruggles claims that when one accounts for demographic constraints, it looks as though most of those who could live in extended families did so (1987, pp. 121–23).

Table 3.1. Labor force participation rates of elderly males and females

Year	Canada		Great Britain		United States	
	35–64	65 +	45–64	65 +	45–64	65 +
Males						
1890–91	—	—	93.7	65.4	92.0	68.3
1900–1901	—	—	93.5	61.4	90.3	63.1
1910–11	—	—	94.1	56.8	—	—
1920–21	94.3	71.0	94.9	58.9	90.7	55.6
1930–31	95.8	69.0	94.3	47.9	91.0	54.0
1940-41	95.2	58.9	—	—	88.7	44.2
Females						
1890–91	—	—	24.6	15.9	12.1	7.6
1900–1901	—	—	21.1	13.4	13.6	8.3
1910–11	—	—	21.6	11.5	—	—
1920–21	11.8	19.9	20.1	10.1	16.5	7.3
1930–31	13.5	22.8	19.6	8.2	18.0	7.3
1940–41	15.2	19.9	—	—	20.2	6.1

Sources: British Labor Statistics, Historical Abstract, 1886–1968 (London: Her Majesty's Sta-tionery Office, 1971), p. 207; U.S. Bureau of the Census, *Historical Statistics of the United States, Colonial Times to 1970*, vol. 1 (Washington, D.C.: Government Printing Office, 1975), p. 132; M. C. Urqhart and K. Buckley, eds., *Historical Statistics of Canada* (Toronto: Macmillan, 1965), p. 62.

ages was dependence on the wages or other income of men active in the paid economy (U.S. Bureau of the Census 1960, p. 71; Strong-Boag 1988, pp. 41–43; Quadagno 1982, p. 153). As we shall see, elderly women were a significant part of the "problem of old age," the inability of elderly people to support themselves. Because they were economically dependent on men's wages, many women were "only a husband away from poverty" (to borrow a modern slo-gan which is equally apt for the nineteenth and early twentieth centuries), and widowhood struck the majority of elderly women. Thus, although most elderly men continued to work, and most elderly people of both sexes headed their own households, a significant minority could not head their own households— through loss of jobs, husbands, or other circumstances. Indeed, early pension proposals recommended the establishment of social assistance targeted at that minority of "elderly persons who through chance and circumstance possessed neither jobs nor property"; pensions were definitely not intended to provide "a retirement wage for a population of superannuated elders" (Myles 1984, pp. 8, 16). This minority—increasing slightly due to changing economic con-ditions—was important politically. Given the uncertainties of employment and marriage, their fate was potentially one that could befall most working-class and many middle-class people.

Analysts have highlighted several interrelated ways in which capitalist industrialization operated to constrict employment opportunities for the aged and to increase uncertainty about work. Key are the decline in agriculture, and in self-employment more generally; once people became dependent upon wagework, any number of forces beyond the control of individuals could deprive them of their livelihood. Economic depressions, industrial accidents, or disability due to aging all could lead to unemployment. The shift to the predominance of waged work concomitant with industrialization was the critical factor in the increasing economic vulnerability of the aged. Further, within the industrial sector, processes of capitalist rationalization were destructive for older workers as their skills became technologically obsolete and as employers' interests in making their work forces efficient increased, trends which became particularly evident in the 1920s and 1930s (Quadagno 1982, p. 154; Haber 1983, pp. 34–35; Graebner 1980).

Self-employment serves as an important barrier against forced retirement. Recent quantitative research has confirmed that wagework was increasing and self-employment was declining in the late nineteenth and early twentieth centuries in the United States (Grusky 1986). Sociologist Jill Quadagno's historical study of work force participation of elderly men and women in turn-of-the-century England shows that the decline of opportunities for self-employment led to the loss of job opportunities for the aged (Quadagno 1982, pp. 158–62). The rise of wagework made all wageworkers vulnerable to unemployment; for the elderly, this was often the equivalent of unpaid, forced retirement, a possibility simply not present for elderly people who owned land or small businesses. Farmers and small business owners were much better able than industrial workers to retire partially, for the decision of how much or whether to work was their own, and they also had resources with which to bargain for support if retirement should become necessary with the waning of their physical powers (Quadagno 1982, p. 162; Haber 1983, p. 33; Achenbaum 1978, pp. 96–98).

Older workers suffered especially from the decline in agriculture. As early American social insurance advocate Isaac Max Rubinow wrote in his 1913 book, *Social Insurance*, "What is the modern problem of old age? It is the problem of poverty caused by inability to find employment because the productive power has waned—and waned not temporarily, but forever. Evidently, in this form, the problem could not exist until the majority of mankind became dependent on a wage-contract for their means of existence. . . . In an agricultural community, the usefulness of an old man or woman does not cease until actual senility is established, and actual senility is a comparatively rare phenomenon" (pp. 302–4).

Farmers were often self-employed, particularly in North America, but even waged agricultural work—frequently on a part-time basis—was more often made available (although under worse conditions) to older workers than were positions within manufacturing (Achenbaum 1978, pp. 95–98; Quadagno 1982, pp. 162–66). In Canada, unskilled farm labor was dominated by young, single men, but it was the occupation with the largest absolute number of elderly men (Marsh 1940, pp. 208–9). Indeed, in the United States, analyst Murray Latimer found that the decline in labor force participation for males aged sixty-five or over (as well as that for males aged between forty-five and sixty-four) between 1890 and 1920 was accounted for entirely by the decline in nonindustrial employment (Latimer 1932a, p. 814).[2] There was almost no decline in the participation rates of older American men in industry or in agriculture over the period 1890–1930; total rates did drop off, for rates in the industrial sector were lower than in the agricultural, and the occupational distribution was shifting away from agriculture (Gratton 1986, pp. 63–70). In his study of the elderly in Boston, historian Brian Gratton reports that in urban areas like Boston, older men's labor force participation—almost entirely within nonagricultural sectors—was quite stable over the forty years between 1890 and 1930; indeed, in the fifty largest American cities, the rate fell only eight percentage points, from 61 percent to 53 percent (1986, p. 70). Gratton (1986, p. 67) argues that a new equilibrium level of participation in the labor force may have been reached within industrial occupations, and that there was no inherent reason why healthy aged workers could not have gone on working. Gratton and others (e.g., Myles 1984) stress that it was *after* the introduction of old age assistance and insurance measures that overall participation rates dropped sharply in all three countries.

Analysts have also highlighted technological advancement as a force undermining the position of older workers. Industrial employers concerned with efficiency and the "superannuation" of elderly workers with outdated skills and lower productivity are seen as the agents of this process. Direct displacement of older workers within modernizing industries, however, was actually comparatively rare in the pre–World War I period. In the United States, only after 1920 did the amount of permanent unemployment of the elderly in industrial occupations begin to increase (Latimer 1932a, p. 814). As Quadagno (1982) points out in her study of work and the elderly in England around the turn of the century, the elderly tended to be phased out of the work force in less direct ways. This finding was corroborated by Gratton (1986) for Boston.

2. This point is also made by U.S. historian Andrew Achenbaum (1978, p. 103), who devised drop-off ratios to measure what proportion of workers over age sixty-four in a given economic sector retired. To derive the ratio, the proportion of the total population over age sixty-five in an occupation is divided by the proportion of the population aged forty-five to sixty-four in that occupation and multiplied by 100 percent; in 1900 the ratio for agriculture was 93 percent, while nonagricultural pursuits were 59 percent; in 1920 agriculture was 82 percent and nonagriculture, 53 percent.

The aged were disproportionately represented in traditional jobs and underrepresented in newer occupations, so that as the composition of the labor force changed, there was less room for older workers, though the individual older workers already in these jobs were not moved out (see also Marsh 1940 on Canada). Some older workers did lose jobs when traditional occupations, particularly those in domestic industries such as weaving, were mechanized and moved into factories. The decline of domestic industry hastened the decline of labor force participation of the elderly, for, like self-employment, domestic occupations more readily allowed for partial employment and individual pace-setting of work than did factory employment.

By the 1920s and 1930s a new aspect of industrial capitalism began to impinge upon older workers: "How much each worker produced during a fixed period of time—what we now refer to as productivity—became the crucial measure of a firm's viability in a competitive marketplace. Under such circumstances, it is not difficult to appreciate the new risk faced by older and slower workers" (Myles 1984, p. 11). What was problematic for older workers was not the introduction and use of new industrial technology per se, but the speed with which the machinery had to be operated. The requirement for speed was the result of capitalist dynamics, for speed was necessary if profitability was to be maintained (Graebner 1980, pp. 24–27). This development was part of the general trend toward rationalization in industry which occurred in the early twentieth century; it was manifested in a concern with efficiency and in the transformation of authority in the workplace, with bureaucratic forms replacing personal relationships. As the concern with rationalization and efficiency grew, so too did the notion that the aged were by definition "superannuated" and unfit for participation in the labor force (Haber 1983, pp. 118–29). In the United States and Canada during the 1920s and 1930s, increasing attention was paid to the "problem of the older worker," the inability of the middle-aged or elderly to find employment (Latimer 1932a, p. 18; New York Commission on Old Age Security 1930, p. 78; Rogers 1929). Actual firings of older workers were still rare as personal employment relationships prevailed strongly enough to prevent most employers from dismissing their elderly employees to a life of penury, yet contemporary studies found that if for some reason employment was interrupted (e.g., by lay-offs), it was truly difficult for the older person to start over (Latimer 1932a, p. 836; U.S. Social Security Board 1937, p. 144; Armstrong 1932, p. 387; Gratton 1986 finds similar patterns). The Depression dramatically highlighted this trend: the unemployment levels of older workers were found to be disproportionately high (U.S. Social Security Board 1937, pp. 145–48).

The idea of utilizing pension plans to deal with efficiency concerns attendant on superannuation was widespread in industry in both the United States and Canada prior to the Depression (Haber 1983, p. 118), but the practice was not equally pervasive. Only about four hundred pension plans were found in operation in North America in 1932 in the thorough research of Murray Latimer (1932a, p. 893); this covered less than 15 percent of the nonagricultural labor force (1932a, p. 55). The issues of retirement and the problems of older workers may have gained salience in the 1920s and 1930s, but it is important to remember that mass retirement, predicated on a public retirement wage, is a post–World War II phenomenon. During the Depression, the issue of retirement entered into public discourse on state old age protection programs in the United States (Graebner 1980). This was precocious by world standards, but even in the United States, the retirement wage did not begin to function until after World War II (Myles 1984, pp. 16–21; Derthick 1979, p. 273).

The Vulnerability of Old Age

Although voluntary and state-supported retirement was still not common before World War II, a significant number of elderly men were unable to support themselves if they found themselves unemployed or working less than full time; many elderly women faced difficulties if their spouses were unemployed or if they were widowed. Private savings or pension plans did little to relieve the economic burden of forced retirement among the working classes. Discussions of the need for modern old age income maintenance programs in Britain, Canada, and the United States (both before and after World War II) commonly noted the fact that workers' voluntary schemes of savings, annuities, and insurance—however morally admirable—were totally insufficient to deal with the problem of economic dependency in old age (Bryden 1974, pp. 51–59; Collins 1965, pp. 250–51; for contemporary remarks, see Rubinow 1913, chap. 20; Booth 1894, p. 425; Armstrong 1932, pp. 381–85). Nor did government-subsidized or sponsored voluntary schemes work well. Very few workers ever signed up in Canada, where government annuities were initiated in 1908, the U.S. states, or any of the other countries which had such programs (Rubinow 1913, chap. 21; Bryden 1974, pp. 59–60; Commons and Andrews 1927, pp. 470–71; Armstrong 1932, pp. 398–99). Even in the United States in the 1920s, when economic prosperity and welfare capitalism might have been expected to make private solutions to old age need more possible, Armstrong estimated (1932, p. 393) that industrial pensions relieved only about 5–6 percent of the potentially dependent elderly, while trade union benefits aided another fraction of a percent. Clearly, private plans did not adequately prevent dependency.

Personal saving was not a viable alternative for most workers either, although in an analysis of the aged in early-twentieth-century America, Gratton and Haber (forthcoming) note that a substantial middle class did have significant assets. Many investigators note the difficulties of saving, given that the proportion who did not make more than a "living wage" was so large (Booth

1894, p. 425; Arthur Huddell, quoted in Massachusetts Commission on Old Age Pensions 1910, pp. 336–37; Epstein 1922, chap. 6, provides a summary of U.S. research on the "living wage"). Charles Booth's early work on the working-class poor of East London (1889, 1891) showed that 30 percent of the population there had incomes judged, by Booth's far from extravagant standards, to be inadequate for the support of their families, making savings an impossibility (Rose 1972, pp. 27–28). Seebohm Rowntree, in his classic investigation of York, *Poverty: A Study of Town Life* (1901), found that 28 percent of the population had incomes inadequate to purchase the necessities of life, much less to save for old age. Similar findings were recorded for North American cities (Ames 1972 on Montreal; see Squier 1912, pp. 35–50 for a survey of American studies). Current research also suggests that saving was an impossibility for a large proportion of workers in all three countries (on Britain, see Treble 1979; Rose 1972; on Canada, Copp 1974; Darroch 1983; Bryden 1974, pp. 24–34; on the United States, Bremner 1956a). A modern historian of American poverty estimates that, using seven hundred dollars as a poverty line, 40 percent of wageworkers and clerical employees lived in poverty around the turn of the century (Patterson 1981, p. 11).

Those elderly people who had no income from work or savings had limited alternatives: their families, public social provision, or private charity. Families did not abandon their responsibilities to their aged kin, but by the end of the nineteenth century, more of them were called upon to offer support to elderly relations. Changes in the character of public social provision intensified the burden represented by the nonworking elderly, while simultaneously leaving the aged who had neither job nor family in an unprecedentedly vulnerable situation. Private charity accommodated only a fraction of those who needed assistance and could not or would not receive public relief.

Family Structure and Family Economy

Before the initiation of income-maintenance programs for the aged, families were an important economic resource for elderly people unable to support themselves by their own earnings. In thinking about the emergence of demands for new forms of state social provision to address the dependency of the aged, it is useful to consider that such demands can come from two sources—the elderly themselves and the (primarily working-class) adult children and other kin who had to support the nonworking aged. First, we look at the household arrangements of the elderly, to see whether the aged were a group increasingly in need of public care because of declining family support. There is no evidence that adult children became less willing to support their aged parents. Elderly people were not turned out by their kin, but those without families were increasingly vulnerable to destitution or institutionalization as the character of social policy changed. Second, we review the evidence about changing demo-graphic conditions, which affected the extent to which the elderly represented a burden to the younger generation; over the nineteenth and early twentieth centuries, the proportion of adults at risk of supporting an elderly relative in-creased. It may well be that the increasing burden represented by the elderly as it was reinforced by shifts within public policy formed a basis for the demand for new forms of state old age provision.

The Households of the Elderly

Over the latter half of the nineteenth century and the first half of the twentieth, there was a good deal of continuity in the family situations of aged people. Most of the elderly lived with their kin, mostly their children, rather than alone (Smith 1979, 1982; Gratton 1986, chap. 2; Wall 1983; Laslett 1976; Ruggles 1987; Quadagno 1982). There is simply no warrant to believe the myths about families abandoning the elderly as societies industrialized. But this generally positive picture of the circumstances of the elderly should not be allowed to obscure the very real vulnerability of certain groups within the aged popula-tion: widows and the single and childless. Important gender differences in life expectancy, rates of widowhood, and the ability to head households left more women than men dependent on their adult children and other kin. Moreover, the situation of the single and childless of both sexes was less favorable than that of their ever-married counterparts with living children, and the proportion of never-married people increased during the late nineteenth century (Ward 1990, pp. 62–63; Gratton 1986, pp. 44, 49; Anderson 1984, pp. 378–79, 392). In the United States, many more whites remained unmarried than blacks, however (Ruggles and Goeken 1990).

Let's consider the incidence of five ideal-typical household forms among the elderly population: the multiple family household, in which two married couples, one from each of the adult generations, live under one roof, perhaps with young children (this is the ideal-typical peasant household but may also occur in industrial societies under certain conditions); the simple, or conjugal, family household, in which two parents—in this case aged—live with their unmarried children (this can be continued if one parent is widowed); married couples alone (the "empty nest"); an extended family household, in which aged individuals live in households with their kin (typical situations are that of widowed persons living with their married adult children, single women living with siblings, or grandparents taking in grandchildren); and solitaries. By some terminological schemes, both the multiple family household and the extended family household constitute "extended" families, because they con-tain the elderly and their adult children. In evaluating the circumstances of the aged, however, it is important to know whether they were married or single members of the household (co-residence of two married couples is the hall-mark of propertied agrarian social relations). Thus, it is important to be able to distinguish between "multiple" and "extended" household types, and I follow the terminology proposed by Peter Laslett and the Cambridge Group for the History of Population and Social Structure (Laslett 1972, pp. 30–31). More-over, we want to know if the elderly within extended households were heads of households or dependents of the heads. Following modern usage, I will call adult wives as well as widows "heads" rather than "spouses of heads."

The households of the aged today fall into the categories of married couples alone and solitaries. Very few elderly people live with their children. As noted above, the mythology of aging holds that multigenerational households formerly predominated and that the shift away from co-residence occurred due to changing cultural values of the population. In fact, such three-generation families did not predominate in England, at least from the mid-seventeenth century on, or in North America (Laslett 1976). Instead, in England and its former colonies, nuclear families have been the rule for all age groups, although analysts debate whether this reflects cultural preferences or demographic exi-gencies. Most of the aged were self-supporting and headed their own house-holds, living with their unmarried children or on their own once the children married and left home. For that minority of aged persons who became depen-dent, very often upon widowhood, extended family households predominated, for the elderly typically moved in with their children. Note that co-residence of the elderly and their children occurs in multiple, simple, and extended family households, but only multiple and extended households contain more than two generations. Co-residence is not synonymous with extended family living. Much of the co-residence of the past occurred in the context of conjugal family households; the elderly were simply living with their own unmarried children. This form of co-residence has declined as life expectancy has increased and as people have had fewer children, closer together and earlier in life, leading to a longer period of the empty nest (Quadagno 1982, p. 13; Uhlenberg 1978, pp. 88–90; Glick 1977). Extended families in which elderly widows live as depen-dents of their married adult sons and sons-in-law have also all but disappeared, as these women live alone.[3] Such changes in the living situations of the aged, however, occurred after the adoption of pensions and old age insurance in the early decades of the twentieth century and thus cannot be invoked as causes of the initiation of the welfare state.

Let's examine the available evidence about the living situations of the elderly in Britain, Canada, and the United States around the middle of the nine-

---

3. The best evidence about the circumstances of these women suggests that they prefer to live alone, and they have been enabled to live independently by the largesse of the welfare state (Shanas 1979).

teenth century, then contrast this with data from the end of the century and, for the United States, with a study from the mid-1920s. Several reconstructions of local demography have been done for all three countries. Clear patterns are seen in all the studies, representing a broad range of community types.[4] At midcentury in Britain, Canada, and the United States, most of the elderly were household heads. For example, in 1851 England, over two-thirds of the aged in Chilvers Coton were heads (Quadagno 1982, p. 80), as were about three-quarters in Colyton. In Buffalo, New York, most of both the foreign-born and native-born aged—well over three-quarters—headed households (Glasco, cited in Achenbaum 1978, p. 77). Of those who were not heads, most lived with kin (Wall 1986, p. 271; Glasco, cited in Achenbaum 1978, p. 77). Analysts of most of the localities surveyed report that most of the elderly lived with their children or other kin (including spouses). In Chilvers Coton, close to three-quarters of aged men and women lived with their spouses, children, or other relatives; about half the elderly lived with their children (Quadagno 1982, p. 80). In some communities, even higher proportions lived with their offspring: "Well over 80% of those people who had a child alive were, in Preston in 1851, in fact living with one or the other of their children," notes Anderson; given that many older people were childless, about 70 percent of all elderly persons in Preston resided with children (Anderson 1972, p. 224; Thomson 1986, p. 364). Thomson (1986), however, reports finding much lower proportions of the elderly living with their children in a number of English areas (predominantly rural, but some urban)—about 40 percent—than Anderson found for Preston. Adding those who lived with other kin would bring the proportion of the aged up to about half. This is not so far off the figures Anderson reports for the rural areas surrounding Preston, where just under half of the elderly lived with their children (Smith 1982, p. 257).

Most of those residing with kin did so as heads, for most of the elderly lived with their own unmarried children. A much smaller proportion lived with

---

4. Among the studies I have reviewed are Michael Anderson's study (1971, 1972) of 1851 Preston in Lancashire, a cotton mill town, and the surrounding countryside, an area of owner-operated small farms; Richard Wall's study (1986) of 1851 Colyton, a small market town in the agricultural area of southeast England; Jill Quadagno's study (1982) of 1851 and 1901 Chilvers Coton, a ribbon-weaving town where domestic industry predominated to a later date than in the rest of England; and Thomson's studies of rural areas of Dorset and Bedfordshire, Ealing (near London), Bedford borough, and the city of Cambridge, for the years 1851, 1861, and 1871 (though not all years for all places) (1983, 1984a, b, 1986, 1990). In the United States there are studies for Buffalo and Erie County for midcentury (Glasco, cited in Achenbaum 1978, p. 77), and for Providence, Rhode Island, for the mid-to-late nineteenth century (Chudacoff and Hareven 1978). Information is available for the state of Massachusetts by the 1880s and 1890s (Gratton 1986). Daniel Scott Smith (1979) has analyzed samples from the 1880 and 1900 U.S. censuses. In Canada, Michael Katz (1975) surveyed the commercial city Hamilton, Canada West (later Ontario), in 1851 and 1861, and Bettina Bradbury (1979) has investigated industrializing Montreal in 1871.

their married adult children, either as heads themselves or as dependents of their adult children who headed the household (Quadagno 1982, p. 80; Anderson 1972, pp. 224–25; Wall 1986, p. 271; Katz 1975, p. 253). Some communities, particularly ones in which there was a housing shortage or large numbers of mi-grants, seem to have had a slightly higher than average proportion of multiple family households in which married couples lived with their elderly married parents; about one-sixth of the households of the elderly were of this type in 1851 Preston (Anderson 1972, pp. 224–25; Quadagno 1982; Chudacoff and Hareven 1978; Bradbury 1979 finds this pattern for Montreal in 1871).

In 1851 very small proportions of the elderly—under 8 percent in all cases—lived alone (Wall 1983, pp. 270–71; Quadagno 1982, p. 80; Anderson 1977, p. 47; Achenbaum 1978, p. 77; Chudacoff and Hareven 1978, p. 75; Katz 1975, p. 249). Even smaller proportions lived in institutions; about 2 percent of the aged in the United States and about 3 percent in Britain were in poorhouses and similar establishments (Achenbaum 1978, p. 80; Anderson 1977, p. 44). Given the lower level of institutional development in Canada (Strong 1930), there is no reason to believe the proportion of elderly in institutions there would be any higher.

Around the turn of the century, the dominant patterns observed in the living arrangements of the elderly were unchanged: most older persons were heads of households, and most lived with children or other kin. Few lived alone or in institutions. Quadagno's study of Chilvers Coton in England is one of the few which directly compares the household situations of the English elderly in 1851 with those in 1901. Some subtle shifts occurred within the overall con-tinuities of headship and of co-residence with kin (Quadagno 1982, p. 80). Three-quarters of men and two-thirds of women were heads in 1901 as com-pared with 70 percent and 64 percent respectively in 1851, and the proportion residing with kin rose from 73 percent to 83 percent. Living arrangements had changed somewhat: fewer old people lived with nonkin or in "empty nests," more aged parents lived with their unmarried children, and among the minority of multiple family households (about one-sixth of the total), more were formed from old couples moving in with their children than the reverse. Quadagno suggests that "a combination of reduced mortality for the young people and delayed marriage kept unmarried children at home longer and reduced the pro-portion of aged in the 'empty nest' " (1982, p. 83). The increased proportion of aged people moving in with their kin, she explains, was related to reduced work opportunities for the elderly in the dominant silk-weaving industry of Chilvers Coton, which declined during the late nineteenth century (Quadagno 1982, p. 87). Although we do not have direct evidence on this point, it seems quite likely that the slightly declining employment opportunities for the elderly in other parts of Britain and in North America might have had similar results, that is, small increases in the proportion of the aged living as relatives of household heads or, for those without kin, as lodgers or as inmates of institutions. Similar decreases in mortality (Achenbaum 1978, p. 90) might also have increased the proportion of the elderly living with their unmarried children in the United States.

In the United States, studies of household arrangements at the turn of the century find most aged people—black and white, native-born and foreign-born—as independent householders and/or living with kin (for racial breakdowns, see Ruggles and Goeken 1990; Gratton and Haber forthcoming; for ethnic comparisons, see Achenbaum 1978; Gratton 1986). Brian Gratton shows that in 1885 and 1895, about 80 percent of men and 60 percent of women in Massachusetts were householders; of the rest, most lived in the homes of their children or other relations (Gratton 1986, pp. 41, 45, 47). In Daniel Scott Smith's national sample from the 1900 U.S. census, fully three-quarters of people aged fifty-five and over were heads of households. Even among those aged seventy-five and over, more than half were in this position (Smith 1979, p. 290). Only after husbands reached the age of eighty did more than a tenth of married couples fail to maintain a household of their own (Sweet and Bumpass 1987). Smith (1979) points out that if elderly people could not support themselves (and had no assets), they most typically moved in with their married children or other kin. Married children did not move back into their parents' households to maintain them as "heads" but did support them when necessary. In a study of elderly people in New York State in 1925, Sue Weiler (1986) finds comparable patterns. The household arrangements of the single and widowed elderly were quite similar to those reported by Smith for his 1900 U.S. sample: in both cases, about three-quarters lived with their children or other kin, a little over a tenth lived alone, and the rest lived with nonkin (Weiler 1986, p. 81). Among the married elderly, similar proportions lived with their married children (16 percent in the United States in 1900, 12 percent in New York in 1925), and somewhat fewer lived with their unmarried children (42 percent versus 30 percent). New immigrants were more likely than native-born residents to have unmarried children living with them and were more likely to live with their married children when widowed.

Some analysts have argued that unmarried children's willingness to remain in their parents' home—which in many instances could also be a form of transferring resources from young to old—decreased over the period from the mid-nineteenth century to the early twentieth. Gratton notes, however, that in Massachusetts, "contrary to expectation, at every age group between 19 and 60, the percentage of men and women remaining in their parents' households in the twentieth century [using data from 1940 and 1950] exceeds nineteenth-century [1885 and 1895] levels. That is, an adult child, 35 years of age, in Massachusetts in 1950 was *more* likely to live with his aging parents than his peer in 1885" (1986, pp. 51–52).

What changed in the United States was not values and willingness to live with one's elderly kin. Rather, the proportion of elderly people in the population relative to younger people increased; there were fewer adult children to go around, so more were called upon to help in the support of those elderly people who needed it (see also Ruggles and Goeken 1990). Part of the reason the aged among new immigrant groups were more likely to have children at home, then, was that these groups had higher fertility rates (Weiler 1986).

Gratton and Haber (forthcoming) argue that while many elderly Americans might have assets, particularly homes, they might not have stable sources of income. Adult children living with their elderly parents, however, could provide such income, although they might have to forego opportunities to marry or pursue their own education. Indeed, Gratton (1991) contends that through similar strategies of familial income pooling, many working-class families managed to save sums sufficient for the aged to maintain their independent households. He notes that these strategies were helpful to the elderly but certainly increased receptivity to pension proposals among the younger generation, which was giving up control of significant resources in order to maintain the older generation of adults.

In 1901 as in earlier periods, few older people were boarders or otherwise on their own, and small proportions were institutionalized. In England, the institutional population remained a small minority of the aged, but it had grown to about 6–7 percent in 1901 from 3 percent at midcentury (Anderson 1977, p. 44; Thomson 1983). In the United States, the proportion of the elderly living in public almshouses remained stable over the period 1880–1923, at about 1 percent of the total population over age sixty-five (Gratton 1986, p. 133). In 1895, Gratton reports, another 1–1.5 percent of the aged in Massachusetts were in other institutions, such as private old age homes and hospitals (1986, pp. 44, 48). A number of investigations carried out by U.S. state governments in the first decades of the twentieth century also showed very small proportions of the aged—nowhere above 2 percent—living in institutions (Massachusetts Commission on Old Age Pensions 1910; Massachusetts Commission on Pensions 1925; Wisconsin Industrial Commission 1915; Pennsylvania Commission on Old Age Assistance 1919; Ohio Health and Old Age Insurance Commission 1919; California Department of Social Welfare 1929). We would again expect that few elderly Canadians would have been institutionalized in 1900; indeed, counties were not mandated to build poorhouses until 1903, and most had not previously taken advantage of the option to do so (Strong 1930, p. 103).

Gender Differences among the Aged

Men and women did not experience aging in the same ways. Most elderly men headed their own households, living with their unmarried children and wives; a small minority lived as "parent of the head" or with other relations. The experience of elderly women was more mixed. Many lived as "spouses of the head" and headed their own households even when widowed, but large propor- tions of aged widows moved in with their married children or other kin, with the proportion increasing with age. Some studies find that single and widowed men were not much more likely to head households than women in the same statuses (for the United States in 1900, see Smith 1979, p. 288). It is important to remember, though, that men were far less likely to be widowed or single than were women in all three countries (Smith 1979, p. 287; Anderson 1984, p. 379; Thane 1978, p. 33; Katz 1975, p. 254; Chudacoff and Hareven 1978, pp. 73–74). Thus, throughout the nineteenth century, the status of older men showed continuity with their situation in middle age, while women often were unable to maintain the status of their middle years. Tamara Hareven summa- rized the situation of older women and men in the United States (see also Smith 1979, pp. 286–87), but it can also be applied to their British and Canadian counterparts:

> For men surviving to old age, labor force participation and family status generally resembled those of their earlier adult years. Only at very ad- vanced ages, when their capabilities were probably impaired by infirmity, did a substantial number experience definite changes in their household status. These men, however, represented a fraction of their age peers. . . . Because widowhood was a common experience, older women experi- enced more marked transitions [to old age] than did older men, although the continuing presence of [unmarried] adult children in the household meant that widowhood did not necessarily mark a dramatic transition into the empty nest. (Hareven 1982, p. 16)

And, Hareven might have added, it did not necessarily and immediately lead into the dependent status of "parent of household head." Yet as Pat Thane pointed out, "poor women were more likely to be widowed . . . and more likely than men to survive past work into old age and dependency. . . . Women were less likely than men to marry, less likely to remarry if widowed, and were less able to support themselves if unmarried or widowed" (1978, p. 33). Thus women's greater economic vulnerability and their greater propensity to end up in nonmarried statuses combined to make them more likely to depend on kin in old age.

In U.S., Canadian, and British studies from both the mid-nineteenth cen- tury and the early twentieth century, evidence shows elderly men continuing on as heads of household and women living as dependents of kin far more often than men. The minority of men not heading households were less likely to live with kin than women, and more likely to live as boarders. Wall notes that almost all elderly men in Colyton in 1851—over 80 percent—headed house- holds through old age, as there was little "retirement"; only about one in ten men over sixty lived as kin of household heads, and a slightly smaller proportion lived as lodgers or inmates of institutions (Wall 1986, p. 270). "More women over the age of 60 entered the house of a relative (usually that of a son or daughter) than moved into lodgings or headed their own households," although the modal experience for this age group is still that of "spouse of head" (Wall 1986, pp. 271–72). In Chilvers Coton in both 1851 and 1901, more women than men were taken in by kin (Quadagno 1982, p. 80). Anderson's study of Preston showed that elderly men ended up as lodgers more frequently than older widowed women, and less often with kin; fewer men than women lived with their married children (Anderson 1971, pp. 139–40, 145). In the United States, Smith found that "most old men never held what have been called the 'statuses of old age' . . . departure from gainful employment, loss of spouse, and movement from headship" (1979, p. 286). About two-thirds of men aged sixty-five and over were employed, and an even larger majority of aged men were married (even among men aged eighty or more, over half were married). In sharp contrast, over half of women over sixty were widows, and over half of these lived in the households of their kin (Smith 1979, p. 288). Katz (1975, p. 254) found only 20 percent of aged men, but almost half of elderly women, widowed in 1861 Hamilton. Gratton's study of Boston's elderly reports almost identical patterns in the late nineteenth century—men continuing as married, employed heads of households, and women widowed and moving in with kin at far higher rates (Gratton 1986, chap. 2). Weiler's study of the elderly in New York in 1925 also reports these patterns (1986).

There was a life cycle component at work that left women increasingly vulnerable as they aged, as diminishing proportions of women had living husbands. Not all widows were forced to move into the households of their children, of course; those who maintained an independent household worked, depended on the work of unmarried children living at home, or received outdoor relief. Taking in boarders or lodgers was also a key strategy for widows trying to maintain independent households (Katz 1975, p. 234; Modell and Hareven 1973, p. 475; Anderson 1971, p. 146; Weiler 1986). But this might become less viable as children moved out and work was less available or possible; while about half of widowed women aged sixty-five to sixty-nine headed their own households, this figure declined progressively to about 30 percent among women over age seventy-four (Smith 1979, p. 288). Katz (1975, p. 253) found in midcentury Hamilton that older widows were more likely to live with relatives than younger widows (with 45 percent of widows over sixty living as kin of the household head as contrasted with about one-quarter of widows in their fifties, and about one-tenth of widows in their forties).

The Single and Childless Aged
The minority of the aged population that did not marry tended to live with kin. This was more the case for women than men, however. Spinsters were far

more often incorporated into the households of relations than were bachelors, who tended to be boarders, as Anderson reports for England in 1851 (1984), and Smith for the United States in 1900 (1979, p. 292). Thus, in the United States in 1900, over 70 percent of single women over age fifty-four, but only 40 percent of single men, lived with kin (Smith 1979, p. 292).[5] Members of this group, particularly the men, were more likely to be living alone or to be institutionalized than ever-married people with children. In all three countries over the course of the nineteenth century, an increasing proportion of people remained unmarried (Gratton 1986, pp. 44, 49; Watkins, Menken, and Bongaarts 1987, p. 350; Anderson 1984, pp. 378–79, 392; Ward 1990, pp. 62–63). By the turn of the century, therefore, more of the elderly were in this vulnerable status. Families did not respond differently to their elderly kin, but more of the elderly had the sparser family ties that characterize the single. This group was especially vulnerable to shifts within public social provision.

As analysts consistently point out, the institutionalized aged in the nineteenth and early twentieth centuries, as today, were not people rejected by their kin; rather, institutional populations were, and are, biased toward the nevermarried, childless, and widowed (Anderson 1977, pp. 45–46; Thomson 1983; Gratton 1986, chaps. 4–5). Indeed, the available evidence about the preindustrial era suggests that people without kin were relatively worse off than those with families to call upon, and that those without family in industrialized societies fared much as did people in analogous situations in the past (Laslett 1971, p. 11; Haber 1983, pp. 25–27). A 1908 study of the "belongingless poor" in England showed that those without family members made up a disproportionate part of workhouse populations (Sellars, cited in Quadagno 1982, p. 132). In the United States, too, there is evidence that it was principally those without family ties who were forced to turn to public poor relief, before extensive industrialization in the eighteenth and early nineteenth centuries (Haber 1983, pp. 25–27), as well as during and after the transformation from agricultural to industrial society. Historian Michael Katz (1983, pp. 122–23, 268) found that a majority of women and about 40 percent of men aged fifty or more residing in New York State's almshouses in the last quarter of the nineteenth century had no living children. A series of American state reports on the problems of old age dependency and poverty done in the period 1907–19 shows the same pattern: the elderly people found inside almshouses were disproportionately those without a spouse or children able to support them (they were also unlikely to be healthy enough to work for their own support). For example, in Massachusetts, the state that did the most detailed and sophisticated studies of the conditions

---

5. Interestingly, in the United States, childless elderly widows fared less well than aged spinsters in terms of living with kin: most of the former group lived apart from kin (Smith 1979, p. 293).

of the elderly, in surveys done in 1908–9 and in 1924, over 80 percent of aged persons receiving indoor relief had no spouse (Massachusetts Commission on Pensions 1925, pp. 82–84; Massachusetts Commission on Old Age Pensions 1910, pp. 36–41, 61). In a survey of older working-class residents of the cities of Philadelphia, Pittsburgh, and Reading done by the Pennsylvania Commission on Old Age Assistance for their 1919 report, investigators found that 79 percent of almshouse inmates were widowed or single, while only 44 percent of the nondependent elderly were unmarried; 36 percent of almshouse inmates had at least one living child as against 86 percent of those outside poorhouses (Pennsylvania Commission on Old Age Assistance 1919, pp. 20–23).

The evidence historians and historical demographers have amassed about the circumstances of the elderly in the decades preceding the consideration of new public social provision suggests a good deal of continuity. The elderly tended to head their households or, when unable to do so, to be taken in by married children or other kin. Very few ended up alone or in the poorhouse, although it is at least worth speculating that more of the elderly would have preferred single independence to dependence on sons and sons-in-law. Certain groups were vulnerable: the widowed and the single. Aged women, who were more likely to be widowed than were men, were especially susceptible to becoming dependent on their married adult children. Among the single, men were more likely to be living alone in lodgings or in institutions than were women, who were more likely to be cared for by kin. These vulnerabilities were not new, but they did affect a somewhat larger proportion of the elderly as the nineteenth century wore on. But overall, from the point of view of the aged, family status remained fairly stable. When we turn to look at things from the vantage point of adult children of elderly parents or the kin of single elderly people, we see that some significant changes occurred—changes that may well have meant that more resources were flowing to older people than before. Especially when considered in combination with shifts in state social provision, these could have led to increasing receptivity to policy proposals for new forms of state provision for old age.

How do our cases compare? It is hard to get comparable figures, but the ones we do have are suggestive about the cross-national differences in household structure. Quadagno presents a fairly detailed breakdown of the living arrangements of the elderly residents of Chilvers Coton in 1901 which may be compared with U.S. data as presented by Smith (1979, 1982) and Gratton (1986). It is worth noting that Chilvers Coton appears to be on the high end of the scale in terms of the proportion of the elderly living with their children— about 62 percent, as compared with the approximately 40 percent Thomson (1986) reports finding for a number of English places a few decades earlier. Thus, although Quadagno's 1901 figures for Chilvers Coton may not be completely representative for Britain, when compared with Smith's statistics from the 1900 U.S. census and those presented by Gratton for Massachusetts in 1895, we see some impressive differences. Both the Chilvers Coton and the two U.S. studies showed comparable proportions of men as heads of household—about three-quarters. (Indeed, comparable proportions were in the labor force: 61.4 percent in England, 63.1 percent in the United States.) The overall proportion of the elderly living with their children is the same—62 percent (Quadagno 1982, p. 80; Smith 1982, p. 257). But a much higher proportion of men were "relatives of the head," that is, living as dependents of their children or other kin, in the United States and in the state of Massachusetts than in the English town—about two to two-and-a-half times as many. Similar proportions of elderly women—about six of ten—headed households in both countries (in Chilvers Coton, about two-thirds were householders; in Massachusetts, 62 percent; in the United States as a whole, 55 percent). Again, much higher proportions were "relatives of the head" in the United States, with 40 percent, or Massachusetts, with 30 percent, than in the English town, with 14 percent. Thomson (1986) has suggested that differences in household formation within England reflect in large part local variation in the character of public social provision. It is quite likely that cross-national differences in the availability of outdoor relief and other provision contributed to the variation in household arrangements across our cases.

The Elderly in the Households of Their Kin

Michael Anderson's now-famous investigation of 1851 Preston, a cotton mill town in Lancashire, revealed relatively high proportions of extended and multiple family households. Thus he suggests that, in Britain, industrialization and urbanization initially seem actually to have increased the likelihood of aged parents co-residing with adult children over the rates of the eighteenth century and before (Anderson 1971, 1972). Steven Ruggles (1987), in a work examining the extended family in late-nineteenth-century England and the United States, offers an impressive analysis that suggests that there was increased potential for extended family formation resulting from changing demographic circumstances—the average age of marriage, the proportion ever marrying, fertility rates, and mortality rates. He shows with the use of innovative simulation analyses that there were greater opportunities for the formation of both horizontally and vertically extended families in this period than had been the case in the preindustrial period (vertically extended families involve people from two generations; horizontally extended families are created with people from the same generation). From a range of sources, we know that in North America the aged made up an increasing proportion of the population from the mid-century on, so that more elderly people would be "available" to live with their children or other kin.[6] In other words, there would be an increasing proportion of adults with at least one living parent, and at least the potential for more adults to live with an elderly parent (Watkins, Menken, and Bongaarts 1987, p. 349). In all three countries, an increasing proportion of people remained unmarried, and these people also contributed to the pool of kin available for extended family living, for "coresident horizontally extended kin tend to be 'unattached individuals' "—the unmarried, widowed, and orphaned (Ruggles 1987, pp. 69–70). Clearly, not all of the horizontally extended families would have involved elderly people; indeed, Ruggles notes that many of these families were formed through incorporating people in their twenties and thirties. Yet some elderly singles would certainly be included. There is a good deal of debate about whether, where, and why this demographic potential was converted into the reality of greater proportions of extended and multiple family households in the latter half of the nineteenth century. The controversy that has developed around the issues initially raised by Anderson, now joined by Ruggles, is relevant for our purposes because an expanded proportion of extended households could indicate that more people were faced with the need to care for elderly relatives or to contribute to the family economies of households headed by the elderly.

There is some evidence, in addition to Anderson's study, from Britain, Canada, and the United States in the decades between midcentury and 1900 to support the contention that larger proportions of households were extended or multiple than in the periods before or after. Ruggles (1987) reports that the mean frequency of extended family households in studies carried out in a number of British and American communities increased from under 10 percent in the period 1600–1750 to about 20 percent between 1850 and 1885 and began to decline after that. Richard Wall (1983) shows an increase in the mean number of extended kin per one hundred households, using both community and census figures, from about fifteen in the years 1750–1849 to over thirty in the 1851 British census; it has declined steadily since, and it stood at ten in 1970. (Both of these compilations are directed at the issue of the relative proportion of all extended families and thus include those formed with young as well as elderly kin.) Several studies—of Chilvers Coton in England in 1851 (Quadagno 1982), Montreal in 1871 (Bradbury 1979), and Providence, Rhode Island, in the latter half of the 1800s (Chudacoff and Hareven 1978)—find relatively high proportions of newly married couples living with their married parents, as well as

6. The increasing proportion of aged people in the population principally resulted from declining fertility, evident in the United States and Canada from the beginning of the nineteenth century, and from immigration (as it was predominantly people from younger age groups who had come to North America earlier in the century and these migrants were aging by century's end) (Wells 1982, pp. 92, 105, 276; Henripin 1972, chap. 2). Improving life expectancy also contributed to the trend (Achenbaum 1978, p. 90).

numbers of widowed parents moving in with their married children, as Anderson found in Preston. Yet not all investigators find these patterns. Smith (1982) notes that the scattered evidence he reviewed suggests that the United States did not fit the "curvilinear pattern" of rising extended family living at the early stages of industrial development, with a declining proportion of such families later. Katz's study of Hamilton (1975) showed very few young married couples living with their elderly married parents. And as we noted above, Thomson (1986) finds much lower proportions of the aged living with their children in the mainly rural areas he investigated than did Anderson in Preston.

Anderson argued that among the working classes of Preston, extended and multiple family households were formed as a response to frequently occurring "critical life situations," such as widowhood, housing shortages (particularly for the badly paid and/or newly married), illness, migration, and unemployment, in "the almost complete absence of alternatives to the kinship system . . . as sources of help in solving the problems which ensued from these crises" (1971, p. 160). Moreover, Anderson indicates that the relationships between the elderly and their adult children or other relatives were reciprocal ones, involving a "short-run instrumental orientation" (1971, p. 177). If an elderly person was taken into a relative's home, housing and food were exchanged for other services, especially child care, or perhaps for the financial contribution an older person could make to the family economy with the aid of outdoor relief (Anderson 1971, 1972, 1977; see also Quadagno 1982, pp. 17, 89–90). The fact that elderly women were less often lodgers and were found disproportionately less often than aged men inside workhouses in all three countries lends some credibility to the notion that the elderly could exchange services for economic support, for older men had less to offer at this point in their lives than did women (Katz 1983, pp. 122–23; Booth 1894, pp. 321–22, 326). Writing about the situation in Massachusetts, Gratton notes that "women could get outdoor relief (i.e., aid in their own [or, I would add, their children's] residences) more readily, could handle household duties alone more effectively, and, if needy, were more welcome in the homes of their children" (1986, p. 136). When married couples lived with their married parents, they received housing when rents were high and shelter scarce (Katz, Doucet, and Stern 1982, chap. 8; Booth 1894, p. 322; Anderson 1971, 1972, 1977; Chudacoff and Hareven 1978). These multiple family household arrangements seemed sensitive to local housing markets and were not found universally in urban areas. For example, the fact that Katz (1975, p. 253) finds few such families in 1851 and 1861 Hamilton would tend to confirm this explanation, for Hamilton was not experiencing a housing crisis at midcentury. Most married couples in both Preston and Hamilton had their own households, but in Preston many had started their married life living with their married parents, whereas few had followed this pattern in Hamilton. In contrast, the situation of single and widowed elderly people being taken in by kin when unable to support themselves seems more widespread.

Thomson (1986) has suggested that there may be an urban-rural difference in patterns of household formation, with higher rates of co-residence in urban areas, where housing was often scarce and expensive and social provision allowing the elderly to live independently was less prevalent than in rural villages. This seems to fit the English pattern, where Thomson finds low rates of co-residence in rural areas, while analysts such as Anderson (1971, 1972) and Quadagno (1982) find higher rates in urban areas. At least one Canadian city, Hamilton, however, did not display relatively high rates of extended and multiple family households, although Montreal did. Smith (1982) reports that in the United States in 1900, the differential was in the other direction: that is, co-residence was higher in rural than in urban areas. But Gratton and Haber (forthcoming) argue that differentiating rural and urban areas is insufficient for characterizing the U.S. patterns; they argue for a tripartite scheme for categorizing dominant family forms—urban, farm, and small town. They find that co-residence was far lower in small towns than in either cities (defined as places with populations of 2,500 or more) or on farms and suggest that the wealth of the small-town elderly (often retired farmers who had sold their farms) allowed them to live independently. In cities, lower wealth and tighter housing markets led to more extended and multiple families, while the property in land the elderly on farms had to pass on helped to keep their children with them (as is generally the case for propertied groups in agricultural regions).

It seems reasonable to summarize these findings by saying that extended family formation did rise relative to preindustrial levels in many areas and that the increased demographic potential for co-residence with the elderly was at least partially responsible. But it is also clear that the potential was not uniformly converted into actuality. What explains the variation? A range of sources suggest that differences in critical material conditions—the availability and cost of housing, the need for child care services, and the availability of sources of income to permit independent living by the nonworking (outdoor poor relief, pensions, or wealth)—can explain the different levels of co-residence. It certainly appears that independent living was the preferred alternative, of which people availed themselves when either social provision or private resources allowed.

The explanation I have just outlined is consistent with Anderson's argument that decisions about household arrangements depended on short-run material considerations, but it would also imply that where resources were sufficient, adult children or other kin might well assist the elderly on the basis of a longer-run calculation of reciprocity. Indeed, Anderson makes clear that the short-run orientation he describes for Preston operatives was conditional on their very low resources, among other factors (1971, p. 173); he does not rule out the development of longer-term calculations given conditions of sufficient resources and certainty.[7] This would still leave us with a predominantly economic, or, more precisely, material, explanation for variations in patterns of extended family formation over the last two centuries. It does assume an underlying, and relatively unchanging, preference for independent residences that can only variably be acted upon. Ruggles, however, dismisses such an approach, using evidence from the later twentieth, rather than the nineteenth, century: "The rising frequency of extended families in the nineteenth century might simply have been a function of the rise in the proportion who could afford them. . . . But if the high frequency of extended families in the nineteenth century was a consequence of relative prosperity, one wonders why the frequency of extended families has declined in the twentieth century," when income has continued to rise and demographic opportunities for extended family formation have not declined (1987, p. 58). Here, Ruggles does not take seriously his own critique of the new home economics—that they assume away any internal dynamics to the family (1987, p. 20). In discussing rising incomes over the nineteenth and twentieth centuries, Ruggles forgets whose incomes rose when: in the nineteenth, the aged without work were unlikely to have any income; in the twentieth, the nonworking elderly got access to an independent income. And it is once the elderly have access to an independent income above a subsistence threshold that they begin to live alone in increasing numbers.

The fact that the proportion of extended family households increased with income, which Ruggles cites as proof that such families formed in response to cultural preference rather than economic hardship (on the basis of demographic potential in any case), seems to me perfectly consonant with the findings of both Quadagno and Anderson that the poorest families might take in elderly kin to cope with hardship but could not do so without something being given in exchange. Extended family living could be both a "luxury" (Ruggles' point) and a response to hardship (Anderson's). Those who could afford it would take in the elderly (or other kin) whether or not the elderly had something to offer in return; the poorest would only take in the elderly if they could bring in resources or services, for otherwise the drain on resources was too great.[8]

---

7. Ruggles says, "Many persons may have maintained their parents in old age with the expectation that they in turn would be supported by their children," but he maintains that this is not economic exchange but a "reflection of social norms and bonds of obligation," which he ascribes to the cultural realm (1987, p. 57n). The difference here strikes me as one of terminology.

8. Ruggles says he has found that many families were in fact burdened by the addition of extended kin, and thus, their being taken in cannot have been a way to cope with hardship. The measure Ruggles uses to assess the economic impact of adding kin to the household, however, is based solely on whether or not they were employed. This clearly ignores unpaid services or the provision of resources such as housing where it is scarce—a situation which is locality-specific. In fact, Anderson, Quadagno, and Chudacoff and Hareven all claim that the potential for elderly

Social Policy and Family Living Arrangements

A serious problem in much of the discussion of the elderly, extended family living, and the burden such an arrangement may have represented is the neglect of social policy and the subsequent failure to consider the full range of alternatives available to people. In fact, social provision significantly affected living arrangements and the extent to which the elderly were a burden on younger generations. At some points in British history, poor relief may perhaps have been enough to sustain independent living; this was more likely to be the case in rural areas than in urban areas (Thomson 1986). Thus, the urban elderly—even with a bit of outdoor relief—were unlikely to be able to live alone, but they could stay out of the poorhouse if they could pool resources with their kin. Anderson (1977), Quadagno (1982), and Thomson (1984a) also note that poor law authorities began to demand that relatives support the elderly in the 1870s and 1880s—precisely when analysts have found higher proportions of extended families. In England and some areas of North America, outdoor relief was unavailable in practice, and there is evidence of the elderly being forced into the poorhouse or of support being extracted (often under protest) by poor relief authorities from families. Moreover, poor relief was far from universally available; migrants, for example, would face removal to their original "settlement" (place of birth or early residence) in order to claim relief. Is taking in an elderly relative evidence of cultural preference for co-residence, when the only alternative for that person is the poorhouse? Indeed, it also strikes me as difficult to argue that responding to a housing crunch by moving in with one's parents represents a true cultural preference for extended family living. This further suggests that with increasing levels of co-residence as manifested in larger proportions of extended families, at least some of which represented resources flowing from the younger to the older generation, more people would have had an interest in initiating new forms, or returning to old levels, of state social provision. In short, we need not posit changing cultural preferences for co-residence once social policy is considered: without public assistance, people

---

women to baby-sit for working mothers provided an important motivation for taking in kin. Ruggles does not dispute this relationship for Lancashire (1987, p. 48), although he downplays it, but says it doesn't hold up for his U.S. samples. He also downplays the possibility of the elderly providing shelter for their adult children, noting that the aged would not help much with the rent "since the aged were rarely employed" (1987, p. 56). In fact, as we noted above, most of the aged were employed. And his own investigation of the character of extended families among different classes in 1871 Lancashire shows that the bulk of three-generation households among the working classes were in fact headed by the elderly (1987, p. 217). This suggests that married adult children might well have been moving in with their parents prior to establishing themselves independently. This seems quite in line with Anderson's findings about Preston and Quadagno's about Chilvers Coton in 1851, where elderly couples and individuals did take in their married children and grandchildren.

had no choice but to take in their elderly or other nonworking kin unless they were willing to leave them to the poorhouse (some were, of course). Even middle-class people—specifically elderly widowed women—would not have escaped destitution or the degradation of poor relief under the poor law regime without family assistance.

In the late nineteenth and early twentieth centuries, U.S., British, and Canadian families did take in their elderly kin, but for the poorest, such assistance was contingent on the aged relatives being able to offer something in return for their care. Whether or not the elderly would have that something to offer depended in turn on the character of state social provision. Even if insufficient for an independent existence, a state pension or the aid supplied by overseers of the poor as outdoor relief to an elderly person could enable a family to shelter an aged, nonworking relative (Anderson 1977, pp. 50–53; Quadagno 1982, chap. 3; Henderson 1909, p. 277). When such sources of assistance were reduced or cut off, families were hard pressed to care for their elderly kin, if they could at all, and the aged without kin were put in an especially vulnerable position. Thus, we need to consider the shifting character, availability, and levels of public social provision to understand the problems faced by the elderly and their families as opportunities for self-support changed.

4
The New Poor Law
Starting Point for Modern Social Policy Debates

The "new poor law," deterrent poor relief, was the starting point for late-nineteenth- and early-twentieth-century debates and struggles over the character of public social provision for the aged. In assessing the effect of socioeconomic changes in the development of demand for new forms of social provision, it has been all too typical to ignore the role of policy feedback; most accounts of the circumstances of the elderly and their families fail to consider the character of social provision which supported work and familial arrangements, particularly in the preindustrial era when state social provision is often assumed to be minimal or nonexistent. Yet existing social provision mediated the impact of changing demography and work opportunities on the aged and their kin and was a critical independent factor in the formation of political demands and the development of policy discourse. In examining the evidence about the character of nineteenth- and early-twentieth-century social provision, the policy legacy, we will see that pensions and outdoor relief were an important component of many household economies, especially among the working classes. The character of that provision had an important effect on many, if not most, working-class households. When these forms of provision were cut back, the elderly and their families suffered: at worst, older people might be forced into institutions; at the least, families would have to allocate resources to caring for their aged kin that otherwise went to other needs, with a concomitant decrease in living standards. State social policy was far more accessible to human observation than the subtle economic and demographic changes and was an important proximate cause of the break with poor relief and the initiation of modern social provision.

Britain, Canada, and the United States experienced during the nineteenth century what Gaston Rimlinger (1971, p. 35) has aptly called the "liberal break" with early modern, mercantilist notions of poor relief. This is a key similarity of these countries which sets them apart from continental Europe, where more paternalist understandings of social provision remained strong. Paternalist conceptions were embodied in England's Elizabethan Poor Laws (usually referred to as the old poor law), dating from the early seventeenth century, and in the earliest poor relief legislation and practices of England's daughter nations. These laws restricted the mobility of poor people by tying relief to long-term local residency but did offer outdoor relief, supervised subsistence to the poor in their own homes, or work relief to members of the local community who were impoverished, widowed, disabled due to age, injury, or illness, or unemployed, through locally financed and administered institutions (Himmelfarb 1983, p. 4; Heclo 1974, p. 48; Knott 1986, chap. 1; Mohl 1973, pp. 6–8; Katz 1986, pp. 13–14; Haber 1983, pp. 24–25; Strong 1930, part 1; Guest 1980, pp. 9–17). In the new poor law, and its New World followers, paternalism—at least for the able-bodied poor—was swept aside, and a harsher regime was institutionalized.

"Less eligibility," the "workhouse test," and local responsibility were the essential policy precepts adopted in the British Poor Law Amendment Act of 1834—popularly known as the new poor law—and in analogous legislation and the operating rules of voluntary institutions in North America. Under the new poor law, outdoor relief was to be kept to a minimum and abolished altogether for the able-bodied. The able-bodied were to receive help only if they were willing to enter workhouses to do hard work under demeaning conditions for subsistence support at less than any "independent" worker could earn under prevailing economic conditions—the (in)famous principle of "less eligibility." The workhouse thus served as "a mechanistic, self-acting test of destitution on the Benthamite pain/pleasure principle" (Rose 1981, p. 53). Carried over from the old poor law was local administration and financing of relief, and the requirement that relief be given only in one's place of settlement (often one's birthplace or place of very long residence, or, for married women, the settlement of one's spouse) (Abromovitz 1988, pp. 79–83; Brown 1940, pp. 11–13; Heisterman 1933, 1934; Knott 1986, pp. 20–21, 58; Rose 1976). Should persons become destitute away from their legal settlement, the authorities could "remove" them to the place of legal responsibility. Elaborate legal provision was made for reimbursement of localities which cared for the "unsettled poor" (those with no legal settlement) or for those with settlements elsewhere, and disputes over settlement provided occasions for endless legal wrangling between communities, all of which wanted to keep poor relief costs down (see, e.g., Creech 1969, chap. 7). These policy principles shaped the character of public provision in all three countries. Thus the new poor law must serve as our starting point for understanding both how policy mediated people's experience of the changes associated with capitalist industrialization and how existing policy contributed to debates about the future of public social provision which took place around the end of the nineteenth and the beginning of the twentieth centuries.

While the principles of less eligibility and the workhouse test were the basis of state and state-subsidized social provision, there was important variation over time. We can discern several different phases of social provision in all three countries: the early new poor law, under which the elderly were exempted from the harshest practices, beginning in the 1830s; the campaign against outdoor relief and the movement for a "scientific charity," which began in the 1870s and lasted into the 1890s; and a softening of relief practices toward the aged, which began in the 1890s and lasted through the 1900s in Britain and until the 1920s in North America (that is, until the break with poor relief). The common elements of poor relief policy and its development across the three countries can help to account for the similarities in the popular experiences of poverty and in the emergence of demands for policy remedies. There were also notable differences in the ways in which common poor relief policy principles were carried out in the three countries and across localities, which significantly affected policy debates and outcomes, particularly among elite political actors. Moreover, in the United States, Civil War pensions provided a very important additional form of public social provision. These honorable, generous benefits served as de facto old age and disability pensions for a large proportion of elderly Americans as the program was continuously expanded in the years between the 1880s and 1910s.

The New Poor Law

In Britain, policy under the old poor law oscillated between offering outdoor or work relief and providing relief only on condition of entering a workhouse, so-called indoor relief. In England during the 1790s some groups from among the rural gentry who administered local poor relief developed the system called "rates in aid of wages," the practice of giving outdoor relief to aid agricultural laborers whose low wages were insufficient to maintain a family. The "Speenhamland system," named after the town in which it was first developed, tied the level of poor relief to the price of bread (Polanyi 1944, chaps. 7–8; Heclo 1974, pp. 54–55; Himmelfarb 1983, pp. 154–55). The result was the widespread pauperization of the agricultural working class, many of whom received poor relief to supplement their wages. Outdoor relief was also widely available to widows and the "impotent aged" (Thomson 1984a, 1990; Knott 1986, chap. 1). Indeed, Thomson argues that the assistance available to the nonworking elderly constituted the equivalent of a pension.

With the advent of capitalist industrialization in Britain, these Elizabethan poor relief policies came under sustained assault from intellectuals and reformers, adherents of the new theory of political economy, who championed competitive markets and the "freedom" of wage laborers to look after themselves in the emerging economic order based on individual entrepreneurial initiative (Rimlinger 1971, pp. 33–44; Polanyi 1944). Because they encouraged pauperism and impeded labor mobility, the old poor laws were said to be economically inefficient, unjustly costly to property owners, and demoralizing to workers (Rose 1972, p. 8; Heclo 1974, p. 55; a useful collection of excerpts from pieces arguing for the reform of the old poor law can be found in Rose 1971, pt. 1).[1] Nassau Senior and Edwin Chadwick, influential Benthamite political economists who served on the investigatory Royal Commission on the Poor Laws (appointed in 1832), favored amending the poor law to ensure that social policy reflected the "laws" of political economy (Webb and Webb 1910, pp. 1–2; Fraser 1973, chap. 2). In the landmark 1834 report of the commission, they argued that outdoor relief should be kept to a minimum and abolished altogether for the able-bodied, who would be helped only "indoors," that is, in workhouses, under "less eligible" conditions (see excerpts in Rose 1971, pp. 85–86).[2] Only the truly dependent or the desperately needy would then apply for local relief, since the threat of entering the workhouse in order to obtain relief (the "workhouse test") was so forbidding. Thus costs would be kept down and the self-reliance of the working class encouraged.

The principal target of these first poor law reformers was the treatment of the able-bodied poor. Indeed, in their 1834 report they ignored the aged almost altogether, save to note that "even in places distinguished in general by the most wanton parochial profusion, the allowances to the aged and infirm are moderate" (cited in Quadagno 1982, p. 99). In theory, outdoor relief for the "impotent poor," including the aged, was acceptable under the new policy regime, and the aged were not to be sent to poor law institutions unless they were unable to care for themselves (Webb and Webb 1910, pp. 8–9, 18; Crowther 1982, chaps. 1–2; Himmelfarb 1983, p. 161). Specialized institutions were to be set up to attend to those old and sick people who needed care. Thus, the key difference between old and new poor laws was in the attempt to deny all but indoor relief for the able-bodied poor (in fact, there was a reduction but not a complete cut-off). While estimates of the proportions vary, analysts agree that the able-bodied poor received substantial amounts of outdoor relief under the old policy regime (Williams 1981, pp. 40–41; Knott 1986, p. 26). While concern for the handling of the aged poor was initially not particularly intense, however, their treatment under the poor relief system eventually became a spark for the shift to modern forms of state social provision.

1. There is now evidence that the actual results of the old poor law, and specifically the Speenhamland system, may not have been as economically disastrous as people then believed (see Rose 1981, p. 51; Himmelfarb 1983, p. 155; Knott 1986, chap. 1).

2. Although it is widely believed that the new poor law was the fruit of the 1832 Reform Bill, which enfranchised the middle class, it should be noted that the experiments in using workhouses were begun in the 1820s and that the Royal Commission was appointed prior to the seating of members elected under the new franchise. Further, the new poor law was not immediately a party issue, receiving almost unanimous support in Parliament (Heclo 1974, p. 56; Fraser 1973, p. 45).

The new poor law regime for the aged was less harsh than that prescribed for the able-bodied poor, and some analysts, most notably David Thomson (1984a, b, 1990), have argued that both the old poor law and the early version of the new offered a relatively generous allowance to most of those working-class aged who could no longer work.[3] Thomson investigated poor law administrative records, including those for the parish of Ampthill—a rural union which was known for "looseness" under the old poor law, as well as for the harshness of its post-1834 cutback—for the years 1835–44. He discovered that even after the 1834 changes, three-quarters of women aged seventy or over, along with almost two-thirds of men of the same age group, received substantial cash assistance over a five-year period, and that almost 90 percent of these were regular poor law pensioners (their receipt of assistance was no longer subject to more than perfunctory review) (Thomson 1990, p. 7). Thomson notes that even in the lowest-spending unions, relief to the aged was substantial. For example, 36 percent of women and 26 percent of men over seventy were regular recipients of outdoor relief in Barton-upon-Irwell, in the industrial Manchester district (Thomson 1990, p. 8). In considering the question of benefit levels, Thomson has shown in a series of analyses that poor law allowances to the elderly on average amounted to about 40 percent of adult male wages, or about 70–90 percent of the resources available to working-class adults—a relative level higher than that of twentieth-century pensions (Thomson 1984b). Furthermore, in the first years of the new poor law, relatives were not expected to contribute to the maintenance of their elderly parents, much less to the support of more distant kin (Thomson 1984a). Thomson's work is thus critical of many existing analyses of the early years of the new poor law, which have stressed only its harshness and have failed to consider the important role of poor relief in sustaining the nonworking elderly. Yet even when we consider his important corrections to our understanding of poor relief policy, it remains true that older people who received poor relief were subject to the stigma of pauperization and disenfranchisement (if they were eligible to vote). It also proved difficult in practice to establish the specialized institutions called for in the report of 1834, so that the aged who were institutionalized were put in the "general, mixed workhouse" of Dickensian infamy, with the sick, the insane, the unemployed, and unwed mothers and their children, under a regime of "less eligibility" (Rose 1972, pp. 35–36). Although outdoor relief recipients might be treated decently, people certainly had no right to such relief, and the practices of poor law guardians differed across localities.

From the colonial era through the early 1800s, U.S. poor relief policy, embodied in colonial and then state statutes, resembled the old poor law of Britain

---

3. Thomson (1990) notes that these allowances were referred to as pensions and were accepted as legitimate provision for the "worthy aged."

(see Katz 1986, pp. 13–21; Trattner 1979, chap. 4; Brown 1940, pp. 3–13; Creech 1969, pt. 1; Brown 1928, chaps. 2–3; Wisner 1970, chaps. 1–3; Alexander 1980). Outrelief was often available to the "deserving," including the aged, and as the country became more urban, institutions began to be built, particularly in the larger towns. In addition, especially in less developed regions, towns and counties sometimes contracted for the care of paupers or auctioned them off to the lowest bidders. These practices, which often resulted in terrible conditions for the poor, might also be used to their advantage. Indeed, reformers complained about "contracting out," in which poor relief authorities paid people to care for the destitute of a locality. It seems that relatives often took in their kin under this system and received help from the poor rates in doing so (Katz 1986, p. 20; Hannon 1985, p. 241). There was evidence of a "liberal break" in the early decades of the nineteenth century in the United States, too, particularly in the longer-established states such as Massachusetts and New York, where influential investigations of the poor law took place during the 1820s (the reports are reprinted in *The Almshouse Experience* 1971). These reports criticized outdoor relief, auction, and contract and advocated the use of the workhouse, arguing on grounds similar to those used by the British reformers (Brown 1940, pp. 8–9; Mohl 1973). The concern, as in Britain, was the treatment of the able-bodied, rather than the "impotent," poor (Katz 1986, p. 18).

In the United States, as in Britain, poorhouses were built at an increased rate, and officials attempted to cut back on outdoor relief in the decades following the issuance of the influential state reports (Katz 1986, chap. 1; Trattner 1979, chap. 4; Hannon 1984a, b, 1985). For example, following the 1824 Yates report in New York, the state passed legislation mandating the building of county poor relief institutions and disallowing outdoor relief (Trattner 1979, p. 52; Hannon 1985). Furthermore, Hannon documents that the period following the Yates report "brought a dramatic decline in the generosity of poor relief relative to common labor earnings in New York State" (1984a, p. 818). Since the United States lagged somewhat in industrialization and did not experience "overpopulation" in the early stages of the process, however, the anti-Elizabethan ideas were less quickly and unanimously embraced among American poverty reformers before the Civil War—and were less uniformly put into practice (Klebaner 1964; Wisner 1970). Even New York amended its 1824 law to allow local discretion on institution-building and the granting of temporary outdoor relief (Hannon 1985). Coll (1972, pp. 144–45) reports that in the 1850s outdoor relief was apparently favored in New York and Philadelphia for temporary assistance to the unemployed and in the form of a regular "pension" to "aged and infirm persons whose relatives were able to provide shelter but no other subsistence," or to those who could supplement the aid with part-time work or aid from relatives or charity; pensions went as well to the sick and widows with small children (see also Katz 1986, p. 56). Relief was often given in kind, or, if in cash, at a level barely sufficient for subsistence. Furthermore, acceptance of such assistance meant disenfranchisement and sometimes the forced removal to one's place of "settlement" or of long residence as poor relief officials refused to care for the needy of other localities (Coll 1972, p. 145; Abbott 1934; Brown 1940, chap. 1).

Particularly in rural areas where there were few paupers, taxpayers were reluctant to build institutions, and nowhere were they willing to build a network of differentiated institutions to offer proper treatment to the various categories of "deserving" and "undeserving" poor. In the early years of the new poor law in the United States, the "worthy" aged mingled with other categories of the poor in the poorhouse. Similar to those in England, U.S. poorhouses remained "trapped by their contradictory purposes, undercut by poor management and inadequate funds, . . . [unable to] find useful work for their inmates or [to] offer the old, sick, and helpless, not to mention the ablebodied unemployed, much more than a roof and escape from death by starvation" (Katz 1986, p. 35).

Because the United States had no national- or state-level poor relief administration, we have far less information about U.S. poor relief practices than we do for Britain. We know from poor relief statistics from around the turn of the century that elderly Britons received assistance at far higher levels than their American counterparts. Thus, we may surmise that through the 1860s in the United States, modest proportions of the aged and widowed population received outdoor relief, probably at levels somewhat reduced from the eighteenth century, and almost certainly at levels lower than the British. Part of the reason for the lower levels of assistance in the United States was that kin responsibility was taken seriously even before 1870 (Katz 1986, p. 14; Abbott 1934).

In Canada, the Elizabethan poor law was brought by British colonists only to what would later become the provinces of Nova Scotia and New Brunswick. As in early America, in these maritime provinces, there was auctioning off of paupers and boarding out of others at public expense in addition to indoor relief (Guest 1980, p. 11). In Nova Scotia, outdoor relief initially was organized by private philanthropic organizations, but in the 1830s it was attacked in the same way as was public outdoor relief in the United States and Britain. In the wake of the attacks, the organization providing it disbanded (Hart 1953). Colonists in Quebec and Ontario and later settlers in western Canada made no statutory provisions for government responsibility for poor relief, leaving the task of caring for the poor to private philanthropy, the Catholic Church and other religious organizations, and the municipalities (Machar 1898; Guest 1980, pp. 12–15; Strong 1930, pt. 1).[4] Yet the voluntary organizations and institutions

4. The decision not to enact a poor law was deliberate, but the reasons for the colonists' decisions were not recorded (Splane 1973, pp. 278–79).

that predominated in Canadian relief-giving depended heavily on government financial support for their survival, and they, like U.S. and British state welfare institutions, attempted to carry out the principles of the new poor law in Canada from the 1830s on (Baehre 1981a, p. 79). In the years following the 1834 poor law reforms in Britain, settlers of Britain's Canadian colonies opened workhouses, called houses of industry, in Toronto, Montreal, and other cities (Strong 1930, pp. 36–37; Splane 1973; Baehre 1981a). Indeed, Canadian welfare developments in the 1830s and 1840s were directly influenced by British developments arising from the 1834 reform, both through the appointment of a former poor law official as lieutenant governor and by the problems created by the immigration of British paupers to Canada, assisted by British public authorities (Baehre 1981a, b; Angus 1972, pp. 121–22). Outdoor relief was organized through private, often sectarian, institutions (Spiesman 1973, pp. 38–39; Splane 1973, pp. 104–5; Strong 1930, p. 35). By most accounts it was more important than institutional relief for the aged, widowed, and seasonally unemployed, although some did end up in institutions (personal communication from James Struthers; Angus 1972, p. 134). In Quebec, the Catholic Church was the predominant force in relief-giving, as Church-affiliated organizations provided outdoor relief to the Catholic needy, including the aged, and religious orders ran benevolent institutions for those who could not care for themselves. Protestant organizations offered similar help to their adherents (Strong 1930, chaps. 1–2, pp. 139–49; Bradbury 1979). Thus, despite the lack of British-style poor laws in most of Canada, the practices associated with the new poor law were to some extent duplicated (McLean 1901; Bryden 1974, p. 22; Guest 1980, pp. 36–38).

How did these systems of public provision affect the household arrangements of the elderly? In Britain, poor relief allowed a substantial proportion of the nonworking elderly to maintain themselves, on their own or, particularly for aged men, as lodgers, or, particularly for elderly women, as members of the households of their adult children or other kin. In those households, poor relief allowed the aged to contribute to the family economies. Few aged people who could care for themselves were institutionalized. Analysts have emphasized different effects of outdoor relief, some noting that it was most important in allowing the aged to live independently (Thomson's position), others that it allowed poorer families to take in their elderly kin (the position of Quadagno and Anderson). It may well be that this reflects an urban-rural difference in Britain, where outdoor relief was more generous in the villages than in the cities. Either way, there is no support for the view that the elderly were "abandoned" by their kin, and both positions suggest that poor relief provided an important source of support to the aged in Britain.

In both the United States and Canada, outdoor relief was more important than indoor relief for the aged, particularly in rural areas, where institutional development lagged behind the cities. Yet poor relief was less widely available in North America than in Britain. (Indeed, Britain's poor relief system was the most developed in all of Europe.) This may be traced at least in part to the greater importance of agricultural work in North America than in Britain during the early part of the century and to the larger proportion of farm owner- ship among agrarian populations. These factors in turn meant less retirement by aged men in Canada and the United States and, at least for some, signifi- cant resources for retirement if it should occur. In the late 1700s and early 1800s British elites used poor relief to deal with the problems of agricultural wageworkers, elderly and otherwise, rather than with those who owned land. Hannon's work on poor relief in antebellum New York (1984b), too, suggests that relief was a response to the spread of wagework, rather than to industrial- ization per se. For those elderly people who could not work, some were taken in by kin and were able to contribute to the household economy with outdoor relief. Outdoor relief would also have allowed some older people, particularly widows, to survive on their own. Finally, indoor relief provided food and shel- ter to a small proportion of aged people who had no one to care for them. Thus, poor relief was surely an important component of the living arrangements of North American older people, though perhaps not to the same extent as in Britain.

Despite its role in shoring up many a working-class family economy, poor relief always entailed some uncertainty about eligibility, depending as it did on the discretion of poor relief officials, and a certain level of stigma, though this applied less to the "deserving," such as the aged, formerly working poor. Relief was always at a very low level, almost invariably requiring supplemen- tation from other sources—part-time work, kin, or private charity. Even then, relief allowed no more than a subsistence standard of living, if that. Of course, this occurred in the context of generally low living standards for the entire working class and widespread poverty. But the uncertainty, degradation, and inadequacy of poor relief helped to provoke popular reactions against it.

The Campaign against Outdoor Relief

In the late nineteenth century, changes in the policies which had allowed cash awards to the elderly outside of institutions undermined the family support system prevailing among the working classes as well as the capacity of many elderly people to survive on their own. The campaign against outrelief is better documented in Britain than in Canada or the United States, but we do know the broad outlines of this policy shift in North America. A range of reformers in the movement for "scientific" and "organized" charity in all three countries and government officials in Britain and the United States advocated major changes in the administration of poor relief. Arguing that both public relief and private charity were indiscriminate and more likely to perpetuate than eradicate pauperism, they pressed for two key reforms of the public and private systems of relief and a clear division of labor between the two. The "deserving" poor were to be shifted entirely to private charity so that public relief could become fully deterrent in its dealings with the "undeserving." This meant the abolition or severe curtailment of outdoor relief to allow the "workhouse test" to perform its function of forcing able-bodied but lazy paupers to work. At the same time, private charity was to be systematized, to prevent duplication of services, and made "scientific," in order to rehabilitate the "deserving" poor who were to be the prime responsibility of the voluntary sector. These prescriptions were made without too fine a regard for the facts about who was actually drawing outdoor relief (predominantly the aged, widowed, and those otherwise unable to work) or what resources (inadequate) the voluntary sector had for helping the "worthy poor."

The campaign against outdoor relief, which was the main reform for the public relief sector, was embraced unevenly across the three countries. In Britain, it was national in scope, carried out between 1870 and 1890 by the Local Government Board, the central body charged with oversight of poor relief, which remained locally financed and administered. Although outrelief was severely cut back, it was never abolished entirely. In addition to reducing outrelief, British poor law officials for the first time systematically enforced family support rules. In the United States, some municipal governments actually abolished poor relief completely, others cut back, and still others left outdoor relief practices unreformed. In Canada, the intellectual arguments of the campaign against outrelief and scientific charity were espoused by the country's few charity officials and reformers, but there is no evidence that these were effective in changing policy. Wherever reforms were put into practice, aid was cut off to many elderly people who, even under the severe prescriptions of the new poor law of 1834, were entitled to be relieved outside of institutions. The cut-off, along with decisions to enforce family support rules, put pressure on the families of the aged, many of whom already existed only precariously, and caused great difficulties for the elderly without families, who were more often institutionalized. This phase of poor relief policy, with its emphasis on institutionalization, rather than the early new poor law, was the immediate background to the consideration of modern social provision for the elderly. It is largely responsible for the almost unrelievedly negative view of poor relief developed in the course of movements for state old age pensions. Moreover, variation in the campaign against outdoor relief was critical to the reactions of elites to demands for new forms of public social provision. At this point, I will not attempt to explain why the campaign in the three countries varied but will note that much of the answer lies in the structures and capacities of political institutions. Here, I simply want to document that there was in fact variation that led to different sorts of "problem pressures" among the populations of the three countries and to show that these pressures were not the unmediated result of socioeconomic processes such as industrialization.

Across Britain, the proportion of the population receiving poor relief declined from 5.7 percent to 2.0 percent over the period 1850–1910, even as poverty levels remained the same or increased (Rose 1972, p. 53; Heclo 1974, p. 62). This decline was almost wholly due to reductions in outrelief. At midcentury, outdoor relief reached about 5 percent of the population, but by the early part of the twentieth century, this had been reduced to 1 percent. Indoor relief remained fairly stable, going to about three-quarters of one percent of the population. Thus, the new poor law generally had achieved its goal of cutting back on outdoor relief, but the sharpest decline in outdoor relief occurred in the decade 1870–80, following the campaign against outrelief (Rose 1981, pp. 56, 61–64). Moreover, Mary MacKinnon found that "during the Crusade all types of applicants for relief were less likely to obtain outdoor assistance, although the increase in the proportions of paupers relieved indoors was greatest for the elderly . . . and for able-bodied men" (1987, p. 604). David Thomson states that "public assistance to the aged was cut between 1870 and 1890 to onehalf or one-third of mid-century levels. And the proportions continued to fall through the 1890s and 1900s" (1990, p. 18). The relative value of the assistance these smaller proportions of the aged received was cut drastically as well (Thomson 1984b).

A crucial concomitant of the campaign against outdoor relief in Britain was the enforcement of family support rules. Thomson (1984a) has pointed out that this was a departure from the previous practices of poor law guardians (local administrators), who had given allowances to the elderly without regard to family resources. Under the new regime, poor relief officials were to pursue relatives—whether legally liable or not—to provide support, through devices such as "offering the house" if the relatives would not contribute at least partially toward the support of an older person, publishing and publicly displaying lists of paupers, encouraging neighbors to inform on others, and obtaining court orders against adult children (Thomson 1990, pp. 22–24). In examinations of local poor law administrative records, Jill Quadagno (1982, chap. 5) and Michael Anderson (1977) have found that the campaign put pressure on, and in some cases actually broke up, extended families that previously had sheltered the aged from the workhouse. In Britain, in the wake of the anti–outdoor relief order of the Local Government Board, local boards of guardians—themselves pressured by the national board—put pressure on the adult children of aged relief recipients to support their parents, or see them sent to the workhouse (Drage 1914, pp. 83–84; Ashforth 1976, p. 131). A tug-of-war between the guardians and the adult children ensued; as Anderson puts it, "Working class resistance to supporting their parents on a regular, total-support, week-by-week basis was clearly based on their own abject poverty, resulting from low wages" (1977, pp. 55–56). Quadagno finds no evidence of family break-down apart from that caused by the withdrawal of outrelief in the prepension period. On the contrary, she argues that state policy put pressure on the poor-est families, who otherwise would have at least partially supported and housed their aged kin. "The refusal of children to maintain aged parents was due to the economic hardships imposed by the withdrawal of outdoor relief, rather than to filial neglect. Working-class families simply could not survive as eco-nomic units when aged members did not contribute to the family economy" (Quadagno 1982, p. 137). This dynamic could help to explain the pattern found by Ruggles (1987) and others of extended families being more common among the better-off than the poorest.

The Local Government Board policy on outdoor relief had the effect of forcing those without kin—or whose kin could not or would not support them—to the workhouse. Under the earlier policy, many without families might have stayed on their own, helped to survive on part-time work by a small amount of cash relief from the poor law authorities (Anderson 1977, p. 45). Indeed, as we noted in chapter 3, there is evidence of increased institutionaliza-tion of the elderly from 1880 through 1900, with the proportion in institutions doubling between 1851 and 1906 from 3.2 percent to 6 percent (Anderson 1977, pp. 44–45; Thomson 1990, 1983). All but the aged were removed from these institutions (Rose 1981), and thus "workhouses were made deliberately into what popular memory this century has come to remember them—huge, gloomy barracks housing hundreds of elderly men and women, under condi-tions intended constantly to remind everyone of the ignominy of being a public charge. These were an expensive but unavoidable side-product of the reform campaign" (Thomson 1990, p. 20).

Thus, in Britain, specific policy decisions, namely the campaign against outrelief, put pressure on the elderly and their families, causing the poorest to "abandon" their aged kin to the poorhouse, and others to suffer increasing hard-ships in caring for them. It is clear that in the late nineteenth and early twentieth centuries, the elderly were more burdensome to their families, as opportunities to work, even part-time, declined and as public aid dried up. The nonworking elderly without families had few, if any, alternatives to the workhouse.

Canadians were influenced both by Malthusian and laissez-faire political doctrines in the early 1800s and by social Darwinism in the later years of the nineteenth century. Among other things, these intellectual trends criticized out-door relief and encouraged an individualist view of the causes of poverty and pauperism (Wallace 1950b; Splane 1973, pp. 13–17, 278–79). Yet the cam-paign against outrelief never was put into effect in Canada. In Toronto, for example, the city with the largest concentration of the charity reformers who were so influential in promoting the campaign against outrelief in Britain and the United States, the effect of their efforts was limited to the initiation of a work test in 1888 at the house of industry, a publicly subsidized private institution which gave outrelief to the aged and unemployed and was also responsible for indoor care for "tramps," the indigent aged and sick (Pitsula 1980; Spiesman 1973). Charity organization societies were established in Canada's larger cities toward the end of the nineteenth century and in the early twentieth, and they attempted to make relief "scientific," as did their counterparts in Britain and the United States (Copp 1974, chap. 7; Guest 1980, p. 37; Pitsula 1979; Splane 1973, p. 114). Yet outdoor relief was nowhere abolished, even where officials initiated work tests or other means for making assistance more difficult to get. Essentially, these changes had little or no effect on the "impotent" aged; indeed, they were aimed at the able-bodied unemployed, particularly "tramps" (Pitsula 1980). Of course, as in Britain and the United States, not all Canadians who needed assistance got it. With the lack of statutory mandate for the provision of poor relief, old people were sometimes jailed rather than given outdoor relief (Machar 1898, p. 242).

In the United States, too, a crusade against outdoor relief was promoted by organized charity and some local poor relief administrators (Katz 1983, pp. 132–33, 191; Katz 1986, chap. 2). Unlike Great Britain, the United States had no nationally administered poor relief administration, which meant that the anti–outdoor relief campaign had no central organization with sanctioning power over the local officials who were responsible for the financing and administration of relief. As a result, the campaign was only unevenly successful. Contemporary observer Frederick Almy, writing on outdoor relief practices in 1900, noted that "of the 21 cities in this country having a population over 200,000, 10 give practically no out-relief" (1901, p. 138). Outdoor relief was completely abolished in Brooklyn—this was the most celebrated case of the campaign against outdoor relief (Low 1879, 1881)—as well as in Baltimore, St. Louis, New Orleans, San Francisco, Kansas City, New York, and other cities. Others, including Chicago and Providence, cut back significantly on their relief budgets (Mohl 1983, p. 41). Where relief was not abolished entirely, cities often initiated work tests and other devices to make it harder to get (Mohl 1983, pp. 41–42). In New York State, which has unusually good statistical records of poor relief, outdoor relief declined both absolutely and relative to indoor relief in the years 1870–90 (Katz 1986, p. 37). The effect of the campaign against outdoor relief on the aged, or anyone else, however, has yet to be systematically assessed (Katz 1983, pp. 227–28).

Recently, historian Michael Katz examined the impact of the campaign in Brooklyn, where charity reformers claimed they had found evidence that the cutoff of outdoor relief had virtually no effect on the well-being of the poor (Katz 1986, pp. 46–52). His research suggests that, like their British counterparts, poor Americans were severely pressed by this policy shift, despite the protestations of the officials who promoted it. Few turned to the workhouse in Brooklyn, for it was already overcrowded, although in other locations this was not necessarily the case. Many unemployed men turned to crime, while others became vagrants; arrests increased following the cutoff. One of the principal ways the poor coped with the change was by sending their children to local orphan asylums, where the number of children placed nearly doubled in the year following the formal abolition of outrelief. Soon after, contemporary observers noted that private charity was inadequate for the volume of need formerly relieved with public funds, although the political aims of the reformers had already been accomplished and outdoor relief discredited among most elites and middle-class people. Katz did not directly investigate the circumstances of the elderly, but we can make some educated inferences from his research findings. In those cities where public outrelief was terminated, the elderly poor, some of whom were previously considered worthy recipients of outdoor relief pensions (Katz 1986, p. 56; Coll 1972, p. 145), would have little recourse but the support of families, private charity, or the almshouse. There is evidence that more elderly people were sent to mental institutions in the late nineteenth century than in earlier periods (Grob 1983, chap. 7). Among the poorest strata of society, it is hard to imagine that families would continue to support elderly relatives if they could not even keep their own children in their households, and solitary elderly men likely responded as did other nonworking men, by becoming vagrants, sleeping in police stations, and so on. Those families that could afford it would have been pressed to help any elderly kin previously dependent on outdoor relief. Of course, even without the campaign against outrelief, given the stringency of eligibility requirements, many families would have been called upon to support aged kin who could not work. The discrediting of outrelief could only have reinforced the social sanctions among the "respectable" working and middle classes against allowing one's relatives to accept relief. While public relief was under attack and in eclipse by the 1880s and 1890s, however, some elderly people, even in the localities which did abolish outdoor relief, were getting another form of help from the government: military pensions (Katz 1983, p. 233; Haber 1983, pp. 110–13).

Many working-class and lower-middle-class elderly Americans had no old age protection, and even poor relief was not as extensively developed in the United States as it was in Britain. Yet from about 1880 through the First World War, hundreds of thousands of men and women had the equivalent of an old age pension in the form of a Civil War military pension. Figure 4.1 helps to show the evolution of the Civil War pension law from a provision for compensation of combat injuries into a de facto system of old age and disability protection.

Benefits under the original 1862 law were extended only to soldiers actually injured in combat or to the dependents of those disabled or killed. As one might expect, the number of beneficiaries and total expenditures were

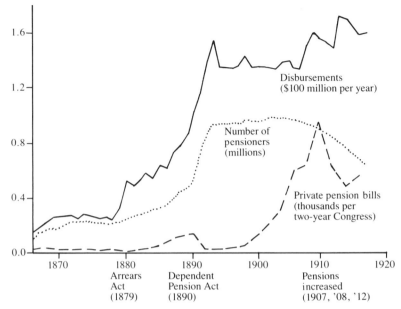

Figure 4.1. The expansion of Civil War pensions, 1866–1917.
Source: Data used to construct this figure were drawn from Glasson 1918, pp. 273, 280.

falling off in the late 1870s. Subsequently, however, legislative liberalizations occurred, the most important in 1879 and 1890 (McMurry 1922; Glasson 1918, pp. 148–247). The 1879 Arrears Act allowed soldiers who "discovered" Civil War–related disabilities to sign up and receive in one lump sum all of the pension payments they would have been eligible to receive since the 1860s. Then, the 1890 Dependent Pension Act severed altogether the link to combat-related injuries. Any veteran who had served ninety days in the Union military, whether or not he saw combat or was injured in the Civil War, could sign up for a pension if at some point in time he became disabled for manual labor. In practice, after the 1890 legislation, old age alone became a sufficient disability (Haber 1983, p. 112). In 1906 the law was further amended to state explicitly that "the age of sixty-two years and over shall be considered a permanent specific disability within the meaning of the pension laws" (U.S. Bureau of Pensions 1925, p. 43). This liberalization of the military pension laws is also clear from the increasing proportions of veterans who received benefits over the years 1870–1910 (see table 4.1).

A high proportion of men of military age were members of the Civil War regiments; about 35 percent of all men between fifteen and forty-five years old in the Northeast and Midwest served with the Union army during the Civil War (Vinovskis 1989, p. 40). Most of these men were in their sixties in the period

Table 4.1. Proportion of Civil War veterans
receiving pensions

Year	Estimated number of veterans in civil life	Proportion of Civil War veterans receiving pensions
1870	1,744,000	5.0%
1880	1,557,000	9.3%
1890	1,322,000	31.4%
1900	1,000,000	75.3%
1910	624,000	93.0%

Sources: U.S. Bureau of the Census 1975, p. 1145;
U.S. Bureau of Statistics 1912, p. 618; Glasson 1918,
p. 145

1890–1910, when the pension system was expanded. Thus it is not surprising that about a third of all elderly men, as well as many old and young widows, were receiving what were in effect federal old age and survivors' pensions during this period. The states, too, aided veterans; by 1910, all but six states had made statutory provision for the relief of Civil War veterans, so that they would not have to apply for poor relief (many gave relief to the veterans of other wars as well) (Brown 1940, p. 20). The benefits were relatively generous: the average pension in the years 1890–1910 was the equivalent of 30 percent of average annual earnings. By way of contrast, Germany's old age and invalidity pensions never reached 20 percent of average earnings, and Britain's pension under the 1908 law was about 22 percent (calculated from data in Phelps Brown and Hopkins 1981, pp. 194–95; Ritter 1986, pp. 155, 191; Sozialgeschichtliches Arbeitsbuch 1978, p. 107; Wisconsin Industrial Commission 1915, pp. 56–59; U.S. Bureau of Pensions 1911, p. 147; U.S. Bureau of the Census 1960, pp. 91–92).

The post–Civil War pension system reached about 15 percent of the elderly in America around the turn of the century. Invalid pensioners (the veterans themselves) made up about 30 percent of all American men over age sixty-five by 1910. Yet the system was uneven in its coverage of the population. In regional terms, it favored the North, Midwest, and West over the South (Bensel 1984, p. 68). For example, the proportions of men over sixty-five receiving pensions in 1910 amounted to 40 percent in Ohio, 48 percent in Kansas, and 45 percent in Indiana (U.S. Bureau of Statistics 1911, p. 652; U.S. Bureau of the Census 1975, pp. 15, 25–37). Confederate veterans, meaning most southern elderly men, were left out of the federal pension system, of course, although most of the southern states began to give much more meager state pensions to Confederate soldiers in the 1890s (Glasson 1907). In Georgia, the southern state with the most liberal and comprehensive pension system, Confederate pensions for "incapacity to perform manual labor" (assumed at age sixty-two) averaged $50 yearly, while U.S. military pensions for the same disability averaged $360 (Glasson 1907, p. 45). U.S. service pensions—as opposed to pensions for specific and service-related disabilities—were somewhat less generous; the average pension in 1910 was about $170 yearly, while annual wages averaged $566 (U.S. Bureau of the Census 1960, pp. 91–92; Phelps Brown and Hopkins 1981, pp. 194–95; U.S. Bureau of Pensions 1911, p. 147). Also excluded were most blacks, although the pensions did go to those who had served in the Union army, and all post–Civil War immigrants, which meant a large proportion of unskilled workers.[5] In ethnic terms, the post–Civil War pension system disproportionately helped native-born whites and early immigrants; in class terms, it assisted the middle class and upper strata of the working class the most (Rubinow 1913, pp. 408–9). Widows did receive pensions, but far fewer were granted to widows than to those who had served in the Union army. Over the period 1890–1900, more than three times as many "invalids" (as the male pensioners were called) as widows and survivors received pensions, while the ratio declined to about 2:1 by 1910 (U.S. Department of Commerce 1916, p. 646). Moreover, the average widow's pension was lower than the average invalid's: $144 versus $172 in 1910 (U.S. Bureau of Pensions 1911, p. 147).

Civil War pensions must have helped many men maintain their own households, particularly in the small towns and farm areas of the North, where a disproportionate share of pensions were received (Sanders 1980) and where, as Gratton and Haber (forthcoming) show, elderly people were most likely to live on their own. Rates of co-residence were higher among immigrants and women than among native-born people and men; while this fact is certainly related to the greater economic vulnerability of these groups, it may also be related to the availability of pensions. Elderly women's rate of receiving pensions was much lower than that for men (a little over 5 percent as compared with about 25–30 percent at the turn of the century). The "new" immigrants from Eastern and Southern Europe had not been in the country to participate in the Civil War and to gain entitlement to military pensions. This would tend to support the contention that the availability of noninstitutional public social provision or sufficient private means allowed elderly people to live on their own, for foreign-born people and women were poorer and would have had less access to Civil War pensions than native-born elderly American men.

What was the overall impact of the Civil War pension system on the elderly? Observers around the turn of the century commonly noted that it allowed many elderly people who could no longer work to maintain their independence or to contribute to their kin who took them in. Not every Civil War pensioner would have been a pauper without this aid, but as social analyst

5. The exclusion was based not on race or ethnicity, but on military service.

Charles Henderson wrote, "many of the old men and women who, in Europe, would be in almshouses, are found in the United States living upon pensions with their children or in homes to which paupers are not sent and they feel themselves to be the honored guests of the nation for which they gave the last full measure of devotion" (1909, p. 277). Thus, Civil War pensions acted as a functional equivalent of old age pensions for an important segment of the aged U.S. population. Indeed, at the same time charity reformers were waging the campaign against outrelief, the military pension system was undergoing expansion. In 1917 charity leader Edward Devine noted that without Civil War pensions, "the problem of old age dependency would have been far more pressing than it has been" (quoted in Gillen 1926, p. 284).

Treatment of the Aged Poor within the Poor Relief Framework

Poor relief policies toward the elderly softened somewhat toward the turn of the century, and in some areas treatment of the "worthy aged poor" improved. This was explicit in Britain, where Local Government Board circulars in 1896 and 1900 allowed for the aged "deserving" poor to be relieved outdoors and gave the elderly better treatment when they entered institutions (Williams 1981, pp. 119, 129; Rose 1981, p. 63). In North America, the shift to more lenient treatment also occurred, though it was unheralded. In the years between 1890 and the First World War, statistical information on the condition of the elderly first began to be collected by social scientists, government officials, and reformers, often in connection with the consideration or promotion of old age pension or insurance plans. These investigations, though not without flaws, allow us to get a more precise picture of the situation of the elderly in regard to access to public provision.

The evidence on dependency rates (the proportion of the elderly dependent on public aid) has sometimes been used to indicate how many of the elderly were potentially in need of a government pension at different points in time (e.g., by Fischer 1978, p. 174; Putnam 1970, p. 5). This was the common use of such material in the period in which public pensions were first under discussion. This is, unfortunately, potentially quite misleading, since it imbues these outcomes of public policy with a status as a causal factor in policy-making produced by socioeconomic developments alone, rather than by socioeconomic and political factors. Moreover, dependency does not simply equal need. Presumably, the acceptance of poor relief indicated that the pauper was at the very least not starving, and many poor faced destitution without public assistance for a range of reasons.[6] Gratton, too, has argued that "we err when we measure

---

6. An analogous distinction can be—and often is—made between poverty and receipt of AFDC or Supplemental Security Income in the present-day United States.

old age dependency by the number of old people receiving relief. The decision about what constitutes 'deserving need' is intensely political" (1986, p. 173). The real issues for contemporaries were the legitimacy of this form of public support for the groups who were receiving it and the possibility that some deserving poor people were without assistance. In this context, a high proportion of paupers among the formerly self-supporting elderly was a problem, as was the existence of unrelieved destitution.

In Britain, national poor relief policy for the aged softened in the 1890s (Collins 1965, pp. 247–48). The Local Government Board's policy of reducing access to outdoor relief for the aged, introduced in 1871, was partially reversed in an 1896 circular, which called for extending liberal outdoor relief to the "deserving" aged poor. In 1900 the LGB called for "adequate" outdoor relief for the deserving aged poor and proclaimed that the aged should not be sent to the workhouse unless they were unable to care for themselves (Quadagno 1982, pp. 111–12). Officials also called for indoor relief to the aged to be made less harsh: the "deserving aged" were to be segregated from "unworthy" inmates and allowed some privileges, such as the right to smoke and have visitors (Williams 1981, p. 119). But as M. A. Crowther notes, "the workhouse in 1900 was criticized less for its cruelty than for its dreariness, its regimented squalor, its failure to deal appropriately with different types of inmate" (1978, p. 36). Moreover, any improved treatment depended on demonstrating "worthiness" to the satisfaction of the guardians (Crowther 1978, pp. 45–46). As pioneering social investigations of the day suggested, these changes within the framework of the poor law were not enough to change the practices of all local boards of guardians, some of which ignored the circulars and continued to be quite harsh (Webb and Webb 1910, p. 354). Nor did the policy changes overcome the dread with which many working-class people viewed poor relief. In essence, the campaign against outdoor relief had done its job too well to allow for thoroughgoing reform.

The pioneering work on the aged poor of Charles Booth in the 1890s, based on census and Local Government Board data, revealed that 29 percent of the elderly in Britain were in receipt of poor relief in the early 1890s: 8 percent were inside poor law institutions, 19 percent received outdoor relief, and an additional 2 percent got medical help from poor law institutions (Booth 1894, p. 14).[7] Aged women were more likely to be receiving outrelief than elderly men: only 6 percent of women, but 11.5 percent of men, were in the poorhouse in 1891, while 23 percent of women got outdoor relief, contrasted with 14 percent of men (Booth 1894, p. 14). The proportions of the aged dependent

---

7. There had been no breakdowns by age in the returns on poor relief prior to 1890, but even as early as the 1840s, well over half of adult paupers were listed as being "aged and infirm" (Rose 1972, p. 19).

on poor relief were even greater in the larger metropolitan areas. For example, 37.5 percent received poor relief in London, and institutionalization was also more widespread there (Booth 1894, p. 14; Thomson 1983). Booth pointed out that if it were possible to break down the pauper figures by class, among the working classes and small traders, the proportion of the aged in receipt of poor relief was likely to be 40 percent or more (Booth 1894, p. 39). Compared with other segments of the population, the aged received poor relief far out of proportion to their representation in the population: investigations of LGB figures by the Royal Commission on the Aged Poor for the year 1891 showed that 5.1 percent of children aged sixteen or under, and only 3.7 percent of adults aged sixteen to sixty-five, received poor relief, but fully 29.3 percent of the aged did (Great Britain, Royal Commission on the Aged Poor 1895, p. xiii). Further, there was evidence that increasing age was associated with increasing proportions of pauperization (Booth 1894, pp. 40–46). This was made clear in Hamilton's analysis (1910, p. 7) of LGB data for 1906, reproduced in figure 4.2. Moreover, as other groups from among the poor, such as children and the insane, were removed from the workhouse to newly established specialized institutions, the elderly came to dominate workhouse populations. About one-fifth of indoor paupers were over age sixty-five in 1851, but this proportion had risen to almost two-fifths by 1901 and was close to one-half in London (Williams 1981, p. 205; Thomson 1983, p. 47). The prominence of aged people in these hated institutions served to dramatize the plight of the elderly poor.

Clearly, on the basis of this widely publicized information, substantial need existed among the elderly of Britain, and it is worth remembering that poor relief was at a relatively low point by the end of the century (Thomson 1990). Yet poor relief statistics exposed only a partial picture of need, for the investigations of Booth, Seebohm Rowntree, and others showed a tremendous amount of unrelieved poverty among the working classes, particularly the elderly (Rose 1972, p. 15; Treble 1979; Booth 1894; Rowntree 1901). Investigations carried out by the 1895 Royal Commission on the Aged Poor also revealed large numbers of elderly people choosing to live in utter destitution rather than to accept the degradation of becoming a pauper or the loss of freedom attendant on entering the workhouse, which was the only alternative in many areas (Quadagno 1982, pp. 103–16). We can also see, in retrospect, that the proportion of the aged living in poverty must have been even greater than the proportion receiving poor relief by examining the numbers of elderly Britons who qualified for pensions after 1908. Prior to the passage of the Old Age Pension Act, the government estimated that about one-third of the population aged seventy or over would be eligible for the pension in 1911; the actual proportion receiving pensions in 1911 was about three-quarters. The income limit for receipt of the full pension was set quite low—at about one-third of average annual earnings—but 94 percent of those receiving pensions were eligible for the

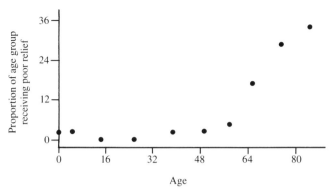

Figure 4.2. The relation between age and receiving poor relief in Great
Britain, 1910.
Source: Data used to construct this figure were drawn from Hamilton,
1910, p. 7.

full amount. The maximum pension was the equivalent of less than a quarter of
average annual earnings at the time (Wisconsin Industrial Commission 1915,
pp. 65–66; Ritter 1986, p. 155; Phelps Brown and Hopkins 1981, pp. 194–95).

In the United States by the end of the nineteenth century, according to historian Michael Katz, "outdoor relief had been reduced radically; state authority
[to supervise charities] had expanded; and special institutions had drawn children and the mentally ill out of poorhouses" (1986, p. 109). The able-bodied,
too, were forced out of poorhouses, leaving the institutions to become homes
of last resort for the aged poor. In the United States, there was no national-
level collection of statistics on poor relief save census surveys of paupers in
almshouses, and most states did not even collect information on the numbers
of their residents who were receiving public relief (Gillen 1926, pp. 38–39).
Information on the characteristics of almshouse inmates show that the almshouse population was aging during the period between 1890 and 1920 (see table
4.2). Even as the number of people under age sixty-five in almshouses declined
between 1910 and 1923, the number aged sixty-five and above increased, as
members of other demographic groups were being removed (Haber 1983, pp.
82–84; Katz 1983, pp. 57–89; U.S. Bureau of the Census 1925, pp. 10–11).
Unlike the situation in Britain, where the proportion of the elderly confined to
poor relief institutions expanded in the wake of the campaign against outrelief,
in the United States elderly people were not going to the almshouse at a greater
rate than before (the rate stayed steady at about nine or ten per thousand between 1890 and 1923; Gratton 1986, p. 133). The work of Gerald Grob (1983,
esp. chap. 7) on the history of mental illness, however, has shown that increasing numbers of elderly people were being committed to mental institutions.
From 1880 to 1923, the proportion of mentally ill persons in the almshouse

Table 4.2. Proportion of the elderly among almshouse
inmates, United States, 1880–1923

Year	Percentage of inmates aged 50 +	Percentage of inmates aged 65 +
1880	45.9	25.6
1890	54.3	31.8
1904	67.7	40.6
1910	73.0	42.7
1923	80.0	53.8

Source: U.S. Bureau of the Census 1925, p. 11

declined sharply, from 24.3 percent to 5.6 percent, but "the number of aged mentally ill persons committed to hospitals was rising steadily" (Grob 1983, p. 181). Grob goes on to note that

> the shift was [largely] . . . a consequence of financial considerations. As states began to adopt and implement principles of state responsibility for all insane persons in the late nineteenth and early twentieth century, local public officials seized upon the fiscal advantages inherent in redefining senility in psychiatric terms. If senile persons were cared for in state hospitals rather than in local or county hospitals, the burden of support would be transferred to the state. To many families, confinement in a mental hospital may have been preferable to almshouse care. Not only did hospitals provide better care, but paradoxically enough the stigma of insanity—especially if an aged person was involved—may have seemed less than that of pauperism. (1983, p. 181)

Thus, the difference between the United States and Britain in proportions of the elderly institutionalized, as reflected in almshouse populations, is more apparent than real. If we include the elderly committed to mental institutions, we can see that in the United States, too, the campaign against outrelief had led to increasing proportions of the elderly being institutionalized and harder choices for the aged and their families. In any event, as in Britain, the aged inmates of the almshouses served to dramatize the problem of poverty and lack of public provision for the elderly in the United States. Almshouses had not become any more inviting places. Petty criminals continued to be sent to many, and tight budgets prevented anything but the most minimal accommodation, even when the institutions came to be called "county homes for the aged" or "infirmaries" rather than poorhouses (see Gratton 1986, chap. 5; Brown 1928, p. 70, and chap. 4; Creech 1969, p. 235; Wisner 1970, pp. 42–47; Evans 1926). Concerns raised by the aging of the almshouse population encouraged the investigation of the circumstances of the aged population more generally.

Until the federal government began to provide emergency relief during the Depression, all relief in the United States was administered locally and continued to be based on settlement laws, which made residency a requirement for relief and allowed for the removal of the poor (see Abbott 1940, pp. 125–257). In her review of public relief in the United States, Josephine Brown condemned U.S. settlement laws: "The intricacies, inconsistencies, and lack of uniformity of these laws have forced great and bitter hardship upon many thousands of helpless and destitute people in the United States, who have been denied relief and shifted back and forth between towns, counties, and states" (1940, p. 12). Localism also allowed for wildly varying standards of relief—local authorities controlled even the basic issue of whether to give outdoor relief—and residency requirements (Abbott 1934; Almy 1899, 1901).

At the turn of the century, many cities continued to deny outdoor relief to needy residents, although in some of these cities, some of the burden was taken up by private relief-giving (Almy 1899, 1901). After 1912, however, municipal public spending on charities increased substantially (Katz 1986, p. 154). Odum (1933, p. 1251) reported that spending on poor relief expanded more than two-fold and outdoor relief spending expanded more than fourfold between 1913 and 1928 in U.S. cities with populations greater than thirty thousand. Gratton's analysis of Boston (1986, chap. 6) showed specifically that outdoor relief eligibility rules for the aged were loosened somewhat; about 4 percent of Boston's elderly were receiving outdoor relief in the 1920s, about double the proportion in the earlier years of the century. It is likely that similar changes underlay the expansion of relief spending in other cities as well.

What was the impact of public social policy on the aged? In the absence of national-level information, one is forced to rely on state-level investigations of the situation of the elderly, as did contemporary writers such as Lee Welling Squier, whose book *Old Age Dependency in the United States* (1912) was important in calling attention to the problems of the aged. By far the most influential and complete of all the reports issued were those from the state of Massachusetts, which carried out three separate surveys of the aged in 1908–9, 1915, and 1924 (Linford 1949, chap. 1). From these surveys we can get some sense of the circumstances of those already depending on some form of aid outside their own work, savings, or help from relatives. No other state took a census of all the dependent aged, and few bothered to conduct empirical research on the situation of the aged. Massachusetts was also the only state in which comparable surveys were undertaken in both the Progressive Era and the 1920s, so we can make some evaluation of changes in the situation of the elderly during the years when pensions were first proposed and adopted. The Massachusetts commissions also conducted surveys of samples of the so-called nondependent aged, which, like most of the few other such surveys done by state commissions and private organizations, were flawed. For example, there

Table 4.3. Aged dependent poor in Massachusetts, 1908–1909 and 1924

	Number of recipients aged 65 +		Proportion of population 65 +	
Type of aid	1908–1909	1924	1908–1909	1924
Almshouses (public)	3,480	4,123	2.0	1.8
Outdoor relief (public)	3,075	3,791	1.7	1.7
Private old age homes	2,598	2,921	1.5	0.7
Outdoor relief (private)	2,312	1,471	1.3	0.7
Veterans' benefits*	15,655	—	8.8	—
Other relief**	—	1,800	—	0.8
Prisons, insane asylums	2,517	3,000	1.4	1.3
U.S. military pensions	27,230	15,000	15.4	6.7
Civil service pensions	—	3,000	—	1.3
Total dependent	41,212	35,106	23.3	15.0
Total dependent, excluding military pensions	13,982	20,106	7.9	8.9
Total aged 65 or over	177,000	225,000		

Sources: Massachusetts Commission on Old Age Pensions 1910, pp. 21–22, 34–35; Massachusetts Commission on Pensions 1925, p. 37
Note: Civil War pension figures, supplied to the Massachusetts Commissions by the U.S. Bureau of Pensions, are approximate.
*Veterans' benefits include soldiers' relief and state and military aid, and are not included in the totals since there is no information about the degree of overlap between recipients of this category of aid and recipients of Civil War pensions.
**Other relief includes aid to the blind and aid provided by trust funds and churches (Massachusetts Commission on Pensions 1925, pp. 39–40).

is no information about how the sample of supposedly nondependent but poor elderly people in the 1908–9 survey was selected, yet the commissioners made recommendations against the adoption of pensions on the basis of the needs of this group (Linford 1949, pp. 23–24). These parts of their investigations are far less informative than one would like, but fortunately, the material on the dependent aged is very telling about the possible sources of pressure for policy change. I concentrate on the 1908–9 rather than the 1915 survey, as the later investigation merely confirmed the findings about the dependent elderly of the earlier and better-known analysis.

The information about aged people depending upon public or private assistance uncovered by the first Massachusetts investigation, published in 1910 by the Massachusetts Commission on Old Age Pensions, Annuities and Insurance, is reproduced in table 4.3. The commission's 1908–9 survey of the aged showed that about 23 percent of the residents of the state aged sixty-five or above depended on some form of public or private aid; the categories of dependents included those in public almshouses, prisons, or insane asylums, those in private benevolent homes, people receiving public or private outdoor relief, and those who received federal military pensions and/or state veterans' benefits (Massachusetts Commission on Old Age Pensions 1910, p. 29). A very small proportion of the elderly in Massachusetts—about 4 percent—received public (indoor and outdoor) poor relief. This is much smaller than the comparable proportion in Britain, which stood at almost 30 percent (Massachusetts Commission on Old Age Pensions 1910, p. 29). Yet when we include the proportion of the Massachusetts elderly receiving veterans' pensions, we see that the shares of the aged populations depending on some form of public provision is far more similar in Massachusetts and Britain (23 percent and 30 percent, respectively) than a comparison of poor relief alone reveals.

It is particularly noteworthy that such a high proportion of public aid in Massachusetts, and indeed throughout the North and West, was given under the rubric of veterans' aid.[8] State and military aid were special categories of state-subsidized relief for veterans and their dependents with no poor law disqualifications or stigma. Soldiers' relief was paid by towns to veterans who somehow did not qualify for any of the very liberal categories under which state and military aid were given, or whose state aid and pension combined were inadequate for their relief and "who would otherwise be receiving relief under the pauper laws" (Massachusetts Bureau of Statistics 1916, p. 30). While a majority of those getting relief in state pauper homes, in almshouses, or in their homes were foreign-born, those receiving aid for veterans and their dependents were, of course, almost all native-born whites or members of the Northern European immigrant groups which had arrived early in the nineteenth century (Massachusetts Commission on Old Age Pensions 1910, p. 62). Civil War pensions went to about 15 percent of people (approximately twenty-seven thousand) over age sixty-five in Massachusetts—more than were aided by all forms of nonveterans' public relief and at a cost to the federal government of over four million dollars, more than four times the cost of state and local welfare aid to the aged, apart from veterans' programs (Massachusetts Commission on Old Age Pensions 1910, p. 29). This stands in vivid contrast with the situation of the dependent elderly in Britain, where dependence on public aid meant degrading poor relief, rather than the honorable veterans' subsidies which many "dependent" elderly Americans claimed.

In the Progressive Era, only three other states collected information about the aged. Ohio, Pennsylvania, and Wisconsin all conducted surveys of the dependent aged, in a somewhat less extensive fashion than had Massachusetts,

---

8. Moreover, the fact that a fifth of the elderly depended on sources of aid outside their own employment or assistance from kin hardly seems congruent with the notion that Americans had little need for public programs of income support, which has occasionally been suggested as the reason for U.S. tardiness in initiating modern social provision.

and also looked at limited samples of the nondependent aged. Their findings about the dependent were quite comparable to those of the 1910 Massachusetts Commission (Wisconsin Industrial Commission 1915, pp. 10–12; Pennsylvania Commission on Old Age Assistance 1919, pp. 16–78, 197; Ohio Health and Old Age Insurance Commission 1919, p. 14). In all three states, very small proportions of the total population over sixty-five—nowhere greater than 5 percent—received poor relief. As had been the case in Massachusetts, all of these state commissions found that those in institutions were unlikely to be married, have living children, or be able-bodied, and more men than women were institutionalized. Significant proportions of the aged were Civil War pensioners: 10 percent of Wisconsin residents over age sixty in 1914, 19 percent of Pennsylvanians aged sixty-five and over in 1917, and about 20 percent of those sixty and over in Ohio in 1916.

The information uncovered by the 1924 Massachusetts investigation—published in 1925 by a new Massachusetts Commission on Old Age Pensions—is compared with the data from 1908–9 in table 4.3. The 1924 survey reported similar findings about dependency of the aged as had its 1908–9 predecessor, with one notable exception. The proportion of the elderly receiving Civil War pensions was more than halved, falling from 15.4 percent to 6.7 percent. This, of course, resulted from political choices, which, though less politically charged than the campaign against outrelief, may very well have had an effect similar to that campaign in Britain. It seems quite likely that this decline in public social provision available to the aged increased the receptivity to new public protections for the aged within the social strata which had formerly received Civil War pensions. Those who reached old age in the years following the First World War could not count on nonstigmatizing public aid in the form of a federal pension as had those a few years their senior. Indeed, the 1915 Wisconsin Industrial Commission report took note of these trends and stated that matters for the aged would worsen as Civil War pensions, which "may be regarded as a form of old age relief," declined with the dying off of the veterans and their widows (1915, p. 10).

In the 1920s, in connection with the consideration of numerous pension proposals, a greater number of American states appointed commissions which investigated the conditions of the aged; some private commissions, fielded by those politically interested in the pension debate, also undertook surveys of the elderly (see summaries in New York Commission on Old Age Security 1930; U.S. Social Security Board 1937). These were the usual surveys of the dependent, which again found very small proportions of the elderly relying on poor relief, and indoor relief limited almost exclusively to those with few if any family ties and unable to work. Civil War pensions clearly had declined in importance as a mode of relieving the elderly by the mid-to-late 1920s. But investigators were also concerned to find out whether most of the elderly, who did not depend on poor relief, needed pensions. Thus, they attempted to establish the level of dependency, broadly understood as reliance on friends or relatives in addition to public or private charity. The reports found a wide range of dependency rates, at least in part because the surveys used different methodologies, none very reliable. For example, in many of the 1920s surveys, the income of married couples was counted twice—once for each partner—making the conditions of the aged look quite a bit rosier than was justified by the facts (U.S. Social Security Board 1937, pp. 150–51). Taking three hundred dollars as the income necessary for survival, the New York Commission on Old Age Security (1930, pp. 52–65) found between 37 percent and 75 percent of aged individuals and between 10 percent and 48 percent of aged couples falling below this "danger line" in the separate surveys it carried out in several New York State communities. Using the same cutoff point, both Connecticut in 1932 and Wisconsin in 1915 found that almost half of the elderly were in need; indeed, the Connecticut survey found that fully one-third of the state's elderly residents had no income at all (U.S. Social Security Board 1937, p. 149).[9] Property ownership might also yield some resources; both the Wisconsin and the Connecticut surveys obtained information about this. Over a third of the Connecticut residents surveyed had no property, and almost 60 percent had property worth less than three thousand dollars. Wisconsin's earlier survey showed half with property worth less than fifteen hundred dollars. Most of these small assets probably represented homes, and as the Depression era investigators noted, "the ownership of a dwelling house does not keep an old person from becoming dependent" (U.S. Social Security Board 1937, p. 150). The situation for the single and widowed elderly was far worse than for the married (U.S. Social Security Board 1937, p. 151). Given that aged women were far less likely than men to be married, this is further evidence of women's greater economic vulnerability. The U.S. Social Security Board summarized the state of information on American old age dependency by saying, "Scattered estimates of the extent of old-age dependency thus indicate that a large proportion of the aged have made no adequate provision for the period when self-support by working is impossible" (1937, p. 152).

The condition of the elderly was affected catastrophically by the economic crisis. During the Depression, the trend of declining labor force participation was considerably accelerated (see table 3.1), and unemployment rates for the elderly were disproportionately high as well. While unemployment for men of all ages stood at 41.2 percent, it was above 50 percent for men sixty and over

9. The Massachusetts survey of 1924 found 30 percent, and the National Civic Federation survey of 1926–27 found 22 percent, of the aged with incomes below the "danger line" of three hundred dollars, but these surveys were among those counting income and property of married couples twice. Hence they were certainly too optimistic about the situation of the elderly (U.S. Social Security Board 1937, pp. 150–51).

(U.S. Social Security Board 1937, pp. 145–48). If as many as 30 to 50 percent of the aged—those whose income was below the "danger line"—were already being supported by their families in the prosperous 1920s, then the effect of general unemployment could have been nothing short of devastating. About seven hundred thousand elderly people were members of families relying on general relief (U.S. Social Security Board 1937, p. 154). In addition, the economic crash destroyed the wealth, much of it in real estate, of many of the nonworking but previously independent elderly (Gratton and Haber forthcoming). Conditions among the aged unquestionably constituted a problem pressure and an issue ripe for use by political entrepreneurs.

In Canada, poor relief policy took an institutional turn around 1900, a shift decried by leading reformer J. J. Kelso, who argued in testimony before the Parliamentary Special Committee on Old Age Pensions in 1911–12, "We ought above all things to avoid creating a workhouse system [although] now the tendency is distinctly in that direction" (Canadian House of Commons 1912, pp. 14–15). Ontario had mandated the building of county houses of refuge—poorhouses—in 1903 (Strong 1930, p. 121). Margaret Strong remarked that "the house of refuge is in fact as in name a refuge for the indigent-aged and infirm of the community" and noted that commitment to such an institution was also a possible punishment for vagrancy (Strong 1930, p. 121). Cities, too, maintained houses of industry. Toronto's house of industry, a private institution funded by municipal revenues, cared for the aged poor both in- and out-of-doors (Strong 1930, p. 134). Nova Scotia, which did have a poor law, allowed for relief only in the poorhouse (Strong 1930, p. 149). In testimony before the Parliamentary Special Committee on Old Age Pensions in 1911–12, John Joy, an official of the Longshoreman's Association, noted that the aged poor had no recourse but the workhouse and in fact dominated the inmate population (Canadian House of Commons 1912, p. 9). Quebec, however, favored religious administration of charity institutions, including those directed at the aged, and outdoor relief, which reached many more Quebecois than institutional assistance (Strong 1930, p. 145).

Unfortunately, no statistical studies were made of the elderly in Canada in these years; indeed, as late as 1928 Canadians were relying on extrapolations made from studies done in Massachusetts to determine the state of need among their own aged population (Committee on Research of the Social Service Council 1928). We can make the educated guess that the situation in Canada was similar to that in those U.S. cities where outrelief was not abolished (cf. Katz, Doucet, and Stern 1982; Bryden 1974, pp. 24–34; Patterson 1981, chap. 1).[10]

10. Certainly, there was a good deal of need. Once the means-tested pensions, with their relatively low income limit, began to be paid out in the 1930s, a very high proportion—ranging in 1931 from 32 percent in Ontario to 58 percent in Saskatchewan—of elderly Canadians qualified for them (Canada, Department of Labour 1932, p. 153).

This would lead us to an estimate of about 5 percent of the aged poor depending upon relief, and many more relying upon their children.

The Legacy of Poor Relief

In all three countries by the late nineteenth century, poor relief had been stripped of any paternalist features it might have had in earlier times. Even by 1900, in locations where "less eligibility" was formally abandoned, at least for the "deserving" aged, its legacy lingered. Uncertainty was an essential aspect of poor relief, for decisions about eligibility remained in the hands of officials. There was no right to relief. Relief practices varied tremendously across localities, which could allow outdoor relief to the aged or deny relief altogether outside the poorhouse. Relief could be denied on the basis of residency requirements, the presumed ability and willingness of relatives to support a person, or the presumed ability of the person to work or gain income from property. Relief could be offered in any amount or form (e.g., in kind as opposed to cash) and for any length of time officials deemed reasonable; it could be offered only within the walls of the workhouse. Officials' sensitivity to local ratepayers prevented relief standards from rising to levels which could support recipients at a decent standard of living, in or out of the workhouse.

In stressing institutionalization, strict relative responsibility, and deterrence, the campaign against outrelief had done its job in making poor relief a policy almost universally loathed by the working classes. In all three countries, the stigma of poor relief left thousands poor but unwilling to accept assistance under the poor law. Those that did accept it faced social stigma on top of the inadequacy of relief and the difficulties to gain eligibility imposed by poor relief officials. The campaign was successful in thoroughly discrediting public or publicly subsidized poor relief as a mode of social provision. The proponents of the campaign attempted to promote private charity as the alternative to public relief for the "worthy," but as the figures on poverty and dependency made clear, their attempt was unsuccessful. Once it was apparent that private efforts could not deal with the poverty of the elderly and other groups, both elite and popular reformers in all three countries pressed for new provision for the aged outside the framework of poor relief.

As we have seen, the policy legacy, and the problems it created, did differ to some extent across the three countries. Poor relief was a more important component of the elderly's sustenance in Britain than in the United States, or even in one of its most urbanized and industrialized states, Massachusetts. In 1895 about 3 percent of men and 2 percent of women over age sixty in Massachusetts were institutionalized (Gratton 1986, pp. 42, 48). National figures for England at the same time showed almost 12 percent of men aged sixty-five and older receiving indoor relief, and about 6 percent of English women in poorhouses (Anderson 1977; Thomson 1983). Later investigations of the Massachusetts elderly also showed that, relative to Britain, smaller proportions of the aged received indoor relief (Massachusetts Commission on Old Age Pensions 1910; Massachusetts Commission on Pensions 1925). No state-level or national investigations showed a higher proportion in the 1910s or 1920s. A significant number of aged people were institutionalized in mental asylums, however, rather than poorhouses (Grob 1983, chap. 7). It also appears that outdoor relief, like indoor relief, was much less widely available to Americans than to the British in the late nineteenth century, as well as the early twentieth, when figures began to be kept. Indeed, whereas British commentators on the state of the elderly inevitably mentioned the high proportion of the aged receiving poor relief, no American studies make such statements (compare Booth 1894; Hamilton 1910; with Squier 1912; Ohio Health and Old Age Insurance Commission 1919, p. 202; National Civil Federation 1925). In his pioneering study, *Workingmen's Insurance*, William Willoughby noted that the "American workingman rarely, if ever, looks to the poorhouse as his inevitable home in old age, as do many laborers in England" (1898, p. 282). Similarly, Canadian commentators on the elderly made no note of poor relief as a significant source of support for the aged. Our comparative analysis suggests that the elderly in the United States were more likely to be taken in by their kin than their British counterparts. Perhaps this was because wage levels were generally higher, allowing more families to assist their aged kin, but it almost certainly also reflects the lower availability of relief. Availability of outdoor relief was a key factor in allowing independent living by the elderly in English rural areas as compared with the cities.

In Britain, the nationwide crusade against outdoor relief increased pressure on the families of the elderly, who were expected to contribute more to their support, and sent increasing numbers of elderly people to the poorhouse, where their plight dramatized the failures of the poor law. In the United States, some of these dynamics of policy feedback were comparably present, as the campaign against outrelief curtailed the assistance made available outside workhouses in many areas. Because no nationwide poor law administrative body existed, however, this policy was only unevenly implemented. As best we can tell, poor relief was a less important component of the family economies of the elderly in the United States than in Britain, so changes in poor relief affected smaller proportions of the population. In Canada, as in the United States, there was no national-level poor law. Indeed, Canada lacked even local or provincial-level poor laws outside Nova Scotia and New Brunswick; relief was given by state-subsidized voluntary institutions. Moreover, the campaign against outdoor relief remained only a preference of the few charity reformers who lived in Canada; it was not ever implemented in Canadian cities. Thus, again, changes in poor relief policy would affect fewer people.

What was the effect of these policy differences? Does the greater availability of poor relief in Britain mean that demand for new forms of public
social provision there was greater? It might as easily be argued that the lesser
availability of poor relief—and the greater proportions of the elderly living
as "dependent of the household head"—in North America resulted in more
unmet need among the aged and a greater burden on families. This, in turn,
might result in greater popular demand for new public social provisions. In fact,
concerns about the effects of supporting elderly relatives on families raising
children were voiced quite often in both Canada and the United States.

The American case is particularly complicated by the existence of the
Civil War pension system. It is quite likely that Civil War pensions served
to dampen popular demand for public old age pensions among native-born
American northern men in the pre–World War I years, while the decline in the
numbers of people receiving military pensions in the 1920s intensified popular
demand for new forms of old age protection in this group. Yet the Civil War
pension system also offered a precedent for modern social provision for the
elderly (see Rubinow 1913) and in this way may have stimulated demands for
comparable coverage on the part of those left out of the system or those who
supported them. Given that much of the burden of aged dependency on relatives came from aged widows and that the working classes who needed help
most were disproportionately foreign-born, this seems a plausible supposition.

5

Answering the Social Question
Labor, Elites, and Social Policy

Capitalist industrialization significantly increased the economic vulnerability of elderly people, principally through the spread of wagework, while demographic changes increased the proportion of younger adults who might have to support elderly parents or other kin. Yet these changes were not experienced directly by the working population; rather, they were mediated by existing public social provision, most importantly by poor relief. By the late nineteenth century, because of the deliberate action of poor relief officials, public social provision in many places offered inadequate protection against destitution, forcing families to help their aged relatives or see them left to slow starvation or the semipenal workhouse. These were the only alternatives for the impoverished elderly without families. Consequently, many of the difficulties created by demographic and socioeconomic shifts for the elderly and their families were exacerbated by political decisions to cut back on outdoor poor relief and to enforce relatives' responsibility and, in the United States, the decision to allow military pensions to vanish with the passing of the Civil War cohorts. In essence, the policy choices made by political elites in the later nineteenth century were an important cause of the perceived crisis of old age poverty and pauperism of the 1890s and beyond. Moreover, the harshness of the ideological and political attack on outdoor relief, even where it was not successful in completely eliminating such provision, contributed to the belief of many elite and popular political actors that respectable aged people should not be forced to depend on poor relief should they become unable to support themselves. The character of social provision, then, was political from the beginning, and the political transformations and shifting political conditions of the nineteenth and early twentieth centuries affected policy developments as much as did economic and demographic changes.

One of the most critical of these political transformations was the enhanced organizational and political strength of the working classes, stimulated

152

by capitalist industrialization and urbanization, as well as by the spread of ideologies of equality and the state-building projects of political elites. The emergence of the working class transformed the political context, giving popular preferences increased salience.[1] Although working-class organizations did not directly shape policy, the preferences of their members were of importance to policy developments because elites had new incentives to respond to popular interests, both from concern about social disorder and from political desires to capture the loyalty and electoral support of popular forces. Collective action on the part of industrial workers—strikes, riots, and demonstrations—raised fears on the part of elites and the middle-class public about the maintenance of social order. In addition, however, the working classes presented new opportunities for politicians; as Reinhard Bendix put it, "leaders of established elites," while concerned about the consequences of giving political rights to the working class, were "fascinat[ed] with the possibilities of strengthening the powers of the nation-state through the mobilization of the working class in its service" (1977, p. 114). Partisan advantages might also be gained by playing to labor's interests in competitive electoral situations. This situation generated what contemporaries called the "social question"—how to cope with the challenges to the status quo posed by the industrial working class (see Brooks 1906). Social policy, which, in the form of poor relief, had helped to create the problem of political alienation in the first place, provided a large part of the answer.

Poor relief was repudiated politically and ideologically as a policy framework by many of the representatives of the population most affected by it. The working classes and working-class organizations were among the earliest supporters of old age pensions. Although members of the working classes were most directly affected by the character of public social provision, their influence on policy-making was indirect, for during the period we are examining, labor organizations and working-class parties were not in a position to form governments and thereby directly affect policy.[2] Instead, the elites—reformers, intellectuals, officials, and politicians—directly shaped policy. Indeed, the proximate cause of the initiation of new public social provision for the aged in all three countries was the coalescence of elite-led cross-class coalitions. Thus,

1. Unionization increased in all three countries over the late nineteenth and early twentieth centuries. In Britain, the franchise was expanded at several points during this period, and in Canada, most of the (somewhat lower) barriers to universal manhood suffrage were removed. Thus, popular influence in the British and Canadian polities and in the already-democratized (for white males) American polity could be expected to be at least potentially important. But the timing of new legislation establishing modern social provision for the aged did not mirror the ebbs and flows of unionization, popular enfranchisement, or social unrest. Popular influence did not simply increase in linear fashion, but rather ebbed and flowed. Moreover, not all nonelite groups benefited equally from the expanded franchise and enhanced organizational capacities.

2. In Britain, the Labour party did form a government in 1924, after the initial adoption of pensions and other welfare legislation.

we need to be attentive to the factors which shaped elite political orientations and actions in the arena of social policy. In addition to concern for social order, the rejection of the deterrent poor law by a significant section of liberal elites was conditioned by intellectual and cultural trends. The development of social scientific understanding of poverty and the fact of interdependence under the industrial regime pushed toward a reworking of liberal ideology, as did changes in the character of the state itself, which in this period was developing new capacities for intervention and regulation. Reform elites in all three countries became convinced that state activity was essential to regulate the economy and society and to preserve individual freedom. These trends—working-class mobilization and elite ideological reorientation—made possible a new force in politics: a cross-class alliance for new state social provision.

In this chapter, I first describe the policy preferences of working-class organizations, which prominently included demands for changes in the character of state social provision for the aged. I then turn to the ideological and intellectual forces shaping the different elite responses to the social question. In all three countries, there were divergent views. One view stressed repression and deterrence, the others reform, as the best way to cope with the challenge. But in all three countries, reformist liberalism made headway in the first decades of the twentieth century (although nowhere did old-line liberalism completely die out), and reformist political elites were willing to work with popular organizations or in response to working-class electorates to introduce some social reforms. Ideological change was necessary, but not sufficient to bring elites to support new social spending initiatives. The policies reformist elites were willing to support differed across the three cases and over time. Social spending, such as would be required for old age pensions or insurance, was not embraced in Canada or the United States before the First World War, although other (regulatory) reforms were successful. In the last section of this chapter, I document the variations in the willingness of elites to enter cross-class coalitions for social spending. Part 3 of the book will explore why these variations existed.

The Working Class and State Social Policy

The features of deterrent poor relief policy generally worked to bolster capitalist economic principles (Polanyi 1944). The new poor law reformers were most concerned with the situation of able-bodied workers, and "less eligibility" and the "workhouse test" helped to force workers into the labor market, as well as undercutting their bargaining power with individual capitalists. Moreover, the changes resulting from the campaign against outdoor relief intensified these effects. And as we have seen, the characteristics of poor relief policy affected not only workers but also those who could no longer work and those who had to contribute to the support of nonworkers. To the extent that deterrence was stressed, the effect was certainly adverse. Knott (1986, p. 275) quotes one of Britain's anti–poor law protesters,[3] George Holyoake: "The hatred of the [new] Poor Law was well founded. Its dreary punishment would fall, it was believed, not upon the idle merely, but upon the working people who by no thrift could save, nor by any industry provide for the future." Thus, it is not surprising that the working classes resisted deterrent poor relief and, where possible, worked politically for different forms of social provision. Working-class and, more generally, popular opposition to deterrent poor relief first materialized in the form of demands for more lenient administrative practices.

The earliest manifestation of popular influence over policy can be seen in debates over the administration of poor relief itself. For example, Knott (1986) and Edsall (1971), among others, have documented that popular protests were able to delay the introduction of some of the most objectionable features of the new poor law in Britain, particularly the widespread use of the workhouse. Poor law authorities backed off on these until the 1870s, when, for reasons to be detailed in chapter 6, state capacities to enforce the "principles of 1834" were enhanced. Where working-class electorates were important, poor relief might be administered leniently. In Britain, the local government franchise and eligibility to sit on local authorities was extended somewhat in the 1890s, and labor was able to influence policy in some areas. Poplar, an overwhelmingly working-class poor law union in the East End of London, gained notoriety for its generous and generally nondeterrent administration of poor relief from the 1890s until 1930, when the local boards of poor law guardians were abolished and national administration instituted. Better treatment for the old, along with outrelief for the unemployed, were among the goals of labor members of the Board of Guardians and the Borough Council (Ryan 1978). In the United States, patronage political machines in large urban centers offered poor relief to the needy among their constituencies in exchange for political support (Katz 1986, chap. 2). Gratton (1986, chap. 6) shows that as Irish-American working-class politicians gained power in Boston in the 1910s and 1920s, poor relief officials made outdoor relief available to the needy working-class aged: "From the point of view of ethnic politicians, the working-class family struggling to raise children and care for feeble Aunt Bridget deserved help." He further contends that "for the elderly, the redefinition of deserving need [inherent in expanding outdoor relief] had special meaning, since it undercut the threat of the almshouse and reduced reliance on children" (Gratton 1986, p. 171).[4]

3. Anti–poor law protests took place for several years after the enactment of the Poor Law Amendment Act (the "new poor law") in 1834 (Knott 1986; Edsall 1971). By the 1840s they died out, as authorities backed down on enforcing the harshest features of the law and as many working-class protesters became involved in the more encompassing political movement of Chartism.

4. There is also some evidence outside the liberal countries for the proposition that working-class political strength would be used to make poor relief more amenable to labor interests. Stein-

Politicians elected by working-class constituencies, from labor parties or not, might administer poor relief in such a way as partially to subvert its deterrent purposes. Yet the entire poor relief framework was increasingly rejected, particularly after the campaign against outdoor relief and as national-level agencies gained more effective control over local relief administration and made it more difficult to implement nondeterrent practices (see Ryan 1978; Katz 1986, chap. 2). Elite attacks on public or publicly subsidized assistance had left a legacy of popular disgust with poor relief, and a determination to provide for the elderly needy outside its parameters.[5] Across all three countries, fraternal group members and unionists constantly insisted on an "old age free from the stigma of pauperism" (Minnesota unionist, cited in Anglim and Gratton 1987, p. 95; see also *Eagle Magazine* 1920–35; Evans 1926; Canadian House of Commons 1912; Canadian House of Commons 1924; Rogers 1973; Pelling 1968). While poor relief and especially the poorhouse were universally condemned, there was not a single, simple working-class response. Working-class organizations pursued the principal reform strategies of self-protection and voluntarism, as well as promotion of more generous state social provision.

Unions and fraternal organizations worked to raise wages, so that workers might actually be in a position to save for a "rainy day," which might come through involuntary retirement or unemployment, either individually or collectively through union or fraternal group schemes. American unions have been celebrated for their embrace of voluntarism (Rimlinger 1971, pp. 80–82; Horowitz 1978, chaps. 1–2), but they were joined by many of their British and Canadian counterparts (Yeo 1979; Thane 1984; Pelling 1968; Jamieson 1973, chap. 1; Robin 1968, chap. 1). Pat Thane quotes from the journals of the Foresters, Britain's second-largest friendly society, in the 1890s, which nicely summarizes this view: "The aim of the working class ought to be to bring about economic conditions in which there should be no need for the distribution of state alms. The establishment of a great scheme of state pensions would legalize and stamp as a permanent feature of our social life the chronic poverty of the aged. The desire of the best reformers is to remove the conditions that make that poverty, so that every citizen shall have a fair chance not only of earning a decent wage for today but such a wage as shall enable him to provide for the future" (Thane 1984, pp. 879–80). This strategy also had the advantage of helping to build up working-class organizations, which presumably would profit from their successes in bargaining with enlarged and more loyal memberships. A related strategy by unions involved offering benefits to members,

---

metz (1987) found working-class political strength in late nineteenth- and early twentieth-century German cities to be associated with poor relief administrative practices that were more favorable to working-class interests.

5. Popular disgust was directed at the way poor relief was administered, not at the public provision of assistance to the poor per se.

which had the goal of maintaining members' loyalty (Quadagno 1988a, p. 53; Lubove 1968, p. 130). Of course, the entire raison d'être of friendly societies and fraternal organizations was to offer benefits. Thus, many times the leaders of these organizations preferred private solutions to the problems of wagework—the strategy of voluntarism or self-protection. Pensions or other forms of expanded state social protection were sometimes seen as offering undeserved advantages to the politicians who initiated them, and these programs might well be financed by working-class taxes to boot.

Working-class organizations might have had good reasons to prefer self-protection to state social protection for their own members. But as Pat Thane (1984) has pointed out, the actual needs of the poorest workers, especially the unorganized, presented these groups with a dilemma. They claimed to represent the disadvantaged, and thus there was pressure to act in the face of mass misery. The poorest workers and women were not going to benefit directly (and perhaps not even indirectly) from a strategy of self-help, while state financial assistance would bring immediate improvement in their situations. But there were also ways in which the interests of the better-off workers were directly affected by the situation of disadvantaged workers (Thane 1978, pp. 84, 91–92). Many members of unions and fraternals were likely to be supporting aged dependents without any state assistance. Moreover, pensions would help to clear the labor market of the most desperate workers, who often served to drive down wages (Quadagno 1982, p. 168). Thus, most unionists and fraternal group leaders came to support new state social provisions, particularly old age pensions. Some emerged as leaders in drives for policy reform. The secretary of the British National Committee of Organized Labour on Old Age Pensions (NCOL), long-time unionist Frederick Rogers, said in regard to his work for old age pensions: "I was not pleading for state help on behalf of strong men who could help themselves, but for those on whom the conditions of modern life pressed heaviest—the weak and helpless" (1973, p. 234). Noncontributory old age pensions were prominent as measures supported by organizations such as the NCOL, for in addition to addressing a need that affected large numbers of both retired and active members of the working class, they would not involve taxing workers and infringed the least upon the voluntary activities of unions and fraternals (Thane 1984, p. 893; Thane 1978; Reed 1930, pp. 117).

Old age pensions would be distinguished from poor relief in fundamental ways: entitlement to honorable benefits as an aspect of citizenship, on the basis of service to society, was key. Labor support for these new forms of social provision did not depend on socialist understandings, although these were present as minority ideological currents in all three countries. Rather, in popular ideology entitlement to state social benefits was based on service to society, broadly understood. This meshed well with the new liberal ideology embraced by reform elites and the broader middle-class public. Labor leaders argued, as did many new liberals and middle-class progressives, that since the labor of workers had been socially useful, society owed them support in their old age, to be paid from the general revenues to which their labor had indirectly or directly contributed (see Rogers 1973; Squier 1912; Canadian House of Commons 1912).

Not surprisingly, given the policy legacy of Civil War pensions in the United States, labor leaders often took off from the existence and legitimacy of military pensions and called for government provision for the "soldiers" or "veterans" of industry. The first pension proposal introduced in the U.S. Congress came from former United Mine Workers leader William B. Wilson in 1909 and borrowed from the positive symbolism of military pensions; it was soon endorsed by the American Federation of Labor along with many state and local labor leaders (Lubove 1968, p. 135; Fischer 1978, p. 171). The Wilson bill would have created an "Old Home Guard" in which all Americans aged sixty-five or over were invited to enlist if their annual income was less than $240 and they owned less than $1,500 in property. Their sole duty was to report to the War Department on the state of patriotism in their communities, for which they would be paid $120 per year (bill reprinted in Massachusetts Commission on Old Age Pensions 1910, pp. 339–40). A labor representative on the Massachusetts Commission on Old Age Pensions, Arthur M. Huddell, expressed his disagreement with the commission's recommendation against old age pensions, citing Civil War pensions as a favorable precedent: "The pensions to the veterans of the Civil War has built up the American family. . . . the old veteran and his widow are made comfortable in their old age . . . and have a feeling of independence that old people should have" (Massachusetts Commission on Old Age Pensions 1910, p. 335). Huddell also endorsed the Wilson bill. Later U.S. legislative initiatives backed by labor at the state and federal level were more similar to European and Canadian proposals; that is, they called for the establishment of noncontributory old age pensions or, in a few cases, contributory old age insurance (Fischer 1978, pp. 171–74; Brandeis 1935, pp. 611–16). Former union officials turned legislators often introduced these proposals. The AFL endorsed pensions in 1909 (Reed 1930, pp. 117; American Federation of Labor 1919, pp. 303–4). But most legislative activity on labor and welfare matters occurred at the state and local levels in the pre–New Deal era (Graebner 1977), and state labor federations were even more enthusiastic supporters of public provision for the aged than the national organization (Anglim and Gratton 1987; Quadagno 1988a, chap. 3; Fink 1973, pp. 161–83; Linford 1949, pp. 6–59; Pennsylvania Commission on Old Age Assistance 1925, p. 83). In addition, predominantly working-class fraternal groups, particularly the Fraternal Order of Eagles, were also important supporters of new public welfare programs in the United States (Quadagno 1988a, chap. 3; Fraternal Order of Eagles 1929; Preuss 1966; Schmidt 1980, pp. 59–61).

Trade union federations in Britain and Canada were among the earliest proponents of old age pensions in their countries, with endorsements of universal pensions coming in 1899 and 1905 respectively (Heclo 1974, p. 168; Bryden 1974, p. 48). The most important working-class organization in the pension debate by the turn of the century was the National Committee of Organized Labour on Old Age Pensions (NCOL), founded in 1899 by union leaders and some middle-class reformers, notably Charles Booth, with the backing of wealthy philanthropists (Stead 1910; Thane 1984, p. 888; Gilbert 1966, p. 193; Quadagno 1982, chap. 7). British fraternal societies were initially opposed to state social provision, particularly contributory schemes, but withdrew into cautious acceptance of noncontributory old age pensions by the turn of the century; several friendly societies joined the NCOL (Williams 1970; Treble 1979; Gilbert 1966, p. 198). The NCOL lobbied extensively for pensions, raising the issue of socially caused old age poverty and the potential solution for national debate. By 1906 several labor leaders, many of them members of the NCOL, sought and gained election as part of the Labour Representation Committee; a demand for pensions was a part of their platform (Gilbert 1966, p. 202). The demands of the NCOL were partially met in the old age pension law of 1908, enacted under the auspices of a Liberal administration. In Canada, early pension proposals in the Dominion House of Commons were backed by Alphonse Verville and Ralph Smith, M.P.'s who had been presidents of the Trades and Labour Congress, which endorsed their efforts (Bryden 1974, pp. 46–47). (Canadian fraternal group members were neutral on pensions; O'Reilly 1904, pp. 12–17; Canadian Fraternal Association 1907, 1908, 1909, 1919.)

Like their American counterparts, British and Canadian labor reformers invoked the imagery of the "aged soldiers of industry" in their campaigns for pensions (Guest 1980, p. 74). Reference to class inequities in access to public provision for old age was also prominent, for, unlike the American policy legacy in which state social provision went to a very broad range of people, the beneficiaries of state largesse in Canada and Britain were predominantly elites. In its campaign for universal pensions, the British Labour party referred to the fact that well-paid upper-class civil servants received healthy pensions amounting to more than twenty times the average worker's annual wage, even for a few years in office, in contrast with the fact that "the workman . . . who has worked all his life gets zero pounds" (British Labour Party 1976). Kenneth Bryden summarized the arguments of Canadian trade unionists in 1907, who claimed that "if the money could be found for 'bounties, subsidies and payment of senators, whose appointment really makes them pensioners of the state,' then money could be found for the aged poor" (1974, p. 49). Canadian senators were appointed for life, rather than elected (they are still appointed, but may serve only until age seventy-five); the appointments were usually rewards for party service given to prominent and well-to-do supporters of the political parties (Van Loon and Whittington 1971, p. 481). Similarly, at the 1911 Trades and Labour Congress convention, speakers noted the government's ability to offer subsidies to business while ignoring the need for old age pensions (Bryden 1974, p. 48).

In the 1920s, despite the organizational problems faced by trade unions and a political atmosphere that was hardly conducive to social reform, labor organizations and working-class fraternal groups in North America remained staunch supporters of pension proposals (Lipset 1976, pp. 38–39; Guest 1980, chap. 6; Bryden 1974, pp. 64–66; Bain and Price 1980, pp. 88, 107; Bernstein 1960, chap. 2; Linford 1949, pp. 55–56; Pennsylvania Commission on Old Age Assistance 1925, p. 83; Gratton 1983, p. 404). In the aftermath of World War I in Canada, the Trades and Labour Congress persisted in its campaign for pensions, and a number of federal and provincial legislators, many from fledgling labor political organizations, introduced pension measures (Bryden 1974, pp. 66–73). The old age pension law was finally enacted in 1927, responding partially to the labor campaign. In the United States, the predominantly working-class Fraternal Order of Eagles was at the forefront of campaigns for noncontributory (and almost always means-tested) old age pensions in most nonsouthern states during the 1920s, working with state labor federations (Lubove 1968, p. 138; Leotta 1975; Chambers 1963, chap. 7; Quadagno 1988a, chap. 3). These popular pro-pension coalitions stressed the arguments that pensions were humane and just. They were earned by older workers through lifetimes of work, and they were also more economical than the degrading poorhouse (see *Eagle Magazine* 1920–35; Fraternal Order of Eagles 1930, 1935a, b; Leotta 1975; Fischer 1978, pp. 174–75). Although other fraternal societies were not as active as were the Eagles, they, too, supported pensions as the only just alternative to the poorhouse for aged, "deserving" workers and their wives. The Fraternal Order of Moose in conjunction with several other orders published *The American Poorfarm and Its Inmates* (Evans 1926), which condemned the poorhouse as the mode of caring for the aged poor. The fruit of the pension agitiation prior to the Depression was rather meager, however: six county-optional laws were passed by 1928, when about one thousand elderly people were drawing pensions (U.S. Social Security Board 1937, p. 161; U.S. Bureau of Labor Statistics 1929, pp. 530–31).

The Eagles-labor coalition did not last until the 1930s, as many labor organizations became disillusioned with the tactics of the Eagles, which while successful in getting laws passed, often resulted in the adoption of less than satisfactory county-optional plans (Quadagno 1988a, pp. 70–71). County-optional pension schemes left the decision of whether to pay pensions up to county boards—most of which did not choose to do so in the states which had such plans—and usually did not include any state financing (U.S. Social Security Board 1937, p. 161; U.S. Bureau of Labor Statistics 1929, pp. 530–31). Yet both the Eagles and the labor federations continued to press for pensions, and they were joined by a predominantly middle-class organization, the Townsend clubs, in demanding greater social provision for the elderly.[6] The American Federation of Labor also emerged as a more enthusiastic backer of national noncontributory public provision for the aged in the 1930s, although the concerns of the leaders of organized labor in this period were more directly focused on organizing and intraorganizational battles for representation than on social security (Quadagno 1988a, chap. 5). A number of state old age pension plans enacted in the 1920s and 1930s and the old age assistance title of the Social Security Act of 1935 partially satisfied the demands of these groups.

Working-class organizations offered a reliable and consistent source of support for modern social provision for the elderly over the first decades of the century in all three countries. Reform and intellectual elites concerned with the situation of the working class were quite interested in social policy as a way to respond to the social question, while some political elites interested in winning working-class support offered policy initiatives such as pensions. In fact, elite or middle-class reformers or politicians worked with labor leaders either in pressure groups such as the National Committee of Organized Labour, which, partially financed by the Cadbury fortune, worked for pensions in Britain, or the Fraternal Order of Eagles. Alternatively, some cross-class alliances for social spending were purely political, as in the agreements forged between Labour M.P.'s Woodsworth and Heaps and Prime Minister W. L. Mackenzie King in Canada. Indeed, elites had a more direct influence on the shape of policy than did the workers who also worked for policy reform.

The Elite Response to the Social Question: Ideology and Social Policy

Elite understandings of poverty and the role of the state in addressing problems of economic insecurity and absolute deprivation were important determinants in shaping the public response to the "social question," for elites directly controlled social policy-making throughout the period. Indeed, it is useful to consider social policies as the institutionalization of given ideologies, though of course they are shaped by a range of other factors as well. Ideologies embody visions of the moral order, and state social provision is a critical way in which the moral order is expressed.

With reference to the welfare role of the state, the array and sequence of

---

6. The Townsendites proposed a two-hundred-dollar monthly pension to be paid to every elderly American, on the condition that it be spent within the month; it was to be financed by a "transaction tax," which was recognized by most as a sales tax by a different name. The plan was to simultaneously solve the problems of old age dependency and the economic depression through increasing older people's income and stimulating the economy with that increased buying power (see Holtzman 1963).

cultural, intellectual, and ideological developments were remarkably parallel from the 1870s onward in Canada, the United States, and Britain—obviously due in part to constant communication between them (Mann 1956; Morgan 1976; Keller 1980, pp. 463–64; Allen 1973, chaps. 1–2; Splane 1973, pp. 13–19; Hareven 1969). Intellectuals, politicians, labor leaders, and charity workers interested in questions of social policy were, in these nations as in Europe and Australasia, a part of an international community of policy discourse which diffused ideas and specific reform proposals relating to the social question and workingmen's insurance far beyond the areas in which they were initially formulated (Heclo 1974, pp. 10, 310). Political actors in the United States and Canada saw Britain as a model both of what was to come in their own nations as "civilization" progressed and of what might be done to cope with unprecedented new social problems (Mann 1956; Wallace 1950b, p. 390; Wallace 1952, p. 125). Canadians were also extremely attentive to the developments in welfare and politics across the border (Hareven 1969; Rutherford 1974; Mackenzie 1908). A regular stream of speakers attended various conventions, assemblies, and meetings of both labor and middle-class reform groups in each of the three nations from the others (Rutherford 1974, p. xii; Logan 1928, pp. 77–79, 190–91).

In all three countries, two basic approaches to answering the social question through social policy may be discerned within the dominant liberal ideologies of elites. The first, based on an individualist understanding of poverty, was tied to a deterrent poor relief policy. Within this individualist approach to poverty, we can see two somewhat different orientations—classic liberalism and scientific charity/social work—which reflected different preferences for the kinds of programs that should be available outside public or publicly subsidized provision. By the late nineteenth century, a second approach emerged, grounded in a structural or sociological view of poverty. Some politicians, charity workers, poor law officials, and intellectuals had come to believe that many of the poor were not personally responsible for their situations, thus justifying the consideration of their needs apart from the principles of less eligibility and the workhouse test (Hareven 1969, p. 88; Katz 1983, pp. 72–89; Rose 1981, pp. 57–61; Marshall 1975, pp. 41–45; Abbott 1941, p. 17). Their understanding of policy and the poor was expressed in "new" or progressive liberal ideology, which supported state action to guarantee the social and economic conditions for individual responsibility. Thus, they looked to reform social policy to reflect this new understanding and preferred modern social provision based on citizenship rights to poor relief. In Britain, Canada, and the United States alike, new liberalism provided the justification for initiatives in social protections for the aged, and new liberal politicians, with the backing of intellectuals and reformers, initiated such provision.

Businessmen and business organizations tended to support a classic liberal position; that is, they opposed new public social provision, particularly if it would involve new taxes. But in each country, some business elites did express social policy views which had some commonalities with the new liberal orientation, such as an acknowledgment that capitalism produced economic insecurity which could not be addressed only by individuals. This has led some analysts, particularly in the United States, to identify so-called corporate liberals as the vanguard of social policy initiatives. This view is not supported by the evidence from any of the three countries. To the extent that collective solutions to problems of income insecurity were embraced, business leaders overwhelmingly preferred that these be kept voluntary and that business control be maximized. Entitlement to benefits based on citizenship was the preference of new liberals, not businessmen. Thus, "welfare capitalism," the provision of corporate-controlled benefits to firms' own workers, rather than the welfare state, the public provision of benefits as a matter of right, was the choice of even "enlightened" corporate leaders.

Classic Liberalism and Scientific Charity/Social Work

Those embracing deterrent policy approaches based their views on an individualist understanding of poverty. That is, they saw poverty largely as the result of the individual failings of the poor; the "worthy" poor were those, such as young orphans, whose fate was clearly not the result of their own actions. The policy tenets of classic liberalism were most clearly enunciated by the new poor law reformers in Britain and by their counterparts in North America. In arguing against the paternalism and "moral economy" of the old poor law, they championed the new theory of political economy and the supremacy of the market (Polanyi 1944). The poor law reformers were concerned to distinguish sharply between the merely poor and the indigent. "Pauperism" or "dependency," clearly differentiated from poverty, was no longer accepted as the inevitable situation of large segments of the working classes, as had been the case under the Speenhamland system. Pauperism, not poverty, was the social problem. It could best be solved by deterring the poor from becoming dependent on public relief, which was condemned as leading to an unhealthy dependency on the part of those receiving it, even when the recipients were classed among the "worthy." The classical or laissez-faire liberal approach expected that deterrent poor relief could enforce the work ethic and discourage dependency more or less automatically, as long as poor relief officials used stringent requirements—most important, not allowing generous outdoor relief. Poverty was not seen as problematic if the poor eked out an independent living, and many argued that poverty was necessary to provide a stimulus to work (Himmelfarb 1983, pp. 163–71). On this basis, these reformers argued that public relief must be deterrent; to the extent that starvation had to be prevented, the situation of the pauper should be "less eligible," or desirable, than that of any self-supporting worker. These views were dominant among elites in the 1820s and 1830s, helping to justify the policy principles of the new poor law, and enjoyed a resurgence in the 1870s and 1880s in association with social Darwinism, this time helping to justify the campaign against outrelief, also known as the "revival of the principles of 1834." Attempts to help the poor were said by such leading intellectuals as Herbert Spencer and William Graham Sumner to lead to greater social distress, since they would impede the work of natural selection, which was to improve the human species by weeding out the "unfit," a category including the poor, along with other "defective" classes (Rimlinger 1971, pp. 46–51; Bremner 1956a, p. 19; Hofstadter 1955; Splane 1973, pp. 13–17; Collini 1979, chap. 6).

The second variant of the deterrent approach, which may be labeled the scientific charity or social work perspective, called for a more positive role for, first, private charity workers and, later, social workers employed by voluntary agencies in "rehabilitating" the deserving poor through friendly visiting and, later, casework. Movements to put individualist ideas about the poor, charity, and relief on a "scientific" basis began in Britain with the formation of the first Charity Organization Society (COS) in London in 1869. The first American COS was founded in Buffalo in 1877, and the first Canadian group in Toronto in 1898 (Mowat 1961; Guest 1980, p. 36; Splane 1973, p. 19; Hareven 1969, p. 85). City-level organizations also gathered in national groups which became important forums for the dissemination of news about policy experiments and "expertise." In the United States, the National Conference of Charities and Correction (NCCC) began meeting in 1879 after several preliminary gatherings under the auspices of the Conference of Boards of Charities and the American Social Science Association (Bruno 1957, chap. 1). Canadians often attended the NCCC meetings in the United States, and the Canadian conference was formed when a number of Canadian reformers and charity workers attended the meeting of the NCCC in Toronto in 1897 and organized a separate group. The first Canadian conference was held in 1898 (Canadian Conference of Charities and Correction 1899, pp. 25–26). These movements called for the coordination of charitable and governmental efforts and the careful investigation of individuals asking for relief or charity. They advocated the firm separation of the "deserving" poor, who should be helped by "friendly visitors" from voluntary associations, from the "undeserving" poor, who should be left to the discipline of the marketplace, to force them to take responsibility for themselves or to enter the miserable workhouse if they were unwilling to work (Fraser 1973, pp. 121–23; Mowat 1961; Bremner 1956b; Spiesman 1973; McLean 1901). The COS and some members of the NCCC were the most important advocates of the abolition of all outdoor relief in the 1870s and 1880s, joining with the Local Government Board in Britain and with some municipal governments in the

United States in crusades against outrelief (Rose 1981, pp. 61–62; Katz 1983, pp. 132–33, 191). Charity workers in Canada, too, attempted to cut back on outdoor relief, although they had less success than their counterparts in Britain and America (Pitsula 1980).

As popular demands for assistance to the aged poor emerged in the late nineteenth and early twentieth centuries, both classical liberals and adherents of scientific charity rejected the idea that social forces produced poverty, as well as public, collective solutions to the poverty of the aged. These groups saw the problems of pauperism and poverty in old age as part and parcel of the overall problem of the poor, who were expected to save for a "rainy day," a category of misfortune which included the need to retire in old age due to increasing infirmities along with unemployment, illness, or industrial accidents. A spokesman for the British Charity Organization Society argued, "Old age is a condition to which all must look forward, and for which there is a whole lifetime to prepare. . . . The expectation of old age is part of the discipline of life . . . and probably has a beneficent effect upon the average of humanity" (Committee on Old Age Pensions 1903, p. 67). In this scenario, then, the aged poor were simply those who had failed in their task of self-maintenance. The testimony of several Local Government Board inspectors to the 1895 Royal Commission on the Aged Poor about the aged paupers they saw in their work reflected the classical liberal viewpoint. It was summarized in a popular tract on the aged poor: "The majority of inmates of workhouses are undeserving, and have come there through their own fault. Drink, improvidence, and general want of 'backbone,' have been contributory causes in reducing them to pauperism" (Drage 1895, p. 19; original testimony in Great Britain, Royal Commission on the Aged Poor 1895). State pensions were seen as having the potential to do great moral and practical harm (Guest 1980, p. 24; Bryden 1974, p. 24; Collins 1965, p. 250; Hoffman 1908; Mowat 1961, pp. 142–44; Committee on Old Age Pensions 1903). A typical comment came from a Canadian commentator on the British 1908 pension act and proposals for similar legislation in Canada, who noted, "If we take away from a working man the responsibility that rests upon him to provide for his old age . . . we will have deprived that man of an important stimulus to self-control and industry" (Mackenzie 1908, p. 262).

Those who held views based on classical liberalism and scientific charity advocated thrift and family assistance as solutions to the increasingly recognized problem of poverty among the elderly. The Massachussetts Commission on Old Age Pensions (1910, pp. 324–25) formally recommended the teaching of thrift in the public schools as an alternative to pensions. If personal efforts were insufficient, then these groups advocated family responsibility for the elderly, often to be encoded in legislation or administrative rules requiring that adult children assist their destitute elderly parents. Even grandchildren and other relatives were under certain circumstances required to offer financial help. Such laws and regulations were indeed passed in the late nineteenth and early twentieth centuries before being bypassed by later enactments of public provision for the aged, including those with children (Canadian Conference of Charities and Correction 1904, p. 29; Creech 1969, p. 118; Linford 1949, pp. 17, 37; Thomson 1990). Self-help and familial reciprocity might be judiciously supplemented by private assistance from charities. In all three countries, some charities did offer limited help to a few of the "deserving" elderly, but this assistance was both limited and based on recipients demonstrating "proper" behavior (Mowat 1961, pp. 97–98; Gratton 1986, chap. 5).

In the early twentieth century, the workers of the charity organization societies—both paid agents and volunteer friendly visitors—moved to claim professional standing as social workers, and "casework became the 'nuclear skill' on which social work rested its claim to expert authority" (Katz 1986, p. 165). The professionalization project of social workers was most advanced in the United States; Canadian social workers lagged behind their American counterparts in establishing professional schools and societies (Struthers 1987, pp. 111–12). Essentially, the caseworker was a "trained, professional friendly visitor" working to help poor clients adjust to their environments (Katz 1986, p. 165; Richmond 1917, 1922; Lubove 1973, pp. 47–49). After the war, social workers moved further from their charity roots by embracing Freudian psychology, which, in Katz's words, allowed social work to "bypass the new social and economic theories that had undercut scientific charity and return with scientific authority to individual explanations for dependence," albeit based on psychological rather than moral understandings (Katz 1986, p. 166; see also Lubove 1973; Gratton 1983). As Paul U. Kellogg, editor of the reform journal *The Survey,* wrote to a friend in 1927, "psychology rather than labor legislation is on the map" (quoted in Chambers 1971, p. 77). The intellectual framework of casework was less important to developments in old age policy than in some other areas, such as provision for widowed mothers and their children. Most caseworkers were interested in cases that at least potentially could be rehabilitated, and there was no such possibility for people at the ends of their lives. But because old age pensions would represent the "right to relief without determination of need by a trained [social] worker," social workers often opposed the enactment of pension legislation, which usually pointedly called for these benefits to be administered by governmental units other than the departments of public welfare or social service that employed social workers (Gratton 1983, p. 403).

Those embracing laissez-faire were typically more concerned with keeping social spending and taxation low than with rehabilitating even the "deserving" poor. This view did not encourage support for the projects of social workers. Yet the two groups did find common ground in their steadfast insistence that the causes of poverty were individual and in their disparagement of public provision for the needy, either in the form of relief or of new forms of public protection such as old age and mothers' pensions (see Leff 1973; and Guest 1980, p. 52, on the opposition of the private charities to mothers' pension legislation in the United States and Canada, respectively). As answers to the social question, both laissez-faire and scientific charity/social work ultimately failed politically. They were unable to stop the enactment of new public protections, although they did hobble some programs with provisions flowing from the individualist standpoint. The fact that the social question was largely resolved through social policy in Britain, Canada, and the United States is related to other elite ideological currents, especially the emergence of new liberalism.

New Liberalism and State Social Policy

The rejection of poor relief and the embrace of modern social programs, both pensions and social insurance, on the part of an important segment of policy-makers and elite political actors were related to several major sociopolitical changes. First, like other elites, they reacted to the social question, the challenge to social order posed by the political emergence of the industrial working class. But unlike those embracing a solution of maintaining deterrence in social policy, these "new liberal" elites preferred reform aimed at incorporating workers into the social and political order. Moreover, they tended to tie the demands of workers to growing inequality and the concentration of wealth generally (see Brooks 1906). The rejection of the deterrent poor law was conditioned by significant intellectual and cultural trends. The development of social scientific understanding of poverty and the fact of societal interdependence under the industrial regime pushed toward a reworking of liberal ideology, creating a situation in which the aged were increasingly seen as "deserving" of better public provision than was offered by poor relief. Changes in the character of the state itself also encouraged the new policy approach; in this period the state was developing new capacities for intervention and regulation and offered new opportunities for middle-class and elite "experts" and professionals. In all three countries, reform elites and many in the middle-class public became convinced that state activity was essential to regulate the economy and society and to preserve individual freedom. Liberal ideology was also reworked to accommodate state activities that modified the operations and consequences of the market, so that the social question could be answered, in part, through social policy. These changes helped to create a situation in which politicians and officials were interested in fashioning solutions to the problems of the poverty of the elderly outside the parameters of the poor law, less eligibility, and the workhouse test, working with popular forces in cross-class political alliances. Indeed, by the turn of the century across Britain, Canada, and the United States, elites concerned with working-class loyalty and parties competing for the votes of working-class electorates and the support of working-class organizations did offer social policy initiatives as an important mode of securing popular support and responding to the social question. These new political orientations flowed out of the new ideological understandings of poverty, individual liberty, and the social and moral order.[7]

In all three countries, the most important intellectual trend underlying elite ideological support for new state social provision was the reworking of liberal ideals away from pure self-help and distrust of state intervention toward new or progressive liberal conceptions (Clarke 1974; Collini 1979; Emy 1972; Freeden 1978; Tishler 1971; Wiebe 1967, chap. 6; Bremner 1956a, chap. 8; Fine 1956; Mowat 1969; Keller 1980, pp. 462–63; Guest 1980, pp. 18–34; Wallace 1950b, 1952; Christian and Campbell 1974, pp. 54–59). This reworking involved changes in the key policy preferences flowing from the traditional liberal emphasis on individual freedom because of a changed understanding of which factors, under modern conditions, were crucial in underpinning personal liberty. Rather than believing that individual freedom depended on the efforts of the individual alone and were best secured by minimizing state interference in civil society, the new liberals came to see that industrial society made people interdependent. As the influential new liberal theorist L. T. Hobhouse noted, individual liberty could be thwarted as much by a lack of life's necessities as by the presence of governmental restrictions (Collini 1979, p. 107). "Is a man free who has not equal opportunity with his fellows of such access to all material and moral means of personal development as shall contribute to his own welfare and that of his society?" asked J. A. Hobson (1909, p. 93) of his fellow liberals, in a book devoted to arguing for shifting the emphasis of liberalism from the purely "negative conception of Liberalism, as a definite mission for the removal of certain political and economic shackles upon personal liberty" to a more positive conception involving the assurance of "presence of opportunity" (p. 92). In modern society, then, the new liberalism recognized government as an indispensable support for individual liberty, providing "equality of opportunity" and security against socially caused misfortunes and regulating competition to undergird responsible personal initiatives (Hobson 1909, pp. 93, 96–113; Seager 1910, pp. 4–5, 148–50; see *Social Welfare* 1919, p. 120). American social reformer Henry Seager argued in a series of lectures given in 1910 to the School of Philanthropy, sponsored by the Charity Organization Society of New York City: "The simple creed of individualism is no longer adequate. . . . we need not freedom from governmental interference, but clear

---

7. The Liberal welfare reforms, said Hobson, have "been mainly directed so as to improve the physical, moral, and intellectual or economic condition of individuals, as to secure for them a larger measure of liberty in the disposal of their lives" (1909, p. 97).

appreciation of the conditions that make for the common welfare, as contrasted with individual success, and an aggressive program of government control and regulation to maintain these conditions" (Seager 1910, p. 5). Thus, new state welfare activities were seen as fully consistent with liberalism's traditional aim of enhancing individual freedom.

The intellectual trends nourishing the new liberal synthesis of collectivist and individualist values were similar in Britain, Canada, and the United States. Of key importance was the increasing social scientific and personal knowledge of the structural or sociological conditions affecting the working classes on the part of elites and the educated middle classes. This encouraged the development of a structural understanding of poverty, which in turn allowed groups previously seen as poor because of their own failings to be redefined as worthy, that is, poor because of events beyond their control. In essence, the progressives had enlarged the boundaries of the category of the "deserving poor" through considering a fuller inventory of nonindividual causes of poverty. Both pensions and contributory programs were suggested as alternatives to poor relief for "worthy" groups, such as the formerly self-supporting aged poor, but many reformers expected that poor relief would continue on as a provision of last resort for the "unworthy" (see Massachusetts Commission on the Support of Dependent Minor Children of Widowed Mothers 1913, pp. 23–24, 30–31; Booth 1892, 1894). Indeed, for many, a clear benefit of taking the "worthy" aged out of the poor law's ambit was that this would allow the "proper," that is to say deterrent, functioning of poor relief vis-à-vis the "unworthy" (see Booth 1892, pp. 238–39). Thus, the transition to new forms of social protection was justified with reference to the problems of groups considered to be worthy of nonstigmatizing treatment—a larger category after the assimilation of social scientific findings about poverty into policy discourse—but the distinction between "worthy" and "unworthy" was not effaced. More structural understandings of poverty and economic insecurity were embodied in the new thinking about policy, but moral distinctions and a vision of a moral economy endured.

Personal knowledge of the poor on the part of a number of middle-class and elite people increased through two important institutions of the late nineteenth and early twentieth centuries: friendly visiting and settlement houses. At first, charity workers embraced the campaign against outdoor relief while promoting "scientific charity" and friendly visiting in the 1870s and 1880s. In time, some of them, through their continuing investigations of the situations of those asking for relief and the personal experience of seeing the slums in which their clients lived, were moved toward the discovery of environmental and economic causes for mass poverty in the urban centers (Bremner 1956a, pp. 55–56; Mowat 1961, chaps. 6–7). The awakening of social awareness and social consciences was also spurred in all three countries through settlement house movements (Davis 1967; Allen 1973, p. 12; Gilbert 1966, pp. 42–45). University- or college-educated young people moved into urban working-class neighborhoods to live with, bring cultural "improvements" to, and learn about the working classes and the poor. Typically, they stayed for a few years and then moved on to careers in the ministry, the professions, public affairs, or teaching. The first settlement house, Toynbee Hall, was established in the East End of London in 1884, and by 1911 Britain had twenty-six settlement houses (Davis 1967, p. 8). Meanwhile, some Americans and Canadians traveled to English settlement houses and carried models home; others arrived at similar ideas without such direct contact. U.S. settlements sprang up in New York, Boston, Chicago, and many other cities, especially in the Northeast and Midwest; from just six in 1891, the number of settlements grew to over four hundred by 1918 (Davis 1967, p. 12). Canada had thirteen settlements by 1913 (Allen 1973, p. 13). Thus Canada and the United States, along with Britain, were well supplied with these unique institutions through which reform-minded, educated young people could investigate urban-industrial conditions, make contact with certain labor leaders, attempt to bring physical and cultural "betterment" to the masses, and discover the necessity of working through politics for social reforms.

Knowledge about the poor was disseminated more generally through the publication in the 1880s, 1890s, and 1900s of celebrated pieces of muckraking and early empirical social surveys which had a stunning impact on middle-class and elite views, disturbing the earlier consensus that all poor individuals were personally responsible for their troubles (Marshall 1975, pp. 31–35; Fraser 1973, pp. 123–27; Hennock 1976; Bremner 1956a, pp. 67–85). Indeed, the titles of some of the best known of these works underline the extent to which the privileged were discovering conditions among the poor unknown to them before: *The Bitter Cry of Outcast London,* by Andrew Mearns (1883), or *How the Other Half Lives,* by Jacob Riis (1890) (see also Booth 1889, 1891; Ames 1972). These works encouraged reformers and social scientists (not mutually exclusive categories by any means) to carry out social surveys as a means to arouse public opinion favorable toward government action on behalf of the poor (Allen 1973, pp. 12–13; Chambers 1971, pp. 32–44; McGregor 1957; among the most important surveys which specifically dealt with the situation of the aged are Rowntree 1901; Booth 1892, 1894; Nassau 1915). The national and subnational governments of Britain, Canada, and the United States in the late nineteenth and early twentieth centuries carried out wide-ranging investigations of all aspects of industrial life, including low wages and unemployment, along with inquiries specifically directed at discovering the causes of and solutions to the increasingly evident problem of old age poverty and dependency. Of particular importance were the *Report of the Royal Commission on the Aged Poor* (summarized in Lubbock 1895); the materials published by Canadian parliamentary committees on old age pensions appointed in the 1911–12, 1912–13, and 1924 sessions (see Bryden 1974, pp. 42, 219); and, in the United States, the reports of a number of state investigatory commissions published during the 1910s and 1920s.[8] Investigators heard from various experts on old age poverty and amassed statistics and testimony of reformers, charity officials, and labor leaders on the problems facing the industrial working class. As the facts about the causes of poverty in unemployment, illness, industrial accidents, low wages, and forced retirement in old age became more widely known, empirical support for new policy positions in regard to the problem of old age dependency and poverty became available. Indeed, the more routine gathering of information by bureaus of labor statistics, established in all three countries by the first decade of the twentieth century, reinforced the findings of the special national commissions.

In the framework of reworked liberalism, the problem of aged dependency and poverty properly could be addressed through state old age insurance or pension programs. State-sponsored old age protection was a part of the general trend to establish a minimum living standard and was certainly seen as a humanitarian measure, given the poverty of so many of the elderly (Freeden 1978, pp. 201, 204–5). But more important than their having a humane effect, pensions were understood by new liberals and progressives as tokens of social justice and communal responsibility to members of society who had given their labor and had earned the *right* to better treatment than that offered by poor relief at the end of their lives (Collini 1979, p. 109). Charles Booth articulated this sentiment in his influential 1892 tract, *Pauperism, A Picture; and The Endowment of Old Age, An Argument:* "The endowment of old age [is] at once a practical and possible means of giving a surer footing to those who now, trying to stand, too often fall and sometimes sink altogether. I advocate it as bringing with it something of that security necessary to a higher standard of life. A security of position which will stimulate rather than weaken the play of individuality on which progress and prosperity depend" (Booth 1892, p. 241).

First, the "deservingness" of almost all of the elderly was established through the understandings that their poverty was socially, not individually, caused and that they had made contributions to society through socially useful labor. Because poor relief was designed for the "undeserving," it was wrong, indeed immoral, to force "deserving" people to have to turn to this despised form of social provision when in need. Drawing on the traditional liberal discourse of rights, reformers articulated a right of deserving, aged citizens to better treatment than that offered by poor relief. Basically, "better treatment" was defined in opposition to poor relief and was modeled on various existing

8. The report of the New York Commission on Old Age Security (1930, chap. 10) contains summaries of these state reports.

forms of honorable state provision, particularly military or service pensions. Poor relief was stigmatizing and inadequate; it was given to those who had "failed," and it entailed giving up citizenship rights. In contrast, old age pensions or contributory insurance was to be an honorable, adequate form of social provision, a right of citizenship rather than an alternative to it.

The new liberal argument for state old age pensions was premised on an understanding of old age poverty as socially caused.[9] The empirical findings of Booth, the American state investigatory commissions, and others revealed that for many workers, thrift was simply an impossibility, given the high proportion of workers who did not earn a living wage (Squier 1912, pp. 35–50; Freeden 1978, p. 202; Collini 1979, p. 109; Ohio Health and Old Age Insurance Commission 1919, pp. 5, 13, 262–63; Wisconsin Industrial Commission 1915, pp. 5–6; Booth 1892, 1894). Leading liberals and reformers recognized that under the regime of laissez-faire, as Hobhouse put it in 1908, "pauperism among the aged . . . is the *normal* fate of the poorer class" and that this was due not to "exceptional shiftlessness and improvidence" but to "insufficiency and irregularity of earnings" (quoted in Freeden 1978, p. 205; see also pp. 201–7; Collini 1979, pp. 109–10). Even in the United States, where pauperism was not so widespread, poverty among the aged was. But a similar response was forthcoming. For example, Franklin Roosevelt, as governor of New York, said, "Poverty in old age should not be regarded either as a disgrace or necessarily as the result of lack of thrift or energy. Usually it is a mere by-product of modern industrial life" (quoted in Fusfeld 1956, pp. 158–59). Earlier American studies of the elderly made these points as well (see Squier 1912; Nassau 1915). Liberal leader and prime minister W. L. Mackenzie King argued that state pensions were needed by older workers "who possess no capital, and who ha[ve] to face the uncertainties of employment, and contend, unaided, against all kinds of vicissitudes" (1918, p. 348). Voluntary savings schemes under such conditions were seen as inadequate to the problem of old age support (Rubinow 1913, chap. 20).

Information uncovered by various social scientific investigations on the issue of the living wage was particularly important to debates about the elderly, for it had an obvious bearing on the question of whether personal savings offered a viable strategy for dealing with old age poverty. In almost all of these investigations, social scientists revealed that large portions of the working classes did not receive a living wage, and even among those who did, saving enough to provide for old age was nearly impossible unless other family needs were neglected (see Squier 1912, pp. 35–50; Freeden 1978, p. 202; Collini

9. Some also argued that wealth as well as poverty was socially created. Since workers had contributed to the development of society's goods, they were entitled to a share of them at life's end. Leading British new liberal L. T. Hobhouse made this point (cited in Clarke 1974, p. 163).

1979, p. 109; Ohio Health and Old Age Insurance Commission 1919, pp. 5, 13, 262–63; Wisconsin Industrial Commission 1915, pp. 5–6; Epstein 1922, chap. 6).[10] Investigations of the aged also dealt with the problem of unemployment and underemployment among the aged (see U.S. Social Security Board 1937, pp. 143–48; Wisconsin Industrial Commission 1915, pp. 2–3; Rogers 1929; Booth 1894). Advocates of pensions often referred to the phenomenon of older workers being relegated to the "industrial scrap heap," to use the rather common terminology of old age pension advocate Abraham Epstein (Epstein 1922, p. 8, and chap. 2; see also Squier 1912, pp. 35–38; *Eagle Magazine* 1920–35; Rubinow 1913; Pennsylvania Commission on Old Age Pensions 1921; Quadagno 1982, pp. 148–62; Booth 1894, p. 321; Canadian House of Commons 1912, p. 23; James Massie, CCCC treasurer, quoted in Canadian Conference of Charities and Correction 1899, p. 10; Gould 1927, p. 340). Generally, they were able to illustrate that forced retirement was a growing problem for older workers, although they tended to understate the extent to which older workers were able to continue working. But even if they overstated the problem of technological displacement of older workers, these advocates did make clear that a good deal of old age poverty was related to transformations in the character of production and employment relations, rather than to workers' personal failings.

The aged were defined as "deserving," for most had worked all their lives—they had been "worthy" citizens—until old age prevented their working any longer. How could it be legitimate to treat them in the same manner as those who had not led worthy lives by forcing them to apply for poor relief, with all the degradation that implied? Mabel Nassau, a student of prominent American Association of Labor Legislation leader Henry Seager, studied the conditions of the aged poor in New York City in 1915 and argued that pensions for most would be well justified: "When people have contributed all their lives to the industry of their state, should they be obliged at the end of their days to depend on charity?" (1915, pp. 95–96). The almshouse was not a "fitting reward for a life of honorable toil," noted the 1915 report on old age relief of the Wisconsin Industrial Commission (1915, p. 5). Franklin Roosevelt echoed this sentiment in the late 1920s: "No greater tragedy exists in modern civilization than the aged, worn out worker who, after a lifetime of ceaseless effort and useful productivity must look forward for his declining years to a poorhouse" (quoted in Fusfeld 1956, pp. 158–59). In the initial debates over pensions in the

---

10. Gratton's research (1991) on the family economy among the U.S. working classes in the early twentieth century suggests that at least some families were able to set aside a "nest egg" for use by the elderly. They did this by pooling the wages of elderly wage earners and adult children. This strategy had drawbacks from the perspective of the children involved, and it was not available to older people who were without children or among those strata of the working classes whose pay was too low to permit any surplus to be accumulated.

Canadian House of Commons, pensions were suggested as a fairer alternative than charity or jail for workers who had helped to build up Canadian society (1907 debate in the House of Commons, quoted in Wallace 1952, p. 126). Writing in the Canadian journal *Social Welfare*, the organ of the Social Service Council, just as the Parliament was preparing to vote on pension legislation, Margaret Gould asked rhetorically: "We, who laud the virtue of work, shall we offer no other payment to the [aged] workers than shameful poverty . . . [or] ek[ing] out their last days in almshouses . . . [or] being burdens on their poor children or on relatives?" (1927, pp. 342–43). Her answer: "The only just system of relief should be that of reward. . . . a social policy, applicable to all citizens, in the form of an adequate State Old Age Pension system" (Gould 1927, p. 343). Charles Booth, Britain's leading expert on the conditions of the aged and an early advocate of pensions, argued that the aged poor were "treated undesirably . . . under the Poor Law: indoor relief lacks humanity and outdoor relief encourages improvidence," as savings would disqualify a person from relief (1892, p. 235). Winston Churchill defended the liberal welfare reforms as promoting a "fairer social organization" for the working classes than had earlier forms of provision (Addison 1983, p. 51).

Reformers understood their efforts at providing "more fitting rewards" as contributing to social order. For example, President Franklin Roosevelt noted in a 1936 campaign speech summarizing the impressive social reform initiatives of his administration, "We were against revolution. Therefore, we waged war against those conditions which make revolutions—against the inequalities and resentments which breed them" (quoted in Greer 1958, p. 39). The American Association for Labor Legislation had the following motto on its letterhead during the 1920s: Social Justice is the Best Insurance Against Social Unrest. Many pension advocates underlined the fear of a penniless old age that affected large portions of the working classes and argued that this "dread promotes the almost-universal industrial unrest," in the words of John O'Donoghue, a Toronto reformer (see also Charles Henderson, cited in Tishler 1971, p. 75; Booth 1892, p. 241). But reformers were not cynically using reform to prevent revolution; they understood that real injustices could provoke political choices on the part of the disadvantaged that they considered to be wrong. Thus, both enlightened self-interest and morality for the middle class and elites pointed to reform.

The language of "rights" was prominent in the writings of the British new liberals and North American progressives arguing for pensions as well as other welfare measures; indeed, almost all advocates of pensions claimed to be fulfilling the rights of the aged. Typifying the discourse of rights that attached to old age pensions in all three countries, Sir Wilfrid Laurier, a former Liberal prime minister of Canada, said in his welcome to a meeting of social reformers in 1914: "Charity is noble in the giving, but it always implies humiliation. The poor, the lowly, and the humble, are coming into their own, not as a matter of grace . . . but on the basis of right" (1914, pp. 8–9).

Collini notes in his analysis of the philosophy and sociology of L. T. Hobhouse that the liberal tradition was "receptive to claims based on rights" (1979, p. 125). T. H. Marshall is famous for his elaboration of a typology of rights—civil, political, and social—which are all necessary for citizens to participate fully in a democracy. "Social rights" include the "right to a modicum of economic welfare and security" and are institutionalized in modern social provision—the welfare state—as well as in the schools (Marshall 1950, pp. 71–72). Carole Pateman asserts that "the moral basis of the welfare state lies in the provision of resources"—revealed as lacking for the poor by social scientific investigations—that allow citizens to participate as equals in a democracy (1988, p. 235). Marshall argued that starting from the establishment of equal rights under the law, political and then social rights were demanded and won by the working classes. Thus, the framework of rights could be and was expanded through political struggles, inspired by "the juxtaposition of legal equality and social and economic inequalities" (Bendix 1977, p. 94) and in response to the "moral dilemma that arises when citizenship is undermined by the operation of the capitalist market" (Pateman 1988, p. 235).

The inequalities Marshall discussed were, however, only those rooted in class. A number of authors have criticized Marshall's evolutionary framework, which does not fit the experience of nonliberal countries and of many groups, most notably women, who gained political and social rights simultaneously or in "reverse" order compared with men. A similar point could be made about blacks in the United States. Some feminist analysts have further contended that the entire "rights" framework in social policy has applied only partially to women, for their citizenship claims are problematic given the image of the ideal citizen as warrior or, in modern welfare states, as worker, and thus, implicitly, as male (see Dietz 1987; Okin 1989; Pateman 1988; Hernes 1987; Nelson 1984; Fraser 1989, chaps. 5–7). Thus, women's claims to benefits were (and are) often couched in terms of "needs" rather than "rights" (Fraser 1989, chap. 7), and women may be politically incorporated through social policies as dependents of men, rather than as independent worker-citizens (Pateman 1988, pp. 235–36).

Policy discourse around social provision for old age was very much concerned with the situation of men, the "soldiers" of labor who did not deserve the poorhouse, but rather honorable treatment at life's end. The poorhouse powerfully symbolized the problems with the system of poor relief: it deprived worthy citizens of their independence, indeed, of their citizenship rights; it took people from the small comforts of home and family; it treated worthy and unworthy alike; it offered care that was inadequate at best and inhuman at worst. Outdoor relief could be similarly criticized, though it was certainly less onerous than institutionalization. Men were far more likely than women to end up in poorhouses. In Britain, the poorhouse was a real threat for aged men; some 11 percent did end up there, as did 6 percent of aged women. In North America, much lower proportions of men went to the poorhouse—about 2–3 percent. But a larger proportion were institutionalized, if we include insane asylums as well as poorhouses (Grob 1983, chap. 7). "Respectable" old men were increasingly seen as having the *right* to better treatment than these sorts of institutions, or even outdoor relief, offered, a right embedded in their citizenship. Impoverished elderly women were much less likely to be in poorhouses, but rather they usually became dependent on sons and sons-in-law; indeed, a fairly large proportion of elderly widows were taken in by their families. This was not a situation decried as trampling on anyone's "rights." Yet reformers did take notice of the troubles caused by these arrangements, particularly for children, whose education and needs might be neglected in order that an elderly parent could be kept from the poorhouse (Weiler 1986; see Rubinow 1913, p. 314; Epstein 1922; testimony of J. J. Kelso and J. C. McConachie to Canadian House of Commons 1912, pp. 14, 20; Booth 1894, p. 326).

The rhetoric of reformers might highlight the troubles of aged and impoverished workingmen, but most assumed that elderly women would be brought under the protection of the new provisions as well, and most old age pension proposals called for women to receive coverage, usually at levels identical to those offered men. It may be that reformers and politicians implicitly took into account the arrangements made by working- and middle-class families to care for their elderly kin, assuming that state assistance was needed and would be appreciated. Typically, then, women's claim to pensions was mixed, involving both rights and needs. When the "right" to social protection was asserted, it was often based on "service to society," which was rather broadly construed and could implicitly cover women. This is nicely illustrated in a propension article that appeared in the Canadian journal *Social Welfare:*

> Governments to-day pension soldiers or war veterans for disabilities incurred in military service and for long service in the army. Why then should there be any objection to extending this form of giving expression to public gratitude, to the men and women who by their physical and mental work have contributed to the social welfare? Are the services rendered by the railway workers, the roadmakers, the telegraphers, the bootmakers, clothing makers, bakers, steel and mine workers, and all that vast host of workers who are the prime factors in maintaining the needs, comforts and conveniences of our modern world, less essential and honorable than those of teachers, judges, or soldiers? (Gould 1927, p. 343)

The need of families for sufficient resources to care for both aged parents and young children also gave older women a claim on an independent income from the state.

By identifying proposed programs as fulfilling rights, the new liberals were able to preempt "any description of them as benevolent 'doles' which might harm the character of the recipient" (Collini 1979, p. 125). The key question was how entitlement to such rights would be established. One possible means of establishing a right to benefits was, of course, through contributions along the lines of private insurance and annuities. Indeed, a number of reformers argued for contributory insurance for just this reason. Yet this had several drawbacks: contributory insurance excluded from coverage the poorest, especially women, and threatened to tread on the territory of working-class organizations, the leaders of which—at the very least—disliked contributory programs (see Rubinow 1913). In addition, in all three countries, the administrative capacities to run contributory programs were not at all well developed.

Many liberals saw service to society as establishing the right to a pension, giving a rationale for distinguishing pensions from doles. Indeed, the most common argument for citizens' rights to state support in old age was that their labor was a service to society similar to military service and, thus, should merit similar treatment in the form of honorable pensions after retirement. British new liberal J. M. Robertson wrote in 1895 that "if pensions are justly payable to State servants so-called—soldiers and sailors, and postmen and policemen— they are equally due to all workers who render lawful services" (quoted in Freeden 1978, p. 201).[11] Prominent reformer and one-time president of the National Conference of Charities and Correction Charles Henderson, a sociologist at the University of Chicago, argued that, since the nation had recognized its duty to aid the aged soldier through the Civil War pension system, "Why should the victims of the 'army of labor' be neglected? They, also, have served their country in occupations even more dangerous and destructive than war and quite as useful" (1909, p. 308). Lee Welling Squier, author of the first American book on old age dependency, advocated pensions for the "worn-out soldiers of industry" (1912, p. 320). J. J. Kelso, Canada's leading social reformer (Jones and Rutman 1981), testified at parliamentary hearings in 1911 that an old age pension system "would be a recognition of service to the country" and claimed that workers who had given such service had earned a "right to pensions" (Canadian House of Commons 1912, pp. 13, 15). Similarly, supporters argued in favor of pensions for the "soldiers of labor" who had helped to build up Canadian society in a 1907 debate in the House of Commons (quoted in Wallace

---

11. The notion that all somehow contributed to society meshed with the new liberals' organic view of society, so that pensions also were desirable in furthering social solidarity (Freeden 1978, pp. 204–5).

1952, p. 126). Liberal leader and prime minister W. L. Mackenzie King saw pensions as important in promoting social peace and as "fitting rewards" for "life-long public service in Industry" by workers (1918, p. 348; see also Craven 1980; Whitaker 1977a).[12] A particularly nice illustration of the new liberal argument about service is provided in a minority report of the Massachusetts Special Commission on Social Insurance of 1917 endorsing noncontributory old age pensions as an "inalienable right of good citizenship" (p. 53):

> It is said that there is no difference between non-contributory old age pensions and poor-relief. . . . but, if we accept the word pensions with its understood meaning, it is a periodic allowance to an individual in recognition of meritorious work or service. We claim that the industrial army and mothers in the home render such work and service to the State, and that such pensions are not degrading and pauperizing, but come as rewards of merit. Poor-relief, in its understood meaning, is a particular kind of . . . gratuity and a pauper's dole [is] given not as a particular recognition of merit or of services rendered, but as charity. We maintain, as they did in Great Britain, that there is a complete distinction between non-contributory old age pensions and poor-relief. (Massachusetts Special Commission on Social Insurance 1917, pp. 55–56)

The new liberals argued that the state should take responsibility for action. Because social forces caused the problems of the aged, it was seen as fitting that collective solutions be fashioned. Reformers believed that it was not fair to put the burden of supporting the elderly entirely on their kin and worried that working adults would have to skimp on resources for their own children in order to support their parents and keep them from the poorhouse. Collective solutions increasingly focused on the state rather than private associations, as public administrative capacities were enlarged, particularly through the incorporation of "experts" into the civil service. Private associations were not viewed as able to deal fully with the problem, as Britain's experience with friendly societies and many countries' experiences with various voluntary schemes revealed (Rubinow 1913, chap. 20). Franklin Roosevelt noted in 1928, "The state itself

---

12. The case for entitlement based on service was quite widespread. Similar arguments were used by the Canadians and Americans who were sponsoring mothers' pensions and other social insurance proposals during the first two decades of this century (see Addams 1964; Henderson 1909; Seager 1910; Squier 1912; Rubinow 1913; *American Labor Legislation Review* 1911–20; the Progressive party platform of 1912 in Porter and Johnson 1970, pp. 175–82, the social policy planks of which were written by reformist liberals and social workers; for Canada, see Allen 1973, chaps. 1–2; Social Service Council 1914; King 1918, pp. 347–48). For example, mothers' pensions in both Canada and the United States were described as a right, not charity, and as "payment for service," rather than as a dole (Leff 1973, pp. 409–15; Strong-Boag 1979, p. 26; Guest 1980, p. 51; Orloff 1991).

is under obligations to those who labor. . . . the citizen who contributes by his toil to the wealth and prosperity of the commonwealth is entitled to certain benefits in return, which only the commonwealth can give" (quoted in Fusfeld 1956, p. 159).[13] Canadian reformers testifying before the House of Commons committee on old age pensions argued that the "state owes to the individual . . . that he should be provided for" after a life of toil (Canadian House of Commons 1912, p. 17). The British new liberals also argued strongly that the state was properly the guarantor of conditions necessary for the full exercise of economic, political, and social opportunities and therefore should sponsor new forms of social protection such as old age pensions (Freeden 1978; Hobson 1909; Collini 1979). Arnold Toynbee, the founder of the first British settlement house and an inspiration to the new liberals, articulated a critical role for the state: "We have not abandoned our belief in liberty, justice and self-help, but we say that under certain conditions the people cannot help themselves and that then they should be helped by the state representing directly the whole people" (quoted in Quadagno 1982, p. 174).

It is with reference to the role of the state that one can most clearly differentiate the views and political orientations of political and reform elites from those of businessmen active in politics. In all three countries, most "rank-and-file" businessmen were hostile to state social provision outside of deterrent poor relief (Hay 1977; Orloff and Parker 1990; Pal 1986). Their views can best be described as fitting the classical liberal mold, and concerns about costs were conspicuous. Among politically active business elites, a more mixed assortment of views was found. Some groups, such as Sir Charles Macara's Employers Parliamentary Association or the rabidly anti–New Deal Liberty League, also embraced classical liberalism and strongly resisted the initiation of new state social provision. But other businessmen came to admit the existence of some problems associated with industrial wagework, particularly in the face of widespread social scientific and public acknowledgment of such difficulties, and accepted that some form of collective provision was needed. This acknowledgment has led some analysts, particularly in the United States, to argue that certain business leaders—so-called corporate liberals—were the key force behind the initiation of modern forms of social provision. To the extent that protection against the loss of employment was acknowledged as a legitimate need of the working classes, however, businessmen tended to prefer voluntary solutions such as industrial pensions, which could be kept firmly under private, business control. Along with some other private welfare

13. As president, Roosevelt offered another, similar rationale when he announced the formation of the Committee on Economic Security in 1934: "If, as our Constitution tells us, our Federal Government was established among other things, 'to promote the general welfare,' it is our plain duty to provide for that security upon which welfare depends" (quoted in Achenbaum 1978, p. 131).

programs, private pensions aimed simultaneously at undermining the bases of unrest, exercising social control, and increasing workers' loyalty to specific firms. This was the strategy known as "welfare capitalism" in postwar North America (Brandes 1976; Brody 1980; Latimer 1932a). Similar schemes of private and voluntary provision for unemployment or retirement were offered by a few British employers in the years before World War I as well (Hay 1977, 1978; Melling 1979).[14] Generally, the reformist business leaders were motivated to embrace new social policies by their concerns with labor (or social) control and "national efficiency," the ability to compete internationally which depended partially on the character of the work force (Hay 1977), rather than by an attachment to social justice and new liberal ideals.

Public provision outside poor relief remained a second choice at best, and nowhere did more than a handful of businessmen advocate universal, generous public provision for the aged or unemployed. Nevertheless, once it became clear that old age pensions or other forms of social provision were very likely to be enacted, some businessmen did become active in trying to shape the character of the new programs. In all three countries, these businessmen focused most attention on unemployment programs rather than on provision for old age (see Pal 1986, 1988; Struthers 1983; Nelson 1969; Hay 1977; Harris 1972). Generally, means-tested assistance for the "worthy" aged did not excite much opposition from the ranks of "progressive" businessmen. In both Canada and Britain, however, the minority of reform-oriented corporate leaders preferred contributory financing for old age provision, although they failed to have this provision enacted in the initial pension measures, passed in 1927 and 1908 respectively (Orloff and Parker 1990; Hay 1977; Mitchell 1928; Finkel 1979, p. 97). In contrast, in the Depression era United States, even the business leaders most sympathetic to social reform were not enthusiastic about provisions for compulsory employee and employer financial contributions; they preferred means-tested, noncontributory benefits for the needy aged and a noncompulsory contributory plan that would allow exemptions for employers who offered corporate plans to their workers (Altmeyer 1966, pp. 40–42; Witte 1962, pp. 157–61). Thus, it would be fair to say that reformist business leaders contributed to the political consensus that developed in favor of reforms such as old age pensions, but they were not the leaders of movements that pressed for policy initiatives. Rather, the reform, intellectual, and political elites and middle-class professionals who

14. In dealing with the problems of those outside the paid labor force, such as aged widows, welfare capitalists often converged with those holding classical laissez-faire views in advocating family solutions to old age poverty (Weiler 1986, p. 79). For example, in the United States, as such solutions implicitly came under attack in the 1920s with proposals for new public old age protections, the U.S. National Civic Federation, an organization of businessmen and reformers sympathetic to the business position, recommended that laws holding adult children financially responsible for their parents be retained (National Civic Federation 1928, p. 3).

embraced new liberalism led in forming cross-class alliances for new public social provisions with working-class organizations.

Cross-Class Alliances and the Initiation of Pensions

We have seen that working-class organizations supported old age pension proposals and that important segments of reform, intellectual, and political elites had developed new liberal understandings of poverty and the possibilities of state action to alleviate economic insecurity and inequality. Indeed, the key proximate factor in the initiation of new social provision for the aged in Britain, Canada, and the United States was the emergence of a cross-class coalition for social spending which encompassed these two groups. Yet such coalitions did not emerge at the same time in the three countries, resulting in the delayed introduction of pensions in Canada and the United States relative to Britain. The specific content of the old age proposals around which the coalitions formed differed across the three countries as well. Even given the general orientation favorable to social reform, there was no guarantee of a commitment specifically to social insurance or state pensions. The particular solution to the social question likely to be advocated by reform, intellectual, and political elites depended on their positions in struggles for authority within state organizations, as well as on their reactions to past policy and general ideological orientation. In the three countries, elite attitudes to social spending and willingness to work with popular forces were not the same. In Britain, pensions were advanced by a cross-class coalition which had no U.S. or Canadian counterpart prior to 1920. After 1920, elite orientations in Canada shifted somewhat, allowing for the coalescence of such a coalition. To a much smaller extent, similar coalitions were built in the 1920s United States, but it was in the 1930s that American elite reformers and popular organizations joined in an informal cross-class coalition for expanded social spending, including old age pensions and insurance.

In Britain, the extraparliamentary National Committee of Organized Labour that agitated for pensions from 1899 on was initiated and financed by upper- and middle-class reformers and flourished through the cooperation of reformers and some of Britain's trade union leaders (Heclo 1974, pp. 165–66; Rubinstein 1973, pp. xxvii–xxviii; Rogers 1973, pp. 222–23; Williams 1970, chap. 5). More generally, from the 1880s onward, social investigators and national commissions acknowledged the problems of the elderly poor and considered various proposed solutions, leading increasingly toward broad acceptance within the British establishment of the inevitability, if not the desirability, of some sort of public support outside the poor law for the aged (Gilbert 1966, chap. 4; Collins 1965). As we have discussed, new liberal thinkers developed justifications for public old age pensions as a recognition of social service by working people (Freeden 1978, pp. 200–206). The Liberals, while still working to incorporate working-class voters in their own ranks, concluded an electoral alliance in 1906 with the still-tiny Labour Representation Committee prior to passing pension legislation in 1908 (Bealey 1956). The alliance between the Liberals and the LRC was partially cemented by old age pensions (Clarke 1974, pp. 173–75).

In the Progressive Era United States, meanwhile, the missing ingredient for a similar cross-class alliance on the pension issue was not the willingness of the member unions of the American Federation of Labor to support proposals for noncontributory public old age pensions. That willingness came a little later than in Britain, but the AFL endorsed a need-based pension scheme in 1909 and reiterated its support in 1911, 1912, and 1913 (American Federation of Labor 1919, pp. 303–4). State labor federations also supported pensions. Instead, it was many American social reformers in the Progressive Era—and, in general, the upper and professional strata from which they came and to which they oriented their arguments—who were reluctant to push for or accept public old age pensions. Events at the elite level in the United States make a telling contrast with those in Britain.

Whereas British elites had laid the groundwork for the legislative enactment of pensions, in the United States exactly the opposite happened. The first serious official investigation of old age poverty occurred in Massachusetts in the wake of the introduction of several old age pension bills in the legislature from 1903 to 1906 (Linford 1949, pp. 11–17; Fischer 1978, p. 161). The Massachusetts Commission on Old Age Pensions, Annuities and Insurance was appointed in 1907 and issued its report in 1910. The investigatory commission, staffed predominantly with professionals and upper-class Bostonians, gathered data on the elderly poor in Massachusetts, considered various pension proposals, and reported that public pensions were neither needed nor morally desirable (Massachusetts Commission on Old Age Pensions 1910). Massachusetts had long been a pioneer in social and labor legislation, serving as a gateway to the United States for British social policy innovations and as an example to other states (compare the social legislation timelines in Fraser 1973 and Whittlesey 1901). Thus, the setback in the Bay State was critical to developments everywhere in American (Linford 1949, pp. 8–9; Lieby 1960; Abrams 1964, pp. 1–13). Indeed, the report dealt a virtual death blow to what had previously been a promising movement toward old age pensions in Massachusetts and elsewhere (Linford 1949, p. 33; Rubinow 1913, pp. 381, 409–10; Achenbaum 1978, p. 83). A labor representative, Arthur M. Huddell, questioned the commission's arguments about the preferability of contributory as opposed to noncontributory pensions, citing Civil War pensions as a favorable precedent, and endorsed the Wilson bill for the formation of an "Old Home Guard" (Massachusetts Commission on Old Age Pensions 1910, p. 335). But the willingness of Huddell and other reformers from labor's ranks to endorse noncontributory pensions for the "veterans of industry" was not complemented by a similar attitude on the part of elites in Massachusetts or in the rest of the United States.

Across the nation, old age pensions were downplayed throughout the Progressive Era even by reform-minded liberal elites, such as those who made up the American Association for Labor Legislation (AALL). The AALL, composed of social scientists, reformers, and a handful of business and labor leaders, was at the forefront of U.S. campaigns for new measures of social protection, beginning with a campaign for workers' compensation across the states (Pierce 1953). In 1913–14, just as the commitment of the American Federation of Labor to old age pensions was solidifying, the AALL moved toward promoting not old age pensions but health insurance as the "next great step" after workers' compensation in the "inevitable" progress toward a comprehensive program of modern social protections in the United States (Numbers 1978, pp. 15–19, 52; Tishler 1971, chap. 8; *American Labor Legislation Review* 1914, pp. 578–79). Following the massive unemployment in the recession of 1913–15, the AALL also advocated a model bill for unemployment insurance, along with other measures to help the jobless (Nelson 1969, p. 10–21; Lubove 1968, pp. 147–49, 168; *American Labor Legislation Review* 1915, pp. 593–95). Yet given the opposition of many labor leaders to contributory insurance, this decision also undermined possibilities for a cross-class alliance for new social spending programs.

The decision of the AALL was critical to developments throughout the American reform community because of the organization's role in initiating social legislation throughout the United States and in diffusing ideas, model bills, and campaigns to areas outside the cosmopolitan centers of the Northeast. Members of the AALL worked within the National Conference of Charities and Correction (NCCC), a larger, umbrella organization of reformers and social workers. Mothers' pensions and workers' compensation were the social welfare reforms supported earliest and most broadly (Tishler 1971, chaps. 6–7). After the success of these kinds of legislation in many states—thirty states passed workers' compensation statutes by 1916, and twenty enacted mothers' pension laws between 1911 and 1913 (with another twenty by 1919)—the NCCC's sessions on social legislation in 1915 and 1916 focused on health insurance and dealing with unemployment, reflecting the emphasis of the AALL (Brandeis 1935, pp. 575–76; Leff 1973, p. 401; National Conference of Charities and Correction 1915, pp. 493–575; 1916, pp. 146–204). When California reformers were appointed to a commission to study old age pensions and social insurance in 1915, one of their first activities was to send one of their members to the East to consult with social insurance experts. The experts advised them not to pursue old age pensions but, rather, to embark on a study of health insurance (California Social Insurance Commission 1917, pp. 10, 15). The 1917 report of the California commission recommended health insurance and an amendment to the constitution enabling the state to establish a health insurance system (pp. 13–17). Although successful in the legislature, the proposed amendment was defeated by the electorate in 1918, victim of a campaign to link health insurance with the traditions of America's war enemy Germany (Numbers 1978, pp. 72–81). It is noteworthy that California reformers did not pursue the chance to develop what might have been an even more popular, cross-class campaign for pensions.

Prior to 1920, in Canada as in the United States, middle- and upper-class reformers focused on issues other than pensions. The attitudes of Canadian reform elites toward state old age pensions do not provide as stark a contrast with those of the British as do those of the Americans. For example, J. J. Kelso, a leading member of both the Canadian and the American conferences of charities and correction, endorsed pensions at parliamentary hearings in 1911–12 (Canadian House of Commons 1912, pp. 13–16). But Kelso's enthusiasm for pensions was not matched by his fellow reformers and charity workers; indeed, Kelso himself put far more energy into various campaigns for child welfare (Jones and Rutman 1981). The most important group of reformers in the pre–World War I years was the Social Service Council, made up of moral reform, church, and labor groups (Guest 1980, p. 23; Social Service Council 1914, p. iii). The council's first legislative campaign had been for the Lord's Day Act, passed in 1906 (Guest 1980, p. 32). Then known as the Moral and Social Reform Council, this group constituted "an unprecedented alliance of labour and church" (Allen 1973, p. 21). The first congress of the Social Service Council, a gathering made up mainly of professionals, with a few labor representatives, met in 1914 to discuss the many aspects of the social question (Allen 1973, pp. 20, 29). The congress endorsed old age pensions along with many other proposals (Social Service Council 1914, p. 358). In making its representation to the government requesting legislation after the meeting, however, old age pensions were not included, despite the endorsement of pensions by organized labor in 1905 and the activity of M.P.'s supportive of labor in Parliament during the 1911–12 and 1912–13 sessions. Instead, the only labor legislation requested was a proposal for workers' compensation; the representation stressed moral reform (Allen 1973, pp. 30–31). Indeed, though the congress dealt with the labor question, the sessions offering solutions to its various facets did not include unemployment or old age insurance or pensions but emphasized bringing Christian principles to industry and the enactment of workers' compensation, mothers' pensions, and labor standards laws (Social Service Council 1914, pp. 33–76). Overall, discussion of moral and political problems and reform proposals dominated the congress.

The kind of legislation Canadian reformers supported was more similar to that backed by their U.S. than their British counterparts. In the years after the

Social Service congress, while the Trades and Labour Congress (TLC) made a decision to concentrate on getting an old age pension law enacted (Bryden 1974, p. 64), as in the United States, the social welfare legislation on which social reformers focused was mothers' pensions and workers' compensation (which the TLC also supported) (Strong-Boag 1979; Guest 1980, chap. 4). In Parliament, M.P.'s Alphonse Verville and Ralph Smith, both former presidents of the TLC, along with several Liberal and Conservative backbenchers from working-class constituencies, introduced various pension bills but failed to receive support from either of the major parties or from major reform organizations (Brown and Cook 1974, p. 124; Bryden 1974, chap. 3, and p. 186). Instead, the debate about reform focused on eliminating patronage in the civil administration (Brown and Cook 1974, chap. 10). What attention old age poverty received was channeled into a successful 1908 proposal to establish a government annuity system (Bryden 1974, pp. 51–53).

In the pre–World War I period, then, the comparative picture of Britain, Canada, and the United States looked like this: Encouraged by elite reformers and building on a climate of broad elite and governmental acknowledgments of a problem requiring new public action, British union leaders were able to campaign effectively for noncontributory old age pensions. In North America, many union leaders, even in the American Federation of Labor, supported noncontributory old age pensions as well. But U.S. and Canadian elites, including most of the prominent reformers, did not coalesce with unions and other working-class organizations to campaign for old age pensions, nor did they pave the way for them through official investigations.

After 1920 a marked shift began to occur in the orientations of reform and political elites in North America toward new public spending for income protection for the aged. In the 1920s both Canadian and American reformers became far more supportive of old age pensions. In the United States, this occurred in a political context rather unfavorable for social reform, but even so, the basic elements that would prove far more successful politically in the 1930s were coming together.

In Canada, reform and political elites became much more supportive of the idea of pensions and social insurance, a position manifested in the increasing number of endorsements of pension legislation. In 1919 the Royal Commission on Industrial Relations recommended inquiry into all forms of state social insurance, and this was supported as well by representatives from the federal and provincial governments, management, and labor who attended the National Industrial Conference, held later that year to consider the commission's recommendations (Guest 1980, pp. 68, 71). The Social Service Council, which before the war had concentrated on moral reform, exhibited a changed emphasis, after 1920, issuing a national program which concentrated on social and industrial issues, including social insurance and pensions (Allen 1973, pp. 65–66).

The council actively lobbied Parliament for these reforms, especially pensions (Allen 1973, pp. 240–41). Political parties, too, showed more positive interest in pensions. The Liberal party endorsed a pension and social insurance plank in 1919, as did M.P.'s sitting as United Farmers after 1921 (Carrigan 1968, pp. 82, 102; Bryden 1974, p. 66; Christian and Campbell 1974, pp. 54–56). In addition, several provincial legislatures passed resolutions in favor of federal pension legislation in the first few years after the war (Bryden 1974, pp. 66–67). In the mid-1920s, the Liberal administration worked with Labour and Progressive (agrarian) M.P.'s for old age pensions, and the governing party utilized pensions to appeal to working-class constituencies. By the 1930s, public provision for the elderly was very widely accepted among both Liberals and Conservatives.

In the years immediately following the war, in the United States the American Association for Labor Legislation endorsed the campaign of the Eagles and state labor federations for state old age pensions (Hering 1923; Lubove 1968, p. 138; Mackenzie 1920). Together, they introduced in many state legislatures a model pension bill, following a draft suggested by the Pennsylvania Commission on Old Age Pensions in 1921 (Leotta 1975, p. 361). State labor federations were particularly important actors in the key states of Wisconsin, California, New York, Massachusetts, and Pennsylvania (Putnam 1970, pp. 17–28; Linford 1949, p. 56; Gratton 1983, pp. 404, 412; Pennsylvania Commission on Old Age Assistance 1925, p. 83; Lubove 1968, p. 138; Leotta 1975, p. 367). Abraham Epstein, long an advocate of new public protections for the aged and the author of two of the most widely read books on the problems of the aged in the United States—*Facing Old Age* (1922) and *Challenge of the Aged* (1928)—worked with several other, European-oriented reformers to establish the American Association for Old Age Security (AAOAS) in 1927 to campaign for old age pensions and insurance, at times working with the Eagles and the AALL (Leotta 1975). Also in the 1920s, several important politicians, including Franklin Roosevelt while he served as governor of New York, progressive Republican governors Gifford Pinchot of Pennsylvania and C. C. Young of California, and Senator Robert F. Wagner, as well as many lesser-known state legislators, supported state-level pension legislation (Fischer 1978, p. 174; Bernstein 1960, pp. 486–87; Putnam 1970, chap. 1; Linford 1949, pp. 55–87; Pennsylvania Commission on Old Age Assistance 1925, p. 78; Huthmacher 1968, pp. 129, 176–77). Both Democratic and Republican progressives were able to aid the pension movements of their states when serving as governors. These developments foreshadowed the events of the 1930s, when even broader forces from the camps of reformers, organized labor, and the Democratic party (joined by several Republican progressives) came together in support of federal programs to help the aged. Yet these coalitions were only a minority movement in the conservative 1920s. The GOP at the national level ignored the issue of pensions and social insurance, and the Democrats' programmatic adherence to social insurance and pensions did not come until 1932 (Porter and Johnson 1970, p. 331). The progressive creeds of Woodrow Wilson and Teddy Roosevelt were certainly politically legitimate and embodied new liberal principles similar to those expounded by W. L. Mackenzie King. Yet it is clear that the progressive wings of the Republican and Democratic parties were vastly overshadowed on the national level by the ascendancy of conservative Republicanism in political debate, legislative agendas, and electoral preference. The propension campaigns of the 1920s thus yielded little fruit.

By the 1930s reform, intellectual, and political elites generally supported new forms of social provision, including old age pensions and insurance. The most liberal reformers in the AALL and AAOAS were joined by the broader reform community, and the relatively few propension progressive politicians, particularly within the Democratic party, were joined by many more. Whereas the reports of state investigatory commissions in the 1910s generally were unfavorable to the initiation of pensions, those issued in the 1920s and early 1930s supported pension legislation (U.S. Social Security Board 1937, p. 159). As working-class voters, particularly those of immigrant background, shifted massively into the Democratic party in the 1932 election that brought Franklin Roosevelt into office, politicians at all levels of government offered social policy initiatives to secure their loyalty. FDR pursued coalition politics with unions, farmers' groups, and other popular organizations through the 1930s as he initiated a number of social policy measures, including the Social Security Act of 1935. The politicians and administrators FDR appointed in the area of social welfare were almost all political and ideological products of the Progressive Era; their commitment to social insurance and old age protection was not a creation of the Depression but drew upon the themes first elaborated in the 1910s. Because the contours of the Social Security Act were most importantly shaped by the preferences of Roosevelt and his close advisers, it was here that the United States felt the strongest political impact of the legacy of reworked, progressive liberalism.

We now are ready to turn to the broader political and institutional context in order to understand the differences over time and across countries in elite willingness to form alliances with labor for the expansion of state activity in income protection for the aged. In Part 3 I offer an analysis of the overall structure of the Canadian, British, and American states and the sequences of democratization and bureaucratization that transformed these polities in the nineteenth and twentieth centuries. Then it will become apparent why the British Liberal party was able and willing to launch modern pensions in 1908 while Canadian and American political and reform elites could not and would not take a similar course before the war, and why and how it became possible for them to do so after 1920.

Part 3
The Break with Poor Relief and the Initiation of Modern Social Provision for the Aged

Introduction to Part 3

The development of cross-class alliances was the key proximate condition for the initiation of modern social provision for the aged. While working-class pressures for pension reform were comparable (if not exactly the same) across the three countries, elite political orientations did vary across the three cases and over time. In Britain, the problems of the aged served as a unifying focus for the political activities of reformers and some labor leaders, helping to cement a cross-class alliance in favor of new social spending measures. In contrast, in the United States the problems associated with the aged—poverty, but also mismanaged Civil War pensions—served to drive apart groups who might otherwise have cooperated politically to press for a modern system of social protection. Even the most socially progressive middle-class American reformers were unwilling to join a campaign for old age pensions that had been suggested by various labor leaders. Once Americans decisively rejected new public social protections in the wake of World War I, it took the political crisis triggered by the Depression of the 1930s—with the failure of existing social policies, intense popular mobilization, electoral realignment, and further administrative reforms—to create a situation in which national social welfare legislation could succeed through the efforts of a cross-class alliance for social spending, as represented in the liberal wing of the Democratic party. The Canadian pattern was not one in which the interests of working-class and middle-class groups were driven apart, but one in which they were simply not brought together. Soon after the war, some Canadian elites did work with labor politicians in introducing pensions, but efforts to enact contributory pensions faltered.

To understand the political orientations of reform elites and of the middle-class public oriented to their leadership, we need to examine the institutional and political context within which they operated. We have already discussed some of the major elements of the political context within which policy-making for the aged took place: capitalist industrialization, as it was mediated by the policy legacy of poor relief; the political emergence of the industrial working class; and the development of new liberal ideology among elites, which offered justifications for new uses of state power to guarantee individual dignity and the "right" to an honorable source of support in old age. We now turn to a discussion of the institutions which structured the political context: parties and state administrations, the organizations which provided the means by which policies were formulated and gained political support.

The institutional context was shaped by processes of state formation, itself the result of a complex set of factors, both international and domestic. The position of a state in international political-military and economic systems, particularly the extent to which it is subject to the threat of war, affects the state-building process. International military and economic pressures have been key catalysts in the process of building and then "reforming"—that is, making more efficient, rational, and bureaucratic—state administrative organs, while domestic arrangements have also affected how easily the state could extract and mobilize resources, and at what costs. Domestic arrangements—the character, capacities, and interests of popular and elite forces, the sequence of democratization and bureaucratization, and the character of the economy—also have significantly affected the process of state-building and the qualities of the institutions which emerged thereby.

In Part 3, we will examine the character of the institutional context within which policy-making took place, discussing the capacities and operating procedures of state administrative organs and of the organizational structure and relationship to the electorate of political parties. We will investigate the process of state-building in Great Britain, Canada, and the United States in order to understand both the institutional context within which the politics of social policy were played out and to assess the extent to which state administrative capacities were in place at key moments in the policy-making process. We have already seen that both popular and elite forces reacted to the character of existing social provision, the policy legacy, in formulating demands for policy reforms. We will put this process of policy feedback into political and institutional perspective, examining the ways in which distinctive policy legacies shaped political struggles over new forms of public social protection. Finally, each chapter offers an account of how cross-class alliances for new social spending for the aged did or did not form.

6

Great Britain

From Oligarchic Patronage to a Modern Welfare State

Capitalist industrialization affected the elderly and their families by constricting employment opportunities, while demographic shifts—in the British case, an increasing proportion of people remaining single—enlarged the portion of the elderly without kin to support them if they became economically dependent. These changes were mediated and intensified by the existing policy legacy, poor relief, upon which large proportions of the aged in Britain depended. Thus, when poor law authorities cut back on outdoor relief in the 1870s, a significant part of the elderly population and their families were affected for the worse. These policy changes helped to create a perceived crisis of old age poverty in the 1890s, which assumed greater political salience in a polity where working-class voters and organizations were increasingly important. Among a segment of elites, important intellectual and ideological changes had created a new liberal understanding of poverty, the role of the state, and citizens' rights to social support. In turn-of-the-century Britain, these forces helped to create conditions under which new liberal elites worked with working-class organizations—and attempted to win working-class votes—in a campaign for new state social spending for old age pensions. Many historical accounts of the emergence of modern British welfare programs have rested on one or a combination of these factors. Yet our comparative analysis has suggested that such accounts are inadequate, for comparable conditions existed in the United States and Canada, but progressive elites in North America did not exhibit similar political orientations toward social spending and did not work with working-class organizations to initiate new forms of state social provision for the aged. I have argued that to resolve the historical puzzle presented by these comparative patterns, we must understand the character of the institutional context and the policy legacy. Specifically, we must investigate the kinds of state administrative capacities available to political actors struggling with questions of social provision.

In Britain, two aspects of the process of state formation were critical to later social policy developments. First, a unified central state was constructed in the wake of the Glorious Revolution. Although England never developed full-blown absolutism, sovereignty was united in the center, subject to significant parliamentary restrictions. Second, bureaucratization of the state administration occurred relatively late by Continental standards. British elites—the landed gentry—had privileged access to government positions, that is, to patronage.[1] They were thus able to thwart the proposals of a coalition for bureaucratic autonomy for the construction of a bureaucratic state through the 1860s. Patronage, at first distributed through social networks, by the 1830s was partially removed to the field of the elitist political parties that emerged in the wake of franchise extension in 1832. Thus, the elimination of patronage had to be accomplished before the capacities to undertake significant social spending could be created. Moreover, patronage politics and their transformation significantly affected social policy, and thus the legacy against which reformers and others struggled. In contrast with the experience in North America, however, patronage was eliminated in Britain in the 1870s, before the full democratization of the electorate, so that it never gained a mass political base. The capacities for state intervention in civil society were enhanced, and political elites were willing to call upon those state capacities in coping with various problems, including old age dependency. The structure of the state channeled the activities of reformers toward gaining the approval of Parliament through partisan struggle. As electoral incentives to take action on pensions emerged and the reaction against the policy legacy of poor relief intensified around the turn of the century, reformers could mount campaigns directed at gaining the approval of parliamentary parties. Around the turn of the century a cross-class coalition of working-class groups and middle-class and elite reformers coalesced in the National Committee of Organized Labour on Old Age Pensions to press for old age pensions. In the context of increasing electoral competition for the votes of working-class voters, Liberal party leaders put through the Old Age Pension Act of 1908, which partially met the demands of the extraparliamentary group.

State Formation in Britain

English politics in the seventeenth century were divided into "court" and "country" alignments, which reflected disputes over state-building. Those in the "court" camp were statist, seeking to build up the power of the central state

---

1. Significantly, British rulers had not had to resort to venality (the sale of offices) to finance extensive war-making in the sixteenth and seventeenth centuries, which left the state administration more flexible and efficient than some European administrations (Brewer 1989, pp. 19–21).

for international competition and to keep order domestically, while "country" forces "expressed strong suspicion of government, might even at times seem isolationist in foreign policy, and preferred to rely upon local resources and institutions for the preservation of domestic order" (Murrin 1980, p. 379; see also Jones 1978; Plumb 1967). The English court was forced by the Glorious Revolution to rely upon the English Parliament to govern the country, but the goals of the monarchy remained much the same: they still worked to extract resources for the military and to have access to enough patronage with which to be able to "manage" the Parliament (Murrin 1980, pp. 379–80). Thus, England's Revolution Settlement "created a centralized system of Court politics and one-party rule, closely tied to the disturbing new world of high finance and the beginnings of intensive economic growth" (Murrin 1980, p. 382).

> In England by the 1720's, the "court" Whigs were controlling, in collaboration with George I, a national government that routinely influenced Parliament, that manipulated elections, that was part of a complex central banking and fiscal system, and that in the course of the wars with France between 1689 and 1713 had built Europe's most powerful navy. . . . The radical "country" case of 1688 had dissolved. . . . mainstream whiggery was transformed into justification of an aristocratic, oligarchic ruling elite . . . [and] a vindication of strong national government. . . . The danger of absolute monarchy may have been averted when James II was forced off the throne, but in its place there emerged a system of strong national government. (Stewart 1986, pp. 2–3)

Britain in the International States System and World Economy

John Murrin (1980, p. 411) has argued that one of the key reasons the court won in England, helping to create a unified central state, was the pattern of international involvement. England, and later Great Britain, was an integral part of the European states system from its inception and was a key agent in imposing that system on the rest of the world. Both war "at home" (in Europe) and the quest for territory and resources abroad stimulated the development of standing armies or, especially in England, given its geopolitical position, navies and state administration to extract the resources needed to maintain them. Thus, like all European states, the English state developed largely in response to war and the pursuit of hegemony and the preparations for these core state activities. In the case of England, competition with Spain, Holland, and especially France was critical to the process of state formation. As Charles Tilly puts it, "From 1066 to 1815, great wars with French monarchs formed the English state, French intervention complicated England's attempts to subdue Scotland and Ireland [and, I would add, England's goal of maintaining her colonies in North America], and French competition stimulated England's adoption of

Dutch fiscal innovations" (1990, p. 26). Britain displaced France altogether in North America before losing the thirteen American colonies but held the colonies which would later make up Canada until the latter half of the nineteenth century. With the final defeat of Napoleonic France in 1815, Britain emerged as the preeminent imperial power in the world.

Tilly has argued that "how much state apparatus emerged" out of warmaking activities depended on the extent of commercialization of the economy and the extent to which kings relied on local power holders for military forces and keeping domestic order, among other things (1990, p. 94). Because of England's geopolitical position and certain features of its domestic economic and social arrangements, the state-building process resulted in a "less bulky" administrative apparatus than was the case in the Continental powers, and one which was bureaucratized relatively late. England's position as a relatively well-protected island meant that the threat of war was less severe than was the case on the Continent (Brewer 1989, pp. 12–13; Badie and Birnbaum 1983, p. 122). England's economic and territorial ambitions certainly pushed its rulers to develop military might, but navies, rather than armies, carried out these goals. (Navies could carry out these objectives given the geopolitical position of Britain, and they also reflected the preferences of local elites that a standing army be avoided; Murrin 1980, p. 417.) As Tilly puts it, "Commercialized agriculture, far-ranging trade, imperial conquest, and war against rival European powers complemented each other, promoting an investment in naval power and a readiness to mobilize land forces for action overseas" in eighteenth-century England (1990, p. 159).

Domestic Economic, Social, and Political Arrangements

The strength of local English power holders—the landed aristocracy, or gentry—forced English monarchs to rely upon them in carrying out the government's domestic functions and to gain their cooperation in financing and carrying out war and imperial expansion, as analysts as diverse as Barrington Moore (1966, chap. 1), Perry Anderson (1974, chap. 5), and Samuel Huntington (1966) have pointed out. The strong network of local elites also took pressure off the state from having to build structures of local control to ensure domestic order. The English Civil War and the Glorious Revolution certainly underlined the power of local elites and established parliamentary limits on royal absolutism, primarily through tying the Crown to annual parliaments in order to gain the financial resources to maintain the government. Yet even before these key political events of the seventeenth century occurred, the Tudors had been significantly more constrained in their exercise of royal power than their counterparts in countries which produced true absolutist states (Brewer

1989; Lachmann 1989; Moore 1966, chap. 1; Badie and Birnbaum 1983, pp. 121–22).

The commercialization of both rural and urban economies made extraction of resources for war and conquest far less difficult than it was in countries where the economy had not been commercialized, such as Russia. The English state developed along what Tilly calls a route of "capitalized coercion," in which capitalists and sources of capital were incorporated into the state as a mode of gaining needed resources—though this did not entirely displace the process of "squeezing the means of war" from the English and other populations.

The result of these factors was an English state that looked quite different from the extensive and bureaucratized administrations of continental Europe. The distinctive state-building process shaped the characteristics of the British polity in the nineteenth century, which formed the context within which struggles over social provision for the aged took place.

The British Polity in the Early Nineteenth Century

In 1800 the British polity was a liberal oligarchy ruled by and for landlords, with political parties which were basically parliamentary cliques, held together primarily by patronage (Namier 1961; Moore 1966, chap. 1; Webb 1974, pp. 53–57; Smellie 1950, chaps. 1–3).[2] England had effective representative institutions, but they constituted representation for the elite, for powers and liberties were largely limited to the propertied classes. The state, though unitary and internationally powerful, did not boast a large central administration or a substantial army, core features of its Continental counterparts.

As compared with its Continental neighbors, the British state governed by means of a relatively small central apparatus, supplemented by a vast system of patronage and local powerholding in which Lords Lieutenant, sheriffs, mayors, constables and justices of the peace did the crown's work without serving as its full-time employees; before the Napoleonic Wars,

2. As English historian Lawrence Stone (1984) pointed out in a review of the historiography of the "new eighteenth century," this description of English politics, most associated with Sir Lewis Namier, has sometimes been inappropriately extended backward to the reign of Queen Anne. Historians have demonstrated that the period between 1679 and 1721 was a time of intense, violent party conflict in a polity with an electorate that "during the time of Anne became not only the largest and most frequently consulted of any in Europe, but proportionately larger than any to be seen again in England before the late nineteenth century" (Stone 1984, p. 43). Thus, the "political stability" of the mid–eighteenth century, the origins of which J. H. Plumb (1967) analyzed, with the aristocracy enjoying power, wealth, and control of patronage, did not descend in any linear fashion from the century preceding but reflected a resurgence of aristocratic power (Stone and Stone 1984), at least partially reflecting the need of the Crown to manage Parliament.

only customs and excise had substantial numbers of regularly appointed officials. Until then, Britain did not maintain a standing army, and relied especially on wartime mobilization of naval power for its armed force. Except in Ireland, the army played a relatively small part, and militias a relatively large part, in control of Britain's domestic population. (Tilly 1990, pp. 157–58)

The power of local elites was reflected in their significant personal and political liberties (Stone 1972, p. 147; Bendix 1978, pp. 319–20) and their large role in the governance of the country, particularly in the institutionalized control of Parliament—a "committee of landlords" (Moore 1966)—over state administration and finances. The gentry dominated domestic administration and policy, and the relatively fewer positions in the central administration were controlled by Parliament, which filled positions through patronage (Namier 1961; Shefter 1977, p. 434). Not surprisingly, patronage went to members of the aristocracy and other propertied classes. Leading radical and free trader John Bright in 1858 described the administration as a "gigantic outdoor relief department of the aristocracy of Great Britain" (cited in Mueller 1984, p. 107).[3] Because of the significant elite control of the state administration through Parliament and the relative ease of extracting resources, patronage-dominated administrative practices were retained well into the nineteenth century. No "coalition for bureaucratic autonomy" emanating from the monarchy could succeed against the aristocracy, the prime beneficiaries of the patronage system. Certainly the ability of England to do well in war and international competition despite its administrative practices blunted the interests of central authorities in pursuing such bureaucratization projects, at least for a while.

Transformations of State and Party in the Nineteenth Century

During the nineteenth century, the stage was set for later changes in social policy as the British polity underwent intertwined transformations: the expansion of national administrative capacities, the step-by-step democratization of the electorate, the reform of the civil service (professionalization and bureaucratization), and the change in the modes of organization and electoral competition of the major political parties. International and internal pressures, military and economic competition, and the increase in complexity and conflict concomitant with capitalist industrialization helped to stimulate these political changes.

---

3. Although appointments in Britain were made on a patronage basis, the spoils system (rotation of offices with every change of administration) never took root as it did in the United States (Moses 1914, pp. 24–25; Brebner 1938, pp. 22–23; Parris 1969, pp. 29–33).

Pressures for Administrative and Political Reform

The 1830s marked the beginnings of the modern interventionist state, as the British central government tackled the problems created by capitalist industrialization in a remarkable series of legislative and administrative innovations (Webb 1974, pp. 239–47; Lubenow 1971), which scholars now recognize as the "Victorian origins of the welfare state" (Roberts 1960). The first British Factory Acts were passed during the 1830s, the Poor Law Amendment Act (new poor law) was passed in 1834, and various health-related inspectorates were created as well (see Fraser 1973, pp. xiv–xv). With new legislative requirements for inspection and regulation, there was a concomitant expansion of national administrative capacities for the collection of social and economic information and, to an increasing extent, for the regulation of local public health and poor relief practices, as well as of economic relationships and labor standards (Roberts 1960; Martin 1972; Midwinter 1972; Fraser 1973, chaps. 1–4; Lubenow 1971). The enactments of the 1830s were followed by a spurt of growth in the size of the civil administration. This expansion began on an ad hoc basis and so continued through the 1850s, at which time there was a lull in the trend of expanding government activities (Roberts 1960, p. 95). Attention focused instead on the rationalization and professionalization of the enlarged civil administration (Mueller 1984, p. 174).

Meanwhile, during the nineteenth century, important, parallel changes also occurred in the operation of the civil administration as a whole. The governmental response to the increasing societal complexity and class conflicts which accompanied capitalist industrialization was manifested in the expansion of state functions in the early Victorian era. But despite expansion and the infusion of some technical expertise into the ranks of the service, particularly in the new agencies created by the reform legislation (Roberts 1960, chaps. 5–6), the methods of appointment and management in the civil administration remained unreformed. Patronage was the cement of the British polity in the early nineteenth century. The Whigs and Tories—more accurately described as elite parliamentary factions than as parties—controlled the appointments to the civil service and depended upon patronage, both personal and partisan, for political support (Parris 1969, chaps. 1–2; Mueller 1984, pp. 96–108; White 1935, p. 1). Then, the enlargement of the electorate after the 1832 Reform Act stimulated the transformation of faction into party, and patronage spread beyond the aristocratic cliques which had composed the government up until that point (Webb 1974, pp. 195–97; Smellie 1950, p. 35). Thus party politicians partly displaced aristocratic cliques as controllers of patronage (Cohen 1941, pp. 75–76), and patronage went increasingly to the middle classes as well as to the aristocracy and gentry (O'Leary 1962, p. 78). Personal patronage was not eradicated, but patronage became an important ingredient in the parties' electoral appeals and competition (Smellie 1950, chap. 2; Parris 1969, pp. 70–72; see Fraser 1976 for a description of these practices within local poor relief administration).

In the wake of the social reforms of the 1830s and 1840s, which added substantially to the numbers of government employees and functions and to government expense, calls were increasingly heard for the rationalization of the civil service, so that it could more efficiently and economically perform its new duties. There were several sources of dissatisfaction with the civil service, intensifying by the late 1840s. In Parliament, there was pressure for retrenchment and economy in government (Hart 1972, pp. 68–69; Mueller 1984, pp. 178–83). Moreover, the demand for patronage far outstripped its supply, leaving politicians with the uncomfortable task of deciding which of many supplicants to reward with the jobs available (see Parris 1969, pp. 53–65). Senior civil servants and leading politicians recognized that patronage was not supplying enough able people to carry out governmental functions properly and that the old personal management of ministries and various agencies had been overwhelmed by the increase in duties (Cohen 1941, chap. 7; Parris 1969, chaps. 1–2). Both defects were seen as amenable to reform through the creation of an efficient, well-trained, permanent higher civil service (Mueller 1984, pp. 173–78).

Britain's imperialist interests within the international states system constituted another important pressure for the reform of state administrative practices. Beginning with the Napoleonic Wars and continuing through the disaster of the Crimean War, international military competition generated concerns about the ability of a patronage-dominated civil administration to cope with geopolitical realities. Closely connected with international military and economic competition, the maintenance of empire forced the consideration of the need for some reform, with the loss of America being credited to the incompetence produced by the patronage system, and fears for the stability of British rule in India (White 1935, pp. 5–6; Smellie 1950, pp. 69–70). Indeed, it was within the colonial administration that the merit system first succeeded. After twenty years of agitation by reformers, the Indian Service, led by the historian and civil servant Thomas Macaulay, instituted open competition for appointments in 1853, which was a precedent for and stimulus to reform in the home service (Moses 1914, chap. 2; Finer 1937, pp. 38–40).

Leading the fight against patronage and for bureaucratization and the introduction of the merit system of appointments were members of Britain's higher civil service and political leadership, supported by some educators (Hart 1972, p. 81; Mueller 1984, chap. 5; Shefter 1977, p. 435). The reformers' arguments were expressed in the 1853 report of a Treasury committee appointed by Gladstone, authored by Sir Stafford Northcote and Sir Charles Trevelyan, two high government officials, which advocated open competitive exams for all positions in the civil service (Moses 1914, pp. 68–70; Shefter 1977, p. 435; Mueller 1984, pp. 168–73; Hart 1972). Posts were to be graded, and a division between intellectual and mechanical labor introduced. For the superior posts, the exam would be based on academic subjects, so that access would be limited to those who received university training at Oxford and Cambridge, the sons of the gentry, aristocracy, and established members of the liberal professions (Mueller 1984, pp. 108–25, 210, 215).

The response to this initial reform proposal was lukewarm at best (Finer 1937, pp. 45–46; Moses 1914, pp. 72–89). In the House of Commons, it was unpopular because "it would deprive members of the advantage of putting their friends and relations into public offices," and there was disagreement within the Liberal Aberdeen cabinet as well (Smellie 1950, p. 71). An important source of opposition was the fear that open competition would undermine the predominance of gentlemen (the gentry, aristocracy, and professional upper-middle classes) in the civil service. The reformers and their supporters, however, argued that the opposite was true: the reforms would preserve, even strengthen, the hold of the elite on government positions (Mueller 1984, pp. 200–217). Along with several other experienced civil servants, Edwin Chadwick, the administrator connected with so many of the social reforms of the 1830s and 1840s and with the inspectorates they created, agreed that patronage should be abolished and an open competition for posts established. But Chadwick's group, along with some businessmen interested in civil service reform, preferred an exam based on the technical needs of government agencies, rather than on a "literary" education which would ensure the selection of gentlemen (Greaves 1947, pp. 31–35, 39–40; Mueller 1984, pp. 214–15).

Faced with such a mixed reception, the Northcote-Trevelyan proposals were not adopted. But the mismanagement exposed in the wake of the Crimean War and a flurry of agitation for reform of the government service along business lines by the Administrative Reform Association, organized by middle-class entrepreneurs, prodded the administration to take some action. In 1855 an Order in Council was issued, creating a relatively weak civil service commission and a "much diluted system of pass examinations," requiring only a minimum of competence from partisan appointees, rather than open competition (White 1935, p. 1; Moses 1914, p. 90).

Despite the initial failure of reform, the internal and international pressures for increased efficiency and elimination of patronage remained and were intensified by the political dissatisfaction generated as the demand for patronage began to outstrip supply. Finally, through an Order in Council in 1870, the merit system of open, competitive examinations for appointments was instituted in the British civil service. A two-tier exam was set up, with a test oriented to the academic education of gentlemen for the higher grade of positions and an exam geared to an "English" technical education similar to that envisioned by the Administrative Reform Association and Chadwick for the lower grades (Shefter 1977, pp. 436–37).

Why did reform succeed then? There was basically no popular or elite pressure at this point. The civil service reform movement had petered out in the wake of the ineffectual 1855 Order in Council, though patronage was alive and well when Gladstone became prime minister in 1868 (Mueller 1984, p. 219). But one critical political fact had changed: in the electoral reform of 1867, the British electorate moved from the "expanded oligarchy" created in the 1832 Reform Act to more substantial democracy, as some nine hundred thousand voters (an increase of 88 percent over the previous electorate) were added to the rolls (Smellie 1950, p. 327; Webb 1974, p. 207). Several authors have suggested that the 1867 electoral reform stimulated the concerns of elites that the civil administration, like the electorate, might be democratized (Mueller 1984, pp. 220–23; Burn 1965, pp. 255–65; Houghton 1957, p. 183). Given the social composition of English higher education at that time, "the 'conservative' implications of the civil service reform might have appealed . . . to an ever-widening circle of men who were worried about the democratizing effects of the second extension of the franchise" on the civil service (Mueller 1984, p. 221). To preserve the monopoly on the higher positions in the civil service enjoyed by the gentry and professional upper-middle classes, while allowing middle-class applicants in at lower levels, formerly disagreeing segments of elites came together behind the reform (Shefter 1977, pp. 436–37). Even though the concerns expressed by Chadwick and other administrators about the necessity of being able to get well-trained professionals for some technical positions were not directly addressed in the 1870 Order in Council, there remained the statutory option of recruiting some specialists "laterally" into such jobs. The Board of Trade and some other statistically oriented bodies took advantage of this (Davidson 1972, p. 245; Davidson and Lowe 1981, pp. 264–77; Cohen 1941, pp. 159–60).

State and Party after Civil Service Reform

Clearly, much of the importance of the British civil service reforms had to do with class politics. They permitted "gentlemen" to retain control of administrative positions as the electorate was democratized. One of the most critical effects of the reform of the civil service in terms of the later consideration of welfare reform proposals was the fact that after the 1870s British elites were no longer concerned with the issue of government patronage. The professionalization of government was accomplished, and the state was now available for new activities, when and if such activities were desired, without the fear—earlier expressed when new bodies, such as the Poor Law Commission, were established—that they would be used for political patronage purposes. The reforms also decisively enhanced the capacities of the British state by allowing for a more efficient bureaucratic reordering of the agencies that made up the civil administration and by bringing into the public service better-trained officials.[4] Historian Emmeline Cohen observed that "the Northcote-Trevelyan report . . . was concerned with reorganizing the Civil Service in such a way that there might be division of labour, the employment of men of different standards of education to perform different kinds of work, and the introduction of the merit system, to enable the best use to be made of able Civil Servants. Whilst appointments remained in the hands of political patrons, none of the other reforms could be implemented. . . . The Order in Council of 1870 not only checked an abused system, but also paved the way for departmental reorganization" (1941, pp. 122–23).

The reforms of the civil service also shaped the development of political parties. With the civil service credentialed after 1870, parties had no choice but to stop relying on elite patronage for electoral and financial support. New methods of raising funds and rewarding activists and new ways to win votes in the expanding electorate had to be, and were, devised. In the 1870s and 1880s, after some years of struggle with those forces that had benefited most from patronage, both the Liberal and Conservative parties created constituency organizations and began to formulate programs to appeal through activists to blocks of voters and financial subscribers (Hanham 1959; McGill 1962; Douglas 1971, pp. 1–17; Cornford 1963; Shefter 1977, pp. 438–41). The move toward programmatic appeals was reinforced by the adoption of the secret ballot in 1872, which made the traditional exercise of aristocratic influence over voters much more difficult to carry out (Clarke 1974, pp. 41–42), and by the earlier development of parliamentary discipline (Webb 1974, p. 399). The new, primarily urban (male) working-class voters were mobilized into politics by the Tories and Liberals on the basis of programmatic appeals. British workers had never enjoyed the fruits of the patronage system, and they came into politics in the 1867 and 1884 electoral reforms under the auspices of programmatically competing parties. Shefter notes that the way the linkage between a party and a social group "initially is established influences the character of the organization the party builds, and what it subsequently must do to hold onto its social base" (1977, pp. 414–15). The fact that the lines of enfranchisement became synonymous with class lines in the years between the 1832 Reform Act, which gave the vote to the middle classes, and the 1867 act, which gave the franchise to many workers, meant that British workers entered the electorate as a class, rather than merely as a set of individuals (see Katznelson 1985). These sequence-related factors—rather than the "strength of labor" in some abstract sense—

4. The morale of civil servants, often tried under the old methods (Parris 1969, pp. 65–66), was improved as well.

largely explain the tendency for British parties to focus on issues and collective appeals, and class-based ones at that, instead of patronage and distributional policies.

We now have a picture of the British institutional context, within which we can situate the politics of social policy. These involved working-class and new liberal reformers and politicians reacting against the cruelties, injustices, and inefficiencies of the poor law in the search for honorable social provision for the working-class aged. These political actors operated in a polity of programmatically competing parties against a backdrop of a state administrative apparatus with expanding capacities for social intervention, which could be influenced by a Parliament elected by a partially democratized electorate. To better understand the specifics of policy proposals to deal with old age dependency forwarded in Britain around the turn of the century, we will examine the political and administrative character of the existing policy legacy.

Policy Feedback: The Break with Poor Relief

The new poor law was the starting point of debates about social policy throughout the nineteenth century and into the early twentieth. Conditions and practices resulting from the campaign against outrelief formed the immediate backdrop for consideration of proposals for new public social provision for the aged. I have already suggested that the legacy of the poor law, as administered in the late nineteenth century, encouraged members of the working classes and some liberal elites to look for alternative forms of provision. I want here to concentrate on the political and administrative aspects of the poor law legacy, in order, first, to suggest how changing state administrative practices contributed to differential capacities on the part of authorities committed to the principles of less eligibility and the workhouse test to actually implement their policy preferences and, second, to fit the reaction to the poor law within the larger political changes of this period.

The Policy Legacy: The New Poor Law

The Poor Law Amendment Act of 1834 marked a critical turning point in British social administration and policy. The new poor law overturned the old administrative system, in which the key units were some fifteen thousand parishes and in which power resided with local officials: justices of the peace exercised general supervisory control, and overseers of the poor (local householders serving unpaid terms) provided for the destitute through the levying of mandatory poor rates (Heclo 1974, pp. 57–58). Under the new poor law, the local administrative units were six hundred poor law unions, each of which combined several parishes; the unions were run by boards of guardians elected by the ratepayers (Fraser 1979, p. 152). For the first time, effective policy-making was done on the national level, and local administration was centrally supervised, even as local financing and election of poor law officials continued. Indeed, Edwin Chadwick, the leading poor law reformer and coauthor of the influential 1834 report of the Royal Commission on the Poor Law, viewed the establishment of central authority as both the most radical and the most crucial of the commission's recommendations (Finer 1952). The very structure of welfare administration in the unitary British polity meant that tensions generated by the workings of the local workhouses, asylums, and sick wards, and by the implementation of other policies to deal with the poor, inevitably and recurrently generated pressures for *national* debates, investigations, and policy changes.

There had been national legislation in the past; the 1601 Elizabethan Poor Law (the "old poor law") and the 1662 Law of Settlement were the most important statutes. This legislation expressed national policy, but while the Elizabethan poor law was developed by the national monarchy, in the context of a European discussion of poor relief policy among a small, educated elite, in practice, policy had depended upon dispersed local elites, primarily the gentry, who had the administrative resources to implement the poor law which the central government did not. (Despite its relative lack of effectiveness in coordinating local policy, however, the Elizabethan legislation did establish secular as opposed to Church powers in poor relief.) In the first few decades after the 1601 statute, a centralizing trend did emerge, with national commissioners of the poor reviewing poor relief information from all over the country. But the English Civil War "decapitated not only Charles I but also this evolving central administration; the trunk, in the form of local justices of the peace and parish officials, was left intact to function with supreme authority" until the passage of the 1834 statute (Heclo 1974, p. 50).

The new poor law was instituted legislatively in 1834, but the actual administration of poor relief underwent considerable change and strengthening at the national level over the course of the century. In the 1830s there was vociferous popular resistance to the new poor law, especially to the proposal to deny outdoor relief to the able-bodied (Lubenow 1971, pp. 42–56; Fraser 1973, pp. 47–48). Local officials, too, resisted implementing the new law. They had an interest in protecting their ability to put poor relief to partisan use, through jobbing, manipulation of the list of ratepayers used in establishing the franchise, and so on. They were also responsive to taxpayers' concern with high rates, which especially applied to reluctance to build and adequately keep up workhouses, to say nothing of the separate institutions for different categories of paupers the poor law reformers of 1834 had envisioned (Roberts 1960, pp. 272–87).

The debates over the proposal for a central poor law body provoked concerns about its potential use in patronage politics, among other things. Some feared that the new Poor Law Commission (PLC) would be a significant source of new patronage (Fraser 1973, p. 45; Lubenow 1971, pp. 47–48). These fears, of course, reflected the condition of the political system, which in the 1830s was still organized primarily around patronage. But in fact, Chadwick, Nassau Senior, and the other poor law reformers were at the forefront of a Benthamite, rationalizing movement aimed at reforming not just the poor law, but all of government, and this meant that they opposed the continuation of the patronage system (Shefter 1977, p. 435). Chadwick was an early advocate of civil service reform, and he hoped to use the central administration to curb the powers and the "extravagant" spending of the local parish "jobocracies" (Lubenow 1971, pp. 61–63; Roberts 1960, p. 165). At Senior's urging, the PLC was set up as an independent body, so that it might escape the influence of party politics (Roberts 1960, p. 133). It was given the most extensive powers of all the agencies established during the early reform period, having the right to inspect, advise, and issue rules and regulations with the force of law and to order prosecutions. Neither the PLC nor the Poor Law Board (PLB), which replaced it in 1847, however, ever received sufficient inspectors or funds to carry out its tasks (Roberts 1960, pp. 120–23). It soon became clear that the central poor law authorities had neither the administrative resources nor the governmental backing to force compliance with the requirements of the law, particularly the ban on outdoor relief, leaving the administration of the new poor law looking very similar to that of the old (Rose 1981, p. 54; de Schweinitz 1961, p. 139). Indeed, resistance died down by the end of the 1840s (Roberts 1960, p. 117; Fraser 1973, p. 48; Heclo 1974, p. 61). The local administration of the poor law played an important part in the dominant patronage politics of the day, despite the attempts by Chadwick and other national officials in the PLC and PLB to prevent this.[5] Political parties vied for control over local poor law administration, not only because it was a significant source of patronage (Roberts 1960, pp. 40, 110, 162–65) but also because it afforded an opportunity to manipulate lists of eligible voters, which were based on the payment of poor rates (Fraser 1976).

It was not until the 1870s that the central poor law authorities finally managed to bring local practice into line with the guiding principles of the 1834 law and to curtail the use of the poor law for partisan advantage. Broader trends contributed to the increased ability of the national poor law officials to enforce their directives. First, with the demise of the patronage system, there was some

5. The Poor Law Commission had been set up as an independent body, but a series of scandals involving workhouse cruelties, tensions between the PLC and recalcitrant boards of guardians, and the continuing concern of legislators with control over poor law administration led Parliament to change the PLC into the Poor Law Board, the head of which sat in Parliament (de Schweinitz 1961, p. 138; Lubenow 1971, p. 32).

tendency in the 1870s toward consolidation and rationalization of the central agencies which had been established in the first half of the century (Roberts 1960, p. 95). In the case of poor law administration, the PLB was finally made a permanent department of state in 1867, after functioning on a five-year renewable basis. It was then combined with public health functions in the Local Government Board (LGB) in 1871 (Webb and Webb 1910, p. 146). The Webbs explained how this affected the LGB:

> The new establishment of the Central Authority on a permanent basis, no longer dependent on temporary statutes, but definitely one of the departments of the national executive, with its President more frequently than not a member of the Cabinet, really strengthened the authority and augmented the confidence with which it dealt with the boards of guardians. And this authority was in these years being fortified by the growth of an official staff, on a more permanent basis than the temporarily serving inspectors of a professedly temporary board. We are already conscious . . . of a growing firmness of touch and an increased consciousness of there being once more a deliberate policy, which the new department will strive to carry out and enforce. (1910, p. 146)

The LGB was also aided by the intellectual developments associated with the scientific charity movement. Orphans and the sick were removed from the workhouses in the 1860s and 1870s, partially in response to the development of the charity organization movement which focused on, and actually gave a considerable amount of aid to, these groups and others they considered to be "worthy." This in turn allowed the full implementation of the workhouse test, without fear that the "worthy" would suffer from a lack of anywhere else to go. The LGB, along with the Charity Organization Society, was thus free to mount a campaign against public outdoor relief, which was successful in that the proportion of the population receiving relief actually declined between 1870 and 1900 (Rose 1981, pp. 61–63; Heclo 1974, p. 62). It was the anti–outdoor relief campaign which, in addition to its substantive focus on implementing the policy precepts of the new poor law, finally subordinated local practices to national direction and represented the culmination of the efforts of national poor law administrators to rationalize and centralize social welfare policy which had continued since 1834 (Quadagno 1982, chap. 5; Rose 1981). The underlying individualist new poor law philosophy, now also influenced by social Darwinism, which recommended private charity for the worthy (and "salvageable") but only public poor law institutions for the undeserving, could be put into practice on a national scale, given the organizational strengthening of the LGB vis-à-vis the local boards of guardians.

The campaign against outrelief carried out by local poor law administrators in the 1870s, under pressure from the LGB, limited outdoor relief, even for the "impotent" aged. Thus, increasing proportions of elderly people, especially those without families or those whose kin could not be "stimulated" into supporting them with a threat of "the house," entered the semipenal workhouses (Anderson 1977; Quadagno 1982, chap. 5; Webb and Webb 1910, pp. 150–53, 229–30). In the 1890s greater awareness of the shockingly large proportions of old people in receipt of relief came through the survey work of Charles Booth and others (Simey and Simey 1960, pp. 161–68). If the poorhouse had been the fate only of elderly members of the "unworthy" poor, it seems that many middle- or upper-class politicians and reformers would not have been concerned. In fact, a large proportion of the formerly self-supporting, respectable, and enfranchised working poor and their spouses were being forced to turn to poor relief in their old age (Booth 1892, pp. 238–39; McGregor 1957; Simey and Simey 1960, p. 161). The fact that the likelihood of entering the workhouse increased with age (Booth 1894, p. 14) made it possible to focus on the conditions attendant upon age itself, rather than simply the "worthiness" of those older people who sought public relief. In addition, Booth argued that as the worthy aged crowded the relief rolls, administration could not deal properly with the "unworthy"; taking the worthy aged out of reach of the poor law allowed for "good administration" of the principles of the new poor law for those who remained on public relief (Booth 1892, pp. 169–80; Simey and Simey 1960, p. 161; Rose 1981, p. 62–63). But neither the objective level of need among the elderly nor increased middle-class awareness of the number of old people forced to turn to the poor law could alone have produced pension proposals.

It is worth remembering that poor relief could simply have been extended and/or the eligibility requirements softened, as more old people became needy. Indeed, the initial governmental responses to reformers' concern about the situation of the elderly in the 1890s was to investigate, then to improve, the conditions of poor relief for the "worthy aged poor," in effect implementing the new ideas about the worthiness of the aged to receive aid outside the realm of the workhouse test and less eligibility within the poor law itself (Collins 1965; Gilbert 1966, p. 195). The LGB issued circulars to this effect in 1896 and 1900; the latter called for "systematic and adequate outdoor relief" for all old people who were "destitute and deserving" and for the upgrading of the conditions of the indoor aged poor (Quadagno 1982, pp. 111–12). Certainly, there was nothing inherently impossible in a technical sense about transforming poor law institutions to carry out a nondeterrent policy toward the worthy poor, including the aged, sick, and orphans. Indeed, it might have been easier in some sense to utilize the existing administrative apparatus rather than to build new organizations. But this was not the course ultimately taken by British public policy.

The Reaction to the Poor Law

The reaction against the policy inheritance of the poor law, as an institution and an ideology, colored all suggestions for reform. In the poor law, the state provided a guarantee of sustenance, but one which by the end of the nineteenth century was no longer accepted as legitimate by key political actors (Collini 1979, pp. 107–9). The 1834 poor law "did its work of deterrence so well that threats to order could not be contained within it nor could such improvements as it was to make gain widespread popular confidence" (Fraser 1981, p. 29). New liberals opposed the poor law on the grounds that "relief carried the stigma of pauperism [which] vitiated its character as a true civic right" (Collini 1979, pp. 108–9). The conditions under which the poor escaped absolute destitution were, in the words of Lloyd George, a leading new liberal member of the administration which was responsible for the social reforms of 1906–14, "so harsh and humiliating that working class pride revolts against accepting so degrading and doubtful a boon" (quoted in Fraser 1973, p. 50). It was apparent to reformers like Booth, politicians such as Lloyd George, and many others that many elderly poor preferred starvation to accepting poor relief, with its concomitant disenfranchisement, degradation, and breakup of the family (Quadagno 1982, pp. 103–10, 184; Great Britain, Royal Commission on the Aged Poor 1895). Not only workers but also reformers who accepted the moral imperatives of new liberalism (Freeden 1978, pp. 200–206) or who feared for social order (McGregor 1957, p. 157) pressed the state to provide an alternative to poor relief, rather than an extension of it.

There were various suggestions for such alternatives, but all embodied the reaction against the policy inheritance of the poor law. This movement for reform also drew on international sources of intellectual reaction against the poor law and on foreign examples of programs (Hennock 1981). Avoiding the deterrence and degradation of the new poor law inherent in the principles of less eligibility and the workhouse test and in the requirement that recipients be disenfranchised was critical. Even if it had been possible to amend the poor law to remove these principles, the administration of poor relief was, for many reformers, tainted by the adherence of LGB personnel to these ideas. Indeed, by the 1890s, the LGB could be described as a "hostile citadel of poor law orthodoxy" (Heclo 1974, p. 173). There were two ways to accomplish the break from the poor law legacy: by making a pension program contributory, so that benefits were "earned," or by making pensions universal—a perquisite of citizenship rather than a dole for the needy—so that no stigma would attach to receiving them. From the 1870s on, both types of programs were proposed (Thane 1978; Gilbert 1966, chap. 4; Collins 1965). In formulating programmatic proposals, reformers also reacted to and drew on the experience of the major private alternative to poor relief: the friendly societies. The friendlies' actuarial deficiencies and less than universal coverage testified against the soundness of voluntary and/or contributory plans; those who needed protection the most—women, the unskilled, casual and agricultural laborers—were not covered and tended not to have the resources necessary to make contributions for future protection against poverty (Collins 1965, p. 251; Gilbert 1966, pp. 177–80). The problems of contributory plans in the eyes of reformers, combined with the opposition of the politically important friendly societies to contributory plans, meant that by the 1890s reformers converged on various versions of noncontributory pension systems (Collins 1965; Treble 1970; Emy 1972).

The issue by the turn of the century was under what auspices the reform of the treatment of the aged and the "worthy" poor would be introduced. The Conservatives—or at least their reform wing, led by Joseph Chamberlain—wanted to link social reform to tariff reform (the establishment of imperial preference and protective tariffs in place of the prevailing free trade) and to imperialism (through the imperial preference in the tariff and through building up the human resources at the core of the empire). Thus the tax base would be broadened through the imposition of indirect taxes on some essentials in order to pay for social reforms (Freeden 1978, p. 142). The new liberals proposed to link social reform with the traditional Liberal commitment to free trade. Reform would be financed through revenue measures that were themselves an integral part of social reform: a tax on the "unearned increment" on land sales and a graduated income tax (Freeden 1978, pp. 134–35, 143; Collini 1979, p. 105). Taxation according to one's ability to pay, along with an old age pension as a reward for a lifetime of industrial service, fit in with the reformers' notion of society as a network of mutual obligations.

By the later years of the nineteenth century, middle- and upper-class reformers felt that the civil administration which would handle the proposed pensions was sufficiently competent and honest to do the job. This confirms the importance of the sequencing of bureaucratization and democratization to policy developments. The potential political use of pension funds or administration was not an issue in the British debate over old age pensions, for the system of patronage and corruption which characterized the administration of the poor law along with other areas of government had been eliminated. After civil service reform, bureaucratic inertia might excite critical remarks about those areas of public service dealing with social issues (Davidson and Lowe 1981), but reformers did not worry about the "political" (i.e., corrupt) use of welfare programs (Heidenheimer 1973, p. 325). In general, government intervention in this area was deemed legitimate, honest, and competent. Political and cultural elites might debate the merits of particular forms and goals of state intervention, but the fundamental issue of whether or not any policy could be carried out efficiently and without corruption was settled.

A Cross-Class Alliance for Old Age Pensions

We are now in a position to see how the historical legacies of the new poor law, along with the state structure and party system in place by the early twentieth century, facilitated the enactment of old age pension legislation in 1908 and, indeed, all of the Liberal welfare reforms of 1906–11. From the 1890s onward, there was widespread dissatisfaction with the way the respectable aged poor were handled by existing poor law institutions. National politicians, Liberal and Conservative alike, became interested in reforming or replacing the new poor law to deal better with the problems of the "worthy poor" (Harris 1972; Collins 1965). Some of their concerns were generated from administrative dilemmas within established programs, as well as by the threat to the whole edifice of local government finance posed by the rising and uneven costs of the poor law (Hay 1975, p. 41). Other concerns arose from the obvious political fact that the votes of working-class men—and the support of their organizations, the unions and the friendly societies—had to be contested for by parties engaged in increasingly programmatic competition, especially after the friendlies withdrew their opposition to pensions and trade unions and their middle-class allies stepped up the campaign for pensions.

During the 1890s the voluntarist resistance of the friendly societies to pensions helped to delay new welfare breakthroughs, and then the Boer War of 1899–1902 provided political diversion and temporary financial excuses for avoiding new domestic expenditures (Gilbert 1966, pp. 179–88, 196). While in office from 1895 through 1905, the Tories failed to institute tariff or social reform, and the best they did for the aged poor was to improve their conditions under the poor law (Quadagno 1982, pp. 111–12). Then, after the war and the defeat of the Conservatives in the election of 1906, old age pension legislation and the other Liberal welfare reforms, which bypassed the new poor law without abolishing or fundamentally reforming it, achieved success along routes structured by the organization of the British state. In the face of the cross-class campaign waged by the National Committee of Organized Labour on Old Age Pensions, the Liberals devised their noncontributory and need-based old age pensions as a tool of programmatic competition with the Tories, who were still trying to woo voters with their combination of tariffs and social welfare spending. The Reverend Francis Stead, a founder and leader of the NCOL, wrote to Chancellor of the Exchequer (later prime minister) Herbert Asquith after the 1907 by-elections on the issue of pensions. Stead raised the specter of the desertion of propension forces to the Conservatives, for if the Liberals did not act soon, might people not "wonder whether any great Social Reform can be secured on a Free Trade basis?" (quoted in Gilbert 1966, pp. 218–19). The Liberals responded to the threat to their free trade priorities, as well as to their new liberal moral concerns, the electoral exigencies they faced, and the hope of reinforcing their alliance with the Labour Representation Committee, with the Old Age Pension Act of 1908. The Liberal administration called upon the Treasury Department to formulate proposals which would enable it to balance the concerns of the various constituencies interested in pensions in a politically acceptable way.

The 1908 pension act established noncontributory pensions, available to British citizens over the age of seventy who met the tests of their means and character. Almost all British pensioners (95 percent) qualified for the full pension of five shillings per week, the equivalent of about 22 percent of average annual earnings, but benefits were given on a sliding scale with an income limit of thirty-one pounds, ten shillings, or about one-half average annual earnings (Wisconsin Industrial Commission 1915, pp. 65–66; Ritter 1986, p. 155; Phelps Brown and Hopkins 1981, pp. 194–95; Thomson 1984b). Married persons received a pension at the same rate as single individuals (Gilbert 1966, p. 224). In addition, applicants had to pass a character test, which disqualified paupers, lunatics, those imprisoned within the last ten years, and those who had not been "habitually" employed in their given occupation (Gilbert 1966, p. 222). While the means test remained in effect during the life of this pension program, the character test was soon amended, then abolished in 1919 (Thane 1978, pp. 103–4). The pension reflected a "flat-rate egalitarianism" which was responsible for practically eliminating outdoor pauperism among the aged. Although the image of the worthy veteran of industry needlessly consigned to pass his dying years in the workhouse had helped to mobilize opinion against poor relief, the reality of indoor relief was that it aided those unable to care for themselves physically, and these aged veterans did not have an alternative to "the house" (Gilbert 1966, pp. 228–29).

Why was this the particular form chosen? Both of the major political parties were preparing to introduce pensions, almost certainly noncontributory ones, especially with so many working-class votes at stake. As we noted earlier, many business organizations did not favor social reform, but some promoted contributory old age insurance, as did a few reformers (Hay 1977; Thane 1978). Compulsory contributory schemes, however, were ruled out, given the lack of governmental collecting machinery and the hostility of the various working-class organizations, especially the friendlies, which might otherwise have served as alternative collection agencies (as did worker-managed benefit funds in Germany) (Heclo 1974, p. 175; Thane 1978; Ritter 1986).[6] Voluntary contributory pensions were championed only by the opponents of the new

6. The potential costs of entirely noncontributory programs for dealing with other hazards (e.g., sickness, unemployment) turned some new liberals, most prominently Lloyd George, to more active investigation of the German system of contributory insurances (Hennock 1981, pp. 85–86; Heclo 1974, pp. 196; Gilbert 1966, pp. 230–31).

liberal welfare reforms and of new liberalism generally: the Charity Organization Society, old liberals, and high civil servants from the LGB (Gilbert 1966,
pp. 217–20). These groups were not particularly influential with the Asquith
wing of the party and, further, were unable to ally with the friendly societies to oppose pensions (Gilbert 1966, p. 166). Finally, reformers preferred a
scheme which could deal with the situation of the neediest among the "worthy"
working class, as noncontributory pensions would and contributory schemes
inherently could not. While noncontributory pensions were embraced by the
new liberals and their labor allies, to make pensions universal would have been
prohibitively expensive; thus, the restriction of means-testing was acceptable
to the Liberal members of this coalition (Freeden 1978, p. 205). The financial
measures suggested by new liberal thinkers—a continuation and increase of
the existing income tax, originally instituted to pay for the Boer War; an added
supertax on high incomes; a duty on the capital value of undeveloped land; and
a tax on the unearned increment on land values levied whenever the land was
sold—were the centerpieces the 1909 reform budget of new liberal Chancellor
of the Exchequer Lloyd George (Webb 1974, pp. 459–60).

The New Liberal Achievement of Old Age Pensions

Stepping back to put this policy departure in broader context, it is important
to emphasize that in this period the administration of social spending was not
fundamentally problematic for British elites. The "corruption" of patronage
politics was behind them, and the state was considered a legitimate actor in
the realm of welfare policy-making and activity. Disputes now tended to focus
on levels and forms of spending, especially on direct versus indirect taxation
(Emy 1972). The Labour party was not yet a major actor in British politics,
and both Liberals and Conservatives were concerned with attracting and retaining working-class electoral support through programmatic party competition.
Pensions looked like a good way to circumvent for the respectable aged poor
the cruelties, inefficiencies, and costs of the new poor law. Such a policy also
looked like an appropriate program to appeal to the working class, involving
them more fully in the life of a united nation, yet under the hegemony of enlightened, professional middle-class leadership. *The Nation,* an organ of the
new liberals, in a 1907 editorial, "Pensions and the Poor Law," captured the
essence of this motivation: "Poor relief is a state recognition of the duty of
succoring those who fall by the wayside of life. . . . Its concern is with men and
women who at the best are failures. . . . The proposal of old age pensions starts
from a totally different principle. It is a recognition at once of the *solidarity* of
society, and of the actual economic situation produced by the play of industrial
forces in the modern world" (quoted in Freeden 1978, p. 203). The adoption

of pensions helped to gain for the Liberals sufficient backing among working-class and reform groups to move forward with contributory unemployment and health insurance. This group of programs has come to be called the Liberal welfare reforms and is recognized as the beginning of Britain's system of modern social provision (Hay 1975; Gilbert 1966).

7

The United States, 1880–1920

From the Great Barbeque to Modern
Social Politics

Socioeconomic and sociocultural trends common to all the countries of the
North Atlantic Triangle—the development of problems of income interruption in a population increasingly dependent on wagework, of new ideological
resources to justify state action to deal with these problems, and of popular
political pressures for such state action—brought new pension and social insurance proposals onto the political agenda in the early-twentieth-century United
States. Large proportions of the aged and their families in the United States
were adversely affected by the character of public provision in the late nineteenth century. By the 1880s outdoor relief was severely restricted in many
areas, and although Civil War pensions held out the promise of security to some
elderly Americans, many others were denied protection. The political reaction
to this policy legacy was in many ways similar to that in Britain: working-class
organizations and voters favored pensions, and elite and popular intellectual
and political figures denounced the poor law and developed new liberal understandings of individuals' right to honorable social provision in old age. Yet in
contrast with the situation in Great Britain, U.S. reform elites during the Progressive Era were unwilling to work with popular forces toward the initiation
of social insurance or pension programs for the aged. Indeed, the absence of a
cross-class coalition for social spending was the proximate cause of the failure
of pensions in this period. But my argument goes beyond specifying that class
forces must come together in an alliance for social spending.

My explanation for the failure of pension legislation in the Progressive Era
United States is twofold. First, social policy developments in the Progressive
Era were constrained by the structural and institutional legacies of state formation. These legacies made the achievement of social policy reform dependent
upon the mobilization of very broad coalitions, which in turn amplified the
concerns of elite and middle-class reformers and the broad political public.
Second, given the importance of these actors to the formation of reform alli-

ances, reactions to the character of the state and to the policy legacy shaped the fate of specific policy proposals during the Progressive Era.

U.S. state formation resulted in a state apparatus even less developed than its British counterpart and more fragmented through structural features such as federalism and the division of power. Continuing "underdevelopment" of the civil administration through the nineteenth and early twentieth centuries may be traced to the distinctive character and sequence of the great political transformations of the nineteenth century in America: full democratization of the electorate preceded the bureaucratization of the civil administration in the absence of an institutionalized coalition for bureaucratic autonomy. Moreover, the American "Revolution Settlement" left the South—a consistently important force against the development of a strong and autonomous federal bureaucracy—in a politically dominant position through the Civil War, and with a disproportionately strong position in the Congress and the Democratic party even after. (Southern influence in the Democratic party was particularly significant for social policy developments during the New Deal.) In the latter half of the nineteenth century, the United States, like Britain, experienced pressures for the expansion of national administrative capacity stimulated by industrialization, urbanization, and the exigencies of international economic and military competition—and for increased governmental efficiency, honesty, and professionalization. But the mass-based patronage system of the United States proved more difficult to uproot than the still-elitist British patronage system when confronted by similar pressures for administrative change. Thus, civil service reforms remained stalemated into the early twentieth century.

The character of the state and political system closed off certain routes by which social policy initiatives were introduced in other countries and imposed particular exigencies on those mobilizing for policy reform. In this regard, of particular importance was the lack of an autonomous civil administration and the general underdevelopment of state capacities, for there were not well-placed bureaucrats to propose policy innovations in the American polity. Political parties in this period were not programmatic in orientation with leaders looking for new programs to attract expanding constituencies, as was the case in Britain and much of continental Europe. Rather, they were patronage parties with an already-mobilized popular following. Indeed, reforms in the United States in this period typically came not from underdeveloped American bureaucracy or from the parties, but through the support of broad coalitions of interest groups, who pressed reform upon state legislatures. Moreover, the fragmentation of sovereignty imposed by the division of power and federalism meant that reform coalitions had to be especially wide and well-mobilized in order to be successful across most of the states and to overcome possible constitutional obstacles. Thus, critical to understanding the fates of different reform proposals was whether or not cross-class coalitions formed to press for them, and the concerns of elites and the middle classes—who would be crucial to any such coalitions—were especially important. Proposals for new social spending initiatives for the aged were made at the very moment when the mass-based patronage party system of America was in the midst of a crisis over the character of its transformation. This was a singularly unpromising conjuncture for the extension of new state activities requiring substantial new resources, the control of which could provoke struggles between opposing political factions or fears over their potential use.

The second part of the argument concerns the orientations of elites and the broad middle-class public toward social provision. Given that the political context gave such importance to broad mobilization for reform, why were these groups less than willing to support initiatives for the extension of social spending for the aged, in contrast with their counterparts in Great Britain? Their hostility to social spending for the aged, I argue, was based on their general reactions to the character of the civil administrations of the federal and state governments, which remained patronage-dominated, and on reactions to the specific U.S. policy legacy, politically expanded Civil War pensions and patronage-dominated poor relief. Elites and the middle classes developed political orientations in the general context of struggles between civil service and patronage and were thus influenced by the lack of government capacities to administer new social programs. Reactions to the policy legacy informed specific policy preferences. Both poor relief and Civil War pensions were entangled with the workings of patronage democracy. Local control of poor relief typically offered patronage politicians a rich store of resources, and the "expert professionals" who had the confidence of elites and the middle class were rarely if ever employed in public poor relief systems. The Civil War pension system had been turned into a de facto old age pension system for hundreds of thousands of elderly Americans, but its administration, too, was embroiled in the operations of patronage politicians. Reformers saw politicians and politically appointed administrators baldly purchasing the votes of beneficiaries with the expansion of benefits and manipulation of pension administration and worried about the potential for similar corruption in any new social spending schemes for the aged. In essence, they feared a reprise of the nation's experience with Civil War pensions. Thus, processes of policy feedback not only reflected concerns about the problems associated with poor relief for the working classes but also created reactions against the potential political consequences of the administration of social programs.

State Formation in the United States

The American state in the early nineteenth century was in many ways different from its European counterparts. The federal government was relatively small, "a midget institution in a giant land," to use John Murrin's words, and the army and navy, too, were far smaller relative to the population than British and Continental forces (Murrin 1980, p. 425). And "if the percentage of a government's revenue derived from internal sources or direct taxes can serve as a reasonable though crude indicator of its power and influence, the United States did not reach the level of eighteenth-century Britain until fifty years ago" (Murrin 1980, p. 429). While European states were concentrating and centralizing sovereignty, power in the United States was divided among territorial units and among the three branches of government (Huntington 1968). According to Stephen Skowronek, "The most striking operational characteristics of early American state organization were a radical devolution of power accompanied by a serviceable but unassuming national government. The national government throughout the nineteenth century routinely provided promotional and support services for the state governments and left the substantive tasks of governing to these regional units. This broad diffusion of power among the localities was the organizational feature most clearly responsible for the distinctive sense of statelessness in our political culture" (1982, pp. 22–23).

Indeed, the national government "had almost no internal functions except the postal system and the sale of Western lands" (Murrin 1980, p. 425). While a "highly developed democratic politics without a concentrated governing capacity made early America the great anomaly among Western states," it is important not to exaggerate American exceptionalism (Skowronek 1982, p. 8). In its legal supports for democracy and capitalism, the American state represented a pattern that would come to characterize all Western states. It "maintained an integrated legal order on a continental scale; . . . fought wars, expropriated Indians, secured new territories, carried on relations with other states, and aided economic development" (Skowronek 1982, p. 19). Thus, the analysis of American state formation is amenable to the same analytic strategies that are applied to the patterns of state-building in other, more visibly statist, countries. But while the analytic elements are the same, their articulation in the United States was distinctive.

In an insightful article, John Murrin (1980) has highlighted some of the unique features of American state formation, as this was given institutional embodiment in the "Revolution Settlement," that is, the outcomes of the American Revolution up to about 1815, when political and institutional arrangements had stabilized and certain institutional options were permanently foreclosed. The American "Revolution Settlement" was in some ways similar to the British, but, Murrin argues, "the two Revolutions came out so differently that the result, to steal a phrase from R. R. Palmer, might well be called America's 'Great Inversion' of England's Revolution Settlement" (1980, p. 411). British and North American politics in the sixteenth through eighteenth centuries were shaped by struggles, largely among competing elites, which many have characterized as "court" and "country," over state-building. "Court" forces favored active central government by the monarchy and associated appointed officials, a bureaucracy loyal to the king, and a standing army—a state on the model of European absolutism. "Country" forces tended to oppose these institutions out of concerns that strong, unchecked central power might undermine their local power (Jones 1978; Murrin 1980, p. 379; Stewart 1986, p. 11). In Britain, the court won; things turned out differently in the United States (see also Huntington 1966). As Murrin puts it, "Only in America did anti-Court forces, so conspicuous in their resistance to the war-making needs of European states between 1550 and 1789, win and retain possession of a central government, designed by its framers, ironically enough, to make the United States competitive with other powers. After 1801, they kept statist impulses in check" (1980, p. 428). Why was the American experience of state formation different from the British and European? Let us turn to a more systematic inventory of the factors which shaped that experience—the position of the United States within the world system of states and the world economy, and domestic economic, social, and political arrangements.

The United States in the International States System and World Economy

The American colonies, were, of course, initially extensions of the English state. Thus, they were affected by the character of English politics, the capacities of the English state, and the interstate warfare in which English interests were involved. Much as England's opportunities to become a great power emerged from the decline of Spanish hegemony in the seventeenth century, so the opportunity for the American colonies to unite into a new state emerged from Britain's inability to control internal colonial affairs. Indeed, Bailyn (1968) has argued that the colonial assemblies grew strong and autonomous because British-appointed governors had insufficient patronage and financial resources to "manage" them reliably, as the Crown and prime minister managed Parliament at home. Murrin also notes the limits on the capacity of the British Parliament to govern the internal affairs of the colonies and argues that "at one level . . . the American Revolution was a crisis in imperial *integration* which London simply could not handle" (1980, p. 387).

The geopolitical position of the American colonies, and later the United States, was of great significance for the character of state-building. Like England itself, North America was profoundly shaped by the wars between the English and French states. The physical separation from Europe by the Atlantic left America relatively well protected from the threat of war, which was endemic in Europe (Woodward 1960, p. 2). Britain's military and administrative capacities were overtaxed by the tasks of governing the American colonies, at least partly because its resources were called upon to defend its interests against the French in Europe. After Britain drove France from North America in the 1760s, Britain attempted to improve imperial control over the colonies, but it was too late. Indeed, the attempt helped to drive the colonies into a unified rebellion (Bailyn 1968; Murrin 1980, pp. 388–97). French involvement in the American Revolution, of course, helped to defeat Britain. Then French-British conflicts shifted to European soil with the coming of the French Revolution and the Napoleonic Wars, leaving the United States with some "breathing space" in which to consolidate its control over territory and to develop stable and workable governmental institutions. Murrin (1980, pp. 411-14), following a "Tillyesque" line of argument, asserts that "the contrasting pattern of international involvement" of the United States and England was critical to the distinctive outcomes of their revolution settlements. He notes that in the years following the Glorious Revolution, 1689 to 1714, England was at war with France in all but six. When the United States did go to war, "many of the pressures that had transformed England after 1689 appeared instantly in America: an enlarged army, a small but proficient navy, and internal revenues . . . plus improved coastal defenses and a new Bank of the United States." In contrast with the British experience, however, "the United States remained at peace in all but six years from 1789 to 1815" (Murrin 1980, p. 411). Murrin also notes that domestic factors pressured governing elites to keep out of "foreign entanglements": "Because America's political antagonisms had a strong sectional base, protracted war with any great power would almost certainly have destroyed the fragile Union long before it could have transformed itself into a modern state, which, in the world of 1800, meant above all a govenment able to fight other governments effectively for an indefinite period" (Murrin 1980, pp. 411–12).

In the immediate aftermath of the American Revolution, Britain's most vital interests centered on the European balance of power, and internal affairs in North America were of decidedly less concern. But in the first decade of the nineteenth century, Britain's customary sources of raw materials in Europe were cut off due to the Napoleonic wars. In this context, the defense of remaining British territory, an alternate source of needed materials, against American citizens interested in continental expansion assumed new importance. Along with this, conflicts over oceanic carrying trade, aggravated by the French-British war, spilled into the final British-American military contest, the War of 1812 (Brebner 1945, chap. 5). The war ended in military stalemate; Americans could not be forced out of their territory or denied access to the British mercantile empire, but the British did keep their territory in North America safe from American depredations. After the Treaty of Ghent, Americans and the colonists who would become Canadians both profited from the British tie—informal in the case of the United States, formal in the colonies which would become Canada (Brebner 1945, chap. 6).[1] Friendly relations with Great Britain, the world's hegemonic military and economic power, allowed the United States to refrain from involvements in war, which threatened national unity, and to turn its attention inward, to territorial and economic expansion.[2]

Released from much of the stimulus to build up its armed forces that wars provided the European states, the American state was under much less pressure to develop state administrative, extractive, and repressive capacities. Nor did the position of the United States in the world economy call forth such development. Certainly America was never the "night watchman" state of laissez-faire mythology, but the United States confronted fewer obstacles to economic development than did the world's late industrializers, including Canada. Thus, dominant classes demanded less from the state (Laxer 1989, p. 59; Gerschenkron 1962). On friendly terms with the world's only industrial power at the time, Britain, and separated from European conflicts geographically, Americans were free to industrialize, drawing on their abundant resources and large internal market (North 1966).

Domestic Economic, Social, and Political Arrangements

Conditions internal to the United States also contributed to the undermining of court-style arrangements and to the fragmentation of sovereignty and development of a limited central state. The U.S. state was formed in violent reaction to the sorts of states that had emerged in Europe, as American revolu-

---

1. In his classic study *The North Atlantic Triangle: The Interplay of Canada, the United States and Great Britain*, historian John Brebner notes, "At bottom, in 1823, Great Britain and the United States found themselves in agreement, both against the Holy Alliance and Metternichian legitimism, and in defense of the Spanish-American colonies which had proclaimed their independence during and after the Napoleonic wars. Their motives may have been mixed and rather highly colored by hopes of commercial advantage for both, of security for British investments, and of territorial advantage for the United States, but the ruling circumstance was their agreement against the reactionary European powers. Great Britain had a navy which could bar the seas, and the United States was rapidly transmuting her original foreign policy of neutrality into the equally congenial and self-defensive principle of denying the right of European powers to intervene in the affairs of the Americas. . . . once sure the British navy would put real teeth in an otherwise rather empty assertion" (1945, pp. 106–7).

2. C. Vann Woodward (1960, p. 2) has commented on the "free security" Americans enjoyed in the nineteenth century, "based on nature's gift of three vast bodies of water [the Atlantic, Pacific, and Arctic oceans] interposed between this country and any other power that might constitute a menace to its safety." He notes that other states were forced to extract and use extensive resources in order to obtain security. Further, he draws attention to the role of the British navy in America's security: "The costly navy that policed and defended the Atlantic was manned and paid for by British subjects for more than a century, while Americans enjoyed the added security afforded without added cost to themselves."

tionaries called upon "country" ideology to justify their struggles with Britain (Skowronek 1982, pp. 20–21; Murrin 1980; Bailyn 1968). The Articles of Confederation were superseded by a Constitution that provided the federal government with some critical functions, such as the power to levy taxes and conduct relations with foreign states. But the architects of the American Constitution deliberately diffused sovereignty among the states, localities, and the federal government, while further checking any centralizing tendencies at the federal level with the division of powers. Even so, in the years following the Revolution, court forces did not simply dissolve. One segment of American political elites, the Federalists, promoted many institutional innovations that worked to overcome this diffusion of power and tended toward the development of a centralized state on the European model: "To Alexander Hamilton and his Federalist followers, Independence freed America to become another Great Britain" (Murrin 1980, p. 405). For example, "for a time the leverage provided by the debt gave Hamilton a virtual placeman system for controlling Congress under a 'prime minister'—creating, in effect, a national faction" similar to those managed by British political leaders (Murrin 1980, p. 410). But these forces were defeated in the election of 1800 by anti-Federalist "country" forces, the Democratic Republican party, led by Thomas Jefferson. The Democratic Republicans remained in power for an extended period, and in its formative years, the American state was deflected from a European-type trajectory of increasing centralization.

Quite simply, the domestic balance of power tended toward the same result as did America's lack of involvement in war; indeed, the two factors reinforced each other. After the Revolution, social, economic, and regional conflicts within the new nation became connected with the political tension between court and country (Murrin 1980). "Country" forces, groups opposed to a centralized state with extensive extractive and repressive powers, were stronger than the Federalists, America's political embodiment of "court" forces. While both Federalists and Democratic Republicans constituted "parties of notables," to use Martin Shefter's term, the former relied on a much narrower social base, the nation's small mercantile elite of the New England and Mid-Atlantic coastal regions (Shefter 1978, pp. 214–18). The Democratic Republicans were "grounded upon a much larger segment of the nation's upper class," and more significantly, "they were prepared to appeal to mass support" in order to defeat the Federalists (Shefter 1978, p. 217). Thus, both commercial farmers of the South and subsistence farmers from across the new country were mobilized against the Federalists' program of building up the powers of the central government. Popular forces were in a relatively powerful position in the new society due to wide property ownership, cultural egalitarianism, readily available land and employment, and military mobilization during the Revolution and the War of 1812. The southern states were "the regional home of Country principles," and the dominant classes of those states were among their strongest proponents; the presence of the South in the United States is critical to explaining the contrasting outcomes of English and U.S. revolution settlements (Murrin 1980, pp. 404, 426; see also Bensel 1984). In the face of country predominance of the federal government, court forces retreated into the judicial system and to state and local levels of government in regions most important to them, where influence could easily be wielded (Murrin 1980, p. 427).

The American Polity in the Nineteenth Century

A coalition for bureaucratic autonomy could not gain a foothold in the United States, as neither court nor country forces were interested in an independent federal administration. Patronage, either based on local networks or political orientation, was accepted by almost all political actors. The Democratic Republicans had mobilized popular support to defeat the Federalists and to prevent the development of a European-style centralized state, but they turned away from such strategies once their position was secure and staffed the administration with loyal notables (White 1951). Thus, the government drew upon informal community networks and hierarchies (Shefter 1978, pp. 217–18; Goodman 1967; William Chambers 1963). But by the 1820s the Jacksonian Democrats, pursuing a political strategy of mass mobilization to defeat the previously dominant Federalists and Democratic Republicans, fully democratized the franchise for white men and built the first mass constituency parties (Williamson 1960). As part of their program of displacing previously dominant elites, the Jacksonians opened the civil administration to the "spoils system" to solidify their hold on the administration (Shefter 1978, pp. 214–25; see also White 1954; Crenson 1975). Parties emerged as the preeminent political institutions of this period, and the spoils system gave them control over the civil administration and offered a way to reward their cadres and followers as they swept into and out of office in the constant rounds of close-fought elections characteristic of nineteenth-century American democracy before and after the Civil War (McCormick 1966a; Keller 1977).

Indeed, Stephen Skowronek has characterized the United States of the nineteenth century as a "state of courts and parties" (1982, chap. 2). Parties and, to a lesser extent, courts offered political officials a way to coordinate and integrate the functions of different levels and branches of government, given the "broad dispersion of governing power" inherent in the structure of American government. Parties "routinized administrative procedures with patronage recruitment, spoils rotation, and external controls over the widely scattered post offices, land offices and customhouses. Local party organizations were tapped to staff these local federal offices and to oversee their operations" (Skowronek 1982, p. 25). Because parties could rely on patronage to cement ties to their followers, they did not develop programmatic orientations (Shefter 1977). U.S. parties represented only the most general policy preferences and ethnocultural identities (McCormick 1979; Skowronek 1982, p. 26; Lowi 1967). The courts, which played a secondary role vis-à-vis parties until after the Civil War, were important in "defining terms of intergovernmental activity . . . [and] the relations between state and society" (Skowronek 1982, p. 27).

The Civil War is the one episode in nineteenth-century American history which we might well expect would have brought change to the state of courts and parties, if, indeed, war is the mother of states. "The war had brought national military conscription, a military occupation of the South, a national welfare agency for former slaves, a national income tax, national monetary controls." Yet because the "state's power was rooted in the new Republican organization and its capacity to channel the actions of governing elites," state officials did not develop as autonomous agents but remained first and foremost representatives of the party (Skowronek 1982, p. 30). Thus, partisan concerns dominated, and as the South reentered the Union, the state returned to its prewar mode of operation. Thus, the late-nineteenth-century American polity was characterized by a lack of an autonomous federal bureaucracy, localism, division of powers, and a distrust of the activist state (Shade 1974). As the state institutional apparatus was reduced while the challenges of industrialization mounted, the courts emerged as regulators of social and economic life (Keller 1977, pp. 355–56, 360–61, 369–70). In that role, the judiciary came to constitute an important institutional barrier to reform in the early twentieth century.

The late-nineteenth-century U.S. polity was characterized by extremely high levels of popular mobilization. Relative to Europe, it was an extremely democratic political system (Burnham 1982, chaps. 1, 4). In contrast with the political exclusion of their British counterparts, working-class white males in America were mobilized into politics by the dominant parties from the 1830s on, and as an industrial working class emerged in the years after the Civil War, workers found the franchise already open to them (Katznelson 1981, 1985; Shefter 1986; Bridges 1986). The early democracy of the United States left relatively less political space for the formation of class-based parties than the more elite-dominated polities of continental Europe, Britain, and even Canada. Party competition and patronage democracy were at their heights in the years between the end of Reconstruction and 1896, when the so-called third party system existed (Kleppner 1979). Morton Keller has argued that "the passionate, ideologically charged political ambience of the Reconstruction years gave way to a politics that rested on the perpetuation of party organization rather than the fostering of public policy" (1977, p. 238). Parties relied on sociocultural rather than ideological appeals and, above all, on patronage and other

distributional policies to mobilize their constituencies. Thus, the entire system worked best at all levels when governmental outputs took the form, not
of programs devised to appeal to functionally organized collectivities, but of
politically discretionary distributional policies, such as financial subsidies or
grants of land, tariff advantages, special regulations or regulatory exceptions,
construction contracts and public works jobs (McCormick 1979). Ideal sets of
distributional policies combined measures that raised revenues or created jobs
with those that allocated them.

Transformations of State and Party, 1880–1920: Attempts at Civil Service Reform and the Persistence of Patronage

Late-nineteenth-century patronage democracy effectively mobilized broad
popular support, but it also produced serious opposition. Populists and labor
groups denounced the links between politicians and the "robber barons," the
capitalists dominating the economy through their control of railroads, manufacturing, and banking, newly national in scope. At the same time, university-
educated professionals and some businessmen criticized especially the "corruption" and "inefficiency" of the personnel practices of the spoils system.
They were dissatisfied as well with the kinds of policies fostered by patronage democracy, which, they charged, lacked any justification in terms of the
"public interest." Instead, noted critics, the development of American public
policy was above all tied to the partisan political exigencies of winning elections. These exigencies did not all preclude—in fact, probably stimulated—
out-and-out corruption and fraud. Even the normal functioning of the patronage system was coming under fire as "political corruption." For example,
the chairman of the committee on the merit system in public institutions of
the National Conference of Charities and Correction, America's leading association of charity workers and social reformers in the late 1800s, forcefully
challenged the rationale and practices of the spoils system, calling that system "treasonable robbery, although not treason in the eyes of the law" (Garret
1896, p. 369).

The "state of courts and parties" came under tremendous pressures for
change from the 1880s on. Indeed, civil service practices began to replace
patronage, and more thoroughly rationalized and bureaucratized organizations
did emerge in the years between the Pendleton Act (America's first national
civil service legislation passed in 1883) and 1920. But the struggle to replace
patronage was profoundly influenced by the existing structure of institutions
and modes of political mobilization. Civil service reformers fought against
patronage, which meant that they fought against democratically rooted political organizations, particularly in the Northeast and Midwest (Shefter 1983),

but their success was very limited. Both the outcome and the timing of the struggles between patronage and civil service practices proved fateful for social policy developments.

Pressures for Administrative and Political Reform

Industrialization and urbanization stimulated institutional growth in American governments, as they had earlier in Britain. U.S. government employment almost quintupled in the thirty years between 1871 and 1901, rising from 53,000 to 256,000 (Skowronek 1982, p. 49). State governments passed factory, social welfare, and public health legislation analogous to the British Factory Acts and public health laws, which in turn led to the expansion of state government employment and functions (Birch 1955, pp. 147–48; Whittlesey 1901; Yellowitz 1965, pp. 10–13; Brandeis 1935).[3] But as the United States became a truly national economy and society in the decades after the Civil War, problems faced by public policymakers challenged the distributional style of patronage democracy, and vociferous demands emerged for civil service reform of both state and federal administrations. The increasing size of government service, along with broader social trends favoring professionalization generally (Haskell 1977; Furner 1975), contributed to pressures for civil service reform in the United States, as they had in Britain and throughout the industrializing West (Skowronek 1982, pp. 4, 42–45; Mueller 1984, pp. 181–83, 188–97).

The initial proponents of ending patronage through civil service reform in the United States were mugwumps, upper- and upper-middle-class reformers located in the Northeast, especially New York and Massachusetts. Like the successful British civil service reformers of the 1870s, the mugwumps wanted public administration taken out of patronage politics, so that expertise and predictability could prevail (Schiesl 1977, chap. 2; Shefter 1978). At first, however, the mugwumps' reform proposals made only limited headway, for American party politicians had secure roots in the fully democratized, tautly mobilized, mass white male electorate. As Stephen Skowronek has pointed out in his study of American state-building, "to build a merit system in American government, government officers would have to move against resources and procedures vital to their power and position" (1982, p. 68).

---

3. An important exception to the rule of economic regulation taking place at the subnational level in America was the field of railroad regulation, which, because of its essentially interstate character, had to be dealt with at the federal level of government. In addition, this area of regulatory activity was closely linked to that federal activity which was most well developed in this period of American history: the underwriting of national economic development through the financing of railroads, sale of lands, protective tariffs, and so on (Keller 1977, chaps. 8, 10–11). These activities were accomplished largely through distributional policies which fit in well with the proclivities of the existing political system.

Through the last quarter of the nineteenth century, the conflict between politicians and the various good government reformers resulted in overall defeat for the mugwumps. Following the extremely close presidential election of 1880 and the patronage-related assassination of President James Garfield, the Republican administration of Chester Alan Arthur and the GOP-controlled Congress in early 1883 approved the establishment of the Civil Service Commission under the Pendleton Act, largely to avoid losing the mugwumps' votes (Shefter 1978, p. 228; Van Riper 1958, pp. 116–18). Analysts agree that the impact of the law was quite limited; Skowronek notes that it dried up "selected pockets of patronage so as to improve efficiency and, at the same time, serve strategic party goals . . . [it] supplemented the dominant patronage relationship rather than supplanting it" (Skowronek 1982, pp. 68–69). In fact, because of the growth in federal employment, a larger number of jobs was available for patronage by the end of the century than there had been before the passage of the Pendleton Act, even with the growth in the proportion of classified (i.e., civil service) jobs. Reformers continued to find fault with patronage practices even after the Pendleton Act became law. For example, the Committee on Politics in Charities and Correctional Affairs was formed within the National Conference of Charities and Correction in 1896. It functioned through the late 1890s and into the early 1900s, focusing on the problems created in public welfare administration by the spoils system (National Conference of Charities and Correction 1896, pp. 368–98; 1898, pp. 237–63; 1902, pp. 324–42).

Not until the first decades of the twentieth century did administrative reform make significant headway in America. In the Progressive Era United States, social demands for reforms in government broadened from the elite mugwumps to include the growing ranks of the educated, professional middle class and, in many places, farmers and organized labor as well (Wiebe 1967, chap. 5; Buenker 1973, chap. 6). In the newly noncompetitive political situation ushered in by the realigning election of 1896, there was increased freedom for officials in the executive branch, especially the president, to move against patronage practices and to establish bureaucratic organizations useful to augmenting executive power (Skowronek 1982, chap. 6; Van Riper 1958, chaps. 8–10). Given the power of the machine politicians, especially at the local level, it was not an easy battle.

By 1920 patronage at the national level had been curbed. Over 70 percent of the executive branch civil service was under the merit system (Skowronek 1982, p. 210). But although some positions in state, local, and federal governments were removed from the spoilsmen, patronage practices continued at all levels of government. For example, traditional storehouses of patronage positions like the postal service were almost untouched by reform (Van Riper 1958, pp. 236–37, 337–38). Some states—Wisconsin, California, and a few others—successfully eliminated patronage, but only ten states had passed civil service legislation by 1920, and the legislation was ineffective in most (Klein 1940, p. 42; Abbott 1936, p. 403). In the Northeast and Midwest, where patronage party machines had put down strong popular roots, reformers were unable to dislodge them (Shefter 1983; Munro 1929, pp. 69–70). Even with the partial successes of civil service reform at the federal level, the development of state administrative capacities was constrained: the new bureaucratic organizations were soon caught in a new, constitutional conflict between Congress and the executive over their control, and the executive was unable to rely on them to carry out programs and policies which might conceivably be promised by his party (Skowronek 1982, p. 204, and chap. 6; Grodzins 1960).

Civil Service Reform in Britain and the United States

In the United States, as in Britain, a number of pressures contributed to a movement for civil service reform. Success was longer in coming, and less complete, however, than it had been in Britain. In both countries, civil service reform was a question of incorporating technical efficiency in the old civil service as well as a struggle over power and authority. In the United States, though, the professional middle class was outside the state and had to fight the party politicians, with their strong base among the enfranchised masses, to gain access to and control over the civil administration. This contrasted with the situation in Britain, where professionals and gentry could come to an agreement with the entrepreneurial middle classes to preserve their monopoly access to civil service positions. Professionalization was a political strategy of the middle classes in both the United States and Britain. Yet in Britain it was a defensive strategy aimed at solidifying the control they already exercised in the face of a potential threat by newly enfranchised lower classes, while in the United States it was an offensive strategy to gain access to positions in the civil administration then controlled by mass-based party machines.

Administrative historian Leonard White's comparison of civil service reform in Britain and the United States follows the line of argument I have presented. White provides a useful summary:

> The transition in Great Britain from patronage to merit was favored by two facts neither of which existed in this country [the United States] at the same period. There was in Great Britain no strongly organized political party with local branches scattered over the country and maintained in order and discipline by the expectation of mass distribution of patronage as the result of success in a national election. The corollary is that the number of persons who were affected by the change from patronage to merit was relatively exceedingly small, as was also the number of persons who had to be convinced that the change was desirable. Tacit agreement

of the leaders was sufficient, without the necessity of carrying along the rank and file of an organized and effective party machine. (1935, pp. 6–7)

White goes on to note the effect of the "rising tide of democracy" on leaders' perceptions of the relative merits of patronage and the merit system, a factor not operative in the American context (1935, p. 7). English historian K. B. Smellie argued that because full democracy had not yet been achieved in Britain at the time civil service reform was being considered by elites, reform was able to achieve relatively complete success: "The very slowness with which, in England, democratic government was substituted for aristocratic privilege made possible the success of our [elite] civil service. It was rescued from private patronage without becoming public spoils. . . . A sudden introduction of universal suffrage might have caused the public service to be enrolled as one of the battalions in the battle between the Ins and the Outs of party warfare" (1950, p. 70).

Of course, in late-nineteenth-century America, the civil administration was just such a battalion. This meant that in the United States, parties were competing, in a relatively nonprogrammatic fashion, for the votes of a democratized white male electorate, relying for their electoral appeal on patronage and distributive policies. The state structure was fragmented, relatively nonprofessional and nonbureaucratized, even by 1900. The reform of the civil administration—destroying the power of the patronage politicians and achieving the professionalization, rationalization, and increased efficiency of government, under the control of professional and expert officials—was still very much on the political agenda.

The fact that civil service reform had not been accomplished prior to the emergence of new social protection measures on the national political agenda in the United States had important ramifications for policy developments. First, continuing lack of development of administrative capacities meant that the initiatives for new social policies would have to come from outside the state; unlike the European situation, reform-minded bureaucrats would not be actors in policy debates. Second, debates over social policy would be affected by the continuing struggle over political corruption and the character of the state administration. The fight against political corruption and for professionalization, so important to middle- and upper-class reformers, took precedence over all others. An unreformed and not yet professionalized state was not considered by reformers as a suitable instrument for many social reform programs; that is, those who controlled the administration were not considered sufficiently honest and efficient to be trusted with the huge flow of financial resources which many new programs, particularly old age pensions, would involve. Third, in contrast with British parties in an expanding electorate, after the realigning election of 1896, U.S. party competitiveness declined dramatically. Republicans and

Democrats emerged as dominant parties in different regions of the country—the Democrats in the South, and the GOP everywhere else. The dominant parties in the United States had not adopted programmatic modes of appealing to their constituencies; rather, they continued to rely on patronage. Thus, they were not typically vehicles of reform during the Progressive Era. Reforms had to be backed by wide coalitions of interested groups able to press their concerns on state legislatures in order to achieve success.

Policy Feedback: The Reaction to Poor Relief and Civil War Pensions

The social question did emerge on the American policy agenda in the late nineteenth and early twentieth centuries, as a wide range of political actors debated what the state should do in the face of the increasingly well-publicized problems of industrial society—poverty, income interruption due to unemployment and old age, social order. Their debates were shaped by what the government was already doing in the area of social welfare, the policy legacy. Thus, they reacted to the poor law but also to the Civil War pension system. Moreover, this reaction was shaped by the ways these forms of social protection fit into the workings of patronage democracy, and how new programs were expected to affect the outcome of the struggle between alternative forms of administrative and political practice.

The Policy Legacy: Poor Relief and Civil War Pensions

In the United States, as in Britain, the elderly who could not count on family or private sources of support turned to poor relief, largely institutional, when they could no longer work. There were, however, two significant contrasts between the American and the British policy legacies. Nineteenth-century America had no national poor law, either in theory or in administrative fact. Instead, mixtures of Elizabethan and new poor law practices were institutionalized in diverse forms in thousands of local communities, where the prime responsibility lay financially (as it did in Britain) and legally (Brown 1940, chap. 1). Reactions against poor law practices would not so readily converge into a series of national debates as they did from the 1830s on in Britain, although the final decades of the nineteenth century did witness the emergence of state-level administrative supervision of charity and social welfare activities and policy debates in places such as Massachusetts (Brown 1940, pp. 22–23). In addition to poor relief, uniquely, there was the Civil War pension system, functioning for many of the aged—as everyone knew—as a de facto old age and disability pension system (see Rubinow 1913, pp. 404–9; Gillen 1926, p. 284; Nassau 1915, pp. 46–48). By the 1890s some one million Americans, including at

least half the native-born white men over the age of sixty-four, along with substantial numbers of widows, were receiving these pensions (U.S. Bureau of the
Census 1960, p. 718; Rubinow 1913, pp. 404–9).

The post–Civil War pension system was an excellent example of a policy
generated by the distributional proclivities of nineteenth-century patronage
democracy, especially from the point of view of the Republicans. It allowed
the Republicans to confer on individuals in many northern localities pensions
financed out of the "surplus" revenues from the constantly readjusted tariffs they sponsored to benefit various industries and sections of industries
(McMurry 1922, p. 27; Bensel 1984, pp. 60–73). Not surprisingly, Civil War
pension laws and practices were transformed from the late 1870s to the 1890s
(see figure 4.1), when electoral competition between the Democrats and Republicans in the North was especially intense. A few hundred votes could make
the difference in politically competitive midwestern and northeastern states like
Indiana, Ohio, Illinois, and New York (Sanders 1980; Glasson 1918, p. 225).
There, veterans of the Union army made up 12–15 percent of the electorate
(McMurry 1922, p. 20), rendering "the soldier vote a prize of great worth"
(White 1958, p. 218). The prize grew in value with the growth of the veterans'
lobbying group, the Grand Army of the Republic (GAR). Stimulated by the
Arrears Act (which, interestingly, was not a product of GAR lobbying), GAR
membership increased from 60,000 in 1880 to 428,000 in 1890, when more
than one-third of the Union survivors of the Civil War had joined (McMurry
1922, p. 23). In addition to supporting recurrent legal liberalizations of the
terms of eligibility, congressmen intervened with the Pension Bureau to help
people establish their eligibility and sponsored thousands of special pension
bills tailored for individual constituents (Keller 1977, pp. 311–12; McMurry
1922, p. 28). For example, in the Forty-ninth Congress (1885–87), fully 45
percent of all House bills and 55 percent of all Senate bills addressed private
pensions (McMurry 1922, p. 28). The U.S. Pension Bureau itself was the
"most uncompromisingly political branch of the late nineteenth century federal
bureaucracy" (Keller 1977, p. 311). There was wide discretion in the process-
ing of claims due to the huge backlog, so that control of the administration
was a potent tool for responding to constituency demands or to political needs
(Sanders 1980, p. 146). The experience of the Pension Bureau nicely underlines the consequences of the civil administration's vulnerability to partisan use
in this period.

At the same time that spending for Civil War pensions was becoming more
profligate (if one takes the attitude of horrified mugwumps, such as Harvard
president Charles Eliot) or more adequate to the needs of disabled and older
veterans (if one listens to the point of view of the GAR), there were movements,
often successful, in many of America's largest cities to end outdoor relief com-

pletely.[4] Drawing inspiration from intellectual and ideological sources similar to those which nourished the "back to 1834" movement in Britain, particularly social Darwinism, elite charity reformers in the United States also reacted against the blatantly partisan, political uses to which such relief funds were put (Brown 1940, pp. 16–17, 39–41; Feder 1936, p. 23; Lubove 1968, p. 93; Mencher 1967, pp. 288–89; Almy 1899, 1901).

The financing and administration of the poor laws throughout nineteenth-century Europe and North America had several commonalities: local administration was the rule, and poor relief was meager and degrading at best. By the latter half of the century, some central administrative supervision of poor relief functions had emerged; in European countries, this was often at the level of the national government, while in the U.S. case, it was at the state level (Brown 1940, chap. 1). Centralizing and professionalizing trends in charity and welfare in the United States, as in Britain, aided in the formation in the post–Civil War era of scientific charity movements, most notably the National Conference of Charities and Correction (Bruno 1957, chap. 1), and of state-level boards of charity to supervise public and private welfare organizations (Brown 1940, p. 22–23). These boards were partial analogues of the British Local Government Board (established in 1871). But in the United States, the continuing problems of patronage in poor relief administration added extra political force to the campaigns against outdoor relief: this crusade was related to the overall movement against the patronage system. Indeed, the distinguishing feature of late-nineteenth-century U.S. poor relief administration was the predominance of patronage practices.

A wide variety of governmental forms existed in American localities, but whatever the form, the patronage organizations of Democrats and Republicans dominated city, town, and county governments (Keller 1977, p. 377). The partisan control of American local governments, like the dominance of patronage politicians in the federal government, meant that administration was nonprofessional and "permeated . . . to the core" by party politics (Hoogenboom 1968, p. 1). Control of poor relief provided politicians with opportunities for patronage appointments and exercising partisan preference in the awarding of contracts for building and supplying poorhouses, asylums, and other welfare institutions (Bruno 1957, p. 79; Breckinridge 1927, sec. 4; Evans 1926; Keller

---

4. Eliot said of Civil War pensions in 1889: "I hold it to be a hideous wrong inflicted upon the republic that the pension system instituted for the benefit of the soldiers and sailors of the United States had been prostituted and degraded. . . . As things are . . . one cannot tell whether a pensioner of the United States received an honorable wound in battle or contracted a chronic catarrh twenty years after the war. One cannot tell whether a pensioner of the United States is a disabled soldier or sailor or a perjured pauper who has foisted himself upon the public treasury. I say that to put the pension system of the United States into this condition is a crime . . . against Republican Institutions" (quoted in Skocpol and Ikenberry 1983, p. 87).

1977, p. 501; Sutton 1991). In addition, local officials had discretion in granting outdoor relief and work relief, so that electoral considerations could enter easily into the determination of eligibility for aid (Brown 1940, p. 16). Describing the use of public works as a relief measure in New York City in the 1890s, sociologist Leah Feder noted that "partisan politics entered into its expenditure; workers referred by social agencies were dropped more quickly than those sent by politicians. . . . carelessness, extravagance, and misappropriation in administration were rife . . . [although] the fund undoubtedly provided an important resource in relieving unusual distress" (1936, p. 188; see also pp. 22, 158). Public relief was sometimes supplemented by the gifts of party bosses, who on occasion distributed food and fuel to the poor. Typically, they paid for this largesse out of the "private" funds they garnered through graft or "macing" (the practice of levying assessments on the salaries of public employees) (Pratt 1961, pp. 396–411; Riordan 1905).

The Reaction to Patronage-Dominated Social Policy

Around the turn of the century, British and other European reformers within and outside the state suggested social insurance and pensions as a means for respectable members of the working classes to avoid the cruelties of the traditional poor law. These measures were also to serve as a means for governments and propertied classes to head off the threat to social order and to their political hegemony posed by leaving no recourse to the lower classes in times of need but the poor law system. Many of the reformers looked to a reformed public administration for the implementation of new welfare programs. To be sure, there were reactions against the poor laws in the United States as in Britain, and the reformers based their arguments on very similar grounds. Americans, too, were concerned about the problem of social order and of how to promote social solidarity and maintain the loyalty of the working-class electorate (see Brooks 1906). In the same period, however, U.S. elites had additional concerns, based on the continuing existence of patronage and what they considered to be political corruption in government.

Reform elites and the middle-class public perceived the "problem" of patronage democracy in relation to the state's welfare functions as a severe one, for local poor relief systems and the national Civil War pension system were dominated by the purposes and practices of patronage political parties. This tended to work at cross-purposes to reformist, anti-poor law intellectual currents. Middle- and upper-class American reformers were struggling against the fiercely competitive, patronage-style political system whose practitioners, in the reformers' view, had utilized the Civil War pension system and expanded pensions for the sake of the veterans' vote, had used welfare institutions to honor the claims of unqualified party activists for jobs or contracts, and had used outdoor relief and public works jobs for the advantage of local machines (see reports of the Committee on Politics in Charities and Correctional Affairs in National Conference of Charities and Correction 1896, pp. 368–98; 1898, pp. 237–63; 1902, pp. 324–42).

The Civil War pension system was targeted by reformers as a particularly egregious example of the problems to which patronage democracy led. Indeed, given the centrality of this system of benefits to the Republican coalition (Bensel 1984, chap. 3), the centrality of pensions in the critique of the patronage political system should not surprise us. By the 1880s and 1890s the pension system's partisan uses were clear to many in the broad middle-class public, despite the attempts of elected officials to legitimate the repeated expansions of the system through the use of patriotic rhetoric and "waving the bloody shirt." In an investigatory article appearing in an 1884 issue of the reform-oriented magazine *Century,* one observer noted: "It is safe to assert that most of the legislation adopted since the war closed, to pay money on account of service in the Union armies, has had for its real motive not justice nor generosity, but a desire to cultivate the 'soldier vote' for party purposes" (Smalley 1884). For the remainder of the nineteenth century and in the Progressive Era of the twentieth, these abuses of the pension system and other "perversions of democracy" associated with mass patronage politics provided a continuing stimulus for political reform, as well as a powerful symbol of all that was considered to be amiss with existing political practices.

These "perversions of democracy" stimulated the reformers' fear of entrusting new activities, particularly in the field of welfare, to public as opposed to private organizations, although it is usual to read in histories of American welfare only that this preference for private agencies reflects the traditional American ideological commitment to private and voluntary, as opposed to public, activity. Britons certainly shared this traditional preference, even by the last quarter of the nineteenth century, as the strength of the friendly societies and charity organization societies attests. But in the face of new problems and political opportunities, a powerful countercurrent in favor of new kinds of public activity was able to develop. Why is the U.S. experience so different on this point? Certainly the fact that public administration of welfare, along with most everything else (most notably, military pensions), was not yet free from patronage politics and the corruption of party machines was a critical difference between the two countries in determining the receptiveness of the broad middle-class political public to the new ideas of the "positive state" (as embodied in specific proposals for new social spending programs such as pensions and social insurance) being promulgated by thinkers on both sides of the Atlantic. This difference in the character of U.S. state organizations as compared with British ones can certainly help to explain why, into the Progressive Era, most reformers focused on political, or "structural," to use the term of historian Melvin Holli (1969), as opposed to social, reform.

The struggle between patronage politicians and civil service reformers in the United States added a dimension to the conflict over new social welfare spending programs—making them much less likely to be adopted—which was simply not present in Britain (Heidenheimer 1973, pp. 325–26). Seth Low, a leading charity reformer and mayor of Brooklyn when outdoor relief was abolished (Katz 1986, p. 46), presented papers at the meeting of the National Conference of Charities and Correction in 1879 and 1881 in which he explicitly linked the campaign against outdoor relief to concerns about its connection to patronage democracy, stating that "both in Philadelphia and in Brooklyn, outdoor relief was attacked primarily because it was prostituted to political ends, and was demoralizing in its administration" (Low 1881, p. 150; see also Low 1879). Of course, similar concerns had existed in Britain in the early years of the new poor law, but by the time the new intellectual trends favoring social insurance and pensions became influential, poor law administration had been freed from use in the partisan battle through the success of civil service reform and the concomitant reorganization of party functioning. Instead, party differences focused on alternative policies and financing questions. The timing of civil service reform, itself determined in large part by the timing of democratization and the position of the state in the international states system, was critical in whether or not the debates over the new workingmen's insurance proposals would be additionally entangled by issues of administrative probity and competence.

In the United States, the political logic of expansion which lay behind the growth of Civil War pensions was presumed to be a constant under democratic conditions and made reformers wary of any kind of government "handouts," that is, any benefit which had no requirement of contributions from the beneficiary to hold back politicians from cashing in on the political payoff of expansion. Reformers were painfully aware of the role that popular pressure had played in expanding Civil War pensions and feared that a similar fate would befall any new programs funded from the general revenues (see Seager 1910, pp. 144–45). Even as proposals for new social insurance or pension schemes were being debated, Civil War pensions continued to symbolize all that was wrong with mass patronage democracy and public policy. In 1911 and 1912 Charles Francis Adams, a well-known journalist and reformer, carried out an investigation of the abuses of the military pension system which was published as "Pensions—Worse and More of Them," in the reform magazine *World's Work* (Adams 1912).[5] The series' title when reprinted as a pamphlet in 1912— *The Civil-War Pension Lack-of-System, a four-thousand million dollar record of legislative incompetence tending to political corruption*—says it all in regard to reformers' view of the link between patronage democracy and pensions. The

---

5. *World's Work* carried many articles on pension abuse even as it championed various social, political, and labor reforms during the years between 1900 and the outbreak of World War I.

political learning in regard to the existing political system and social policies fueled fears about trusting government to carry out any new social welfare functions. The reformers' perception of the inevitability of political pressure for expansion in any noncontributory pension scheme led to their opposition to such systems. This sentiment was expressed in the testimony of John Graham Brooks, a well-known labor reformer and the first American to investigate German social insurance for the government (Brooks 1893), before the Massachusetts Commission on Old Age Pensions: "The condition of our politics is the first difficulty in the way of the working of a pension scheme. . . . We have no end of illustrations of the way that we pension off all sorts of persons in the army; while there are a large number of deserving, there are many thousands who are not,—and pensions are given on account of politics. I do not see how we can save any pension system in this country from running into politics" (Massachusetts Commission on Old Age Pensions 1910, p. 238).

Further, although this fear of pensions might have recommended contributory insurance to guard against politically motivated and popularly demanded expansion of benefits and coverage, both the lack of state administrative capacity and the concerns of American reformers about the continuing power of patronage politicians stood in the way. John Graham Brooks, in a report on the lessons of German workingmen's insurance for Americans to the National Conference of Charities and Correction in 1905, explained the dilemma of reformers weighing the possibility of attempting to implement contributory social insurance in America, "There is the general condition of [American] politics and civil service. The German success, such as it is, has been owing absolutely to a strictly competent and independent administration. They *barely* succeed as it is. With an administration like that which has controlled our army pensions, what would become of industrial insurance? One-fifth of the looseness and extravagance that have characterized that history would wreck any conceivable scheme of industrial insurance in a year" (Brooks 1905, pp. 453–54).

Thus, because social spending measures in general, and old age pensions in particular, were so similar to the Civil War pensions, reformers were extremely reluctant to champion such policies. Even that minority of reformers concerned with social issues and sympathetic to the need for labor and social legislation tended not to give support to measures which were deemed likely to reinforce political corruption. This was true even among those most aware of the widespread nature of old age poverty. Mabel Nassau, in her report on old age poverty in the Greenwich Village section of New York City, wrote, "As these . . . people actually need their war pensions, perhaps others receiving war pensions do also. But in no way do I wish to seem to approve the reckless extension of our war pensions" (1915, p. 47). The Committee on Standards of Living and Labor of the National Conference of Charities and Correction stressed legislation establishing labor standards and workplace safety and favored "some effective system of compensation for the heavy loss now sustained by industrial workers as a result of unavoidable accidents, industrial diseases, sickness, invalidity, involuntary unemployment and old age," the entire set of risks usually associated with state social insurance. But for the risk of old age, the committee did not endorse a public program but called only for state regulation to protect workers' equity in private schemes (National Conference of Charities and Correction Committee on Standards of Living and Labor 1912, pp. 393–94). And Henry Seager, prominent member of the American Association for Labor Legislation, said in 1910, "Our experience with national military pensions has not predisposed us to favor national pensions of any kind" (1910, p. 145). Sociologist Charles Henderson, one of the few elite reformers who favored pensions, was forced to admit that the "extravagance and abuses of the military pension system have probably awakened prejudice against workingmen's pensions" (1909, p. 227).

Now, we can finally make sense of the decision by leaders of the American Association for Labor Legislation and other middle-class social reformers to forego a campaign for old age pensions after their successes in promoting workers' compensation and industrial safety laws. Although such a campaign assuredly would have appealed to organized labor and the broader working-class electorate—as a similar program did in Britain—it is also the case that such a program was unappealing to many of the leaders and members of the AALL itself, as well as to the broader middle-class political public, for all of whom "politics" stood in the way of accepting new government spending for welfare purposes. This point is illustrated in Henry Seager's 1910 lectures on social insurance to the New York School of Philanthropy. Noting that the social reforms he advocated all relied upon state action, Seager said, "It is right here that we find the principal source of opposition to them in the United States . . . [since the characteristic American distrust of the state is] partly the result of painful experience. We do not wish our cities, our states, nor our nation to undertake new and difficult functions, because we know that the functions they now undertake are too often ill-performed" (1910, pp. 150–51). Thus, Seager said, the next step in social reform "must be political reform" (1910, p. 152). Although Seager and other members of the AALL were willing to press for worker's compensation and health insurance, because they believed "the battle for good government is being won," Seager's audience was less likely to believe that "we can safely impose on the government new and difficult functions." Seager went on to argue that the idea "that no new duties must be entrusted to government because it fails in the duties it already has, seems to me no longer admissible" (1910, p. 154). Clearly, though, this notion must still have had many adherents among those listening. Even Seager, who surely was more willing than most progressives to rely on governmental action in social reform, was unwilling to take up a campaign for noncontributory old age pensions.

The Failure of Old Age Pension Proposals in the United States

The legacies of nineteenth-century patronage democracy and the conjuncture of its crisis in the Progressive Era created a relatively unfavorable context for the enactment of social reforms such as old age pensions and social insurance. At the most basic level, the civil administration of the early-twentieth-century American state was quite weak, given the lack of an established state bureaucracy and the dispersion of authority inherent in U.S. federalism and division of powers. Civil service reform, which might have enhanced the capacities of American government for certain types of interventions in civil life, had still not progressed much by the early 1900s. Thus, in contrast with the situation in many European countries, there were in the United States no strategically placed officials to pave the way for new social welfare programs. The still-underdeveloped American bureaucracy was not the source of the reforms which did succeed in the Progressive Era. American political parties did not tend to be the vehicles of reform, either. They were not, as were many of their European counterparts, programmatic parties looking for new policies to attract newly enfranchised working-class voters. Rather, they were patronage parties with an already mobilized working-class following whose mode of operation was under attack as "corruption" by many reformers. The clear challenge for party leaders in the Progressive Era was to find ways to appeal to middle-class reformers and their organizations while not alienating their traditional, patronage-oriented supporters. New social spending measures tended not to meet that challenge, for elites and middle-class groups were still not convinced that officials in control of the state administration had been sufficiently cleansed of corruption to entrust them with such activities. Critically for American social policy developments, the concern of the broad middle-class public was focused on political rather than social reform. Their support would have been critical to the success of any coalition for new social spending programs for the aged. Even social reformers shied away from spending measures such as old age pensions because of their political learning in regard to Civil War pensions and patronage politics generally. The experience of Civil War pensions was apocryphal, and it was invoked by even the most progressive thinkers to reinforce the necessity of first cleaning up politics before turning to the initiation of new state activities which also involved substantial national financial resources.

Although worries about political corruption undermined cross-class coalitions for social spending, especially on old age pensions, some important social welfare innovations did occur in many states during the Progressive Era. In general, middle-class reformers supported the expansion of the regulatory capacity of the government (Heidenheimer 1973, p. 326; Schiesl 1977), which in fact kept pace with European developments (Yellowitz 1965, p. 10). Labor regulations were strengthened, especially for women and children. Mothers' pension legislation, which provided means-tested allowances to widows outside of the poor law, was also widely successful. Workers' compensation laws, too, were enacted by many state legislatures (Leff 1973; see also Lescohier and Brandeis 1935). In Massachusetts and Wisconsin, reformers were able to overcome business opposition to enact legislation establishing savings banks and government life insurance, programs which were not perceived to have a high potential for abuse (Commons and Andrews 1927, p. 471; Squier 1912, pp. 286–91).

Why was it possible for these regulatory programs to be enacted in a political context so hostile to public initiatives that involved social spending? Regulatory activities, unlike social spending programs, could address the new needs of industrial society—and appeal to both working- and middle-class voters—without adding to the potential for political corruption or overtaxing U.S. administrative capacities. The two new welfare programs that were successful in the Progressive Era United States, worker's compensation and mothers' pensions, represented the reworking of government functions already being carried out in the courts and added no significant amount of government spending. Skocpol (forthcoming) has argued that political conditions in the Progressive Era United States did not foster the development of a "paternalist" welfare state, with programs such as old age pensions and unemployment benefits that bolstered the position of male wage earners, but she notes that conditions were favorable to the development of "maternalist" welfare programs, such as protective legislation and mothers' pensions. Yet even though political initiatives to help mothers were popular, the underdeveloped capacities of the American state tended to undermine the implementation of such programs (Orloff 1991). Social spending, even for mothers, remained problematic, though less so than would have the large-scale spending that would have accompanied new protections for the elderly.

In essence, the United States opted not to institute the modern public social provision considered during the Progressive Era, but the attempts to build new realms of public activity free from patronage were not without implications for the future of social policy. Two structural effects were the enhancement of the importance of subnational governments and the intensification of administrative fragmentation inherent in a federal system. Partially because civil service reform had made the most headway at the subnational level, states were the loci of administration for successful labor and welfare innovations in the Progressive Era itself and into the 1920s, and interests in such state-level programs became institutionalized. When social reform again emerged on the policy agenda in the wake of the Great Depression, policymakers would have to contend with this progressive state-building legacy as they designed new programs.

8

Canada

From Elitist to Democratic Politics and
New Social Provision for the Aged

The uncertainties and difficulties of working-class life and the lack of adequate social protection against the threat of destitution encouraged popular interest in new policy initiatives in Canada, as was the case across the industrializing West. But old age pension proposals, although popular among labor organizations, failed to get support from either major party or from most social reformers. A few middle- and upper-class politicians and reformers were sympathetic to the plight of wage earners and saw modern social insurance or pensions as a reasonable alternative to poor relief. Yet no cross-class alliance developed around the pension issue during the late nineteenth and early twentieth centuries, for most middle-class social reformers and politicians were concerned with other issues. "Moral reforms" and regulatory legislation dominated the attention of prominent Canadian social reformers, such as those in the Social Service Council and the Canadian Conference of Charities and Correction, while reform-minded politicians tended to focus on political, rather than social, reforms (Brown and Cook 1974, p. 124; Bryden 1974, chap. 3, and p. 186). The outcome of Canada's politics of social protection in the pre–World War I era, then, was unlike developments in Britain but similar to those in the United States. An old age pension system for Canada's elderly did not gain broad enough political backing to achieve legislative success prior to the war, and a voluntary, government-run annuity program was adopted in its place. Why did a cross-class alliance for social spending not emerge in prewar Canada? Again, we must understand the concerns of middle-class reformers and politicians, who were the available coalition partners for workers in any alliance for social spending, to determine why social spending was not on their agenda— for surely workers favored such measures.

My argument about the failure of pensions in the prewar period has three components. First, although Canadian state formation resulted in a significantly more unified central state than emerged in the United States, the Canadian state was patronage-dominated and lacking in administrative capacity through the First World War. As a result, social reforms in old age provision could not emerge from bureaucratic initiatives, as they did in some European countries. Second, both social and political conditions fostered greater elite predominance than was the case in the United States. Parties were both elitist and oriented to patronage, which meant that popular demands were relatively muted in the prewar Canadian polity and that reform elites were more concerned with civil service than with social reform. Third, the distinctive Canadian policy legacy did not lead to perceptions of crisis in public policy as was the case in Britain and the United States; this also reinforced elite disinterest in social policy reform.

State formation was shaped by the concerns of British colonial and Canadian elites to protect Canada from American military and economic pressures and to prevent a repetition of the American experience of, first, "too much" democracy and, second, a weak and fragmented state. Thus, a unified and elite-dominated federal state with a parliamentary system was constructed, and Canadians opted for dominion status, described by Laxer as "a midpoint between colony and full nationhood" (1989, p. 149), which kept them under the military protection of the British Empire (see also Morton 1972, p. 40). Elites were committed to the use of patronage, and state administrations before and after confederation were patronage-dominated. As parties emerged in the colonial era and early years of confederation, they relied upon patronage to secure their following, and they continued to do so through the First World War. As a consequence, most political elites opposed civil service reforms, and state capacities remained undeveloped and parties nonprogrammatic in orientation. In the early years of the twentieth century, as labor leaders began to propose new public social protections, reformers were most concerned with political and administrative reforms. But perhaps more important, in this political context where popular demands and interests were muted, proposals for new programs for the elderly poor, even if "worthy," did not excite much elite interest. Elite disinterest may also be traced to the character of Canadian provision for the poor. In contrast with the United States and Britain, poor relief in Canada was almost wholly voluntary, though state-subsidized. Thus, questions about the character of social provision were more difficult to bring into the public political arena there than in countries where administration was public and therefore more clearly political.

State Formation in Canada

The Canadian state that emerged from confederation in 1867 looked more like its European counterparts than its neighbor to the south. The elite Canadian and British colonial officials who made the political and administrative arrangements for the new Dominion constructed a unified state based on the British cabinet system, in which an executive committee of Parliament exercised power only so long as it enjoyed the support of the majority in Parliament. Canada did differ from Britain in its federal structure. The provincial governments, too, were unified, and they emerged as the strongest rivals of the federal government, significantly circumscribing its unilateral power. The distinctive characteristics of the Canadian polity were rooted in the colonial experience. There was no Canadian revolution comparable to the English and American, but we can still compare the stable arrangements that emerged from a formative period in which political and institutional arrangements were in flux. In England, this was the period from 1688 through the 1720s, in the United States, the 1760s through the 1820s, in Canada, the 1790s through the 1840s.

In his book *The Origins of Canadian Politics,* Gordon Stewart (1986) has very usefully extended the work of John Murrin (1980) to the Canadian experience of state formation. By characterizing the forces important in that experience in terms of "court" and "country," Stewart sketches the contrasts between the outcomes of Canadian, American, and British state formation. Unlike the pattern of national government shaped by "country" principles and interests that emerged in the nineteenth-century United States, Stewart argues, "court" arrangements prevailed in the Canadian colonies, which directly influenced arrangements made at confederation for Canada. "By the middle of the nineteenth century, Canada seemed clearly to have developed a statist system of government. In terms of government's reach into society, in terms of party leadership, and in terms of endemic and pervasive patronage, Canada was far removed from the small, frugal and spare government of classical 'country' ideology" (Stewart 1986, p. 95).

By the 1840s government was dominated by party, and party leaders used patronage to build their own power and the powers of the administration. The United States and Canada differed not in terms of the dominance of partisan patronage, but in two other factors: the extent of democratization of the electorate and the character of the state dominated by the parties. The Canadian electorate was more constricted than the American, and its parties were more elitist in orientation. Furthermore, the American state was simply far more fragmented than the Canadian and had penetrated less into civil society. Moreover, where American politics in the formative period of state-building were structured by country-court struggles in which the "country" won, in Canada, "the 'country' challenge to 'court' orientation was paltry, but rival 'court' governments in the provinces did the job of circumscribing central power" (Stewart 1986, p. 97). As in the United States, regionalism was key to Canadian political developments, but, unlike the American case, this did not lead to the strengthening of "country" forces. Instead, French Canadians and, later, provincial Liberal leaders representing western agrarians in Ontario "were powerful countervailing forces working against the triumph of a national government" by building "provincial duplicate[s] and rival[s]" to the federal government (Stewart 1986, p. 96). As the Dominion expanded, other provincial governments also entered the fray, leading to a pattern of policy-making in which policy outcomes were affected by negotiations between the federal government and provincial leaderships as well as by partisan conflict (Leman 1980, pp. 19–21, 136).

Canada in the International States System and World Economy

The initial conditions for state formation in the territory that became Canada were set in the context of the rivalry between France and Britain. In the early 1700s Britain succeeded in driving the French from Acadia. As the result of the victory over France in the Seven Years' War in 1763, the British gained control of Quebec, which was later divided into Upper and Lower Canada, the colonies which became the provinces of Ontario and Quebec (Morton 1972, p. 9; Brebner 1945, chaps. 2–3). Quebec was transferred to British rule and opened to settlement by British emigrants and Loyalist Americans. Soon after France was removed from the scene, the American colonies fought for and won independence, and from then on, relations between the new United States and Britain became a critical force shaping events in Canada. After the Revolution, Britain was preoccupied with European rather than North American affairs, but with the Napoleonic Wars resulting in difficulties in getting access to needed resources, British interests in its North American territories—and in keeping the Americans out of them—assumed new importance. After the War of 1812 the British and Americans developed friendly relations, but the British remained resolute about keeping the Canadian colonies out of the American republic. As Brebner noted, "The underlying reason for Canada's salvation [from American annexation] lay in the improved relations between Great Britain and the United States," which in turn depended on Anglo-American recognition of mutual strengths and interests (1945, p. 106).

British elites and the leaders of the colonies that later made up the Canadian confederation, and then Canadian political leaders, were preoccupied with maintaining control over their economy and territory, which meant, predominantly, warding off American economic intrusions and the growth of pro-American popular sentiment (McNaught 1982, chaps. 6–7; Lipset 1970, pp. 58–61). Indeed, the formal founding of the independent Canadian federal state in 1867 was precipitated by Canadian and British elites' fears of possible American economic expansion into or even formal annexation of Canadian territory—a proposal for such action had gained popularity after the Civil War—and their continuing antipathy to American-style democracy (Lipset 1970, p. 58; McNaught 1982, pp. 116–17; Brebner 1945, chap. 10). Confederation added Nova Scotia and New Brunswick to Quebec and Ontario, and the enlargement of the polity helped to solve domestic political stalemate while responding to geopolitical concerns. Manitoba and British Columbia entered the federation in 1871 (Brebner 1945, p. 180). At confederation, Canada's founders were determined to "construct a strong national state," both to maintain firm control of the territory and in reaction against the weaknesses of the more divided American state as manifested in the Civil War (McNaught 1982, p. 133). Thus, retaining the structural features of the colonial regimes, the Canadian state was significantly less fragmented than the American state, since the cabinet system and parliamentary government, rather than the division of powers, were adopted.

British forces left Canadian soil after confederation, but Canada continued to rely upon "protection behind the British shield" and did not raise a standing army (Laxer 1989, p. 149). With the signing of the Treaty of Washington, which settled American-British disputes flowing out of the Civil War, in 1871, the American military threat was gone. Indeed, the United States and the Monroe Doctrine became an additional shield (Brebner 1945, pp. 192–97). This, of course, had implications for state-building; without preparations for war to stimulate the development of extractive and repressive state capacities, the administration of the Canadian state—like the early American state—remained "underdeveloped."

Economic development was a critical part of nation-building for early Canadian leaders (Whitaker 1977b, p. 45), and this put Canada in a somewhat different position than the antebellum United States. The Dominion's geographic extent, its difficult terrain and climate, its status as a late industrializer, and its small population base made it important for the government to act in the absence of sufficient capital or markets to sustain economic development, especially as Canadian elites were anxious that the vacuum not be filled by economic expansion from the powerful United States (Aitken 1967, pp. 204–10). The heart of the late-nineteenth-century "National Policy" pursued by Conservative prime minister John MacDonald was to strengthen Canada's east-west axis through building a transcontinental railway which would offset the north-south pull of U.S. markets and make westward expansion possible (McNaught 1982, pp. 166–68; Fowke 1973). As it was not feasible for the state directly to undertake these tasks, the federal government provided increasingly generous assistance to private builders and developers (Aitken 1967, p. 206). The pattern of strong state support to private enterprise in the service of nation-building through economic development was to be characteristic of Canada for years to come, although state assistance to private enterprise was initiated by the government, rather than private interests (Whitaker 1977b, p. 43; Aitken 1967, pp. 209–10). Canada's elite founders were interested in political independence and power, not merely economic returns, and subsidizing economic development provided a way to achieve both ends. It assumed particular importance given Canada's geopolitical position. By the turn of the century, America was seen largely as an additional guardian rather than as a military threat, and Canadian leaders were willing to allow and indeed to encourage American investment and the establishment of branch plants of U.S. firms in Canada.[1] Yet by this time, basic institutional arrangements were set, and the leadership certainly retained an interest in its independent political and cultural existence.

Domestic Economic, Social, and Political Arrangements

Domestic factors as well as Canada's international situation fostered court-style arrangements and elitism. Governing elites from the colonial period through the early years of the twentieth century were unified in opposing majoritarian democracy, republican arrangements, and universal manhood suffrage. They had the capacity to do without popular support, given the British connection (Whitaker 1977b, 1987; McNaught 1982, pp. 116–20, and chap. 9; Laxer 1989, pp. 129–40). In contrast, American elites were split on the issue of building up the central state and, partly as a consequence of this disagreement, differed on the issue of further democratization in the early 1800s. The political reforms of the Jacksonian era—including the spoils system and an extension of the franchise to all white adult males—resulted from the political mobilization of the white male population by elite groups using this to defeat their political rivals. There were certainly differences between English and French Canadian elites, but Quebec did not reprise the U.S. South by supporting "country" principles in struggles over state-building in Canada. Both Canadian groups agreed on the need for a strong central administration.

The initial British government of Canada after the conquest consisted of an appointed governor and council.[2] The governor was soon given unchecked power to collect revenues; moreover, all governors were officers of the British army. The decision not to establish any elected institutions in the colony stemmed from a range of factors: Canada had been acquired by force of arms, the population was almost entirely French-speaking, and there were already concerns about rebellious tendencies developing in the American colonies, centered in their elected assemblies. Until the Loyalist influx after the American Revolution spurred a change in these arrangements, "Canada had

---

1. Gordon Laxer has linked the absence of military threats to Canada to the willingness of elites to allow foreign investment and the development of branch plants as a route to economic development (what he calls "dependent industrialization"). "Canada's voluntary position as a dependency of the Empire until near the end of the First World War . . . and the absence of a real military threat from the Americans coincided with the period when the industrial structure was established in its branch-plant mould" (Laxer 1989, p. 150).

2. In this and the following paragraph, I rely upon Stewart's analysis (1986, chaps. 1–2).

the most extreme form of 'court' constitution ever seen in Britain or her other North American colonies" (Stewart 1986, p. 21). The arrival of large numbers of English settlers convinced British authorities that representative institutions would have to be established, but in the wake of the experience with the American colonies, they remained wary of democratic forms. Thus, the new government of the Canadian colonies, established through the Constitutional Act of 1791, included representative assemblies. But these were weak, and the executive retained control of all patronage and the ability to collect revenues without having to gain legislative approval. This was clearly quite unlike the American system of the division of powers, but it also differed from the actual workings of Britain's vaunted "mixed constitution," under which the Crown had to rely on the elected House of Commons to raise revenues. Colonial elites deliberately created a strong administration, giving extensive powers to colonial governors, and these arrangements helped to build up the power of local notables, thereby contributing to the elitism of Canadian politics, which persisted through the nineteenth and early twentieth centuries.

From 1791 through the 1830s, the Canadian assemblies demanded responsible government and access to patronage for the notability beyond the colonies' small ruling cliques. In both French Lower Canada and English Upper Canada, however, the opposition remained statist in orientation and supported the monarchy, although each had slightly different reasons. Key to French Canadian support of the monarchy was the position of the Catholic Church, which depended upon the Crown for its existence in British North America. In Upper Canada, members of the assembly accepted the need for a strong government and the monarchy to ward off American threats. Yet Canadian reformers interested in responsible government and gaining access to patronage were increasingly frustrated by intransigent colonial officials, and rebellions finally broke out in 1837 and 1838. The rebellions failed, but British officials eventually conceded responsible government, agreeing with critics that the executive needed to work with leaders of a representative body. With only isolated exceptions, the elite political actors who formulated colonial governmental arrangements after the rebellions were committed to court-style government and differed only on how access to the powers and patronage resources of such a government were to be arranged. Through a series of struggles in the assembly of the Union of the Canadas in the 1840s, gubernatorial powers were shifted to political leaders. "When responsible government came it [was] party-government and not governor-government," and governors remained basically as figureheads representing the tie to Britain, not leaders of the administration (Stewart 1986, p. 51). Party leaders gained access to the patronage that the British had originally put at the disposal of the colonial governors. Thus, patronage became the principal tool of the parties which emerged in the 1840s to ensure the support of local notables across the Canadas. From confederation through the First World

War, patronage remained the cement that held the Conservative and Liberal parties together (English 1977, chap. 1; Whitaker 1987).

Popular groups were successful in pressing for greater democracy in the United States, but Canadians, from the colonial period through the unsuccessful popular rebellions of 1837 until the First World War, were not. Gordon Laxer (1989, pp. 129–40; 1985, pp. 90–94) suggests that Canadian popular political weakness stemmed in large part from cultural, religious, and regional differences between French and English Canadians, traceable to events flowing from the conquest of Quebec, which undercut political cooperation between democratic forces from the two cultural groups (see also Brodie and Jenson 1980, pp. 26, 39–44).[3] Laxer argues that "in contrast to the elites in French and English Canada, which did manage to forge alliances, the early popular-democratic movements found it difficult to establish working relations across ethno-national lines. Elite unity and popular disunity have been constant elements in Canadian history ever since" (1989, p. 135). Canadians were also hampered from expressing democratic demands by "the proximity of the democratic republic. . . . Moving too far towards some democratic check on the executive, a natural development even in Britain, was easily portrayed in the Canadas as an attempt to introduce American-style republicanism which would not simply reform government but would weaken it," threaten the monarchy and the British connection, and pave the way for annexation by the United States (Stewart 1986, p. 30; see also Underhill 1960). Popular sentiment, particularly among Loyalists and later British settlers, was generally favorable to the monarchy and hostile to "country" ideology.

The elitist foundation of the Canadian state offered much less encouragement to a rapid extension of the franchise than had the Revolution and subsequent political struggles in the United States. By showing that sovereignty rested in Parliament rather than in the people, "Confederation itself . . . gave no impetus to democracy in Canada, but rather the reverse" (Morton 1943, p. 76). Similarly, Whitaker points out that in marked contrast with the founding of the United States, no democratic or popular authority was involved in the establishment of the Canadian state, for "the British North America Act was an act of the British Parliament, passed on the advice of a small elite of colonial politicians" (Whitaker 1977b, p. 45; see also McNaught 1982, chap. 9; Laxer 1985, p. 91). In addition, after the defeat of popular rebellions in the 1830s, popular sentiment largely sympathized with developments which ruled out majoritarian democracy. Both cultural groups that came together in the

---

3. For example, in the 1850s, the Clear Grits (agrarian democrats based largely in the rural areas west of Toronto) opposed a publicly supported Catholic school system in Canada West (Ontario), while the Rouges (the popular democratic group in Quebec), despite their anticlericalism, saw religion as a critical institution for maintaining the national identity of the Quebecois (Laxer 1989, p. 135).

Canadian federation needed a central government which could assure minority rights and a British connection to ward off American and democratic threats to their survival. Without the tie to Britain, English Canadians feared becoming "a portion of the republic which adjoins us" (Canadian M.P. in 1867, quoted in McNaught 1982, p. 132). French Canadians were forced to choose the lesser of two evils with confederation: "Quebec, . . . threatened as it felt it was by English-speaking Canadians so far as maintenance of its ways of life and thought was concerned, was still more afraid of engulfment in the omniverous, all-digesting culture of the United States" (Brebner 1945, p. 179).

The Canadian Polity in the Nineteenth Century

In Canada's formative years of state-building, neither British nor Canadian officials were interested in constructing an autonomous bureaucracy; they assumed that patronage would be necessary for any executive to establish an effective administration, much as the British Crown was then relying on patronage to manage Parliament. In any event, Canada lacked "a national, intellectual or traditional elite" which could have staffed the civil administration. Thus, administrations in Canada from colonial times through the early twentieth century relied on patronage given to local notables to staff positions, to enhance the powers of the central government, and, after the achievement of responsible government, to cement party loyalties. Patronage was "political lifeblood" for Canadian politicians, who used public jobs for their own electoral and organizational ends (Bryce 1921; Van Loon and Whittington 1971, pp. 416–17; Stewart 1986; Brebner 1938, pp. 23–27). The "Canadian method of appointment to public office was . . . a blend of British and American practice" (English 1977, p. 26). Political patronage "controlled every phase" of the civil service (Dawson 1933, p. 287; 1929, pt. 1), which is to say that all *new* appointments were of a partisan nature (English 1977, p. 26). Reflecting the greater elitism of the Canadian polity, however, Canadian practices never approached "pure Jacksonianism," for permanent tenure for most officials was recognized and there was no spoils system as there was in the United States (Burnham 1935, p. 62).

The degree of democratization determined which groups in the population would receive the fruits of patronage; this in turn had profound effects on the course of administrative reform. Until World War I, Canadian elites opposed full democratization, and formal property qualifications for the federal and provincial franchises remained in effect through the 1880s (and longer in Nova Scotia and Quebec) (Ward 1950, pp. 216–24). Typically, provincial political differences were played out in struggles over the franchise. Conservative leader John MacDonald, as part of his nation-building project, wanted a uniform federal franchise based on property qualifications; the Liberals, stronger at the provincial than at the federal level of government, had lowered the qualifications for the franchise in those provinces where they held power and pressed for the continued use of provincial franchises. MacDonald succeeded in 1885 in securing a uniform federal franchise with "low but complex property qualifications" (Ward 1950, pp. 216–23). When the Liberals gained power in 1896, however, they returned the franchise to the provinces, for "the perpetuation of a property qualification for federal purposes was . . . becoming increasingly difficult in most of the provinces, yet the national adoption of manhood suffrage was a political impossibility" due to opposition from Quebec, and "the easy way out of the dilemma was to resort to provincial franchises once more" (Ward 1950, p. 224). Enfranchisement in cities was based on property qualifications much higher than those in effect at the provincial and federal levels, which undermined the development of urban, mass-based political machines such as those which existed in the United States (Weaver 1977b, p. 222; Magnusson 1983, pp. 7–8, 12; Anderson 1979, pp. 80–82). Still, a number of socioeconomic conditions mitigated the elitism of Canadian politics: the open frontier and labor shortage allowed for widespread property ownership, so that even with a property-based franchise, the electorate was relatively broad-based (Morton 1943, p. 73). Thus, by the 1870s and 1880s the Canadian electorate was more democratic than the British, which excluded approximately 40 percent of all adult men (Blewett 1965), but was somewhat more constricted than the American electorate, which was based on universal white manhood suffrage.

Thus, around 1900, parties in Canada depended for their electoral appeal and organizational cohesiveness on patronage and politically discretionary distributive policies (Munro 1929, chap. 2; English 1977, chap. 1; Fowke 1967, pp. 237–42). Canadian parties were described by turn-of-the-century observers as merely "machine[s] for winning elections" (Andre Siegfried quoted in English 1977, p. 8), rather than as ideologically or doctrinally motivated groupings (English 1977, pp. 8–9). Leadership of local Liberal and Conservative party organizations came primarily from locally based ruling cliques (Whitaker 1977b, pp. 37–38). "Politically appointed public servants, their relatives and friends normally formed the core of continuing party organization within the constituencies" (English 1977, p. 27). In this way, they resembled America's pre-Jacksonian "parties of notables" more than the post-Jacksonian parties led by groups of political professionals (Keller 1977, chaps. 7–8; Shefter 1978). Although popular electoral participation was not as extensive in Canada as in the United States, many farmers, workers, and lower-middle-class people in the areas of oldest settlement (the central and eastern provinces) were mobilized into politics by the Liberals and Conservatives, primarily through the distribution of provincial and federal patronage and on the basis of ethnic and religious, rather than class, loyalties, with the result that loyalties to the established, patronage-based parties among nonelites were relatively strong (Heron

1984, p. 47; Kealey and Palmer 1982, chap. 6; Robin 1968, p. 279). In the more newly established western prairie provinces (Saskatchewan and Alberta became provinces only in 1905), ties to the Liberals and Tories were not as deeply rooted. These areas became the home of a number of third-party challenges to old party dominance in the years after World War I (Brodie and Jenson 1980, chaps. 2–3).

The support of elites was secured through government spending and contracts, or "corporate patronage" (Whitaker 1987, p. 60) in addition to political appointments. The "young Canadian state desperately needed the support of the powerful entrepreneurial class" in order to carry out the economic development mandated by geopolitics and elite interest (English 1977, pp. 24–25). Thus, legislative corruption and bribery in the interest of private enterprise—"corporate patronage"—were common, in addition to the "administrative patronage" which mobilized the party faithful (Whitaker 1987, p. 60). The strong state role in economic development in Canada did not by any means imply that the state's autonomous capacity to act was well developed. In fact, the situation was quite the reverse: "The state as such was far too poorly organized, far too ridden with political patronage and inefficiency, and far too enmeshed with the private sector, to allow for an autonomous role in direct economic activity. Instead, the state offered an instrumentality for facilitating capital accumulation in private hands and for carrying out the construction of a vitally necessary infrastructure" (Whitaker 1977b, p. 43).

Canadian elites profited disproportionately from distributive policies—the "pork barrel," promotion of development, and so on—which served as an instrument of elite accommodation and a way for the parties to hold together across diverse regional economies and cultural traditions (Munro 1929, pp. 55–57, 69; Underhill 1960, pp. 17–18; Dawson 1933, pp. 194–200; McNaught 1982, p. 166). The protective tariffs, subsidies, patronage, railway building, and economic development which made up the "National Policy" pursued by Conservative prime minister MacDonald especially advantaged Canadian industrialists and commercial elites, while offering relatively smaller benefits to workers and farmers (Creighton 1943; Fowke 1967, pp. 237–43; McInnis 1982, pp. 410–11; Kealey and Palmer 1982, pp. 215–20). In both the United States and Canada, government depended largely on protective tariffs which aided the manufacturing sector, and both funneled the largest part of their revenues to payments on the national debts. Canada's next largest expenditure was financing the development of the country's transportation infrastructure and national economic development generally. In contrast, the second largest portion of government revenues in the United States for the years 1885–97 went into Civil War pensions, which reached hundreds of thousands of elderly Americans. The Canadian Pacific Railway became identified with MacDonald's Tories in its uses as an instrument for achieving national unity, as a source of patronage, and as a conduit of public funds toward private business sources (McInnis 1982, pp. 388–89). Military pensions, meanwhile, were a centerpiece of the GOP coalition in the United States, although of course the Republicans also offered significant inducements to business.

Transformations of State and Party, 1880–1920: Attempts at Civil Service Reform and the Attack on Patronage

Movements for the reform of patronage practices in the interest of increased government efficiency developed in Canada in the late nineteenth and early twentieth centuries as they did in the United States and most of Europe, in response to similar pressures from industrialization and urbanization, from the growth in the size of the state and in the complexity of state activities, and from similar professionalizing trends among the middle classes (Splane 1973, pp. 18–19; Hodgetts et al. 1972, pp. 16–19; Corry 1939, chap. 1). The first efforts to reform the civil administration occurred in the late nineteenth century, and the Civil Service Act, analogous to America's Pendleton Act, was passed in 1882 (Marx 1957, p. 76). The movement against the "patronage evil" and for civil service reform grew in intensity around the turn of the century, especially among the professional middle classes, the counterparts of America's progressive reformers (Borden 1931, pp. 6–14; Hodgetts et al. 1972, p. 37; English 1977, pp. 10–11). Despite this movement and the appointment of several government commissions to investigate patronage and suggest alternative administrative practices, effective civil service reform was not attained until World War I dramatically altered the political landscape (Hodgetts et al. 1972, p. 8; Dawson 1933, p. 287). Canadian politicians, like their American counterparts, depended upon patronage for their organizational coherence and electoral appeals (English 1977, chap. 1). Neither Americans nor Canadians faced the kind of pressures that would push them into accepting an "implicitly self-denying" (Hodgetts 1973, p. 51) reform of the civil service, as had British elites in 1870, nor did they face so challenging a geopolitical environment. Without the intense military competition that characterized Europe, state administrations in Canada, as in the United States, were given less stimulus for growth and administrative reform than were European states.

Several factors combined to bring civil service reform onto the political agenda again in the first decade of the twentieth century (Hodgetts et al. 1972, p. 19). As in the United States, one-party dominance in Canada turned some politicians to advocacy of civil service reform. The Tories had been cut off from federal patronage since their 1896 defeat, and without the promise of political appointments to attract electoral support, they had turned to advocating positions that would appeal to groups dissatisfied with the Liberals, such as middle-class reformers and businessmen interested in seeing an end to administrative corruption (English 1977, pp. 25, 34–35). (Not surprisingly, corporate patronage never excited the kind of opposition from elites as did the "administrative corruption" that offered jobs to politically connected but less-than-expert members of the lower-middle or working classes.) These groups saw a reformed, more efficient civil service as a "necessary corollary" to further national development, especially in the economic sphere (Brown and Cook 1974, p. 190). Scandals in the Liberal government involving patronage made news in 1906 and 1907. Pledged to the initiation of a merit system, the Conservatives, under the leadership of civil service reformer Robert Borden, pressed for action (English 1977, pp. 34–35). The Liberals appointed a royal commission on the problem in 1907, and then in 1908 passed the Civil Service Act, which reformed the "inside service" (government workers at the capital, Ottawa) through the use of competitive merit examinations in appointments and established a Civil Service Commission to recruit personnel for still-autonomous departments (Dawson 1933, p. 287; Hodgetts et al. 1972, p. 40; Marx 1957, p. 76).

A beginning had been made in the transformation of administrative practices, but the 1908 law did not result in an end to patronage practices even in Ottawa, and partisan appointments continued completely unchecked in the "outside service" (federal positions in bureaus outside of Ottawa) (Burnham 1935, p. 69; Hodgetts et al. 1972, p. 41). Even after he took office as prime minister in 1911, Borden was unable fully to eradicate patronage—although he did initiate merit-based hiring in the higher reaches of the administration—for many members of his party continued to depend on patronage (English 1977, chaps. 2, 4; Brown and Cook 1974, chap. 10). The delay, then the very partial success, of civil service reform had important ramifications for prewar social policy debates. When Canadians began to consider new public social protections around the turn of the century, the political system was still dominated by patronage practices. The administrative capacities needed for complex social interventions were decidedly lacking, nor was there a group of state bureaucrats who might have helped to bring together social groups interested in reforms, as there was in some European countries. Moreover, among the reform-minded, the priority was civil service reform, and few saw the state administration as a likely instrument for social spending initiatives (English 1977, pp. 70–71). Finally, political parties of the time still depended on patronage rather than programmatic appeals in mobilizing their constituencies, rendering social policy initiatives relatively uninteresting to party leaders. These factors undermined the prospects for social spending, an outcome reinforced by policy feedback.

Policy Feedback: The Reaction to State-Subsidized Voluntary Social Provision

Privatism and reliance on the public subsidization of voluntary institutions characterized Canadian poor relief practices. This arrangement complemented the domination of political parties and the civil administration by elite groups of local notables. Moreover, wide variation in poor relief practices undermined tendencies toward a national political debate over social policy. Thus, in contrast with the United States, Britain, and much of Europe, Canada had less of a public policy inheritance in poor relief practices against which reformers and people in general could react and build upon. Comparing the Canadian experience with the British and American makes clear that the absence of a public poor law perceived to be "in crisis" was critical to Canadian elites' lack of interest in new public spending programs.

The Policy Legacy: State-Subsidized Voluntary Provision

Throughout the nineteenth-century Anglo-American world, social policy practices, both public and private, were dominated by the principle of less eligibility, the tenet of England's (in)famous 1834 poor law that ensured that the position of any pauper should be no better than that of the poorest laborer and, indeed, that paupers should forfeit the rights of citizenship (Splane 1973, pp. 13–17). Despite that common ideological attachment, however, the institutions of social policy were quite different and engendered distinctive reactions. In Britain, poor relief was administered by a central governmental organization, the Poor Law Commission, later the Local Government Board (Webb and Webb 1910), which provided a national focus for policy debates as administrative, political, and financial problems increased over the course of the nineteenth century. In the United States, the public character of provision for the poor put the issue on the political agenda. Canada had no uniform legislation or centralized governmental body to coordinate and supervise local poor relief practices. Outside the older Maritime provinces of Nova Scotia and New Brunswick, where poor laws were enacted soon after settlement, there was no statutory recognition of public poor relief responsibilities at all until the 1900s (Guest 1980, pp. 11–12). Instead, an array of differing, permissive statutes covered relief administration and funding (Strong 1930, pp. 113–49).

Even without a poor law, colonial government authorities found that there was a need for some institutional way to handle relief (Baehre 1981a, b). The means they developed—municipal and provincial subsidization of voluntary charity groups and institutions—dominated Canadian social policy well into the twentieth century (Spiesman 1973, pp. 40, 46–48; Struthers 1983, chap. 1; Machar 1898; Strong 1930; McLean 1901; Splane 1973, pp. 79–116). The need for institutions was met for the most part by publicly subsidized private philanthropy, as public authorities—not surprisingly given resistance to higher rates—did not take advantage of the right to build houses of refuge (almshouses), as permitted under statute (Bryden 1974, p. 22). Policies and institutions for dealing with old age dependency were quite disparate, but outside Nova Scotia and New Brunswick, where public poor laws were still in effect, public subsidization of private charity was the rule. Both municipal and provincial governments dealt with the problem of relieving the poor by subsidizing voluntary welfare institutions rather than directly administering poor relief (Spiesman 1973, pp. 40, 46–48; Struthers 1983, chap. 1; Pitsula 1980; Machar 1898). These arrangements allowed for the political use of welfare funds to subsidize private activities and put the local elites in charge. For example, Quebec relied most heavily of all the provinces on private philanthropy (McLean 1901); in this way, public funds helped to maintain the welfare activities of the politically predominant Catholic Church. In Toronto, Protestant elites who ran the city's house of refuge received public monies (Pitsula 1980). Thus, the Canadian policy legacy, in sharp contrast with the American, left patronage democracy relatively unimplicated in the problems of social welfare practices but complemented the political dynamics of its notability-dominated polity.

The pattern of public subsidization of private relief-giving groups and institutions can be illustrated with reference to Ontario, where the work of Richard Splane (1973) and others has unearthed more information than is available for the other provinces. Here voluntary efforts were encouraged by the Charity Aid Act of 1874, which required the province to give financial subsidies for voluntary institutions, contingent upon the acceptance of provincial supervision (Splane 1973, pp. 80–81, 98). Because public institutions did not receive comparable aid, the "development of voluntary institutions may well have removed the pressure for the establishment of public institutions in many communities" (Splane 1973, p. 99). With the House of Refuge Act of 1890, Ontario gave provincial support to public institutions to be devoted to the "care and custody of the aged, helpless and poor" (quoted in Splane 1973, p. 99). Because terms of support remained more favorable to private institutions, however, not all counties immediately built houses of refuge (Splane 1973, pp. 99–102). Yet outside the population centers, institutional development lagged, and "vagrants"—often so due only to the misfortune of being old and poor— were jailed (Bryden 1974, pp. 23, 49). In 1891 the Ontario Royal Commission on the Prison and Reformatory System "found large numbers of homeless elderly who were lodged in local jails on charges of vagrancy because there was no other place for them" (Guest 1980, p. 14). By the early 1900s counties did begin to build poorhouses, although officials were no longer carrying out the principle of less eligibility (Splane 1973, p. 97). As in Britain and the United

States, in Canada the majority of those in the poorhouses in most localities were the aged (Canadian House of Commons 1912, pp. 9–10, 14).

The Reaction to Provision for the Poor

The remnants of the Dickensian harshness of traditional poor relief encouraged some reformers, politicians, and labor leaders to consider modern social welfare programs as an alternative. But the administrative patchwork and lack of centralization of social policy gave Canadians little focus for national public debate as localized administrative and financial problems developed in relief-giving activities and as prevailing beliefs about how best to deal with the poor changed. Not only were problems of financing and administration of poor relief scattered over many municipalities, but they were also the responsibility of many private organizations and institutions that the public merely subsidized. Problems of poor relief did not impinge as strongly on voters and public administrators as they would have if public officials had had direct responsibility for administering poor relief and social welfare institutions. Without uniform, *publicly run* social welfare institutions, Canadians, particularly among elite strata who did not suffer personally from the operations of the social welfare systems, experienced little sense that something needed reforming. A perceived nationwide crisis of public welfare institutions was lacking in Canada. This stands in marked contrast with Britain, with its centralized, public, and increasingly crisis-ridden relief apparatus, or even with the United States, whose decentralized, but still public, poor relief administration had widely recognized shortcomings.

It is somewhat risky to argue that there is an absence of something, yet I contend that Canadian elites were not intensely concerned with patronage in welfare and that *disinterest* is a better characterization of their attitude. In my examination of the proceedings of the Social Service Council (1914) and the Canadian Conference of Charities and Correction in the prewar years and of the personal papers of some of Canada's leading social reformers, J. J. Kelso, Charlotte Whitton, and James Woodsworth, I found almost no references to "politics in welfare," a perennial topic of central importance among U.S. charity and social reformers that was explicitly cited as a reason for not initiating new government social protections. In comparison with the United States, Canada saw less reaction against public social spending, and elites did not manifest the profound opposition to social spending measures that was so important in American social policy debates of the Progressive Era. Indeed, there was almost no public welfare administration in Canada to be permeated by the patronage practices reformers abhorred, and no patronage-dominated pension and poor relief systems to serve as a negative precedent. (Contemporaries also noted that there was no Canadian analogue of a nationally administered

Civil War pension system tied to the federal patronage party system; Bryce 1921, pp. 500–501; Skelton 1915.) The more extensive democracy in America meant that many distributive policies, including Civil War pensions, urban-machine-controlled poor relief and public works jobs, benefited nonelites and implicated them in perceived problems of social welfare policy. Popular interests were given more political expression in the United States, but elite concerns about patronage overshadowed these pressures, turning reform elites away from democratically controlled spending by a state still dominated by patronage.

The Failure of Old Age Pension Proposals in Canada

In the first decade of the twentieth century, reacting to the insufficiency of existing provision for the aged and the example of European and Australasian countries, a number of Canadian M.P.'s, including former presidents of the trade union federation, introduced pension legislation in the House of Commons. Their efforts produced a series of hearings, at which labor leaders and a few reformers testified to the need for public action to relieve the suffering of the "worthy" aged poor and their families (Canadian House of Commons 1912). Yet the hearings did not lead to action by either the Liberal administration or the Conservative opposition, nor did they spark the interest of reformers outside Parliament. Concern about pensions, never very high to begin with, died out as the country's attention was drawn to the issues arising from Canadian involvement in the First World War.

The underdeveloped capacity of the state, the legacy of Canada's experience of state formation, was a key factor in the lack of success of old age pension proposals in prewar Canada. The state was still patronage-ridden due to the failure of civil service reform, and thus administrative resources remained undeveloped. In Britain, policy innovators within the state played key roles in negotiating the details of policy reforms and thus helping to cement cross-class alliances, but such actors were absent in the Canadian state. Given that reform could not occur through bureaucratic initiatives or negotiations, the concerns and orientations of middle- and upper-class political actors were critical. The elitist and nonprogrammatic orientation of Canadian parties blunted the appeal for political leaders of social spending measures that would benefit workers and, to a lesser degree, farmers. Parties continued to mobilize their constituents through patronage and did not face impending franchise extensions that might have highlighted the demands of working-class voters. There was little impetus for issue entrepreneurship using pensions or social insurance given continuing reliance on patronage and a stable electorate. Moreover, Canadian reformers, who did not see the state as a feasible instrument in which to entrust administratively complex programs or funds vulnerable to partisan use, focused on political reforms. Farmers, who might have provided an alternative coalition partner for workers, opposed labor on a number of key questions, notably the tariff and many labor regulations, and had not yet been loosened from existing party loyalties based on patronage, the tariff, and ethnicity (Laxer 1989, p. 137; Brodie and Jenson 1980, pp. 68–77, 137–38). Finally, Canadian social policy was not institutionalized in a way that encouraged elite attention to problems of poor relief, nor did it engender common working-class and elite interests in enacting social spending programs that would overcome the difficulties of poor relief. All of these factors added up to elite disinterest in social spending reforms, and in general, reform-minded politicians in Canada manifested more interest in political than in social reform (English 1977, pp. 70–71).

Basically, Canadian elites' failure to work with popular groups for pensions stemmed from the elitist character of the political system and the private organization of social policy, both of which insulated elites from popular pressures for social reform. American elites' unwillingness to ally with popular forces stemmed from their reactions to U.S. patronage democracy, which led them to oppose public spending. Canadian elites' failure to support new social programs for the aged reflected their disinterest in appealing to popular forces, while the failure of analogous measures in the United States stemmed in large part from American elites' clear and explicit rejection of any expansion of state social spending until patronage practices were "cleaned up."

The pattern of social policy that did emerge in Canada in the years before the war bears the imprint of these factors. Regulatory reforms were most successful in prewar Canada, as they were in the United States: workers' compensation, minimum wage laws, and mothers' pensions all were established by provincial governments in this period (Corry 1939, pp. 57–59, 65–66; Strong-Boag 1979). In addition, legislation establishing arbitration in labor disputes was passed in 1907 (Craven 1980). Regulation was a possibility because it did not overtax a state with relatively undeveloped administrative capacities, and it called for few expert or professional personnel. Perhaps more important, regulation did not demand social spending—for nonelites—on a large scale, which to still-dominant elites would seem an open invitation to corruption or ineptitude given the continuing dominance of patronage practices.

To deal with poverty among the aged, political elites preferred government annuities to noncontributory pensions. In 1908 the Liberal administration proposed a government annuities program as a substitute for pensions, which were under consideration in the House of Commons, several proposals having been made since 1906 (Bryden 1974, pp. 47–49). The Liberal government's spokesman, Sir Richard Cartwright, argued that government annuities rather than state pensions were needed, since "people of limited means were not willing to entrust their savings to private companies" and could not afford the terms necessary when such plans were offered by profit-making companies (Bryden 1974, pp. 49, 51–52). Annuities would simultaneously allow the working class to practice the virtue of thrift, prevent corrupt business interests from profiting at the expense of the poor, and keep the state from having to initiate large spending programs. The bill passed, despite insurance industry opposition (Bryden 1974, pp. 50–53). It is interesting to note that business groups were not strong enough to prevent passage of old age annuities, which they opposed, in 1908 (Bryden 1974, pp. 50–53). But like other elites, they seemed uninterested in the issue of pensions. They did not testify at the hearings held by parliamentary investigatory committees in the period 1911–13 (Canadian House of Commons 1912; Bryden 1974, pp. 42–43), and the subject was rarely mentioned in major business association journals such as *Industrial Canada,* the organ of the Canadian Manufacturers' Association. Ultimately, like voluntary old age protection programs everywhere, annuities did little to lessen the problem of dependency in old age, which reflected the inability of working-class people to save for a rainy day, given prevailing wage levels (Rubinow 1913, chaps. 19–21). But the elderly and their families would have to wait for more propitious political conditions, which came in the decade after the Great War.

Balance-of-Power Politics and New Provision for the Elderly in the 1920s

In the mid-1920s a parliamentary coalition of Liberals, Labourites, and Progressives formed the support for old age pensions, and old age pension legislation was finally enacted at the federal level in 1927. The law provided 50 percent federal funding for means-tested, noncontributory pensions paid out by a province under enabling legislation. Five provinces—British Columbia, Ontario, Alberta, Manitoba, and Saskatchewan—passed the enabling laws by 1929 (Bryden 1974, p. 81). The governments of the other provinces, unable and/or unwilling to contribute 50 percent toward pensions for their elderly residents, lobbied for increased federal funding. Federal funding went to 75 percent in 1931, and by 1936 all the remaining provinces had joined the program (Bryden 1974, chap. 5). Attempts to move toward a contributory old age insurance system in the mid-1930s were thwarted, however, when legislation sponsored by Prime Minister R. B. Bennett's administration was declared *ultra vires.* The 1927 system remained in place until after the Second World War, with only minor changes (Bryden 1974, chap. 5).

Canada's involvement in World War I was the critical factor in changing conditions which had previously stood in the way of the formation of a cross-class coalition for old age pensions. The war created an opening for civil service reform, allowing for the development of new state capacities, and wartime mobilization ushered in the full democratization of the electorate. These changes in the character of the Canadian state and electorate had profound implications for the party system. Parties moved to more programmatic appeals, third parties emerged, elites faced new incentives for attention to the demands of farmers and workers, and the problems of poor relief were thrown into sharper relief in the new, more democratic political context. In addition, with civil service practices in place in the federal government, the concerns of reform elites would not be so focused on political reform. Finally, new and positive policy precedents for old age pensions came with the enactment of soldiers' insurance. The failure of contributory old age insurance in the 1930s is related to some of the features of the Canadian polity which did not change in the wake of World War I—the strong provincial governments and the remaining constitutional tie to Britain.

State and Party after the War: Democratization and Civil Service Reform

Canada's geopolitical position—in particular, its tie to Britain—had important consequences for Canadian politics during and after the First World War. Canada was involved in fighting almost immediately, with the concomitant political battles over participation and conscription and government attempts to mobilize the population for the war effort (Brown and Cook 1974, chaps. 11–16). At war's end, Canada joined with the international community of nations in signing the Treaty of Versailles and entering into the International Labour Organization, whose charter endorsed labor legislation and social insurance (Guest 1980, p. 67). The effects on domestic social politics were profound. Indeed, World War I marks the initial, tentative turning of Canadian politics toward a British model of programmatic parties and an interventionist state. The contrast with the United States is quite striking, for America participated relatively reluctantly in the war and then withdrew into isolationism in the 1920s, rejecting the Versailles treaty and British-style social policy and politics.

The Administrative State

Given the exigencies of the patronage political system, it took a noncompetitive electoral situation to allow civil service reform to make further headway in early-twentieth-century Canada. This came with Canada's participation in World War I and the formation in 1917 of a bipartisan Unionist government, under Robert Borden (Borden 1931, pp. 17–20). It was a "unique opportunity to enact reform," and the government first issued executive orders, then passed the 1918 Civil Service Act, strengthening the Civil Service Commission and extending the merit system to the outside service (English 1977, pp. 162–63; Hodgetts et al. 1972, p. 50). By the early 1920s patronage had been largely eliminated from the federal service (Owram 1986, p. 126; Hodgetts et al. 1972, p. 115; Hodgetts 1973, pp. 51–54; English 1977, pp. 224–25). This cleared the way for the enhancement of state capacities. It also meant that patronage was no longer the primary concern of reformers, who turned increasingly to expanding the expertise of the state administration and extending state activities that depended upon social science (Owram 1986, pp. 128–32). Although provincial governments were not subject to the civil service reform, the increase in welfare and labor regulatory functions—resulting from reform efforts before and during the war—had left a legacy of commissions staffed by experts and separated from the patronage-dominated governmental agencies to run the new programs (English 1977, pp. 226–27; Bryden 1974, pp. 97–98; Munro 1929, pp. 71–72; Guest 1980, chaps. 4–5). Thus, social welfare expertise in provincial and federal governments was increasing, while the demise of partisanship in federal government appointments enhanced the capacity of political elites to use the federal state to oversee and control provincial activities.

The Party System

Canada's involvement in the war brought an end to the old party system, ushering in the full democratization of the electorate (Englemann and Schwartz 1975, p. 48), stimulating the emergence of new parties, and contributing to the reorientation of the old parties. With the end of federal patronage, parties became less dependent on the spoils of office and more programmatic in their approach to the electorate (Munro 1929, pp. 69–72; English 1977, pp. 224–26). This transformation was first manifested in Borden's ultimately unsuccessful attempt to rally support to the Unionist government based on a newly invigorated nationalism (Brown and Cook 1974, chap. 16; English 1977, p. 228). Then, beginning with the Liberals in 1919, all the parties, including a number of newly formed ones, held party conventions to select programs (Dawson 1933, pp. 357–58). The Unionist administration pursued conscription, franchise, tariff, and other policies that set English Canadians against other ethnic groups, and labor and western farmers against eastern business groups (English 1977, chap. 7; Brodie and Jenson 1980, pp. 88–98; Brown and Cook 1974, chap. 13). When the universal franchise was established in 1920 and the wartime manipulations of the franchise rescinded, a large number of Canadians were ready to use votes to retaliate against the Conservatives, the dominant party in the Unionist coalition. Some working-class groups rejected the harsh repressive policies of unionism, including conscription, and turned to independent labor politics (Robin 1968, p. 199). Quebec remained Liberal, most French Canadian members of the party having rejected the Unionist coalition and conscription. In the West, however, the Liberals had "disappeared as a distinguishable party and possible contender for support," while the Tories' protectionist stand made them unacceptable to most farmers (Brodie and Jenson 1980, p. 97). In this new context, traditional party loyalties were undermined for some groups, and mass-based, programmatic, and reform-oriented parties emerged.

Most notable was the Progressive party, made up primarily of western farmers (it would eventually combine with workers in the Cooperative
Commonwealth Federation in the 1930s). The Progressives, who campaigned
for broad-ranging social and tariff reforms and eschewed party organization,
tapped western farmers' discontent with the two old parties' "partyism," corporate patronage, and the National Policy that privileged "the interests" of
central Canada (Morton 1950; Whitaker 1987, p. 60). A number of Labour candidates, of varying party affiliations, also ran for provincial and federal office
in the postwar years (Robin 1968, chaps. 13–16). The 1921 election marked the
entry of new parties and newly politically independent constituencies—western farmers and labor—in the Canadian polity, which helped to create greater
incentives for elites to enter coalitions with popular political representatives.
This was manifested in the programmatic changes made by both old parties
to attract these voters and in the fact that third-party electoral success created
the conditions under which the two main parties depended on alliance with
minority parties to form a parliamentary majority. In fact, in neither the 1921
nor the 1925 elections did the Liberals or Conservatives receive majorities, as
third parties supported by disgruntled farmers and workers collected unprecedented numbers of seats. While some analysts (most notably Horowitz 1968)
have focused on the "Tory touch" and concomitant collectivism in Canadian
ideology to account for the ability of working-class-oriented third parties to
survive, the institutionalist analysis offered by analysts such as Robin (1968,
p. 273) and Lipset (1976, pp. 36–39) is arguably more relevant to the issue of
why such parties (and agrarian-based ones) could gain parliamentary representation. Under the Canadian federal parliamentary system, third parties could
exist separately and were not excluded from the highest levels of politics, as
they helped to form coalitions in the House, mitigating the sense that a third-
party vote represented a vote for the greater of two evils, as in the United States
(Lipset 1983, p. 56).

Policy Feedback: New Precedents for Old Age Pensions

In the wake of the war, given the intensified salience of popular demands and
the importance of accommodating third-party demands, the problems of poor
relief assumed new political importance. Moreover, civil service reform and
the war were associated with the establishment at the national level of two
important positive precedents for old age pensions: civil service pensions and
soldiers' insurance, both of which had the effect of legitimating federal pension
and insurance activities. Civil service pensions were established in Canada in
1924 to deal with the problem of superannuated government employees (Hodgetts et al. 1972, pp. 166, 172). As an essential part of mobilizing for the war,
Canada set up a wartime program for soldiers and their dependents, the first

large-scale public program for military men and veterans, which by its "reason-ableness . . . served to highlight similar categories of need among the civilian population" (Guest 1980, p. 50; see also Brown and Cook 1974, pp. 221–23).

By the early 1920s Canadians had also had some experience with the state-run voluntary annuities program, established in 1908, which had not been a success by anyone's standards (Bryden 1974, pp. 52–53). The perceived shortcomings of the voluntary government program eased the acceptance of a public pension system that could reach all those in need, especially since the public poor relief system, still the only alternative to government annuities, continued to be plagued by unevenness of coverage and perceived illegitimacy as a remedy for the poverty of the "worthy" aged. Indeed, by the 1920s only Quebec still lacked county houses of refuge, but local public responsibility for relief was gaining ground elsewhere (Strong 1930, pp. 105–6). With increasing public responsibility for relief after the war, the relative lack of visibility of social provision began to change. The problems of the poor—especially the aged, who dominated almshouse populations—entered more fully into politi-cal discourse. Increased resources were going into poorhouses at a time when these were losing favor in the international social policy community; reformers such as J. J. Kelso argued that Canada should avoid poorhouses and initiate pensions instead (testimony in Canadian House of Commons 1912, 1924).

Pension Politics after the War: A Cross-Class Coalition for Pensions Emerges

National discussion of pensions had been cut short by World War I (Bryden 1974, p. 61), but the war itself was critical in the reemergence of pensions on the political agenda. Changes in the state administration and party system, re-sulting from full democratization and the success of civil service reform, along with new, positive policy precedents for public pensions, created a favorable context for the enactment of state old age pensions. The coming together of a propension political alliance was not predetermined, but events did produce an agreement among Labourites, Progressives, and Liberals after the election of 1925.

In 1919, immediately following the war, the Liberals developed a new program which endorsed pensions and selected a new leader, former Labour minister W. L. Mackenzie King, a recognized Liberal expert on social and labor issues and proponent of pensions and social insurance. The holding of a party convention to develop a platform represented the transition to a more programmatic mode of appeal on the part of the national Liberal party, in the wake of the demise of federal patronage (Brown and Cook 1974, p. 329) and the declining appeal of traditional liberal issues. Indeed, it was after the Liberal defeat in 1911 on the tariff issue that party leader Sir Wilfrid Laurier called for a reconsideration of the party platform, and the National Liberal Advisory Committee was established to provide material for the postwar convention. A social welfare subcommittee, which consulted extensively with King, recommended old age and widows' pensions and a study of other social insurance programs (Bryden 1974, p. 66; Dawson 1959, p. 259; English 1977, pp. 133–34). These recommendations were accepted by the 1919 convention, so that when King became prime minister after the election of 1921, his administration was expected to act on the social welfare planks of the party platform, especially as the Royal Commission on Industrial Relations had recently (in 1919) recommended pensions as well (Carrigan 1968, pp. 80–84; Bryden 1974, pp. 65–66).

Despite King's commitment as a progressive Liberal, however, there was no immediate action on pensions or any other social welfare measures from his Liberal administration, which was preoccupied with balancing its distinctive sources of support: the conservative, Quebec wing of the Liberals on the one hand, and the pro–social reform western and urban liberals within the Liberal party and Progressive M.P.'s on the other (Neatby 1963, pp. 8–31; Bryden 1974, p. 66). The 1921 election results left the Tories as the third party, behind the Liberals and sixty-five Progressive M.P.'s. Liberals focused attention on the Progressives, for their support was essential to the formation of a W. L. Mackenzie King administration (Morton 1950, chap. 5, p. 245; Brodie and Jenson 1980, pp. 136–42). Finally, in 1924 King could equivocate no longer as political pressures mounted for action on pensions from within the Liberal party, from the Trades and Labour Congress, from provincial legislatures, and from third-party M.P.'s in the Dominion House of Commons. He established a committee in the House to investigate old age pensions. The committee issued a favorable report and a proposed pension plan, virtually identical to the law adopted in 1927 (Canadian House of Commons 1924; McNaught 1959, p. 216). Next, a second special committee was established in 1925 to consider the 1924 committee's recommendation in relation to the provincial governments; provincial responses were not encouraging, especially regarding financing (Bryden 1974, p. 67). Then pro-pension advocates tried to get a purely federal plan, but this too was rejected. Pensions "dropped off the government's agenda altogether," without even a mention in the Liberals' 1925 election propaganda (Bryden 1974, p. 68; Carrigan 1968, pp. 96–98).

As it turned out, however, even without the Liberals' pledge, the results of the 1925 election produced a situation in which pensions were forced to the top of the political agenda. The Liberals again received only a minority of seats in the House and thus continued to rely on third party M.P.'s to form an administration (Morton 1950, pp. 245–47). Even the support of the two Labour M.P.'s was needed (Robin 1968, p. 273; Bryden 1974, pp. 69–72). The Labour members, A. A. Heaps and noted reformer James Woodsworth, pre-

cipitated the consideration of the pension issue by offering both Conservative
leader Arthur Meighen and Liberal leader W. L. Mackenzie King a deal, which
in essence demanded the introduction of a pension bill as the price of their
support (McNaught 1959, pp. 217–19). The Conservative leader turned down
Woodsworth and Heaps, but King decided to accede to their request. It was,
after all, in keeping with the recently adopted Liberal program, the requests
of important Liberal constituencies and politicians, and King's own opinions
on social legislation. It also allowed King to maintain leadership of the closely
divided House. In 1926 the Liberals introduced a pension bill, against which
"no one," even Conservatives "was prepared to vote" (Bryden 1974, p. 70).

Opposition to pensions was voiced more openly in the nonelected, Tory-
dominated Senate—the very existence of which reflected Canada's elitist political tradition—than it had been in the House of Commons, and the bill was
defeated there. By then, the King adminstration was in trouble over other
issues, and the prime minister resigned (see Graham 1967); new elections were
held in 1926. The Liberals now appealed to the voters on the basis of several
issues for which they had passed legislation in the House of Commons but that
had been defeated by the Senate, including, prominently, old age pensions.
Pensions won sizable numbers of votes for the Liberals (Bryden 1974, pp.
71–74) and contributed to the cooperative electoral arrangement at the constituency level engineered by Liberal party organizers between Liberals on the
one hand and Progressive and Labour candidates on the other in the 1926 election (Young 1978, p. 36). Thus, pensions represented a critical programmatic
cement for the cross-class coalition in Canada, as embodied in this electoral
alliance. Farmers, while opposing the "interests"—corporations, railroads,
and so on—had until this point not been a particularly attractive coalition partner for organized labor. They disagreed on the tariff (workers' organizations
adopted a protectionist stance; Brodie and Jenson 1980, p. 138) and on social
welfare measures where the farmers as employers of farm laborers might suffer—this was the case in regard to unemployment insurance (Struthers 1983,
p. 43) and the eight-hour day (Brodie and Jenson 1980, pp. 137–38). Protection for the aged did not fall into this category, however, and Progressives
generally supported the Liberal administration's initiatives regarding pensions.
Thus, King could agree with Heaps and Woodsworth's demand about pensions
with confidence that doing so would not undermine his support among western
Progressives. Quebec, however, remained problematic; the Liberals hoped that
by leaving some issues to be worked out in the upcoming Dominion-provincial
conference, they could circumvent Quebec's opposition.

The Old Age Pension Act established federal funding for provincial programs giving small old age pensions, which were to be means-tested and restricted to British subjects aged seventy or over who had resided in Canada for
many years (Guest 1980, p. 77). The maximum pension was $240 for those

with no income, and total income could not exceed $365 (Bryden 1974, p. 62). (Compare these levels with the living wage for a single, independent woman living in Toronto—$653—set by the Ontario minimum wage commission; Guest 1980, pp. 73, 76.) Woodsworth tried to get a larger proportion of the funding from the federal government and more lenient eligibility requirements, but he could gain no support for this position in Parliament (McNaught 1959, p. 220). This pension program was quite comparable to the British system that had been created in 1908 (Heclo 1974, pp. 174–76) and, indeed, to most of the noncontributory programs established in Europe, Australia, and New Zealand prior to the war (Rubinow 1913, chap. 23; Myles 1984, pp. 16, 38–39). Benefit levels in Canada, as in all early plans including the contributory ones, were low, yet pensions represented the beginning of a citizen's wage in Canada and prevented many elderly Canadians from having to depend on their families or to turn to charity or an almshouse.

By leaving the initiation of pensions to provincial discretion, the Liberals responded to constitutional, administrative, and political realities. The Department of Justice, responding to the inquiry of the 1924 House of Commons committee about constitutional jurisdiction, said that because old age pensions came under the heading of property and civil rights, the British North America Act made them a provincial function. Thus, compulsory contributory plans were ruled out, but a federal grant-in-aid to provinces enacting noncontributory plans was allowed (Maxwell 1937, pp. 228–29). Relegating the administration of pensions to the provinces reflected the fact that federal activities in social welfare were close to nonexistent, while the provinces had some experience in administering analogous programs, such as workers' compensation and mothers' pensions (Bryden 1974, p. 97; Owram 1986, pp. 128–32). The federal government, however, could assert financial control through audits and examinations (Bryden 1974, p. 99), which could be expected to curb any provincial attempts to use pensions in the service of partisan or patronage interests. Politically, the grant-in-aid form was useful as well, for it allowed the federal government to enact pension legislation unilaterally, sidestepping the opposition from Quebec, Nova Scotia, and New Brunswick (Maxwell 1937, pp. 229–30).

The Old Age Pension Act passed in both houses of Parliament in 1927, as the Liberals, finally successful in absorbing many Progressives (Morton 1950, chap. 8), had been returned to the House of Commons with a majority, and the Senate, chastened by the Liberal victory, finally accepted the legislation. Yet this did not complete the institutional arrangements necessary for the payment of pensions to Canada's older citizens to begin, for there still remained the problem of working out differences between the provincial governments over implementation of the joint federal-provincial program. There continued to be substantial differences of opinion between the Quebec and the urban-western wings of the Liberal party. The Quebec wing, never very favorable to pensions, asked that the federal government refrain from signing agreements with any of the provinces until the plan had been discussed with all of them at an upcoming federal-provincial conference in 1927 (Bryden 1974, pp. 72–73). But Labour minister Peter Heenan, a former trade union leader who had run as a Liberal-Labour candidate, and his allies in the Liberal provincial admin-istration of British Columbia forced the issue by getting a pension scheme set up and tentatively approved (by him!) for that province. King and the federal Liberals had no choice but to give final approval to the British Columbian plan (a statutory prerequisite for the plan's functioning) if they were not to waste the political advantages—especially the alliance with western Progressives and Labour party members—they had won with the pension law in the first place (Bryden 1974, p. 73). At this point, confronted with British Columbia's *fait ac-compli*, the 1927 Dominion-provincial conference concentrated on issues other than pensions. By 1929, all the western provinces and Ontario had adopted enabling pension legislation (Bryden 1974, p. 81).

Once pensions had demonstrated their potential political appeal, the Con-servatives pledged that they would implement full federal funding if elected. This was particularly useful in mobilizing in Quebec and financially strapped Nova Scotia and New Brunswick, the voters of which were seeing their fed-eral taxes go toward the payment of benefits to the aged citizens of the more prosperous provinces without their own provinces being able to spare the funds necessary to set up pensions. After the Conservative victory in 1930, party leader R. B. Bennett partially honored his electoral pledge by raising the fed-eral contribution to 75 percent of the cost of the provincial pension programs (Bryden 1974, p. 74), and by 1936 all the provinces were participating in the plan. Bennett expected this to be a temporary situation, as he worked to enact a comprehensive social insurance package, which would include contributory old age insurance (McConnell 1969).

Bennett's plans to introduce a contributory program meshed with the pref-erences of major business groups. In contrast with the opposition of business groups in the United States to old age pension legislation during the 1920s, old age pensions seem not to have stirred the interest of Canadian businessmen. A search of *Industrial Canada* for the period 1920–27 shows little interest in old age pension legislation; in the two years preceding the passage of the Old Age Pension Act, no major articles dealt with the issue, and only a handful of short pieces described the progress of the bill. In February 1928 an article ap-peared asking, "What Will Old Age Pensions Cost Canada?" (Mitchell 1928). The author, a professor of political economy, noted, "With the general prin-ciple of old age pensions nobody can quarrel. That the aged and deserving poor should be able in their declining years to live without bearing the stigma of charity is a worthy and humane ideal." Then he went on to caution his readers that the costs of such a system should be considered, and precautions taken to ensure they did not get out of hand. Clearly, this was a warning for the provinces—which were then considering whether or not to come into the system—to provide adequate safeguards to contain costs. It was also a more positive message about public old age assistance than American manufacturers were giving in the 1920s. In 1929 the Industrial Relations Department of the Canadian Manufacturers' Association published an article in *Industrial Canada* calling for reconsideration of Canada's decision to adopt a means-tested pension scheme; it would be better, argued the spokespersons for the CMA, to enact contributory social insurance for the elderly (Canadian Manufacturers' Association Industrial Relations Department 1929). Again, this position was quite different from that taken by their counterparts in the United States, where old age pensions for the very poor would become acceptable to some by the early 1930s, but contributory public schemes remained anathema.

Bennett's "Canadian New Deal," "an impressive program of unemployment, old age and health insurance, cost-shared social assistance and public works, and measures to help people with mortgages and to help farmers obtain higher prices" was successful in Parliament but was struck down by the Judicial Committee of the Privy Council, an imperial body based in England, on constitutional grounds (Leman 1980, p. 35; Guest 1980, pp. 88–90; Finkel 1977). Again, provincial-federal relations were important in this outcome. A suit contesting the role of the federal government in demanding mandatory contributions from individuals had been brought by Ontario, Quebec, and New Brunswick. The Privy Council, whose jurisdiction resulted from the decision of Canadian elites to remain within the British Empire, "for decades had interpreted the Canadian constitution to prohibit the federal government from infringing on many areas traditionally reserved for the provinces," and its veto was allowed to stand (Leman 1980, p. 35).

After the defeat of Bennett's social insurance legislation, the Commission on Dominion-Provincial Relations was appointed to recommend the constitutional changes necessary to redistribute financial and legislative powers between the two levels of government more rationally, so that federally funded and administered contributory social insurance could become practicable. Unemployment insurance was finally (re)enacted in 1940, and consideration of reforms of the old age pension program began soon after as a part of wartime reconstruction planning (Owram 1986, pp. 276, 298–99). In 1951 a new, universal pension plan was initiated (Guest 1980, p. 145). The Old Age Pension Act of 1927 had paved the way for Canada's version of a modern welfare state.

Third-Party Pressures and Pensions

The coalescence of a cross-class coalition of Liberal, Labour, and Progressive M.P.'s in the mid-1920s was the proximate cause for the success of pensions in Canada. The enhanced state capacities created with the success of federal civil service reform and the development of provincial welfare and regulatory administrative agencies appears to have been important to the formation of the cross-class coalition for spending. In considering a pension program, reformers could turn to the provinces and expect that the federal government could control any new functions and spending. Indeed, following the initial enactment of the pension plan, the federal government continuously extended its control over pension administration and spending in the provinces, forcing the provincial governments to protect pensions from partisan use (Bryden 1974, pp. 98–101). Problems in existing policy formed the backdrop to consideration of old age pensions, especially as popular concerns received greater attention through third-party representation. But clearly the coalition that backed pensions was predicated on the balance-of-power situation existing in Parliament during the early-to-mid 1920s, which emerged in the changed, less elitist, political context following the war. The presence of third-party M.P.'s in the House of Commons was critical to the success of federal pension legislation in 1927. Third-party representation was also important at the provincial level, where legislators from the Labour and Progressive parties were instrumental in getting provincial legislatures to take positive action on pensions: first to put pressure on Ottawa, then to enact enabling legislation (Bryden 1974, chap. 5). Parliamentarism allowed the prime minister to create a programmatically based coalition with minor party M.P.'s and to carry the rest of his party along with his initiatives (Meisel 1967; Epstein 1964). Political entrepreneurs had to win over party leadership to proposed policies but could count on party discipline to pass legislation once the party had a majority in Parliament—a sharp contrast with the fragmented American state and its multiple veto points to reform. In short, the distinctive character of the Canadian state structure and statebuilding channeled popular pressures for new government social activities into third parties and allowed such parties to influence policy outcomes.

9
The United States, 1920–1940
Belated Breakthrough to Modern Social
Protection for the Aged

Americans entered the post–World War I era under quite different circumstances than did their Canadian neighbors. Without the British tie of the Canadians, Americans participated in the war more reluctantly, and at war's end,
they decisively rejected the British model of social politics and new public
social protections. They embraced instead the ideal of "welfare capitalism,"
under which businessmen were to offer necessary protections to their employees through company welfare programs, to be supplemented by private charity
for those outside the labor force (Brandes 1976; Brody 1980; Clarke Chambers 1963). A number of working-class groups, sometimes backed by small
professional reform associations, called for noncontributory old age pension
programs at the state level, but their political success was minimal (Fischer
1978, pp. 173–74; Leotta 1975). State-level pension legislation, first introduced in 1903 in Massachusetts (Linford 1949, p. 9), finally scored its first
success in 1923, when Montana, Nevada, and Pennsylvania adopted old age
pension laws. Pennsylvania's law was declared unconstitutional by the state
supreme court, but by 1928 four more states had passed pension laws (Fischer
1978, pp. 173–74). The passage of these laws was mainly a symbolic success,
for they left the payment of pensions to county option; only about one thousand
elderly people were actually receiving pensions in 1928 (U.S. Bureau of the
Census 1975, p. 738; Fischer 1978, pp. 173–74; Massachusetts Commission
on Pensions 1925, p. 37; U.S. Social Security Board 1937, pp. 160–61).

It was only with the political crisis triggered by the Great Depression
that a large number of states passed pension programs and the federal government finally initiated nationwide public social protection for the elderly, with
the passage of the charter legislation of the U.S. version of a modern welfare
state, the Social Security Act of 1935. In 1929 California became the first state
to pass a mandatory pension law, with contributions from the state (Putnam
1970, p. 19). With the onset of the Depression, there were many more legisla-

269

tive successes for pensions, including those in the key states of Massachusetts and New York in 1930. Most states followed California's lead in establishing mandatory systems with state financial assistance (U.S. Social Security Board 1937, p. 161). By the time the Social Security bill was introduced in Congress in January 1935, twenty-eight states had already enacted pension laws, and about 236,000 people were receiving benefits. By the time Congress passed the Social Security Act in August 1935, an additional eight states had passed laws, while other states amended their laws so that they would comply with the provisions of the act (U.S. Social Security Board 1937, pp. 161, 166). The old age assistance section of the Social Security Act (Title I) provided 50 percent federal funding to all state pension programs which met the federal requirements, subject to the approval of the Social Security Board (U.S. Social Security Board 1937, pp. 218–20).[1] Every state had pension legislation on the books by 1939. But more innovative and ultimately more important politically and in terms of numbers covered and expenditures, the Social Security Act also included a purely national contributory old age benefits system, which covered the nation's paid work force, with the exception of employees in agriculture, domestic service, government, and nonprofit institutions (U.S. Social Security Board 1937, p. 222). (This program was not called "insurance" until after the act had been declared constitutional by the Supreme Court in 1937; see Cates 1983, chap. 2.) With the 1939 amendments to the Social Security Act, benefits were extended to wage earners' dependents.

The political legacy of the American state-building experience had profound effects on the course of policy-making in the decades between the wars. Patronage had been dealt some blows by the civil service reforms of the 1910s, but it showed greater staying power in the United States than in Canada and remained a concern of elites into the 1930s (Shefter 1978; Whitaker 1987, p. 61; Abbott 1936). The fear of democratic patronage that had so long characterized American political elites did not simply evaporate. Indeed, it helped to shape the provisions of the legislation introduced by the Roosevelt administration. Although concerns about patronage remained, action on social provision was politically necessary, and political elites in the Roosevelt administration felt they had to take action or face the passage of "politically unwise" legislation. Because the capacities of some state administrations, most notably in Wisconsin and New York, were enhanced in the wake of Progressive Era political reforms, Roosevelt could draw on the service of experienced social policy experts to help him formulate and run new federal social programs.

---

1. The most important of these requirements was that the plans be statewide in operation, administered or supervised by a single state agency, at least partially financed by the state, and contain certain maximum eligibility requirements, notably an age limit of sixty-five rather than seventy, as required by most state laws up until that point (U.S. Social Security Board 1937, pp. 218–20).

In the context of the divided American state and the continuing absence of an autonomous bureaucracy, the success of any political initiative, including new public protection for the aged, depended on mass and elite pressure being exerted on Congress to overcome the many potential vetoes and to get coordination among the various branches of government. That is, success depended on the mobilization of a broad-based, cross-class coalition. As in the Progressive Era, the concerns of political elites in the interwar period were important in determining whether or not such a coalition could be developed. Critically for the outcome of reform efforts in the 1920s, the polity was characterized by popular demobilization, the demise of third parties, and single-party dominance in both North and South. Thus, political incentives to elites for attention to popular demands for social spending were minimal. Liberal political elites in the United States were generally uninterested in working with working-class groups through the 1920s, despite the fact that the war had brought a number of positive policy precedents for old age protection. In contrast with the political demobilization of the 1920s, the 1930s saw high levels of popular political mobilization. The success of the Social Security Act and state-level old age pension laws rested on the high level of popular mobilization around the pension issue, which was needed to overcome congressional and other resistance to new legislation and to make social insurance or pensions a political necessity, as well as an attractive option from the electoral point of view. The serious crisis of existing relief institutions and the failure of private welfare programs helped to convince many middle-class and elite reformers, politicians, welfare administrators, and voters that public action was required to deal with the problems of the aged poor, the unemployed, and others. Thus, they became willing to enter into political coalitions with workers and other popular groups to that end.

The State and Parties after the War

The fragmented character of the U.S. state was not changed by the political transformations accompanying the Progressive Era and World War I. The American state structure was so divided that coordination among the various branches and levels of the government required the creation of extremely broad coalitions, especially in the period before the emergence of the bureaucracy as a factor in policy-making (Leman 1980, p. 135; 1977, p. 264). In "normal" times, such as existed in the 1920s, the existence of numerous veto points set up prerequisites for policy change which were (and are) difficult to overcome, since "no single agent [had] the initiative" if there was disagreement, which there usually was (Leman 1977, p. 264). But in "crisis" times, it was more likely that very broad coalitions could be pieced together by entrepreneurial policymakers or politicians (Leman 1980, p. 165) and that pressure would be brought to bear on all government organizations at once, though the specific proposals of these coalitions would be less important for policy-making than their simple demand that something be done. Thus, in contrast with the Canadian state, which allowed for executive initiative in response to political exigencies even in the absence of high levels of popular mobilization (in W. L. Mackenzie King's case, the need to respond to the demands of Heaps and Woodsworth to stay in office), the U.S. state imposed high barriers to the initiation of reform.

After the war, parties in the United States became somewhat less dependent on the spoils of office (Munro 1929, pp. 69–72). This, however, did not mean a turn toward European-style mass membership parties making programmatic or ideological appeals (Lowi 1967). Rather, U.S. parties continued as constituency parties, in which each politician responded to his or her electoral base in whatever manner necessary to get and stay elected. Some politicians might make use of programmatic appeals, while others continued to rely on patronage, particularly in those regions of the country which had composed the heartland of the nineteenth-century patronage party system (Shefter 1978, 1983). What was new was that patronage no longer played the integrative role across the levels of government that it had in the past, and American parties were left perhaps more internally divided than ever. Skocpol and Ikenberry point out that during the New Deal, "while the Democratic party certainly 'aggregated' voting blocs into ad hoc state and national coalitions, it did not combine popular demands into broad policy programs, nor did it transmit group ideas into inner circles of policy-formation" (1983, p. 122). Thus, U.S. parties did not serve as vehicles of reform in the way that programmatically oriented European parties in this period did.

The achievement of a partially reformed civil service at the federal level meant that, within the sphere of the civil administration, concerns after the war focused on the techniques of administrative management and the implementation of professional ideals, in addition to the issue of partisanship and patronage versus professionalization and bureaucratization (White 1958, pp. 395–96). Officials appointed under merit rules had a foothold in the federal civil service. Yet the kind of bureaucratic corps of officials who could fashion policy initiatives and shepherd them over the necessary political hurdles was not widely in evidence in the U.S. federal government.[2] Patronage, particularly in the states east of the Mississippi, did not simply go away (Shefter 1978, p. 237; 1983). Officials appointed under merit rules, however, were quite important to social

---

2. There were a few isolated exceptions. The experts of the U.S. Children's Bureau were instrumental in the success of the Shepard-Towner Act, which provided grants to states to promote maternal and infant health (Skocpol forthcoming, chap. 10).

policy developments in those states where civil service had been most successful, such as Wisconsin, and in certain "islands of expertise" within some
state governments, such as New York's Industrial Commission, even though
patronage may not have been thoroughly expunged from the entire state administration (Shefter 1978, pp. 229–37; White 1933; Abbott 1936; Zimmerman
1981; Amenta et al. 1987). These state officials also emerged as key actors
in the New Deal, as Franklin Roosevelt called upon them to formulate and
implement his main social policy initiatives. In most states during the 1920s,
however, the incompleteness of the progressives' civil service (and social) reforms encouraged elites to prefer private solutions to public problems, and a
circumventing of state administration rather than its utilization. After all, only
ten states had passed civil service legislation by 1920, and the legislation was
not effective in most of these; not until the late 1930s did states again begin
passing such laws (Abbott 1936, p. 403; Klein 1940, p. 42). Then, because
private solutions were institutionalized and legitimated, they had to fail before
public policy could again emerge on the political agenda. This is exactly what
happened with the Depression.

The United States entered the Depression with federal, state, and local
administrations only partially delivered from the patronage system (Van Riper
1958, chap. 12). This state of affairs in the civil administration of federal and
state governments had important effects on the course of social policy-making
in the 1930s. To the extent that the bureaucratization and professionalization
of the civil service incorporated experts and reformers into the administration,
an increase occurred in the state's capacity for investigation of problems of
income interruption and dependency and for administration of programs designed to alleviate them (Achenbaum 1978, p. 130). In the United States these
developments were especially important at the state level: the industrial commissions, worker's compensation agencies, and state bureaus of labor statistics
which were established or strengthened (with the additions of inspectors and
statisticians) in the wake of the labor and social legislative successes of the Progressive Era (Brandeis 1935) could be utilized in collecting information about
and proposing solutions for the perceived problems of the older worker and
aged dependency. In Wisconsin, an especially powerful industrial commission
and an important legislative reference library flourished even in the 1920s,
with strong ties to the academic community at the University of Wisconsin. It
was from this state government–academic complex that Roosevelt found many
of the key personnel for the Committee on Economic Security (CES) and the
Social Security Board (Schlabach 1969, chaps. 3, 5; Harter 1962; Cates 1983,
pp. 23–25, 27).[3] Roosevelt also drew on people who had served in social and

3. What the achievement of civil service reform in Wisconsin meant for considerations of new
public social programs is well-illustrated in the following quote from John R. Commons, the Uni-

labor agencies in his home state of New York (Charles 1963, p. 23; Bernstein 1985, pp. 43–45; Perkins 1964, chaps. 1–2).[4]

With the economic crisis, the demands for government to take on new duties increased once again. This in turn led to pressures for reforming administrative practices and struggles on the part of patronage politicians to defend these practices (Shefter 1978, pp. 237–43). Thus, debates about social insurance and pensions again took place against the backdrop of a continuing struggle for control of the civil administrations of the federal and state governments between those who favored civil service reform and patronage politicians. Liberal elites, mainly progressive politicans and social reformers, argued for initiating new social programs while simultaneously reforming administrative practices (Abbott 1936). Despite his progressive background, however, in his first administration FDR did not immediately attack the patronage system. Given the continuing strength of patronage politicians, to have done so would have been extremely difficult (Polenburg 1966, p. 10). In fact, Roosevelt was perfectly willing to use patronage to help out the machine bosses who supported him (Dorsett 1977; see also Patterson 1969, chap. 7). But administrative reform and reorganization and the establishment of enduring public welfare programs were both part of the long-term political agenda of Roosevelt and his allies within liberal professional elites (see Abbott 1936). When permanent public programs were to be established, the CES recommended mandatory merit practices in the state administration of social insurance and assistance. The CES was rebuffed by Congress, however, showing the resilience of the patronage system. The Social Security Act was stripped of the provisions man-

---

versity of Wisconsin labor economist who was associated with much of his state's innovative labor and social programs of the Progressive Era and 1920s and was the teacher of both Edwin Witte and Arthur Altmeyer: "[The] devotion to civil service rules . . . gained for the Commission the confidence of employers to whom we were supposed to be antagonistic. . . . Progressive legislation could not be made enduring . . . and, in our case, conciliatory toward organized employers and employees, except by a civil service law in which the Progressives, like their great leader [Robert La Follette], denied themselves political preference for jobs" (quoted in Abbott 1936, p. 405).

4. Among the most important of Roosevelt's appointees were Secretary of Labor Frances Perkins, Assistant Secretary of Labor (later head of the Social Security Board) Arthur Altmeyer, Federal Emergency Relief administrator Harry Hopkins, and executive director of the CES Edwin Witte. Perkins had been industrial commissioner of New York State under Roosevelt, a Department of Labor official under Governor Al Smith, and a lobbyist for the Consumers' League (a group interested in securing regulatory labor legislation, especially applying to women workers in the "sweated" trades) during the Progressive Era (Martin 1976). Altmeyer and Witte were both students of John Commons at the University of Wisconsin and served on the Wisconsin Industrial Commission; Witte headed the Legislative Reference Library in Wisconsin prior to taking on the directorship of the CES (Bernstein 1985, p. 45). Harry Hopkins was active in settlement house and charity work in New York City until his appointment as director of New York State's Temporary Emergency Relief Administration under Governor Roosevelt in 1931 (Schlesinger 1957, pp. 391–92).

dating states to implement merit systems (Altmeyer 1966, pp. 35–36). The Roosevelt administration did not give up in the fight against patronage in social welfare administration, however; the struggle to institutionalize the program and the power of the New Deal led to initiatives—some successful, some not—by the Roosevelt administration to create and reorganize government institutions in the late 1930s (Shefter 1978, pp. 237–43).

Policy Feedback: New Policy Precedents for Old Age Pensions, the Rise and Demise of Welfare Capitalism, and the Continuing Problems of Poor Relief

In the United States, as in Canada, civil service reform and the war were associated with the initiation of two national programs—civil service pensions and soldiers' insurance—which eventually served as positive precedents for old age pensions. Both of these programs had the long-run effect of legitimating federal pension and insurance activities, for both were run in a way compatible with the desiderata of reform elites oriented to professionalism and rationalization. The political and social learning from the experience with this newest addition to the policy inheritance, in terms of evaluating the state administration, was bound to be more positive than that from earlier federal activities, such as the checkered history of (mis)management of soldiers' pensions. Further, the success of these programs provided testimony against ideological claims that "government handouts" inevitably destroyed the moral fiber and family ties of their beneficiaries. Yet it is important to keep in mind that the feedback from these programs was indeed long-term; its influence was not felt widely until new public programs were again on the political agenda in the 1930s.

As part of the general transformation of the civil administration, civil service pensions were established in the United States in 1920, following arguments about the necessity of some form of retirement system to solve the problems associated with superannuated, that is, "inefficient," government employees (U.S. Social Security Board 1937, p. 179; Graebner 1980, p. 57). Indeed, the justification for the civil service retirement system was quite similar to that invoked by enthusiasts for private pension plans (Graebner 1980, chap. 3). In the United States, an unintended outcome of the end of the spoils system had been the aging of the bureaucracy, as job tenure became secure and agency heads were unwilling to dismiss elderly employees, even those perceived as "inefficient," in the absence of a retirement provision for them (Graebner 1980, pp. 57–59, 64–66). For example, in 1912 a high official in the War Department characterized the prevailing practice as a pension system "without retirement" (quoted in Graebner 1980, p. 66). Early civil service pension proposals were opposed at least partially on grounds derived from the political learning about the Civil War pension system: "Opponents of early pension proposals, most of which called for contributions by employees only, anticipated that the public would ultimately be called upon to contribute. Tax-payers, acutely aware at this very moment of the budgetary consequences of the commitments made years earlier to Civil War veterans, shuddered at the thought of creating yet another army of clerk pensioners" (Graebner 1980, p. 60). But finally, as the merit system scored further victories and more attention focused on efficiency, superannuation became an intolerable problem for the service. Moreover, politicians found potential advantages in acceding to the demands of civil service employees' unions for some kind of retirement provision (Graebner 1980, pp. 86–87; Skowronek 1982, pp. 201, 208).

For Americans, setting up a new program for World War I soldiers and veterans was seen as especially essential, for in the absence of new legislation by Congress, the general law pension system would have applied to World War forces (Glasson 1918, p. 283). This, of course, was the system under which Civil War veterans had collected such an astounding amount of the nation's largesse over the half-century since Appomattox. While neither Democratic nor Republican politicians were willing to attack directly the Civil War pension system, no one was ready to see a fresh extension of the life of the general pension laws.[5] Officials in the Wilson administration drew up plans for a system of soldiers' insurance at the outset of U.S. involvement in the war, and it was enacted into law in October 1917. The new law was, in the words of Civil War pension historian and critic William H. Glasson, a "radical departure from the existing pension system" (1918, p. 283). While the existing pension laws were not disturbed in their application to veterans of America's previous wars and their administration continued under the commissioner of pensions in the Department of the Interior, the new War Insurance Law was to be administered in the far more trustworthy Treasury Department, where a new Bureau of War Risk Insurance had been established (Glasson 1918, p. 283).

Reformers in the American Association for Labor Legislation were quite sanguine about the positive effects the examples of civil service pensions and soldiers' insurance would have on the American social insurance movement (Andrews 1920; Lindsay 1919). In his 1919 presidential address to the AALL, Samuel McCune Lindsay, professor of social legislation at Columbia University, said of U.S. war risk insurance, "This single experiment, successful beyond the fondest hopes of its proponents, constitutes so striking a forward step that it may almost be said to atone for our previous backwardness and to place the United States abreast of the European countries in the development and use of this modern method of social organization. Those who believe in social insurance will do well to see that our next step shall be to hold on to this

5. Both parties' platforms continued to endorse the expression of the "nation's gratitude" through the granting of pensions to the veterans of the Union army through the Progressive Era (see Porter and Johnson 1970, pp. 140, 161, on the 1908 campaign).

gain" (1919, p. 111). Lindsay went on to call for the conversion of soldiers' insurance, then for the extension of all forms of social insurance to civilian government employees and, eventually, to the American public as a whole (1919, pp. 113–14), perhaps hoping to make use of a dynamic similar to that which had led to such generous provision for veterans in the past—but in the service of well-run contributory social insurance programs. Why did the hopes of the AALL reformers turn out to be so ill-founded, and these policy precedents bear so much less fruit in 1920s America than in its neighbor to the north? The reaction to the war was quite different in the United States than it had been in Canada, where the British connection brought League of Nations and International Labour Organization membership. In the United States, with the political predominance of conservative Republicanism, Europe and its social policy arrangements were rejected as possible examples for future development, and welfare capitalism was lauded as a suitably American replacement (Brandes 1976; Brody 1980).

The conservative Republican presidents of the 1920s were not at all interested in building a professional bureaucracy to administer social programs. Although the federal government was now considered to be less patronage-dominated than it had been around the turn of the century (see White 1933), *public* solutions to welfare problems, if and when these were even recognized to exist, were out of fashion. Political learning in relation to social insurance and pensions was influenced by revulsion with Europe generally after the war, and with its social policy experiences in particular. Most notably, the "dole" seemed to confirm fears of earlier critics that social spending programs were inevitably subject to uncontrollable mass political pressures for expansion (Nelson 1969, pp. 22–23; Romasco 1965, pp. 132–33; Skocpol and Ikenberry 1983, p. 114). The Republicans embraced the vision of an antibureaucratic "associative state" developed by Herbert Hoover, who served as secretary of commerce for presidents Warren Harding and Calvin Coolidge before becoming chief executive himself in 1929. Hoover worked in his capacity as a public servant to encourage research, planning, and cooperation on the part of private groups; these activities would help citizens, under the "enlightened" leadership of corporate capitalists, to "meet the needs of industrial democracy without the interference of government bureaucrats" (Wilson 1975, p. 89, and chap. 4; Hawley 1974).[6]

In the 1920s reformers and political leaders, as well as many average

6. A striking example of the "associative state" approach to social problems was the 1921 President's Conference on Unemployment, organized by Hoover to gain backing from the invited politicians, labor leaders, and social policy experts (incuding some from the AALL) for plans—already largely formulated—to deal with the severe recession of that year. Harding and Hoover ruled out any kind of governmental action from the beginning, and the conference was left to recommend better coordination of private and local charitable efforts (Chenery 1921, 1922; Grin 1973; Wilson 1975, pp. 90–93).

Americans, believed that businessmen could and would look after the American economy and Americans' economic well-being. To the extent that the problems of income insecurity associated with industrial capitalism were given any recognition at all, they were to be addressed through welfare capitalism—programs run by employers for their workers—or private and local charity (Clarke Chambers 1963; Brody 1980; Brandes 1976). Welfare capitalist schemes reached only a very tiny proportion of the work force, and there was little growth in the number of programs during the latter half of the 1920s, even before the Depression caused the failure of many schemes (Berkowitz and McQuaid 1980, pp. 79–81; McQuaid 1978, pp. 346–51; Lubove 1968, pp. 127–28; Latimer 1932a, p. 59; Nelson 1969, pp. 47–48). The most comprehensive study of industrial and trade union pensions in the United States was published in 1932 by Murray Latimer, later a member of the technical board of the Committee on Economic Security under Franklin Roosevelt.[7] Latimer found that, at a maximum, about 14 percent of American workers were nominally covered by the 397 pension plans he was able to find in his exhaustive survey, though the future solvency of such plans and their own eligibility were very far from assured (Latimer 1932a, pp. 49, 55, and chap. 19). In 1932 pensions were going to only 140,000 retirees (Latimer 1932a, p. 893), out of an over-sixty-five population of about 6,500,000. Trade union retirement or disability benefits were given by some twenty-five unions with a total membership of 1,500,000; union pensions were going to about 18,000 people in 1931 (Latimer 1932b, pp. 110, 116). Armstrong (1932, p. 393) estimated that industrial pensions relieved about 5–6 percent of the potentially dependent elderly, while trade union benefits aided another fraction of a percent. The Committee on Economic Security noted in the mid-1930s that "even within the field which these voluntary pension systems embrace, the terms of the plans are restricted so that relatively few employees qualify for pensions" (U.S. Social Security Board 1937, p. 176). Clearly, private plans were not adequate for preventing dependency, but they were important in the 1920s as a cultural ideal in opposition to public social efforts.

By the 1930s the claims of proponents of welfare capitalism were belied by crisis. Social scientific experts such as Abraham Epstein noted as early as 1919 the inadequacy of corporate welfare schemes; Latimer summarized his

---

7. Latimer's findings had been foreshadowed in the work of Abraham Epstein, working for the Pennsylvania Commission on Old Age Pensions through the midtwenties. The commission (1919, pp. 116–18) noted the inadequacy of the very few existing private or municipal pension plans. Eligibility requirements were difficult to meet, and the plans most often remained discretionary. The commission identified only twenty plans in the state, from a survey of every corporation employing five hundred or more people along with some smaller companies known to give pensions. The National Industrial Conference Board (1925) also surveyed private pension plans, finding 245 in operation, but it was far more sanguine about their potential than was Epstein or Latimer.

research by saying that "by and large the bulk of industrial pension plans are insecure. . . . the depression which started in 1929 has brought out in clear perspective the instability of industrial pension systems" (1932a, pp. 902, 938). Roosevelt's officials, including Latimer, did examine the experience of the welfare capitalist schemes, but they came to the conclusion that this experience demonstrated precisely that voluntary schemes were unworkable and that public, compulsory programs were essential (U.S. Social Security Board 1937, p. 176). Not only were the numbers covered under the much-vaunted private welfare schemes (including pensions) tiny, but the majority of these programs were also abandoned under the onslaught of the Depression (Armstrong 1932, pp. 392–93).

Welfare capitalism and private charity were widely preferred to public relief by many social reformers through the 1920s, but in most localities, public relief played a far more important role in supporting the needy, including the needy aged (Gratton 1986, chap. 6; Katz 1986, p. 167). The Depression made this fact evident to all. Workhouses had been transformed into old age homes, rather than institutions to scare the able-bodied into the labor force, but public outdoor relief in the 1920s and 1930s was still based on the poor laws, with their principles of local responsibility, settlement (residency requirements), and family responsibility. Leading social reformer Edith Abbott titled an article reviewing the state of public relief in the early 1930s "Abolish the Pauper Laws." She argued that

> The old principle of local responsibility has resulted in very inadequate standards of public aid and very antiquated methods of giving service to those in need. . . . [It] has led to corruption and graft among petty officials at the expense of the destitute. It has meant the use of deterrent methods in the giving of relief, such as the publication of the names of those receiving relief in the local newspaper, depriving the person receiving aid of the right to vote, the humiliation and degradation of unfortunate men, women, and children. . . . Another antiquated poor law principle that should be abolished is that of *legal family responsibility*—that is, the *prosecution of the members of the family* of the client . . . when those members are unwilling, but are believed to be able, to contribute to the client's support. (Abbott 1934, pp. 10, 15)

Working-class constituencies were sometimes able to pressure local politicians to partially abrogate these principles in the administration of poor relief. Gratton (1986, chap. 6) found this to be true for Boston in the 1920s. Such principles became considerably harder to sustain as the Democrats worked to win working-class voters permanently to their party in the 1930s. Where local officials could not be moved, state and later national politicians stepped in. Essentially, dissatisfaction with poor relief remained a prime motivation behind the enactment of old age assistance and other programs of modern social protection in the 1920s and into the 1930s.

Private welfare agencies, along with local and state welfare officials, were quickly swamped by the economic crisis of the 1930s, undermining the claim of superiority of private or nonfederal sources of aid for the needy. In fact, the leaders of these groups, earlier among the most vocal advocates of voluntarism, first sounded the call for federal action in the early years of the Depression, though Hoover ignored them (Brown 1940, pts. 2–3; Bremner 1956a, p. 262). In this way, middle-class and elite opinion moved more into line with popular demands, expressed through the Progressive Era and into the 1920s, for modern provision for the elderly as an alternative to demeaning and inadequate poor relief. And at that point, the perceived failures of public welfare policy—regarding either the Civil War pension system or the connection between local relief and a thriving party patronage system—stood further in the historical background and were overshadowed by the massiveness of the collapse of locally controlled poor relief, private charity, and welfare capitalism.[8] The continuing concerns of cosmopolitan, middle-class reformers with the connection between relief and patronage at the subnational level (see Abbott 1936) plausibly could be dealt with through imposing controls from the federal level. In any event, in the 1930s, in contrast with the 1920s, there was little choice politically about enacting new programs.

The Movement for Old Age Pensions in the 1920s: Dress Rehearsal for the New Deal

American social reformers recognized that the 1920s were a remarkably unpropitious time for advocating public solutions to the problems of industrial capitalism (Chambers 1971, p. 77). Many—most important, the American Association for Labor Legislation—accommodated themselves to the new political climate by downplaying state initiatives and emphasizing the so-called preventive approach, associated with the work of University of Wisconsin economist John R. Commons (Harter 1962; Lubove 1968, chap. 7; Nelson 1969, chap. 6). Commons and his disciples called for labor and social insurance legislation that would give individual businessmen tangible financial incentives for increasing

8. For example, the U.S. Committee on Economic Security's 1935 report to the president (1985), which recommended old age insurance and pensions, along with other welfare and insurance measures, made no references to the experience of Civil War pensions, a standard in the reports of the prewar pension commissions. The reports of commissions serving in the 1920s, while noting the numbers still covered under the pension laws, did not note the political implications of the Civil War pension experience, which had been discussed in earlier considerations of the subject of public pensions (compare Massachusetts Commission on Old Age Pensions 1910, pp. 237–38, with Massachusetts Commission on Pensions 1925, p. 38).

workplace safety, stabilizing employment, and otherwise improving workers' and social welfare. It was in his home state of Wisconsin, with its unusually strong network of ties between state government and the state research university, that this type of administration was best developed. The Wisconsin Industrial Commission was staffed by labor economists schooled in the Commons philosophy. The commission engaged in research and was empowered by the legislature to enforce and adjust all the state's industrial regulations (Lubove 1968, p. 33). In the absence of other reform activity, the AALL became increasingly oriented to the experiences and policy ideas of the Wisconsin Industrial Commission, where—almost alone among state government agencies in the 1920s—social reform-minded "experts" (albeit of the "preventive" stripe) were still in a position of political influence. Only in the state of Wisconsin did continuing activity occur around proposed unemployment insurance legislation through the 1920s. In 1921 an unemployment insurance bill based on the preventive approach and including employers' incentives came close to passing in the state legislature. The reformers continued their campaign until a similar bill finally succeeded in 1932—the first in the United States (Nelson 1969, chap. 6).

Popular political activity for welfare reform in the 1920s outside Wisconsin consisted almost exclusively of state-level campaigns for noncontributory old age pensions led by the Fraternal Order of Eagles, a predominantly working- and lower-middle-class, white fraternal order. At times, the Eagles worked in uneasy alliance with professional, middle-class reformers of the AALL or the newly formed American Association for Old Age Security (AA-OAS), later the American Association for Social Security. A handful of progressive Republican and northern Democratic politicians supported the pension cause as well (Leotta 1975; Fraternal Order of Eagles 1929; Fischer 1978). The American movement for pensions actually was mobilized on a greater scale than was the Canadian, yet its proponents in Congress were never in the strategic position of Canadian Labour M.P.'s Woodsworth and Heaps (Leotta 1975, pp. 371–75).

In a situation of one-party dominance and popular demobilization in the North and the South, there was little political incentive for politicians of either party to use pensions to increase their appeal, especially for Republicans and southern Democrats, when this sort of program was at odds with their philosophies. The dominant stalwart faction of the Republican party at the national level called for a "return to normalcy" under President Warren Harding and agreed with the probusiness policies of President Calvin Coolidge (Schlesinger 1957, chaps. 7–10). During the administration of Herbert Hoover, the most progressive of the presidents of the 1920s, some elites were committed to welfare capitalism as the solution to the remaining defects of industrial society (Wilson 1975; Schlesinger 1957, chap. 11). Private pension plans, along with other private welfare programs were to address simultaneously the need of aged workers for retirement support and the need of employers for a more efficient, stable, and controllable work force (Graebner 1980, chaps. 2, 5). Indeed, Hoover and congressional Republicans worked against old age pension bills (Leotta 1975, p. 374). Urban "wet" (anti-Prohibition) Democrats in the North did have an electoral incentive to promote new programs, but they could not mobilize the national party behind pensions because of the deep schism between themselves and the conservative southern wing of the party (Ladd and Hadley 1978, pp. 48–49; Schlesinger 1957, chaps. 12, 16).

On the state level, in a foreshadowing of the cross-class policy coalition that emerged in the 1930s, some northern Democrats, most notably Franklin Roosevelt, in the legislatures or governors' mansions formed alliances with representatives of the AAOAS, the AALL, the Fraternal Order of Eagles, and state federations of labor to work for pensions in the 1920s (Leotta 1975, pp. 367–69; Gratton 1986, chap. 6; Anglim and Gratton 1987). Another group with an electoral incentive to support pensions was what remained of the progressive contingent within the GOP, especially in states such as California and Wisconsin, where electoral competition after the Progressive Era took the form of intraparty struggles between progressive and stalwart factions. Progressives such as governors C. C. Young of California and Gifford Pinchot of Pennsylvania allied with the Eagles, Democratic legislators, state social welfare personnel, and organized labor to push for pensions, in the California case, successfully (Putnam 1970, pp. 18–24; Fischer 1978, pp. 173–74).

Analysts stressing the importance of "corporate liberalism" in the 1930s in connection with the enactment of the Social Security Act have tended to ignore public policy developments during the 1920s, concentrating on the private "welfare capitalist" schemes that were widely touted during that time. Yet in many respects, business opinion in the more innovative thirties was foreshadowed in the course of debates over state old age pensions. In brief, almost all business leaders were vociferous opponents of the few proposed public policy reforms, most notably old age pensions (Leotta 1975). "Corporate liberal" organizations such as the National Civic Federation, which had supported workers' compensation legislation and some regulatory reform in the Progressive Era, along with the conservative National Association of Manufacturers, worked to defeat the old age assistance legislation introduced in many state legislatures and in the U.S. Congress, even when it was of the tamest, county-optional variety (Lubove 1968, p. 140; see also National Civic Federation Industrial Welfare Department 1929; Sherman 1923).

In only a few states were propension forces politically positioned so as to be able to get legislation enacted in the 1920s. Thus, despite the efforts of the Eagles, state labor federations, and reformers in the American Association for Old Age Security and the American Association for Labor Legislation, pension legislation was passed only in a handful of states prior to the Depression. But by 1928 the only fruit of the extensive campaigning for new public spending for old age protection was six state-level pension laws, all of them "county-optional," meaning that counties were allowed, but not mandated, to pay pensions to some of their aged residents. As it turned out, not many counties exercised their option, and only about one thousand elderly people were receiving these pensions in 1928, fewer than those who were still collecting Civil War pensions (U.S. Bureau of the Census 1975, p. 738; Fischer 1978, pp. 173–74; Massachusetts Commission on Pensions 1925, p. 37; U.S. Social Security Board 1937, p. 161). Even the initial county-optional efforts were important, however, for when propension forces summed up the results of their efforts in the midtwenties, they made a decision to press for mandatory pension laws in the future due to the disappointing results with the optional legislation (Putnam 1970, p. 20). In spite of the relatively small impact of the pension laws on the conditions of the elderly, the fact that state action preceded federal eventually did have important ramifications for the shape of the federal program.

The Depression, the New Deal, and the Success of New Public Provision for the Aged

It was during the Great Depression that the United States initiated nationwide programs of social protection through the passage of the Social Security Act of 1935. The economic crisis transformed the American political world as it had existed in the 1920s and set into motion political changes that allowed for the success of the New Deal social welfare legislation. Nationally, the ideological and policy inheritance represented by welfare capitalism was utterly discredited. American citizens, politically quiescent throughout the 1920s, became politically engaged on a mass scale. The social insurance and assistance legislation passed during the Depression era bears the imprint of these factors, but it was also shaped by institutional arrangements and policy feedbacks that were themselves the legacy of the struggles for civil service reform and social welfare innovation of the late nineteenth and early twentieth centuries.

By the time of the 1932 election, close to four years of the Great Depression had shattered the ideas that businessmen could guarantee the economic and social well-being of Americans and that very limited private and local charity and corporate welfare programs could serve as a substitute for public social provision in times of economic downturn. President Hoover had responded to demonstrably increased need and to rising demands for federal relief within the framework of his voluntarist philosophy, in which the state's welfare role was limited to encouragement of private philanthropic efforts (Wilson 1975, pp. 157–59, chap. 5; Romasco 1965, chaps. 7–9). With the continuing economic crisis and the blatant failure of voluntary efforts to alleviate need, the demands for federal action to cope with the economic crisis mounted. Popular and expert interest again turned toward public policy solutions to alleviate economic and social problems. Indeed, the policy crisis that emerged from the failure of welfare capitalism and existing systems of private and public relief was decisive in the elections of Franklin Roosevelt and a Congress with a strong liberal Democratic contingent. These elections in turn were critical to the enactment of the Social Security Act, as were the elections of sympathetic state politicians to the passage of state old age pension programs.

Popular Pressures for Social Spending in the Depression

With the onset of the Depression, old age pension bills, tirelessly introduced into the state legislatures through the 1920s by various social reformers, trade unionists, and Eagles, were easily accessible proposals for legislators to support in order to demonstrate responsiveness to citizens' needs in the face of economic catastrophe (see, for example, the discussion of the adoption of pensions in Massachusetts in 1930 in Linford 1949, pp. 74–85). Indeed, pensions were the only welfare proposal on the table at this point in most states, with the exception of Wisconsin, where, uniquely, unemployment insurance had remained on the political agenda throughout the 1920s (Nelson 1969, chap. 6). Political interest in pensions was much higher after 1929 than before (Clarke Chambers 1963, pp. 166–67). In state legislatures across the nation, the economic crisis and the political mobilization it helped to engender brought liberal politicians into power, and the demands of the propension coalitions found much more receptive audiences. Nineteen bills passed between 1929 and 1933, compared with six in the previous decade (U.S. Social Security Board 1937, pp. 160–61). Activity aimed at reforming the character of public provision for the aged also emerged at the national level.

    In 1932 the American electorate expressed an overwhelming rejection of the voluntarism of Hoover and the Republicans by giving Franklin Roosevelt and the Democrats a landslide victory. Democratic political and reform elites, unlike their Republican predecessors, showed some willingness to work with popular forces to introduce new social spending programs to alleviate the problems of unemployment and old age dependency. Roosevelt hardly had a definitive mandate for the national policies he would pursue to achieve economic recovery or to end economic insecurity. The 1932 platform of the Democrats pledged only old age and unemployment insurance at the state level (Porter and Johnson 1970, p. 331). Yet Roosevelt was known as a reformer—when he served as governor of New York, he encouraged the initiation of public programs for old age protection—and though he made no pledge about what he would do beyond "bold experimentation," his campaign promised to involve the federal government actively in dealing with the problems caused by the economic crisis (Holt 1975, p. 29; Fusfeld 1956, pp. 158–59). Frances Perkins, FDR's close adviser and labor secretary, later wrote that it was "basic in the appeal for votes that suffering would be relieved immediately" through federal action, a stance completely different from Hoover's (Perkins 1964, p. 182).

The democratic upsurge in American politics did more than sweep Roosevelt into office, of course. Mass political activity increased throughout the decade: in addition to an increase in voting among new-stock urban-dwellers, there were marches of the unemployed, sit-down strikes, and farmers' protests. Of critical importance to New Deal social policy developments, social movements also arose, demanding extended government welfare activities and new public social spending: Huey Long's Share Our Wealth movement, Father Coughlin's National Union for Social Justice, and Dr. Francis Townsend's old age pension movement (Holtzman 1963; Brinkley 1982). It is certainly true that such pressures played a significant role in the formation of the American system of social insurance and welfare, but the Social Security Act was not a direct product of mass movements.

How, then, did popular demands for new state welfare activity affect the course of policy development? During the 1930s the mass movements dedicated to expanded public social protection provided continuing pressure for state action; indeed, they made such action a political necessity. Yet popular demands were not directly transmitted into the circles of policy formation. U.S. political parties were still far from being programmatic or committed to coherent social policies, and they were not organized to channel the policy proposals of groups to the elected and appointed officials who actually made policy, as did many European parties. As I have stressed, however, given the notable lack of bureaucratic resources of the American state structure in the 1930s, executive policy initiatives depended for their success on mass pressure being exerted on Congress. Without popular pressure, and the electoral incentive it represented to congressmen, the policy initiatives taken by the Roosevelt administration probably would not have been successful. Secretary of Labor Frances Perkins, a key policymaker for social security, saw popular political activity as creating a unique political opening for enacting social insurance programs (Martin 1976, p. 341). She later recalled, in reference to the passage of old age protections in the New Deal, that "without the Townsend Plan it is possible that the Old Age Insurance system would not have received the attention which it did at the hands of Congress" (Perkins 1964, p. vi). The lobbying of the Townsend movement was particularly effective due both to the high propensity of the elderly to vote and to the fact that the Townsend clubs were "distributed fairly uniformly in all the states and congressional districts" (Bernstein 1985, p. 66;

see also Witte 1962, pp. 95–98). This organizational structure was most conducive to bringing pressure to bear on the government, given the structure of the American state.[9]

The strength of mass movements pressing for the extension of state welfare activities had a somewhat paradoxical effect: it reinforced the fears of Roosevelt and his advisers that "unwise" legislation might be enacted and thereby strengthened their cautiousness on matters of social policy and their determination to exclude radical voices from policy discussions. This effect was augmented by the fact that Roosevelt and his closest advisers had reached political maturity during the Progressive Era and took seriously progressive concerns about the legacy of patronage democracy in social benefits programs. Moreover, they reacted quite negatively to European experiences with unemployment insurance in the 1920s; at least partially in response to popular political pressure, benefits in Europe had lost any connection to contributions and had become a "dole." Thus Roosevelt noted in a 1934 address, "Let us profit by the mistakes of foreign countries and keep out of unemployment insurance every element which is actuarially unsound" (Roosevelt 1938, pp. 453–54).

This cautious approach in response to mass pressure is perhaps best illustrated in the case of old age protection. The Townsendites were the largest and politically best connected of the various organizations pressing for new state welfare activities. The movement consisted of thousands of elderly Americans, many of them middle-class, organized into Townsend clubs. A local Townsend club existed in almost every congressional district (Bernstein 1985, p. 66; Holtzman 1963; Achenbaum 1978, pp. 129, 132). In contrast with the usual maximum monthly payments of about thirty dollars under the state old age assistance programs that had proliferated after 1929, the Townsendites advocated a rather remarkable two-hundred-dollar monthly pension for all Americans aged sixty or more, given on the condition that they cease working and spend the pension payment within thirty days (Achenbaum 1978, p. 129). (The average monthly earnings for a full-time employee in 1935 was only ninety-five dollars; U.S. Bureau of the Census 1960, p. 95.) The Townsend plan and others like it, though clearly popular with many Americans, were completely dismissed by the Roosevelt administration officials drafting the Social Security Act's old age pension and insurance provisions (Schlabach 1969, pp. 109–10). FDR insisted to his advisers that any program instituted be on a sound actuarial basis, as opposed to the "unsound" Townsend plan and other popular "panaceas." This meant some sort of contributory scheme, as opposed to one drawing exclusively on general revenues (Leff 1983). Noting that "Congress can't stand the pressure of the Townsend Plan unless we have a real old age insur-

9. The Townsendites were decidedly non-working-class, and working-class-based movements were quite unlikely to be distributed optimally for influencing Congress.

ance system," FDR resolved to take the initiative in the development of social programs and to maintain careful control of the entire process of legislating social security (Perkins 1964, p. 294). Looking toward the future, Roosevelt was especially concerned to insulate programs created by his legislation from popular and political pressure for expansion by including contributions from beneficiaries.

Roosevelt's timing in introducing permanent as opposed to "emergency" measures also reflects the cautiousness of his approach. Planning for social insurance initiatives was undertaken immediately, but no legislation was proposed by the administration. By contrast, the president introduced federal emergency relief legislation almost immediately upon taking office, thus responding to the plight of the unemployed—and the not inconsiderable protests of state and local welfare officials, whose agencies were overwhelmed financially by the proportions of need produced by the crisis (Bernstein 1985, chap. 1; Katz 1986, pp. 216–22; Piven and Cloward 1971, chap. 2). By 1934, when Roosevelt appointed the Committee on Economic Security (CES), the group responsible for drafting the administration's proposed social security legislation, the most urgent demands for relief had been satisfied by public works and relief programs. The permanent program to be designed by these advisers therefore could more easily be kept separate from the "dole" so abhorred by FDR but so politically necessary in the first months of his administration (Perkins 1964, p. 284).

What, then, can be said of the role of mass pressures in stimulating the development of new state social spending measures in the United States? Given the character of the U.S. state structure, popular pressures were critical in providing an opening for elite initiatives. Popular political activity encouraged policymakers in the Roosevelt administration to take initiatives, but they were largely able to insulate the process of formulating policy from popular demands. There is no doubt that some kind of social welfare initiative was politically necessary, but the specific form it took was shaped by the institutional arrangements of the American state, the power of certain congressional groups, and the reaction of New Deal policymakers to the U.S. policy inheritance.

Presidential Initiative on Social Security

Roosevelt had long harbored political ambitions—personal as well as for the Democratic party and the cause of progressive reform—and he eagerly worked to build and lead a cross-class coalition for social policy reform at the national level. The Depression produced an increase in the number of pension bills introduced in Congress, as in the state legislatures, especially after the Democratic landslide of 1932. Two dozen were offered in Congress in 1934 alone (Leotta 1975, p. 377). Yet Roosevelt was interested in developing a comprehensive approach to social security, as well as in taking political credit for any legislation that did succeed. Given the magnitude of his popular support, as evidenced in the 1932 and 1934 elections and the leadership he exercised over the Democratic party and Congress as a whole, leading Democratic congressmen were willing at this juncture, to defer to his preferences (Witte 1962, pp. 3–7; Leotta 1975, pp. 377–78). Roosevelt seized the initiative in formulating policy and was able to maintain control over the policy-making process by setting up the Committee on Economic Security (Bernstein 1985, pp. 41–42, 51–53; Witte 1962, pp. 4–7, 18). This group of cabinet officers, established in early June 1934, was chaired by secretary of labor and long-time social reform advocate Frances Perkins (Martin 1976, pp. 205–6). The CES was to study social insurance and assistance, aided by an expert staff, and have a legislative proposal ready for the start of the 1935 congressional session. The key position of executive director was filled by Edwin Witte, a veteran of years of administrative service in Wisconsin (Schlabach 1969, chaps. 2–3).

Roosevelt's choice of personnel for the important task of drafting the social security bill reflected his generally cautious approach to social policy. FDR and the people he chose to be the architects of the Social Security Act, as products of the progressive movement, shared its concerns with "good government" and fiscal "responsibility." Moreover, they had received their political training and developed their distinctive outlook in the "expert," state-level administrative agencies dealing with labor and social legislation that were the enduring result of progressive state-building and social reform efforts. In particular, Roosevelt's social policymakers came from backgrounds that ensured their concern with fiscal "soundness." They would attempt to build programs able to withstand what they perceived as ever-present dangers of democratic pressure for expansion of government benefits into fiscally irresponsible and politically motivated "handouts" (Perkins 1964, chaps. 1–2; Bernstein 1985, pp. 43–45; Schlabach 1969). Social policy experts who advocated more liberal policies were excluded from the inner circles of policy formulation, relegated to relatively powerless positions within advisory bodies, or left out of the official policy-formation process altogether (Lubove 1968, p. 176; Skocpol and Ikenberry 1983, pp. 127–28).

Not only liberal reformers were excluded from the inner circles of policymaking. Politically active "corporate liberal" businessmen were also marginalized. In the United States, this group has received an inordinate amount of scholarly attention, and some analysts have argued that the Social Security Act reflected its influence (see Quadagno 1984, 1988a; Berkowitz and McQuaid 1980; Radosh and Rothbard 1972; Weinstein 1968; Ferguson 1984; Jenkins and Brents 1989; Graebner 1980). Much of the corporate liberal argument rests on the fact that some of the prominent welfare capitalists who were members of the Business Advisory and Planning Council (BAC) of the Department of

Commerce also served on the CES Advisory Council and were consulted by Witte early in the policy-formulation process (Witte 1962, p. 16). The Advisory Council indeed included five prominent corporate liberal capitalists: Gerard Swope, president of General Electric; Morris Leeds, president of Leeds and Northrup; Sam Lewisohn, vice president of Miami Copper Co.; Marion Folsom, treasurer of Eastman Kodak; and Walter Teagle, president of Standard Oil. All but Teagle were from firms that had corporate unemployment compensation schemes, although Teagle was head of the BAC committee on unemployment insurance (Witte 1962, p. 50). (The Advisory Council also included representatives of organized labor, who by all accounts were less active than were the businessmen, and a good many "representatives of the public," including social workers, university officials, and fraternal organization leaders.) The businessmen are alleged to have had decisive influence on the provisions of the Social Security Act, yet it is clear that the Advisory Council basically served only a public relations function (Schlabach 1969, p. 101; Altmeyer 1966, p. 19). More critical to the corporate liberal argument, the Committee on Economic Security did not accept much advice from the Advisory Council. This was at least partly due to the fact that the CES and its technical staff began work in the summer of 1934, while the Advisory Council did not meet until mid-November—only two weeks before the CES report was due, and only four weeks before it actually was written—leaving little time for genuine consultation.

The Deliberations of the Committee on Economic Security

From the very outset of the deliberations of the CES, the tension between national standards and coordination and state-level autonomy and diversity was of overriding importance in debates about the character of the programs the group would propose (Schlabach 1969, pp. 114–15). Substantial obstacles to national uniformity and centralized administration existed in the 1930s. Policymakers faced the threat that any national social insurance programs they recommended might be declared unconstitutional by the Supreme Court. In addition, they had to cope with the political exigencies represented by the distribution of power within the Democratic party, which favored the representatives of conservative and states'-rights viewpoints as much as or more than those of urban liberalism. In particular, the extraordinary political leverage of southern representatives in Congress, out of proportion to the population and economic might of their states, was a fact that could never be neglected as FDR and the CES formulated the bill (Perkins 1964, p. 291; Altmeyer 1968, pp. 14–15, Quadagno 1988a,b). Moreover, the fact that states had been the principal actors in social policy until the mid-1930s meant that diverse programmatic and administrative interests in the various state programs were politically well entrenched and difficult to bypass by the time the CES began its work. Indeed, Roosevelt, Witte, and Perkins, all of whom had been involved in state-level labor and welfare administration, actually preferred to maintain the states as important administrative actors, even as they hoped to increase the uniformity and adequacy of social programs. Other politicians representing the interests of progressive northern states, such as Senator Robert Wagner of New York, the Roosevelt administration's chief ally in the Senate, also took some stances which undercut nationalizing trends for programmatic uniformity in order to protect favored state legislation (Huthmacher 1968).

The tension between nationalizing and decentralizing tendencies played itself out in the area of old age protection and was complicated by the politically sensitive issue of whether to include contributions from future beneficiaries. CES policymakers had to contend with the growing strength of Townsendism and other movements calling for noncontributory federal pensions and the fact that members of Congress were far more supportive of pensions than of contributory insurance for the aged. But none of the proposals offered by popular or reformist organizations—Townsend clubs, the AALL, the AAOAS, or the Fraternal Order of Eagles—were fully implemented in the 1935 law. All of these groups preferred noncontributory pension plans, such as the one embodied in the various bills introduced by Senator Dill and Representative William Connery, which proposed to give federal grants-in-aid equal to one-third of expenditures to states which initiated old age assistance programs (Leotta 1975; Achenbaum 1978, pp. 129–31). The Townsendites demanded noncontributory pensions at a very high level to be paid by the federal government. Roosevelt and Witte, reacting to a policy inheritance which dramatized the dangers of politically motivated expansion of benefits, were determined to keep the federal government out of the business of giving direct grants to citizens and never wavered from a commitment to contributory features for whatever permanent old age program was settled on. The arguments of liberal New Dealers for a different approach found no favor. A vivid example of this came when Harry Hopkins, Federal Emergency Relief administrator and member of the CES, eloquently argued for noncontributory old age and unemployment benefits as a matter of right for citizens. FDR saw this as being "the very thing he had been saying he was against for years—the dole" and vetoed all such proposals (Perkins 1964, p. 284).

Roosevelt, Perkins, and Witte preferred to develop what they saw as the only reasonable and fiscally sound long-term solution to the problem of old age dependency: a contributory program of old age benefits, to be firmly distinguished from noncontributory social assistance. Even so, Witte and the members of the CES were willing to include a governmental contribution to the old age insurance fund once payroll taxes and the contributory principle were well established. The draft bill used by the CES showed a subsidy from federal revenues beginning in 1965 (Schlabach 1969, pp. 127–28; Perkins 1964, pp. 294–96). Yet Roosevelt, upon discovering at the last moment that the CES plan included a future subsidy from general revenues, demanded a redrafting of the proposed legislation so that the program would always be self-sustaining from employer and beneificiary contributions alone. Even a governmental contribution to the social security fund was problematic for FDR, with his "prejudice about the 'dole' " (Perkins 1964, pp. 294–96; Leff 1983). In the end, Roosevelt's view prevailed, and the U.S. social insurance program for the aged received no financial input from federal coffers, a logical outcome of Roosevelt's and Witte's concern to preserve a sharp distinction between social assistance and social insurance programs. Indeed, the lack of government contributions to the contributory social insurance fund has been a cross-nationally unusual feature of U.S. social provision for the aged ever since.

Given the preferences of the CES and FDR himself for state-level administration, one must explain the fact that the contributory old age insurance system was the only one of the several programs included in the Social Security Act that was purely national. To some extent this reflected the fact that Witte and Perkins were preoccupied with resolving the disputes about unemployment insurance, which by all accounts occasioned the most attention from the members of the CES and the policy experts who advised them (Altmeyer 1968, chap. 1; Witte 1962; Schlabach 1969, chap. 6). The staff members in charge of developing the old age security portions of the program strongly favored establishing a national old age insurance system. They and the CES actuaries were unanimous in advising that, given extensive labor mobility, a federal-state scheme involving contributions over workers' lifetimes would be unworkable from a technical point of view (Schlabach 1969, pp. 111–12; Altmeyer 1968, pp. 25–26). Moreover, old age insurance was the only area of policy in which the states had not enacted legislation and, hence, the only one in which there were no state-level vested administrative and political interests to defend, as there were in the old age assistance and unemployment programs.

Despite their strong commitment to establishing contributory old age insurance, CES members believed that some sort of old age assistance was needed to cope with existing poverty among the aged, at least until the contributory schemes matured (Achenbaum 1978, p. 134; U.S. Committee on Economic Security 1985, pp. 4–5). The fact that four times as many elderly people were collecting benefits under federal relief programs as under state old age assistance systems worried Roosevelt administration policymakers, who did not want to encourage Americans to look to the federal government to take care of the needs of aged citizens directly through noncontributory programs (U.S. Committee on Economic Security 1985, p. 27; Schlabach 1969, p. 110). State old age assistance programs, with their inadequate financing and benefits, would have to be strengthened if the federal government was to be kept out of direct relief to the aged. The CES therefore recommended the enactment of the old age assistance program, a federal subsidy (of 50 percent) for state old age assistance plans that met certain minimum requirements. Most important, the draft legislation required that plans be statewide in operation and that pensions be paid at a level that would ensure the "health and decency" of elderly recipients (Achenbaum 1978, pp. 134–35). The old age assistance program, though not seen by CES members as a long-term solution to poverty among the aged, would please congressional Democrats and allow the popular enthusiasm for public old age protection to be harnessed to the Social Security Act as a whole.

Advocates of the corporate liberal argument have claimed that the character of the social security programs, in particular the fact that the two main programs, unemployment and old age protection, were contributory in nature, represents the "acceptance of private welfare plans as models for the new law" (Berkowitz and McQuaid 1978, pp. 132–33). This is more than a little misleading. Many programs in addition to voluntary business welfare schemes served as precedents, most notably, the public social insurance and pension schemes of other countries, many of which were contributory schemes (see U.S. Social Security Board 1937). In his speech to Congress on June 8, 1934, Roosevelt noted of his plan to establish public social protections: "This is not an untried experiment. Lessons of experience are available from the States, from industries, and from many nations of the civilized world" (cited in Altmeyer 1966, p. 3). Furthermore, many social reformers, ranging from liberals like Barbara Armstrong (1932) and Paul Douglas (1936) to socialist Isaac Max Rubinow (1913, 1934; Lubove 1968, pp. 35–40, 43–44, 176), also endorsed contributory social insurance as the plan most likely to provide universal, adequate benefits to the elderly and unemployed. Roosevelt's officials did examine the experience of the welfare capitalist schemes, but they came to the conclusion that this experience demonstrated precisely that voluntary schemes were unworkable and that public, compulsory programs were essential (U.S. Social Security Board 1937, p. 176). The committee's report on existing old age provision notes that "the half-century of experience with voluntary plans has shown that they have been inefficient and inadequate as sound social insurance measures."

The Advisory Council spent little time discussing programs for the aged, but after the introduction of the Economic Security Bill in Congress in early 1935, the Roosevelt administration's approach appeared to be at odds with the voluntary approach favored by welfare capitalists. Business leaders were not the ones calling for contributory old age insurance to be financed by a payroll tax; rather, the political leaders—most important, Witte, Perkins, and FDR himself—pressed for a contributory scheme, and Roosevelt insisted the scheme be entirely self-financing (Perkins 1964, p. 294, and chap. 23). Most businessmen preferred a means-tested assistance program for the needy aged poor, rather than a contributory program reaching much of the aged population. Many business leaders also were uncomfortable with the prospect of large reserves building up under the control of government administrators, as envisioned by the CES proposal (Schlabach 1969, pp. 144–45; Cates 1983, chaps. 1–2). Welfare capitalists were willing to have the state step in to provide residual care to the aged poor or to force less "progressive" employers to participate in government-run programs, but they did not want to give up their discretion to maintain their firms' voluntary schemes (Lubove 1968, pp. 132, 140; McQuaid 1978). They showed no interest in compulsory insurance for themselves.

Almost all of the welfare capitalists backed the Clark Amendment to the Economic Security Bill, a provision offered in the Senate which would have given exemptions to employers with private plans with provisions as liberal as those of the government-run program, but they were unsuccessful in this attempt to soften the compulsory aspects of the bill (Altmeyer 1966, pp. 40–42; Witte 1962, pp. 157–61). As conservative analyst Carolyn Weaver notes in her critique of U.S. social security programs, this amendment would have reduced substantially the redistributive possibilities of the program, limited though they were, and forced the government to operate the program more in conformity with the market (Weaver 1982, pp. 89–94). The Clark Amendment passed by a large majority (fifty-one to thirty-five) in the Senate, where senators had been lobbied extensively by insurance company representatives who had sent circulars to all employers with voluntary pension plans and stimulated a flood of mail from home backing the exemption for welfare capitalists (Witte 1962, pp. 102–8, 160–62). Roosevelt and his officials refused to support the amendment, FDR even saying he would not sign the bill if it was included. Labor groups and social insurance activists and experts spoke out against it, too. In the end, the refusal by the House to include the amendment killed it, and the Social Security Act became law without this pro-welfare capitalist provision (Douglas 1936, pp. 121–25, 278–89).

The fact that patronage practices continued unabated in many states and had not been completely eradicated even from the federal government meant that the CES faced a challenge in constructing realms of administration that could manage the new programs while avoiding entanglements in patronage politics. That the group was willing to face the challenge, rather than awaiting the development of a public administration more suited to its preferences, is testament to the crisis atmosphere produced by the Great Depression and the CES members' conviction that the continuing popular pressure for some kind of federal action on the social welfare front would produce "unwise" legislation if they did not act. Yet the CES carefully included as many guarantees against corruption, patronage, and mismanagement as possible in its proposed permanent social security legislation (Aronson 1950, p. 3). The members also tried to design programs capable of withstanding periodic democratic onslaughts demanding "unwarranted" expansion.

The Social Security Act: Charter Legislation of America's Welfare State

The legislative recommendations of the CES included a federal-state contributory unemployment system, federal subsidies to state programs for the needy aged, dependent children, and the blind, and a purely federal contributory old age benefits program. To deal with concerns about the constitutionality of the fully national old age insurance program, separate titles were used to establish taxes and benefits. The CES depended on the taxing power of the federal government to ensure the plan's constitutionality (Achenbaum 1978, pp. 136–37). The pragmatic formulators of the CES social security proposals had opted for substantial state-level autonomy in most of the programs they recommended. Yet the CES report also recommended the establishment of minimum national standards, such as the "health and decency" requirement for old age assistance benefit levels, and practices which would lead to administrative regularity, such as the recommendation for merit personnel systems in state-level administration of the programs. Moreover, the CES hoped to see all social insurance administration united within a single social insurance board located in the Department of Labor, with the social assistance programs grouped together under the aegis of the Federal Emergency Relief Administration. Finally, the CES recommended continuing research and planning for national coordination of the new social welfare activities, endorsing the establishment of a national planning board (U.S. Committee on Economic Security 1985, p. 9).

The CES proposal had been designed to propitiate important congressional interests, of course, especially those representing the South. These had largely determined that a federal approach would be taken. But even more concessions were wrested from the congressional sponsors of the administration bill by southern lawmakers and other conservatives (Witte 1962; Perkins 1964, pp. 296–301; Achenbaum 1978, pp. 134–35; Altmeyer 1968, p. 35; Finegold 1988; Quadagno 1988b). Federal standards in general came under fire. The CES recommendation that all employed persons be included in the old age insurance system was not accepted by Congress, with the result that agricultural, government, and domestic workers were excluded from coverage (Witte 1962, pp. 131, 152–53; Perkins 1964, pp. 282–83). This meant that social security would not reach many women workers and most American blacks, who were still overwhelmingly concentrated in rural agricultural regions of the South (Weiss 1983, pp. 166–68). Southern senators and congressmen led the fight for "states' rights" and against national standards and universal coverage. They especially attacked the provision of the old age assistance legislation that mandated that states pay pensions sufficient to provide, "when added to the income of the aged recipient, a reasonable subsistence compatible with decency and health," fearing it would represent an entering wedge for federal interference in their states' system of segregation and discrimination (see Quadagno 1988b; Alston and Ferrie 1985). In the end, the southern-led bloc won the fight, and the requirement was dropped (Witte 1962, pp. 144–45). The result was that states were free to pay whatever benefit level they chose (in 1938–39, average grants varied dramatically across states, ranging from as little as seven dollars in Mississippi to as much as thirty dollars in California, as compared with average monthly wages for full-time workers of $105 in 1939 [U.S. Bureau of the Census 1960, p. 95]), and southern states found ways to pay different benefits to blacks and whites (Quadagno 1988b, p. 245).[10]

The CES proposal that state programs be administered along merit system lines had to be dropped as a result of congressional pressure, and some state administrations did make use of the new programs and positions created through the old age assistance and other programs for patronage purposes (Aronson 1950, p. 3; Witte 1962, pp. 101, 144–45). Roosevelt noted in an address to Congress that "in some states incompetent and politically dominated personnel has been distinctly harmful" (quoted in Aronson 1950, p. 3). The Roosevelt administration did not simply give up on the fight against patronage in social programs, however. Federal administrators at the new Social Security Board were able to convince some states to adopt merit practices in their social security programs (Altmeyer 1966, p. 65). Also, New Dealers did succeed in establishing a requirement for state merit practices in the 1939 amendments to the Social Security Act after engaging in continued struggles with patronage politicians who were attempting to use the new public assistance funds for their own purposes (Aronson 1950, 1956; Quadagno and Meyer 1989; Altmeyer 1966, chaps. 3–4). The aim of the program's drafters was "to ensure that locally dominant political forces would not gain control of the administration of the program and be strengthened by it. Rather, they wanted the flow of these new benefits to be controlled from the center, and the political advantages of the program to accrue to the administration which enacted it" (Shefter 1978, pp. 239–40).

Analysts of corporate liberalism have argued that significant fractions of monopoly presumably represented by the BAC/welfare capitalist group, offered crucial support for the Social Security Act. This claim is belied by the

---

10. Quadagno reports that "national authority in program administration was carefully circumscribed. Cash grants to blacks were monitored [by state governments] so as not to undermine prevailing wage rates and to intrude as little as possible into the planter-tenant relationship. Although discrimination was illegal, the southern states were allowed to pay blacks lower grants than whites by using different criteria for determining need, and by paying Confederate veterans and their dependents the maximum grants" (1988b, p. 246).

fact that the BAC nearly broke up and did lose several members in the course of the drafting and congressional consideration of the law. By mid-1934 key members of the BAC who cooperated in the administration of the National Industrial Recovery Act had already resigned from the BAC and started an intense, well-funded campaign against Roosevelt and the whole range of New Deal legislation, including social security, through the Liberty League. The men who left the BAC to establish the Liberty League included Pierre DuPont and John J. Raskob, one of the corporate leaders with whom Witte conferred prior to the break (McQuaid 1979, pp. 699–700; 1976, p. 176). (As executives of DuPont and General Motors, they represented sectors of industry that many versions of the corporate liberal argument predicted would be in the forefront of social policy-making.) The Liberty League's vigorous opposition to all aspects of the New Deal (Pietrusza 1978; Rudolf 1950) echoed loudly among other businessmen and business organizations, including the National Association of Manufacturers, an organization led by big business by the 1930s (Burch 1973), and the Chamber of Commerce (McQuaid 1978, p. 362).

The corporate liberals' position within the business community eroded after these events, and business opinion fragmented and shifted away from the administration. Further cooperation between the administration and businessmen occurred on an individual basis, and even executives with the most ambitious corporate liberal proposals, such as General Electric's Swope, no longer supported the administration publicly (McQuaid 1978, pp. 362–63; 1977, pp. 35–37). At the Chamber's May 1935 convention, Henry Harriman, a prominent figure in most of these arguments, was ousted as president, and the conventioneers passed resolutions critical of social security and other New Deal policies (Wolfskill and Hudson 1969, pp. 157, 159–66). When Roosevelt attempted to downplay business opposition by inaccurately citing a confidential memo as evidence of the BAC's strong support for the proposed social security legislation, the organization nearly collapsed. Three executives resigned immediately, and three more followed them within two months, including Chase National's Winthrop Aldrich (McQuaid 1979, p. 702; 1976, pp. 178–79). A September poll conducted by the Chamber of its fifteen hundred member firms found opinion running thirty-five to one against New Deal policies (Wolfskill and Hudson 1969, p. 157). The position of the National Association of Manufacturers went from a cautious support for the principle of public action on social security to opposition to the specifics of the Social Security Act, while there were threats that BAC members, including many of the original participants, were going to resign en masse. If the BAC was the staunchest advocate of social security within the business community (Collins 1978, p. 372), as theorists of corporate liberalism say, then there was hardly any support at all among businessmen.

Although business accommodated itself to social security in the years after the act's passage, businessmen were almost uniformly opposed to the passage of the act in the first place, and the few pro–social insurance liberals remaining in 1935 were almost completely isolated within the corporate community. Despite business (and Republican) opposition, the act passed overwhelmingly, showing the political weakness of U.S. business as an interest group at this juncture of American history. This would fit in with the claims that business typically opposes public social protections and that the weakness of the Right is an important condition for social policy breakthroughs. Individual businessmen were connected to government policy-making but were far from being leaders in the drafting process.

The Social Security Act was finally signed into law in August 1935. States soon acted to pass legislation establishing programs under the act, and by 1937 the programs were nationwide in operation. Also in 1937, the act was declared constitutional by the Supreme Court, and the first payroll taxes were taken out of covered employees' paychecks, though benefits under the old age insurance program were not scheduled to begin until 1942. Yet before the first benefit check was ever mailed, important changes were made in the contributory old age benefits part of social security. A new Advisory Council began discussions in 1937 on certain controversial aspects of the social security program (Schlabach 1969, chap. 8). In addition to dissatisfactions with some of the more technical aspects of the law, there was widespread support for adding survivors' benefits. As a result of the council's recommendations and new negotiations in Congress, the 1939 amendments to the Social Security Act were passed. The most notable changes included a shift from full reserves to a modified pay-as-you-go system, and, in an early demonstration of the potential for expansion that even contributory social insurance systems can have in the United States, benefit payments became payable two years earlier (in 1940), payroll tax increases were delayed, and benefits for wage earners' dependents and survivors were added (Achenbaum 1978, pp. 136–37; Altmeyer 1968, chap. 3). The addition of the dependents' and survivors' program institutionalized a particular set of assumptions about gender relations which were not so evident in non-contributory programs. This new program assumed women's dependence on men's wages and penalized dual-earner families and single people, giving advantages to "housewife-maintaining" couples, to borrow Barbara Bergmann's phrase (1986). But whatever its shortcomings as a system of social protection, social security clearly represented an expandable set of social programs, despite the intentions of its formulators.

The Social Security Act represented one of the most important of all the New Deal reforms of American social and political life. Along with such legislation as the National Labor Relations (Wagner) Act and the Fair Labor Standards Act, it established critical social rights for American citizens. Yet these rights were compromised by uneven national standards, the sharp distinction between assistance and insurance, and the omissions of programs for nonelderly constituencies such as needy children from two-parent families. This reflected the inability of Roosevelt administration officials to overcome the deep resistance of Congress and some congressional constituencies to reform and, ultimately, the larger obstacles represented by the legacies of American state-building and state structure.

The fragmentation of authority encouraged by federalism and the division of powers has consistently undermined coordinated national welfare initiatives in the United States, even in the periods most hospitable to reform. The patronage practices intially encouraged by early mass democracy and the lack of bureaucratic state-building deprived reformers of readily available institutional capacities for carrying out new social spending activities. Successful reforms have had to work around the obstacles represented by America's institutional and policy legacies and have built the bureaucratic capacity for social intervention slowly when it has been possible to build at all. We have seen as well that American policy innovators and reformers have developed policy preferences in response to earlier state social interventions and policies, from the days of the progressives' reactions against the excesses of the Civil War pension system and patronage democracy to the New Dealers' preference for contributory social insurance. Moreover, the historically varying possibilities for cross-class coalitions—joining elite, middle-class, and working-class interests—have been critical for explaining the fates of failed and successful social spending programs. In the Progressive Era it proved impossible to unite these interests around new social spending programs, but during the New Deal a cross-class coalition was able to coalesce around the Social Security Act, ushering in America's version of a modern welfare state.

10
Conclusion

The conjuncture of factors that resulted in the break with poor relief and the initiation of modern public provision for the aged in Britain, Canada, and the United States was in certain respects distinctive to each country, although all can be analyzed within a common framework. Nonetheless, some rather striking commonalities exist across the three countries in the conjuncture of forces leading to the initiation of modern social provision for the aged. The demographic changes and economic transformations associated with capitalist industrialization and urbanization affected citizens of Britain, Canada, and the United States as they did their counterparts across continental Europe, Latin America, and the Antipodes. These changes created conditions under which the support of the elderly could emerge as a social and political problem. Yet in no case were such changes experienced by the elderly and their families directly. In each country, the existing system of social provision mediated the impact of declining employment opportunities and changing family patterns. Policy was (and is) political. In the politics of social provision, one finds divergence among countries with different class-structural, institutional, ideological, and political characteristics, both across and within regime types.

In Britain, Canada, and the United States, the initiation of modern social provision for the aged was the work of (predominantly male) cross-class coalitions of liberal political entrepreneurs, social reformers, and working-class groups operating within and outside of legislatures. Thus, it was premised on the entry into electoral politics of the working class and their political mobilization, as well as on the ideological reorientation of liberal reform, political, and intellectual elites through the development of new liberalism. In Britain, the support of reformers, social scientists, and reformist politicians was joined to the efforts of trade unionists and labor politicians in the National Committee of Organized Labour, in the electoral agreement between the Labour Representation Committee and the Liberal party, and in the Liberal party's reform initiatives, directed at working-class voters. In Canada, W. L. Mackenzie King led his Liberal party in responding to the demands of Labour M.P.'s James Woodsworth and A. A. Heaps, who had carried the demands of the Trades and Labour Congress and scattered labor political representatives into the Dominion House of Commons. The backing of reformers such as J. J. Kelso and reformist organizations such as the Social Service Council had helped to pave the way for the acceptance of pensions. In the United States, the cross-class coalition looked somewhat different than those in Canada and Britain, where labor and liberal parties actually concluded explicit agreements. Extensive discussion of the social question and possible policy solutions among social scientists and reformers such as those in the American Association for Labor Legislation laid the basis for political elites' actions. Political entrepreneurs and social reformers came together in Franklin Roosevelt's administration, as Frances Perkins and the policymakers on the Committee on Economic Security fashioned the Social Security Act, which was partially aimed at securing the support of fraternal and labor organizations, as well as working-class and middle-class voters, for the Democratic party and the bureaucratic agencies it would leave to institutionalize New Deal policies. In Canada and the United States before World War I, such coalitions had failed to emerge in response to initial expressions of support by labor and a few reformers, for most political and reform elites, and the middle-class public generally, were uninterested in initiating social spending programs for the aged.

Working-class groups, such as unions and fraternal organizations, supported nondeterrent provision for the aged from very early on, first within the poor relief framework, but increasingly in the form of noncontributory pensions. Yet pensions only achieved political success when political, intellectual, and reform elites and the middle-class public oriented to their leadership became committed to enactment. There were similarities across the three countries in what produced elite and middle-class willingness to support social spending initiatives. Shifts in liberal ideology accompanied and, indeed, helped to motivate, the emergence of debates over social provision in all three countries. But even a general interest in solving the social question and the availability of intellectual and ideological resources for justifying new forms of state social provision were not sufficient for elites to become willing to support social spending, as the experience of Canada and the United States in the prewar period attests. We can point to clear short-term political advantages that would accrue to political entrepreneurs who seized the moment for policy initiatives: in Britain, competition between Liberals and Tories for working-class votes was intense; in Canada, whichever party agreed to the demands of Labour M.P.'s Woodsworth and Heaps would gain the support necessary to form an administration; in the United States, the Democratic leadership was interested in solidifying the New Deal coalition, including working-class voters and organizations, after decades of Republican dominance. Thus, popular forces had to be able to command the attention of elites, a condition that was only partially met in prewar Canada. Moreover, these initiatives responded to problems in the existing systems of public social provision. Reactions against poor relief animated popular organizations and voters and new liberals alike, but elite interest in reform was also motivated by administrative and financial difficulties within existing social provision. In the United States, it is not an overstatement to call the situation in the 1930s a policy crisis. But similar political moments did not always lead to policy initiatives, and the problems of poor relief had been in existence for a long time. Clearly, factors at work over the longer term paved the way for acceptance of new social spending programs.

   This analysis suggests that countries with a liberal policy regime share a distinctive experience of state formation. Canada, the United States, and Britain all shared a more protected geopolitical environment than the continental European countries, a domestic social structure characterized by the power of significant groups who blocked the emergence of a coalition for bureaucratic autonomy, and a commercialized economy. These factors, which significantly shaped the character of states and parties, help to explain the relative lateness of bureaucratic transformations of government administrations in the three states. The delay in civil service reform meant that state capacities to administer modern social programs were also slower to develop, and indeed, relative to the countries of continental Europe, policy innovation was delayed in the Anglo-American world.

   The character of what I have called the institutional context—the state and political parties—also affected the possibilities for the formation of cross-class alliances. In all three countries, bureaucratic state administrations were less developed than in continental Europe. This meant that democratic politics were relatively more important, and bureaucratic initiatives less important, to policy developments than was the case in some European countries, such as Germany or Sweden (Heclo 1974; Flora and Alber 1981; Ritter 1986). This circumstance in turn magnified the importance of elite and middle-class willingness to form alliances with popular groups for social spending. The existence of state administrative capacities or readily creatable capacities and some safeguards against patronage were critical to elites' willingness to join with popular forces to initiate social spending programs for the elderly. Where patronage practices predominated, elite attention focused on political rather than social reform. Once civil service practices had gained some hold in the state, capacities could be created for bureaucratic interventions in the policy process, even if they were limited at first to such activities as information gathering or working out details of policy initiatives pressed on the state from without. Furthermore, the reaction of elites, particularly liberals, to the state became more positive, as social spending was removed from possible entanglements with patronage politics. Thus, in all three countries, one sees not only the importance of cross-class coalitions, but also the significance to the formation of those coalitions of state capacities and the overcoming of patronage practices.

Within this group of countries, of course, there was significant policy variation, which we have related to differences in the development of state bureaucracies and in the democratization of the electorate, which are also related to the experiences of state formation and building. The timing, sequence, and character of bureaucratization and democratization were particularly critical in determining whether or not there would be necessary capacities at the time pensions and other social reforms first emerged on the political agenda. These factors also affected the character of political parties, which might or might not be the agents of policy reform. In Britain, civil service reform was accomplished before the full democratization of the electorate, and when pension proposals gathered steam, a bureaucratized civil service and programmatically competing political parties had been in place for some time. Social spending for the aged was not problematic on the grounds that it would feed a corrupt patronage system. In contrast, democratization of the electorate preceded bureaucratization in Canada and the United States, which resulted in conditions that undercut the formation of cross-class alliances for social spending in several ways. Only with the partial success of civil service reform did policy breakthroughs occur.

Pension proposals failed in both Canada and the United States before World War I due to the common lack of state capacity to initiate or manage relatively complex social welfare programs, the legacy of their experiences of state formation. Patronage, rooted in democratic politics, dominated the organization of political parties and state administrative practices, so that civil service reform was stymied. This had two important results. While in Britain state officials played a role in negotiating the details of policy reforms and thus helped to cement cross-class alliances, such actors were absent in the Canadian and American states. The character of the administrative states was also important as it affected the policy preferences of political and business elites and the broader middle-class public. Until the resolution of concerns about the capacity and honesty of state officials generated by the workings of patronage democracy, political entrepreneurs were unlikely to be willing to adopt social reform measures which involved significantly increasing the flow of resources through the civil administration. Again, the situation in Britain contrasted with those in North America; for Britons, the administration of spending was not considered problematic.

Canadian and American policy developments in the prewar period differed in other ways. As a result of the Canadian state-building process, postconfederation political parties were significantly more elitist in orientation than were American parties, and the fruits of the Canadian patronage system were enjoyed more disproportionately by elites than was the case in the United States. Thus, there was little impetus for issue entrepreneurship using pensions or social insurance given continuing reliance on patronage and a stable electorate. In addition, policy feedback created different conditions in Canada than in the United States. In contrast with the United States, Britain, and much of continental Europe, Canada had less of a public policy inheritance in poor relief practices which reformers and people in general could react against and build upon. Comparing the Canadian experience with the British and American makes it clear that the absence of a public poor law perceived to be in crisis was critical to Canadian elites' lack of interest in new public spending programs. There was less of a reaction against public social spending in Canada than in the United States, and Canadian elites did not display the intense opposition to social spending measures that was so important in American social policy debates of the Progressive Era. In the United States, the administration of local poor relief and national Civil War pensions was permeated by the patronage practices reformers abhorred, and both kinds of public provision were completely entangled in the workings of patronage political parties. During the Progressive Era, American reformers and charity workers worried about "politics in welfare" and explicitly cited this as a reason for not initiating new government social protections. The more extensive democracy in America meant that many distributive policies, including Civil War pensions, urban-machine-controlled poor relief, and public works jobs, benefited nonelites and implicated them in perceived problems of social welfare policy. Popular interests were given more political expression in the United States, but elite concerns about patronage overshadowed these pressures, turning reform elites away from democratically controlled spending by a state still dominated by patronage. Thus, the failure of social spending measures in the United States clearly can be attributed in part to their political unacceptability among elites obsessed with the need to clean up politics before entrusting the government with new social responsibilities, while the failure of Canadian elites to support analogous spending measures seems more a sin of omission than of commission.

The fate of pensions and old age insurance in Canada and the United States during the interwar years can be explained with reference to the same set of factors. The reaction to World War I in the two countries was quite different, a legacy of their differing geopolitical positions and relations to Britain. The character of their political institutions, forged in the process of state-building, was likewise distinctive. The extreme fragmentation of sovereignty combined with federalism in the United States raised exceptionally high barriers to reform. Very wide coalitions had to be put together to overcome the many potential vetoes lurking at multiple points in the complicated American polity. Such coalitions partially substituted for parties as agents of reform, as the deep hold of patronage among the American electorate and its only partial eclipse meant that U.S. political parties were never transformed into programmatically competing organizations as were their British counterparts. Canada presents another pattern: a unitary federal government confronted unitary provincial governments, so that federal-provincial power struggles and negotiations were important to policy developments. Third parties played a crucial role in the success of pensions in Canada; their role in the United States was minimized by electoral rules. The legacy of patronage, too, was important. The greater success of Canadian civil service reform helped to lay the basis for a relatively more statist political culture and the acceptance of state social interventions and spending by elites once political incentives for these sorts of initiatives emerged. In Canada, once the elitism of politics had been mitigated somewhat by the extension of the franchise after World War I, parties became more programmatic and more responsive to popular concerns in periods of high levels of electoral competition. In the United States, the 1920s were characterized by electoral demobilization and one-party dominance. Thus, in Canada, a cross-class coalition for old age pensions could be constructed in the 1920s, while such a coalition could not coalesce in the United States. Developments in the 1930s, as in the 1920s, were shaped by the distinctive institutional contexts of Canada and the United States. In the United States, the shift from poor relief to modern social provision at the national level occurred in a "big bang" of innovation (Leman 1977), as popular political mobilization and enhanced state capacities created the conditions for a cross-class coalition for social spending to emerge and an opportunity for reform initiatives by the Roosevelt administration and its allies in Congress. Canadian old age policy stalled in the 1930s, as constitutional arrangements thwarted the establishment of a contributory program, and then overcoming the difficulties associated with enacting unemployment insurance took precedence over innovating for the elderly.

Implications for Future Research

This study underlines the necessity of considering the political and institutional context, as well as the interests and capacities of political actors, in explaining how and when policy breakthroughs may or may not occur. Indeed, the whole complex of factors associated with the state—structure, capacity, policy legacy, character of administration (patronage or civil service, or a combination), character of political parties, relations between branches and levels of government, personnel—was useful in this analysis of social policy developments. The dynamics of state-building, rooted in the international states system, contributed to the specific policy developments which occurred in early-twentieth-century Canada, Britain, and the United States as much as did class and other societal dynamics. But clearly we should conceive of these dynamics as inextricably intertwined: state formation affected the strategies and institutions available to social groups active in policy-making, while the capacities and structure of social groups affected political transformations as well.[1]

This analysis also demonstrates the fruitfulness of the concept of social policy regimes. By looking at a set of countries within the liberal grouping, I have been able to suggest some of the common factors in their policy developments, which may in future research be constrasted with other regime types. In addition, I have been able to specify some of the dimensions within which they differ. Earlier formulations of the policy regime concept have focused on the characteristic class coalitions underpinning the different policy regimes. But it does appear that there is a distinctive complex of state and political institutions and a distinctive set of experiences of state formation and state-building, as well as a specific sort of class coalition, associated with liberal policy regimes. Would civil service reform in these three countries have been relatively late if they had been subject to harsher military competition? Aren't their underdeveloped state capacities linked to elites' preferences for policies that respect the market, even as this orientation also reflects the power of capitalists as opposed to other sorts of dominant classes? But, again, this is not merely a matter of "add 'the state' and stir." It also seems quite clear to me that the dynamics of the international states system and the development of modern states on the one hand and the dynamics of capitalism and the development of classes on the other have been mutually influential. Would the "country," anti-central state planter elites of the American South have been able to maintain their influence if the new United States had been drawn into a prolonged series of military engagements? Could democratization have gone as far in a different geopolitical context? Certainly both the presence of southern elites and the early development of mass democratic politics, particularly in the North, shaped the development of the American state throughout the nineteenth century, which in turn had profound implications for social policy developments in the 1930s and beyond. Would Canada's colonial elites have maintained their position, and the antidemocratic bias of the governments they controlled, without Britain's support? Would Britain have been as interested in North America if it had not been engaged in competition with other European states? The distinctive power of Britain's aristocracy was reflected in the absence of a true absolutism in England, but wasn't this outcome strengthened by England's relative protection from military pressures? It would make sense for future investigations of policy regimes to focus on distinctive profiles of both class structures and coalitions and state structures, capacities, and institutional contexts, even as analysts work to incorporate social structures based on gen-

---

1. Over the past few years, sometimes the state-centered versus class-centered debate approached the level of silliness and vacuity that had earlier accompanied the politics versus economics debates over the expansion of social spending.

der, race, and ethnicity, about which I have not said enough. Finally, I would note that the in-depth investigation of particular countries within a regime type, using comparative-historical analysis, seems particularly well suited to specifying the particular conjuncture of state and social factors leading to distinctive policy regimes.

The Importance of the Policy Legacy

My analysis has shown not only that institutions are significant for policy developments but also that the specific characteristics of the policy legacy shape subsequent debates and outcomes. This clearly has analytic implications: we cannot comprehend policy developments outside of their historical context and without an understanding of how policies are embedded in political, administrative, and ideological contexts. I hope, too, that the political implications of this analysis are apparent. Too often, such implications come in the form of deducing alleged "lessons from the past," which is not my intent. There is, for example, no unchanging liberal orientation to social policy to be gleaned from this research. Indeed, it is useful to recognize that variation over time in how people have evaluated social provision is linked to the character of the specific policy legacies, the coalitions they engendered, and the capacities they built, which they have reacted against and built upon.[2]

Allow me to illustrate the importance of the policy legacies set in place in the early twentieth century with the U.S. case. I choose to use the American example both because I know more about the history of policy developments in the United States after the 1930s and because, politically, I am more engaged with American developments. Since the New Deal, the divisions between social assistance, including but not limited to old age assistance, and contributory social insurance built into the system of U.S. public social provision by the Social Security Act have been reflected in the ideology of program administrators, in the political coalitions that have solidified around those divisions, and in the state administrative capacities built up for different sorts of intervention. These in turn have set limits on the sorts of policies that have been pursued.

In the 1930s there was widespread support for noncontributory approaches to income maintenance, especially old age pensions, flowing from notions of entitlement based on socially useful labor. But contributory social insurance was the clear preference of President Roosevelt and most of his closest social policy advisers, largely because of their experience as progressive state politi-

---

2. It has always distressed me to see an unchanging individualist, liberal ideology invoked as the cause of America's many lacunae in the area of social provision, for this deflects our attention from the political factors which I suspect are far more important to the various welfare backlashes our country has witnessed.

cians reacting to even earlier social policy legacies. They succeeded in establishing old age insurance as a contributory program, although old age assistance and ADC, later AFDC, building upon existing state-level programs, were included in the Social Security Act as well. In the early years of social security, it was not clear that social insurance would become the preferred, more generous of the two kinds of programs, and those implementing policy could have developed either program type to this status. Fatefully for those depending on public assistance programs, in the decades following the passage of the Social Security Act, FDR's appointees in the Social Security Administration deliberately pursued a political strategy of building up a notion of entitlement based on contribution and simultaneously attacking the originally more widespread idea of entitlement as based on social service or socially useful labor (Cates 1983).

Coalition-building by the administrators of social insurance has been important for the increasing political strength of contributory old age insurance. After the passage of the Social Security Act in 1935, social security administrators worked effectively within the federal executive and with key congressional committees to build up contributory social insurance (Derthick 1979). At key junctures when it seemed as if noncontributory assistance might become more popular than contributory insurance, these administrators and their congressional allies extended coverage or raised benefits prior to raising taxes (labeled "contributions"). Over time, maturing social insurance programs came to pay out benefits to more and more regularly employed Americans and their dependents, finally overtaking social assistance programs in terms of the numbers of people receiving benefits by the mid-1950s. Thus, by the late 1950s social security had developed a remarkably solid base of congressional and electoral support. Behind the banner of social security were grouped not only all retired people currently collecting benefits, including many middle-class and even wealthy people, but also their families who might otherwise have had to support them, along with most of the working-aged population, who as they made payroll "contributions" gained a stake in the future benefits to which they now felt entitled. This was exactly the kind of virtually universal coalition of citizens that social security administrators had deliberately tried to build as they worked to make social insurance politically secure. Their efforts proved so successful that by the 1980s, when retrenchment of social expenditures was supposedly the order of the day, congresspeople of every political persuasion vied to be seen as the staunchest defenders of social security. (As of this writing, that situation has not much changed.)

Perhaps inevitably, the consolidation of such support for social security was accompanied by the political marginalization of programs assisting those Americans not adequately included in contributory social insurance, particularly people of color and women. Not only did social security administrators sometimes deliberately work to denigrate public assistance, but in addition, the expansion of contributory insurance—to cover more of the elderly in place of old age assistance and, with the passage of the 1939 amendments, to cover widows and orphans of employed workers in place of AFDC—meant that social security siphoned off the most appealing categories of public assistance recipients, leaving "welfare" with politically weak clients, such as unwed or divorced mothers. Thus, as the scope and inclusiveness of social security expanded, so did its supporting coalition, while the possibilities for securely extending generous social assistance beyond its fold correspondingly diminished.

In the 1960s welfare and social security policies were reexamined, and opportunities opened for reform. But developments in social welfare, including the initiation of public medical coverage, reinforced the inherited divisions within public social provision. It was difficult to muster the political force to address problems of poverty and insecurity comprehensively, but social security administrators, calling upon the entrenched social security coalition, were able to intervene effectively for the elderly. Contributory social insurance expanded with the passage of Medicare for the elderly in 1965 and cost-of-living indexing of old age benefits that transformed them into a retirement wage in the years 1969–72 (Myles 1988). Finally, old age assistance was transformed into a fully federal—and more generous—program, Supplemental Security Income, which is effectively a nationally guaranteed income for the elderly and disabled not sufficiently covered by social insurance (see Quadagno 1988b). There was also some expansion of provision aimed at the poor: food stamps (Finegold 1988) and Medicaid (passed along with Medicare in 1965), both of which engaged the interests of nonpoor constituencies, farmers and the Department of Agriculture and medical and hospital groups. But proposals for universal health insurance failed, as did a guaranteed income for all the poor. AFDC, which had become the largest public assistance program, was not nationalized and continued to offer assistance only to certain categories of the needy (Burke and Burke 1974).

The bifurcation of social policy has also been furthered by the uneven and limited administrative capacities of the American state, which have made certain types of interventions efficacious and politically secure while undermining others, notably those aimed at eradicating poverty among the working-aged poor. Despite the slow and uneven development of administrative capacities, some "islands of expertise" became capable of expanding or improving the social programs under their aegis when reform opportunities opened up. The Social Security Administration is an excellent illustration of this. This agency enjoyed unusual jurisdictional autonomy, freeing its administrators to plan and rationalize new policies and to develop stable ties with key congressional committees and federated associations of locally influential groups. Moreover, the success of the programs championed by this agency was facilitated by reliance on mechanisms, such as simple cash transfers, that were technically and politically viable. (From Civil War pensions to social security, the U.S. government has excelled at putting checks in the mail.) More complex sorts of interventions, involving direct, targeted interventions into the social activities of local communities, for example, have been far more difficult to carry out. Indeed, the requisite administrative capacities have not been readily available or easy to create. Given options between constructing new national bureaucracies and relying on third parties to administer programs in return for subsidies and under loose supervision, the federal government has usually relied on the latter. Thus, the expansion of U.S. social expenditure that occurred after World War II did not bring proportionate growth of the administrative apparatus of the federal government. Instead, reliance on third parties, while allowing programs to be launched fairly quickly, undercut the ability of the federal government to control expenditures and target precisely programmatic interventions. This process has been played out rather spectacularly in the health field: Americans pay more of their income for less health care than do citizens of any other rich capitalist democracy. In the few instances where the federal government has attempted to administer programs directly, as in the employment programs of the Great Society, such efforts have foundered in patronage or in bitter disputes over local versus federal control (Weir 1988).

In the end, the political energies mustered for reform in the 1960s and early 1970s were channeled into programs that did not function to draw together the constituencies separated by the social policy decisions of the 1930s. Instead, they worked to increase the political isolation of the poor, especially the black poor, from the working and middle classes. Therefore, a bitter legacy of the Great Society and its aftermath—whatever the real social gains of some of its programs, such as better medical care for those receiving Medicaid—was a deepening of the rifts within the ranks of actual and potential supporters of U.S. public social provision. By the mid-1970s a narrow "welfare" coalition—blacks and the leaders of organized labor, with white workers and much of the base of the traditional Democratic party having deserted—was facing a "backlash" coalition newly strengthened by the inclusion of working- and middle-class whites increasingly unwilling to pay taxes for social programs perceived as benefiting only the (black) poor but willing to put up a significant fight at any suggestion of cuts in social security.

The asymmetry in power between the coalition supporting social security and that defending the lower tier of public assistance programs became apparent with the generalized retrenchment of domestic social programs that began under Jimmy Carter and became a crusade under Ronald Reagan. Policymakers announced plans to cut all social spending, but lower-tier programs were by far the easiest to cut back on politically; among lower-tier programs, those working through established institutions and with middle-class providers have fared better than those providing direct benefits to the poor even when they have been more costly. The powerful social security coalition has helped to ensure that America's elderly are relatively well-off by international standards (Myles 1984) and relative to other social groups (although clearly, not all of the aged are equally well served). The general delegitimation of public programs save those serving the retired has worked against the development of innovative employment policies linked to industrial planning or programs that might serve working-aged people and their children.

While the current condition of American social provision and the politics that sustain it are causes for despair, there are some clues in the policy legacy that might enable us to do better (see Weir, Orloff, and Skocpol 1988). The success story of social security in particular should alert us to the sorts of features that might engender a more generous and equitable set of social protections. The near-universal coverage of social security is critical to its political success, for it has institutionalized a cross-class coalition in defense of the program.[3] In contrast, the targeting of social assistance programs has undercut their political efficacy. We need to look for programs that unite rather than drive apart the diverse constituencies that make up our heterogeneous country. (In the late nineteenth century, the GOP had a clear idea of this strategy in its "package" that supported tariffs, pensions, and industrialization.) Utilizing the social security trust fund to finance the education and training of America's young people, so that they may in their turn build up the society and help to finance the retirement of earlier generations, as suggested by Barry Bluestone and his associates (1990), seems to me to be the sort of program that could work in this way. Likewise, provision for the diverse sorts of caretaking that America's families must undertake—for the young, old, and ill—within a single program, perhaps partially financed by contributions, would also join the interests of different generations and engage a wide range of Americans.

The Idea of Rights Based on Service to Society

I will close on an ideological note, for we need ideas, notions of the moral order, as well as political calculation to sustain the sorts of programs just discussed. As I carried out the research into new liberal ideological formulations, I was struck by the potential of the idea that people's entitlement to state benefits is based on their service to society for expanding the parameters of policy debates within a liberal framework. The elderly were among the first cases for whom this idea was articulated. In particular, the formulation of honorable provision for "soldiers of industry" was based on men's rather than women's experience

---

3. Targeting within this universal coverage has been somewhat effective in reaching the elderly poor, arguably more so than purely targeted programs at reaching the nonaged poor (Skocpol 1990).

and obviously drew upon men's experiences as soldiers in the "real" army. Yet new liberal reformers, particularly in North America, rather quickly expanded the notion of service to include women's work (Pederson 1989; Orloff 1991). Indeed, while such a concept could easily be harnessed to notions of separate spheres, it did valorize the work many women were in fact doing—mothering, which, detached from separate spheres ideology, could be expanded to caretaking and nurturing more generally. As opposed to the alternative ways in which people have secured claims—on the basis of contributions or of "need"—claims based on service seem to me to have the greatest potential for gender, race, and class egalitarianism, as well as for building the notion of a collective good.

The idea that rights are and ought to be based on contributions clearly has taken over the political field in the United States. In the recent past, the Social Security Administration, the congressional committees with which it worked, and a public weaned from earlier ideas of service-based entitlement came to agree that those who received social security benefits had "earned" them on the basis of their contributions, rather than their service to the larger society, while those who depended on public assistance were "undeserving." Organizations of old people defended their entitlement to benefits—supported by most future retirees—and saw these benefits as flowing from financial contributions made by individual wage earners to the social security trust fund, rather than from their labor, collectively useful to the entire society. Yet this thinking about entitlement is subject to rather severe distortions. Many commentators on the contemporary social security "crisis" have pointed out that today's retirees are getting back far more in benefits than they paid in contributions, even when inflation is taken into account (see Longman 1987). The working-aged population is indeed subsidizing the old through payroll taxes and may in fact want to subsidize those who worked before them, to offer them an honorable retirement after a lifetime of service. But the mythology of contribution obscures this budgetary fact, while the notion of contributions as the sole means of entitlement makes it difficult to discuss the claims of others who are serving society. If the old deserve an honorable retirement because they served society, then there are other groups—who might not be in a position to make contributions—who also can claim that they are serving a collective good—the country's caretakers of the young, disabled, and elderly, for example. And the notion of entitlement based on service might well be extended to investments in the future of those who will contribute their labor. Defining entitlement on the basis of socially useful work, or "service to society," defines a public good to which we all contribute.

Service-based claims seem to me also to be superior to claims based on "need." They embody a notion of reciprocity that is missing from claims based on need and thereby empower those doing the claiming. Definitions of "need" are subject to contestation (Fraser 1989), but on the basis of a power imbalance, the needy are asking for help from the powerful, taxpaying, "responsible" public. "Service" is a more universalist category than "need," for all can serve, but not all will be needy. Thus, politically, coalitions built on concepts of service would likely be more encompassing than those built to defend claims based on need. Indeed, they could be more encompassing than even contribution-based coalitions, and contributions need not (probably should not) be displaced entirely. Entitlement based on service, rather than on need, also valorizes people for their contribution to society. It is here that the superiority of this framework for women may show itself most clearly, for this formulation offers them a way to claim honorable social support for the nonwaged work they do.

Originally, provision for the aged embodied notions of reciprocity: the working-aged population supported the elderly in return for their socially useful labor in building up the society. We have lost that sense, and too often we simply argue about taxes and financial contributions. Reclaiming reciprocity and the notion of socially useful labor as the basis of our claims on the state might move us closer to a better solution to our own set of social questions.

Bibliography
Index

Bibliography

Aaron, Henry. 1967. "Social Security: International Comparisons." In *Studies in the Economics of Income Maintenance,* edited by Otto Eckstein, 13–48. Washington, D.C.: Brookings.

Abbott, Edith. 1934. "Abolish the Pauper Laws." *Social Service Review* 8:1–16.

Abbott, Edith. 1936. "Public Welfare and Politics." *Social Service Review* 10:395–412.

Abbott, Edith. 1940. *Public Assistance: American Principles and Policies.* Vol 1. Chicago: University of Chicago Press.

Abbott, Grace. 1941. *From Relief to Social Security.* Chicago: University of Chicago Press.

Abrams, Richard. 1964. *Conservatism in a Progressive Era: Massachusetts Politics, 1900–1912.* Cambridge: Harvard University Press.

Abromovitz, Mimi. 1988. *Regulating the Lives of Women: Social Welfare Policy from Colonial Times to the Present.* Boston: South End Press.

Achenbaum, W. Andrew. 1978. *Old Age in a New Land.* Baltimore: Johns Hopkins University Press.

Achenbaum, W. Andrew. 1983. *Shades of Gray: Old Age, American Values, and Federal Policies since 1920.* Boston: Little, Brown and Co.

Adams, Charles Francis. 1912. *The Civil-War Pension Lack-of-System.* Pamphlet reprinted from *World's Work.*

Addams, Jane. [1902] 1964. *Democracy and Social Ethics,* edited by Anne F. Scott. Cambridge: Harvard University Press.

Addison, Paul. 1983. "Churchill and the Working Class, 1900–1914." In *The Working Class in Modern British History,* edited by Jay Winter, 43–64. Cambridge: Cambridge University Press.

Aitken, H. G. J. 1967. "Defensive Expansion: The State and Economic Growth in Canada." In *Approaches to Canadian Economic History,* edited by W. T. Easterbrook and M. H. Watkins, 183–221. Toronto: McClelland and Stewart.

Alber, Jens. 1987. "Cross-National Evidence on the Crisis of the Welfare State." Paper presented at the annual meeting of the American Sociological Association, Chicago, Illinois.

Alexander, John. 1980. *Render Them Submissive: Responses to Poverty in Philadelphia, 1760–1800.* Amherst: University of Massachusetts Press.

Allen, Richard. 1973. *The Social Passion.* Toronto: University of Toronto Press.

The Almshouse Experience: Collected Reports. 1971. New York: Arno Press and the New York Times.

Almy, Frederick. 1899. "The Relation between Private and Public Outdoor Relief—II." *Charities Review* 9:65–71.

Almy, Frederick. 1901. "Public or Private Outdoor Relief." In *Proceedings of the National Conference of Charities and Correction,* 134–45. Boston: George Ellis.

Alston, Lee, and Joseph Ferrie. 1985. "Labor Costs, Paternalism, and Loyalty in Southern Agriculture: A Constraint on the Growth of the Welfare State." *Journal of Economic History* 45:95–117.

Altmeyer, Arthur J. 1966. *The Formative Years of Social Security.* Madison: University of Wisconsin Press.

Amenta, Edwin, and Bruce Carruthers. 1988. "The Formative Years of U.S. Social Spending Policies." *American Sociological Review* 53:661–78.

Amenta, Edwin, Elisabeth Clemens, Jefren Olsen, Sunita Parikh, and Theda Skocpol. 1987. "The Political Origins of Unemployment Insurance in Five American States." In *Studies in American Political Development,* vol. 2, edited by Karen Orren and Stephen Skowronek, 137–82. New Haven: Yale University Press.

American Federation of Labor. 1919. *History, Encyclopedia Reference Book.* Washington, D.C.: American Federation of Labor.

American Labor Legislation Review. 1911–20. Vols. 1–10.

American Labor Legislation Review. 1914. "Social Insurance." 4:573–80.

American Labor Legislation Review. 1915. "Unemployment Survey, 1914–1915." 5:475–600.

Ames, Herbert. [1897] 1972. *The City below the Hill,* edited by P. Rutherford. Toronto: University of Toronto Press.

Anderson, James D. 1972. "Non-Partisan Urban Politics in Canadian Cities." In *Emerging Party Politics in Urban Canada,* edited by Jack Masson and James D. Anderson, 5–21. Toronto: McClelland and Stewart.

Anderson, James D. 1979. "The Municipal Government Reform Movement in Western Canada, 1880–1920." In *The Usable Urban Past,* edited by Alan Artibise and Gilbert Stelter, 73–111. Toronto: Macmillan of Canada.

Anderson, Michael. 1971. *Family Structure in Nineteenth Century Lancashire.* Cambridge: Cambridge University Press.

Anderson, Michael. 1972. "Household Structure and the Industrial Revolution: Mid–Nineteenth Century Preston in Comparative Perspective." In *Household and Family in Past Time,* edited by Peter Laslett, 215–35. Cambridge: Cambridge University Press.

Anderson, Michael. 1977. "The Impact on the Family Relationships of the Elderly of Changes since Victorian Times in Governmental Income–Maintenance Provision." In *Family, Bureaucracy, and the Elderly,* edited by Ethel Shanas and Marvin Sussman, 36–59. Durham, N.C.: Duke University Press.

Anderson, Michael. 1984. "The Social Position of Spinsters in Mid-Victorian Britain." *Journal of Family History* 9:377–93.

Anderson, Perry. 1974. *Lineages of the Absolutist State.* London: Verso.

Andrews, John. 1920. "Old Age Insurance for Federal Employees." *American Labor Legislation Review* 10:127–28.

Anglim, Christopher, and Brian Gratton. 1987. "Organized Labor and Old Age Pensions." *International Journal of Aging and Human Development* 25:91–107.

Angus, Margaret. 1972. "Health, Emigration and Welfare in Kingston, 1820–1840." In *Oliver Mowat's Ontario*, edited by Donald Swainson, 120–35. Toronto: Macmillan.

Armstrong, Barbara. 1932. *Insuring the Essentials*. New York: Macmillan.

Aronson, Albert. 1950. "Merit System Objectives and Realities." *Social Security Bulletin* 8:3–33.

Aronson, Albert. 1956. "Merit Systems in Grant-in-Aid Programs." *Public Personnel Review* 17:231–37.

Ashforth, D. 1976. "The Urban Poor Law." In *The New Poor Law in the Nineteenth Century*, edited by Derek Fraser, 128–48. London: Macmillan.

Babcock, Robert. 1974. *Gompers in Canada: A Study in American Continentalism before the First World War*. Toronto: University of Toronto Press.

Badie, Bertrand, and Pierre Birnbaum. 1983. *The Sociology of the State*. Chicago: University of Chicago Press.

Baehre, Rainer. 1981a. "Paupers and Poor Relief in Upper Canada." *Canadian Historical Association, Historical Papers*, pp. 57–80.

Baehre, Rainer. 1981b. "Pauper Emigration to Upper Canada in the 1830s." *Histoire Sociale/Social History* 14:339–67.

Bailey, Kenneth D. 1978. "Document Study." In *Methods of Social Research*. New York: Free Press.

Bailyn, Bernard. 1968. *The Origins of American Politics*. New York: Knopf.

Bain, George, and Robert Price. 1980. *Profiles of Union Growth*. Oxford: Basil Blackwell.

Baker, Paula. 1982. "The Domestication of Politics: Women and American Political Society, 1780–1920." *American Historical Review* 85:620–47.

Baldwin, Peter. 1990. *The Politics of Social Solidarity: Class Bases of the European Welfare State, 1875–1975*. New York: Cambridge University Press.

Banting, Keith. 1982. *The Welfare State and Canadian Federalism*. Montreal: McGill-Queen's University Press.

Bealey, Frank. 1956. "The Electoral Arrangement between the Labour Representation Committee and the Liberal Party." *Journal of Modern History* 28:353–73.

Beman, Lamar, ed. 1927. *Selected Articles on Old Age Pensions*. New York: H. W. Wilson Co.

Bendix, Reinhard. 1977. *Nation-Building and Citizenship: Enlarged Edition*. Berkeley: University of California Press.

Bendix, Reinhard. 1978. *Kings or People: Power and the Mandate to Rule*. Berkeley: University of California Press.

Bensel, Richard F. 1984. *Sectionalism and American Political Development: 1880–1980*. Madison: University of Wisconsin Press.

Bergmann, Barbara. 1986. *The Economic Emergence of Women*. New York: Basic.

Berkner, Lutz. 1972. "The Stem Family and the Developmental Cycle of Peasant Household: An Eighteenth-Century Austrian Example." *American Historical Review* 77:398–418.

Berkowitz, Edward, and Kim McQuaid. 1978. "Businessmen and Bureaucrats: The Evolution of the American Welfare System, 1900–1940." *Journal of Economic History* 38:120–41.

Berkowitz, Edward, and Kim McQuaid. 1980. *Creating the Welfare State: The Political Economy of Twentieth-Century Reform.* New York: Praeger.

Bernstein, Barton. 1968. "The New Deal: The Conservative Achievements of Liberal Reform." In *Towards a New Past: Dissenting Essays in American History,* edited by Barton Bernstein, 268–80. New York: Pantheon Books.

Bernstein, Irving. 1960. *The Lean Years: A History of the American Worker, 1920–1933.* Baltimore: Penguin Books.

Bernstein, Irving. 1985. *A Caring Society: A History of the American Worker, 1933–1940.* Boston: Little, Brown and Co.

Birch, A. H. 1955. *Federalism, Finance and Social Legislation in Canada, Australia and the United States.* London: Oxford University Press.

Bjorn, Lars. 1979. "Labor Parties, Economic Growth, and the Redistribution of Income in Five Capitalist Democracies." *Comparative Social Research* 2:93–128.

Blewett, N. 1965. "The Franchise in the United Kingdom, 1885–1918." *Past and Present* 32:27–56.

Bluestone, Barry, Alan Clayton-Matthews, John Havens, and Howard Young. 1990. "Generational Alliance: Social Security as a Bank for Education." *American Prospect* (Summer):15–29.

Booth, Charles. 1889, 1891. *Life and Labour of the People of London.* London: Williams and Norgate.

Booth, Charles. 1892. *Pauperism, A Picture; and The Endowment of Old Age, An Argument.* New York: Macmillan.

Booth, Charles. 1894. *The Aged Poor in England and Wales.* New York: Macmillan.

Borcherding, Thomas. 1977. "One Hundred Years of Public Spending, 1870–1970." In *Budgets and Bureaucrats: The Sources of Government Growth,* edited by Thomas Borcherding, 19–44. Durham, N.C.: Duke University Press.

Borden, Robert. 1931. "The Problem of an Efficient Civil Service." *Canadian Historical Association: Report of the Annual Meeting, with Historical Papers,* pp. 1–34.

Borg, S. G., and F. G. Castles. 1981. "The Influence of the Political Right on Public Income Maintenance Expenditure and Equality." *Political Studies* 29:604–21.

Bradbury, Bettina. 1979. "The Family Economy and Work in an Industrializing City: Montreal in the 1870's." *Canadian Historical Association, Historical Papers,* pp. 71–96.

Brandeis, Elizabeth. 1935. "Labor Legislation." In *History of Labor in the United States, 1896–1932,* vol. 3, by Don Lescohier and Elizabeth Brandeis, 399–700. New York: Macmillan.

Brandeis, Louis. 1911. "Workingmen's Insurance: The Road to Social Efficiency." In *Proceedings of the National Conference of Charities and Correction,* 156–63. Forty-first annual session. Ft. Wayne, Ind.: Fort Wayne Printing Co.

Brandes, Stuart. 1976. *American Welfare Capitalism, 1880–1940.* Chicago: University of Chicago Press.

Brebner, J. B. 1938. "Patronage and Parliamentary Government." *Canadian Historical Association: Report of the Annual Meeting, with Historical Papers,* pp. 22–30.

Brebner, J. B. 1945. *North Atlantic Triangle: The Interplay of Canada, the United States and Great Britain.* New Haven: Yale University Press.

Breckinridge, Sophonisba. 1927. *Public Welfare Administration in the United States: Select Documents.* Chicago: University of Chicago Press.

Bremner, Robert H. 1956a. *From the Depths.* New York: New York University Press.

Bremner, Robert H. 1956b. " 'Scientific Philanthropy,' 1873–93." *Social Service Review* 30:168–73.

Brewer, John. 1989. *The Sinews of Power: War, Money and the English State, 1688–1783.* New York: Knopf.

Bridges, Amy. 1986. "Becoming American: The Working Class in the United States before the Civil War." In *Working-Class Formation: Nineteenth-Century Patterns in Western Europe and the United States,* edited by Ira Katznelson and Aristide Zolberg, 157–96. Princeton: Princeton University Press.

Brinkley, Alan. 1982. *Voices of Protest: Huey Long, Father Coughlin and the Great Depression.* New York: Knopf.

British Labour Party. [1906] 1976. "Who Gets Old Age Pensions?" Labour party leaflet no. 19. *The Archives of the British Labour Party, Series 2.* Hassocks, Eng.: Harvestor Press.

Brodie, M. Janine, and Jane Jenson. 1980. *Crisis, Challenge and Change: Party and Class in Canada.* Toronto: Methuen.

Brody, David. 1980. "The Rise and Decline of Welfare Capitalism." In *Workers in Industrial America: Essays on the Twentieth Century Struggle,* by David Brody, 48–81. New York: Oxford University Press.

Brooks, John Graham. 1893. *Compulsory Insurance in Germany.* Special report of the U.S. Bureau of Labor. Washington, D.C.: Government Printing Office.

Brooks, John Graham. 1905. "Report on German Workingmen's Insurance." In *Proceedings of the National Conference of Charities and Correction,* 452–56. Portland, Oreg.: Press of J. Heer.

Brooks, John Graham. 1906. *The Social Unrest.* New York: Macmillan.

Brown, J. Douglas. 1956. "The American Philosophy of Social Insurance." *Social Service Review* 30:1–8.

Brown, Josephine. 1940. *Public Relief, 1929–1939.* New York: Henry Holt.

Brown, Robert, and Ramsay Cook. 1974. *Canada, 1896–1921: A Nation Transformed.* Toronto: McClelland and Stewart.

Brown, Roy M. 1928. *Public Poor Relief in North Carolina.* Chapel Hill: University of North Carolina Press.

Bruno, Frank J. 1957. *Trends in Social Work, 1874–1956.* New York: Columbia University Press.

Bryce, James. 1921. *Modern Democracies.* New York: Macmillan.

Bryden, Kenneth. 1974. *Old Age Pensions and Policy-Making in Canada.* Montreal: McGill-Queen's University Press.

Buenker, John. 1973. *Urban Liberalism and Progressive Reform.* New York: Norton.

Burch, Phillip. 1973. "The NAM as an Interest Group." *Politics and Society* 4:97–130.

Burgess, Ernest. 1960. *Aging in Western Societies.* Chicago: University of Chicago Press.

Burke, Vincent, and Vee Burke. 1974. *Nixon's Good Deed: Welfare Reform*. New York: Columbia University Press.

Burn, William L. 1965. *The Age of Equipoise: A Study of the Mid-Victorian Generation*. New York: Norton.

Burnham, Phillip. 1935. "The Historical Development of Public Personnel Administration in Canada." In *The Civil Service Abroad: Great Britain, Canada, France, Germany*, by Leonard D. White, Charles H. Bland, Walter R. Sharp, and Fritz Morstein Marx, 62–71. New York: McGraw-Hill.

Burnham, Walter Dean. 1982. *The Current Crisis in American Politics*. New York: Oxford University Press.

Butler, David, and J. Freeman. 1969. *British Political Facts, 1900–1960*. 3d ed. New York: St. Martin's.

California Department of Social Welfare. 1929. *Old Age Dependency: A Study of the Care Given to Needy Aged in California*. Sacramento: California State Printing Office.

California Social Insurance Commission. 1917. *Report*. Sacramento: California State Printing Office.

Cameron, David. 1978. "The Expansion of the Public Economy: A Comparative Analysis." *American Political Science Review* 72:1243–61.

Cameron, David. 1986. "The Growth of Government Spending: The Canadian Experience in Comparative Perspective." In *State and Society: Canada in Comparative Perspective*, Keith Banting, research coordinator, 21–51. Toronto: University of Toronto Press.

Canada, Department of Labour. 1932. *Report for the Fiscal Year Ending March 31, 1931*. Ottawa: King's Printer.

Canadian Conference of Charities and Corrections. 1899. *Proceedings, Second Canadian Conference of Charities and Corrections*. Toronto: n.p.

Canadian Conference of Charities and Corrections. 1904. *Fourth Canadian Conference of Charities and Corrections*. Toronto: n.p.

Canadian Fraternal Association. 1907. *Journal of Proceedings*. Guelph, Ont.: H. Gummer.

Canadian Fraternal Association. 1908. *Journal of Proceedings*. Guelph, Ont.: H. Gummer.

Canadian Fraternal Association. 1909. *Journal of Proceedings*. Guelph, Ont.: H. Gummer.

Canadian Fraternal Association. 1919. *Journal of Proceedings*. Hamilton, Ont.: Heath and Fairclough.

Canadian House of Commons. Special Committee on an Old Age Pension System for Canada. 1924. *An Old Age Pension System for Canada: Proceedings of the Special Committee appointed to make an enquiry into an old age pension system for Canada*. Ottawa: F. A. Acland.

Canadian House of Commons. Special Committee on Old Age Pensions. 1912. *Proceedings of the Special Committee on Old Age Pensions, Comprising the Evidence Taken during the Parliamentary Session of 1911–12*. Ottawa: C. H. Parmalee.

Canadian Manufacturers' Association Industrial Relations Department. 1929. "Old Age Pensions: Their History and Results." *Industrial Canada* 29 (March): 57–58.

Carnoy, Martin. 1984. *The State and Political Theory.* Princeton: Princeton University Press.

Carrigan, D. Owen. 1968. *Canadian Party Platforms, 1867–1986.* Urbana: University of Illinois Press.

Castles, Francis G. 1978. *The Social Democratic Image of Society.* London: Routledge.

Castles, Francis G. 1982. "The Impact of Parties on Public Expenditures." In *The Impact of Parties,* edited by Francis Castles, 21–96. Beverly Hills: Sage.

Castles, Francis G. 1985. *The Working Class and Welfare: Reflections on the Political Development of the Welfare State in Australia and New Zealand, 1890–1980.* Wellington: Allen and Unwin.

Castles, Francis, and R. McKinlay. 1979a. "Public Welfare Provision, Scandinavia, and the Sheer Futility of the Sociological Approach to Politics." *British Journal of Political Science* 9:157–71.

Castles, Francis, and R. McKinlay. 1979b. "Does Politics Matter?: An Analysis of Public Welfare Commitment in Advanced Democratic States." *European Journal of Political Research* 7:169–86.

Castles, Francis G., and Deborah Mitchell. 1991. "Three Worlds of Welfare Capitalism or Four?" Australian National University Graduate Program in Public Policy Discussion Paper no. 21.

Cates, Jerry. 1983. *Insuring Inequality.* Ann Arbor: University of Michigan Press.

Chambers, Clarke. 1963. *Seedtime of Reform: American Social Service and Social Action, 1918–1933.* Minneapolis: University of Minnesota Press.

Chambers, Clarke. 1971. *Paul U. Kellogg and the Survey.* Minneapolis: University of Minnesota Press.

Chambers, William. 1963. *Political Parties in a New Nation: The American Experience, 1776–1809.* New York: Oxford University Press.

Charles, Searle F. 1963. *Minister of Relief: Harry Hopkins and the Depression.* Syracuse: Syracuse University Press.

Chenery, William. 1921. "Unemployment at Washington." *The Survey* 37:47.

Chenery, William. 1922. "The President's Conference and Unemployment in the United States." *International Labour Review* 5:359–76.

Cherlin, Andrew. 1983. "Changing Family and Household: Contemporary Lessons from Historical Research." *Annual Review of Sociology* 9:51–66.

Christian, William, and Colin Campbell. 1974. *Politics, Parties, and Ideologies in Canada.* Toronto: McGraw-Hill Ryerson.

Chudacoff, Howard, and Tamara Hareven. 1978. "Family Transitions into Old Age." In *Transitions: The Family and the Life Course in Historical Perspective,* edited by Tamara Hareven, 217–44. New York: Academic Press.

Clarke, P. F. 1971. *Lancashire and the New Liberalism.* Cambridge: Cambridge University Press.

Clarke, P. F. 1972. "Electoral Sociology of Modern Britain." *History* 57:31–55.

Clarke, P. F. 1974. "The Progressive Movement in England." *Transactions of the Royal Historical Society,* 5th series, 24:159–82.

Cohen, Emmeline. 1941. *The Growth of the British Civil Service, 1790–1939.* London: George Allen and Unwin.

Cole, G. D. H. 1941. *British Working Class Politics, 1832–1914.* London: Routledge.

Coll, Blanche. 1972. "Public Assistance in the United States: Colonial Times to 1860." In *Comparative Development in Social Welfare,* edited by E. W. Martin, 128–58. London: George Allen and Unwin.

Collier, David, and Richard Messick. 1975. "Prerequisites versus Diffusion: Testing Alternative Explanations of Social Security Adoption." *American Political Science Review* 69:1299–315.

Collini, Stefan. 1979. *Liberalism and Sociology.* New York: Cambridge University Press.

Collins, D. 1965. "The Introduction of Old Age Pensions in Great Britain." *Historical Journal* 8:246–49.

Collins, Robert. 1978. "Positive Business Responses to the New Deal: The Roots of the Committee for Economic Development, 1933–1942." *Business History Review* 52:367–91.

Committee on Old Age Pensions of the Charity Organization Society. 1903. *Old Age Pensions.* London: Macmillan.

Committee on Research of the Social Service Council. 1928. *Preliminary Report on Old Age Pensions.* Toronto: Social Service Council of Canada.

Commons, John, and John Andrews. 1927. *Principles of Labor Legislation.* New York: Harper and Brothers.

Conkin, Paul. 1967. *FDR and the Origins of the Welfare State.* New York: Thomas Y. Crowell Co.

Copp, Terry. 1974. *The Anatomy of Poverty: The Condition of the Working Class in Montreal, 1897–1929.* Toronto: McClelland and Stewart.

Cornford, James. 1963. "The Transformation of Conservatism in the Late Nineteenth Century." *Victorian Studies* 7:35–66.

Corry, J. A. 1939. *The Growth of Government Activities since Confederation.* A study prepared for the Royal Commission on Dominion-Provincial Relations. Ottawa: n.p.

Coughlin, Richard M. 1979. "Social Policy and Ideology: Public Opinion in Eight Rich Nations." *Comparative Social Research* 2:3–40.

Cowgill, Donald. 1974a. "The Aging of Populations and Societies." *Annals of the American Academy of Political and Social Science* 415:1–18.

Cowgill, Donald. 1974b. "Aging and Modernization: A Revision of the Theory." In *Late Life: Communities and Environmental Policy,* edited by J. Gubrium, 123–46. Springfield, Ill.: Charles C. Thomas.

Cowgill, Donald, and Lowell Holmes. 1972. *Aging and Modernization.* New York: Appleton-Century-Croft.

Craven, Paul. 1980. *An Impartial Umpire: Industrial Relations and the Canadian State, 1900–1911.* Toronto: University of Toronto Press.

Creech, Margaret. 1969. *Three Centuries of Poor Law Administration.* Chicago: University of Chicago Press.

Creighton, D. G. 1943. "George Brown, Sir John MacDonald, and the 'Workingman.' " *Canadian Historical Review* 24:362–76.

Crenson, Matthew. 1975. *The Federal Machine: Beginnings of Bureaucracy in Jacksonian America.* Baltimore: Johns Hopkins University Press.

Crowther, M. A. 1978. "The Later Years of the Workhouse, 1890–1929." In *The Ori-*

gins of British Social Policy, edited by Pat Thane, 36–55. Totowa, N.J.: Rowman and Littlefield.

Crowther, M. A. 1982. *The Workhouse System, 1834–1929.* Athens: University of Georgia Press.

Cuneo, Carl. 1980. "State Mediation of Class Contradictions in Canadian Unemployment Insurance, 1930–1935." *Studies in Political Economy* 14:37–65.

Cutright, Phillips. 1965. "Political Structure, Economic Development and National Social Security Programs." *American Journal of Sociology* 70:537–50.

Darroch, G. Gordon. 1983. "Early Industrialization and Inequality in Toronto, 1861–1899." *Labour/Le Travailleur* 11:31–61.

Davidson, Roger. 1972. "Llewellyn Smith and the Labour Department." In *Studies in the Growth of Nineteenth Century Government,* edited by Gillian Sutherland, 227–62. London: Routledge.

Davidson, Roger, and R. Lowe. 1981. "Bureaucracy and Innovation in British Welfare Policy, 1870–1945." In *The Emergence of the Welfare State in Britain and Germany, 1850–1950,* edited by W. J. Mommsen, 263–95. London: Croom Helm.

Davis, Allen F. 1967. *Spearheads for Reform: The Social Settlements and the Progressive Movement, 1890–1914.* New York: Oxford University Press.

Dawson, Robert. 1929. *The Civil Service of Canada.* London: Oxford University Press.

Dawson, Robert. 1933. *Constitutional Issues in Canada, 1900–1931.* London: Oxford University Press.

Dawson, Robert. 1959. *William Lyon Mackenzie King: A Political Biography, 1874–1923.* Toronto: University of Toronto Press.

Derthick, Martha. 1979. *Policy-Making for Social Security.* Washington, D.C.: Brookings.

de Schweinitz, Karl. [1943] 1961. *England's Road to Social Security.* New York: A. S. Barnes and Co.

DeViney, S. 1983. "Characteristics of the State and the Expansion of Public Social Spending." *Comparative Social Research* 6:151–74.

Dietz, Mary. 1987. "Context Is All: Feminism and Theories of Citizenship." *Daedalus* 116(Fall):1–24.

Dorsett, Lyle. 1977. *Franklin D. Roosevelt and the City Bosses.* Port Washington, N.Y.: Kennikat Press.

Douglas, Paul. 1936. *Social Security in the United States.* New York: McGraw-Hill.

Douglas, Roy. 1971. *The History of the Liberal Party, 1895–1970.* London: Sidgwick and Jackson.

Drage, Geoffrey. 1895. *The Problem of the Aged Poor.* London: Adam and Charles Black.

Drage, Geoffrey. 1914. *The State and the Poor.* London: Collins.

Dye, Thomas. 1966. *Politics, Economics and the Public: Policy Outcomes in the American States.* Chicago: Rand-McNally.

Eagle Magazine. 1920–35.

Edsall, Nicholas C. 1971. *The Anti-Poor Law Movement, 1834–44.* Totowa, N.J.: Rowman and Littlefield.

Emy, H. V. 1972. "The Impact of Financial Policy on English Party Politics before 1914." *Historical Journal* 15:103–31.

Englemann, Frederick, and Mildred Schwartz. 1975. *Canadian Political Parties: Origin, Character, Impact*. Scarborough, Ont.: Prentice-Hall of Canada.

English, John. 1977. *The Decline of Politics: The Conservatives and the Party System, 1901–1920*. Toronto: University of Toronto Press.

Epstein, Abraham. 1922. *Facing Old Age*. New York: Knopf.

Epstein, Abraham. 1928. *Challenge of the Aged*. New York: Vanguard Press.

Epstein, Leon. 1964. "A Comparative Study of Canadian Political Parties." *American Political Science Review* 58:46–59.

Esping-Andersen, Gøsta. 1985. *Politics against Markets*. Princeton: Princeton University Press.

Esping-Andersen, Gøsta. 1989. "The Three Political Economies of the Welfare State." *Canadian Review of Sociology and Anthropology* 26:10–36.

Esping-Andersen, Gøsta. 1990. *The Three Worlds of Welfare Capitalism*. Princeton: Princeton University Press.

Esping-Andersen, Gøsta, and Walter Korpi. 1987. "From Poor Relief to Institutional Welfare States: The Development of Scandinavian Social Policy." In *The Scandinavian Model: Welfare States and Welfare Research*, edited by R. Erikson, E. J. Hansem, S. Ringen, and H. Uusitalo, 39–74. Armonk, N.Y.: M. E. Sharpe.

Evans, Eric. 1978. *Individualism, Collectivism and the Origins of the Welfare State*. London: Routledge.

Evans, Harry C. 1926. *The American Poorfarm and Its Inmates*. Des Moines: Loyal Order of Moose.

Evans, P. B., D. Rueschemeyer, and T. Skocpol, eds. 1985. *Bringing the State Back In*. Cambridge: Cambridge University Press.

Feder, Leah. 1936. *Unemployment Relief in Periods of Depression*. New York: Russell Sage.

Ferguson, Thomas. 1984. "From Normalcy to the New Deal: Industrial Structure, Party Competition, and American Public Policy in the Great Depression." *International Organization* 38:41–94.

Fine, Sidney. 1956. *Laissez-Faire and the General Welfare State*. Ann Arbor: University of Michigan Press.

Finegold, Kenneth. 1988. "Agriculture and the Politics of U.S. Social Provision: Social Insurance and Food Stamps." In *The Politics of Social Policy in the United States*, edited by M. Weir, A. Orloff, and T. Skocpol, 199–234. Princeton: Princeton University Press.

Finer, Herman. 1937. *The British Civil Service*. London: George Allen and Unwin.

Finer, Samuel E. 1952. *The Life and Times of Sir Edwin Chadwick*. London: Methuen.

Fink, Gary M. 1973. *Labor's Search for Political Order: The Political Behavior of the Missouri Labor Movement, 1890–1940*. Columbia: University of Missouri Press.

Finkel, Alvin. 1977. "Origins of the Welfare State in Canada." In *The Canadian State: Political Economy and Political Power*, edited by Leo Panitch, 344–72. Toronto: University of Toronto Press.

Finkel, Alvin. 1979. *Business and Social Reform in the Thirties*. Toronto: James Lorimer.

Fischer, David H. 1978. *Growing Old in America*. New York: Oxford University Press.

Flora, Peter, and Jens Alber. 1981. "Modernization, Democratization and the Development of Welfare States in Western Europe." In *The Development of Welfare States in Europe and America*, edited by Peter Flora and Arnold Heidenheimer, 37–80. New Brunswick, N.J.: Transaction Books.

Flora, Peter, and Arnold Heidenheimer. 1981. "The Historical Core and Changing Boundaries of the Welfare State." In *The Development of Welfare States in Europe and America*, edited by Peter Flora and Arnold Heidenheimer, 17–34. New Brunswick, N.J.: Transaction Books.

Folks, Homer. 1899. "Report of the Committee on Municipal and County Charities." In *Proceedings of the National Conference of Charities and Correction*, 106–83. Boston: George Ellis.

Fowke, V. C. 1967. "The National Policy—Old and New." In *Approaches to Canadian Economic History*, edited by W. T. Easterbrook and M. H. Watkins, 237–58. Toronto: McClelland and Stewart.

Fowke, V. C. 1973. *The National Policy and the Wheat Economy*. Toronto: University of Toronto Press.

Frankel, Lee K., and Miles Dawson. 1910. *Workingmen's Insurance in Europe*. New York: Russell Sage, Charities Publications Committee.

Fraser, Derek. 1973. *Evolution of the British Welfare State*. London: Macmillan.

Fraser, Derek. 1976. "The Poor Law as a Political Institution." In *The New Poor Law in the Nineteenth Century*, edited by Derek Fraser, 111–27. London: Macmillan.

Fraser, Derek. 1979. *Power and Authority in the Victorian City*. New York: St. Martin's.

Fraser, Derek. 1981. "The English Poor Law and the Origins of the British Welfare State." In *The Emergence of the Welfare State in Britain and Germany, 1850–1950*, edited by W. J. Mommsen, 9–31. London: Croom Helm.

Fraser, Nancy. 1989. *Unruly Practices: Power, Discourse and Gender in Contemporary Social Theory*. Minneapolis: University of Minnesota Press.

Fraternal Order of Eagles. 1929. "The Fraternal Order of Eagles: What It Is, What It Does, What It Stands For." Kansas City, Mo.: Organization Department, Fraternal Order of Eagles.

Fraternal Order of Eagles. 1930. "Old Age Pensions—Just, Humane, Economical, and Inevitable." South Bend, Ind.: National Old Age Pension Committee, Fraternal Order of Eagles.

Fraternal Order of Eagles. 1935a. "Report of the National Old Age Pension Commission." South Bend, Ind.: Fraternal Order of Eagles.

Fraternal Order of Eagles. 1935b. "Famous Words and Pens." South Bend, Ind.: Fraternal Order of Eagles.

Freeden, Michael. 1978. *The New Liberalism: An Ideology of Social Reform*. Oxford: Clarendon Press.

Friedel, Frank. 1956. *Franklin D. Roosevelt: The Triumph*. Boston: Little, Brown and Co.

Furner, Mary O. 1975. *Advocacy and Objectivity: A Crisis in the Professionalization of American Social Science*. Lexington: University Press of Kentucky.

Fusfeld, Daniel. 1956. *The Economic Thought of Franklin D. Roosevelt and the Origins of the New Deal*. New York: Columbia University Press.

Garret, Philip. 1896. "The Merit System in Public Institutions." In *Proceedings of the*

National Conference of Charities and Correction, 368–82. Boston: George Ellis.

Gerschenkron, Alexander. 1962. *Economic Backwardness in Historical Perspective.* Cambridge: Harvard University Press.

Gibbons, Kenneth. 1976. "The Political Culture of Corruption in Canada." In *Political Corruption in Canada,* edited by Kenneth Gibbons and Donald Rowat, 231–49. Toronto: McClelland and Stewart.

Gilbert, Bentley. 1966. *The Evolution of National Insurance in Great Britain: The Origins of the Welfare State.* London: Michael Joseph.

Gilbert, Bentley. 1970. *British Social Policy, 1914–1939.* London: Batsford.

Gillen, John. 1926. *Poverty and Dependency.* New York: Century Co.

Glasson, William. 1907. "The South's Care for Her Confederate Veterans." *American Monthly Review of Reviews* 36:40–47.

Glasson, William. 1918. *Federal Military Pensions in the United States.* New York: Oxford University Press.

Glick, Paul. 1977. "Updating the Life Cycle of the Family." *Journal of Marriage and the Family* 39:5–13.

Gompers, Samuel. 1916. "Contributory Social Insurance versus Voluntary." *American Federationist* 23:333–57, 453–66, 669–81.

Goodman, Paul. 1967. "The First American Party System." In *The American Party Systems,* edited by William Chambers and Walter Dean Burnham, 56–89. New York: Oxford University Press.

Goody, Jack. 1972. "The Evolution of the Family." In *Household and Family in Past Time,* edited by Peter Laslett, 103–24. Cambridge: Cambridge University Press.

Gordon, Linda, ed. 1990. *Women, the State and Welfare.* Madison: University of Wisconsin Press.

Gould, Margaret. 1927. "The Need for Old Age Pensions in Canada." *Social Welfare* 9:340–43.

Gough, Ian. 1979. *The Political Economy of the Welfare State.* New York: Macmillan.

Graebner, William. 1977. "Federalism and the Progressive Era: A Structural Interpretation of Reform." *Journal of American History* 64:331–57.

Graebner, William. 1980. *A History of Retirement.* New Haven: Yale University Press.

Graham, Roger, ed. 1967. *The King-Byng Affair, 1926: A Question of Responsible Government.* Toronto: Copp, Clark.

Gratton, Brian. 1983. "Social Workers and Old Age Pensions." *Social Science Review* 57:403–15.

Gratton, Brian. 1986. *Urban Elders: Family, Work, and Welfare among Boston's Aged, 1890–1950.* Philadelphia: Temple University Press.

Gratton, Brian. 1991. "The Family Economy and the Welfare State." Paper presented at the annual meeting of the Social Science History Association, New Orleans, November.

Gratton, Brian, and Carole Haber. Forthcoming. *In The Steps of the Old: A Social History of the American Elderly.* Bloomington: Indiana University Press.

Gray, Virginia. 1973. "Innovation in the States: A Diffusion Study." *American Political Science Review* 67:1174–85.

Great Britain, Department of Employment and Productivity. 1971. *British Labour Statistics: Historical Abstract, 1886–1968.* London: Her Majesty's Stationery Office.

Great Britain, Royal Commission on the Aged Poor. 1895. *Report*. London: His Majesty's Stationery Office, by Eyre and Spottiswood.

Greaves, H. R. 1947. *The Civil Service in the Changing State*. London: George C. Harrap and Co.

Greenstone, David. 1969. *Labor in American Politics*. New York: Vintage.

Greer, Thomas. 1958. *What Roosevelt Thought*. East Lansing: Michigan State University Press.

Griffin, John. 1939. *Strikes: A Study in Quantitative Economics*. Columbia University Studies in History, Economics, and Public Law Number 451. New York: Columbia University Press.

Grin, Carolyn. 1973. "The Unemployment Conference of 1921: An Experiment in National Cooperative Planning." *Mid-America* 55:83–107.

Grob, Gerald N. 1973. *Mental Institutions in America: Social Policy to 1875*. New York: Free Press.

Grob, Gerald N. 1983. *Mental Illness and American Society, 1875–1940*. Princeton: Princeton University Press.

Grodzins, Morton. 1960. "American Political Parties and the American System." *Western Political Quarterly* 13:974–92.

Grønbjerg, Kirsten, David Street, and Gerald D. Suttles. 1978. *Poverty and Social Change*. Chicago: University of Chicago Press.

Grusky, David. 1986. "American Social Mobility in the 19th and 20th Centuries." Center for Demography and Ecology Working Paper no. 86–28. Department of Sociology, University of Wisconsin–Madison.

Guest, Dennis. 1980. *The Emergence of Social Security in Canada*. Vancouver: University of British Columbia Press.

Haber, Carole. 1983. *Beyond Sixty-Five: The Dilemma of Old Age in America's Past*. New York: Cambridge University Press.

Haber, Samuel. 1964. *Efficiency and Uplift: Scientific Management in the Progressive Era, 1890–1920*. Chicago: University of Chicago Press.

Hage, J., and R. Hanneman. 1980. "The Growth of the Welfare State in Britain, France, Germany, and Italy: A Comparison of Three Paradigms." *Comparative Social Research* 3:45–70.

Hajnal, John. 1965. "European Marriage Patterns in Perspective." In *Population in History*, edited by D. V. Glass and D. E. C. Eversley, 101–43. Chicago: Aldine.

Hamilton, Lord George. 1910. "A Statistical Analysis of the Problems of Pauperism." *Journal of the Royal Statistical Society* 74:1–34.

Hanham, H. J. 1959. *Elections and Party Management: Politics in the Time of Disraeli and Gladstone*. London: Longmans, Green and Co.

Hannon, Joan Underhill. 1984a. "Poverty in the Antebellum Northeast." *Journal of Economic History* 44:1007–32.

Hannon, Joan Underhill. 1984b. "The Generosity of Antebellum Poor Relief." *Journal of Economic History* 44:810–21.

Hannon, Joan Underhill. 1985. "Poor Relief in Antebellum New York State." *Explorations in Economic History* 22:233–56.

Hareven, Tamara. 1969. "An Ambiguous Alliance: Some Aspects of American Influence on Canadian Social Welfare." *Histoire Sociale/Social History* 3:82–98.

Hareven, Tamara. 1976. "Modernization and Family History: Perspectives on Social Change." *Signs* 2:190–206.

Hareven, Tamara. 1982. "The Life Course and Aging in Historical Perspective." In *Aging and Life Course Transitions: An Interdisciplinary Perspective,* edited by Tamara Hareven and Kathleen Adams, 1–26. New York: Guilford.

Harris, Jose. 1972. *Unemployment and Politics.* London: Oxford University Press.

Hart, George. 1953. "The Halifax Poor Man's Friend Society." *Canadian Historical Review* 34:109–23.

Hart, Jennifer. 1972. "The Genesis of the Northcote-Trevelyan Report." In *Studies in the Growth of Nineteenth Century Government,* edited by Gillian Sutherland, 63–81. London: Routledge.

Harter, Lafayette. 1962. *John R. Commons: His Assault on Laissez-faire.* Corvallis: Oregon State University Press.

Hartz, Louis. 1964. *The Founding of New Societies.* New York: Harcourt, Brace and World.

Haskell, Thomas. 1977. *The Emergence of Professional Social Science.* Urbana: University of Illinois Press.

Hawley, Ellis. 1974. "Herbert Hoover, the Commerce Secretariat, and the Vision of an 'Associative State,' 1921–1928." *Journal of American History* 61:116–40.

Hay, J. R. 1975. *The Origins of the Liberal Welfare Reforms, 1906–1914.* London: Macmillan.

Hay, J. R. 1977. "Employers and Social Policy in Britain: The Evolution of Welfare Legislation, 1905–14." *Social History* 4:435–55.

Hay, J. R. 1978. *The Development of the British Welfare State, 1880–1975.* London: Edward Arnold.

Heclo, Hugh. 1974. *Modern Social Politics in Britain and Sweden.* New Haven: Yale University Press.

Heidenheimer, Arnold. 1973. "The Politics of Public Education, Health and Welfare in the U.S.A. and Western Europe." *British Journal of Political Science* 3:315–40.

Heisterman, Carl. 1933. "Statutory Provisions Relating to Legal Settlement for Purposes of Poor-Relief." *Social Service Review* 7:95–106.

Heisterman, Carl. 1934. "Removal of Nonresident State-Poor by State and Local Authorities." *Social Service Review* 8:289–301.

Henderson, Charles. 1898. "Poor Laws of the United States." In *Proceedings of the National Conference of Charities and Correction,* 256–71. Twenty-fourth annual session, Toronto, 1897. Boston: George Ellis.

Henderson, Charles. 1909. *Industrial Insurance.* Chicago: University of Chicago Press.

Henderson, Rose. 1914. "Mothers' Pensions." In *Report of Addresses and Proceedings,* 109–15. Social Service Congress, Ottawa.

Hennock, E. Peter. 1976. "Poverty and Social Theory in England." *Social History* 1:67–91.

Hennock, E. Peter. 1981. "The Origins of British National Insurance and the German Precedent, 1880–1914." In *The Emergence of the Welfare State in Britain and Germany, 1850–1950,* edited by W. J. Mommsen, 84–106. London: Croom Helm.

Henripin, Jacques. 1972. *Trends and Factors of Fertility in Canada.* Ottawa: Statistics Canada.

Hering, Frank. 1923. "Awakening Interest in the Old Age Protection." *American Labor Legislation Review* 13:139–44.

Hernes, Helga. 1987. *Welfare State and Woman Power.* Oslo: Norwegian University Press.

Heron, Craig. 1984. "Labourism and the Canadian Working Class." *Labour/Le Travail* 13:45–76.

Hewitt, Christopher. 1977. "The Effect of Political Democracy and Social Democracy on Equality in Industrial Society: A Cross-National Comparison." *American Sociological Review* 42:450–64.

Himmelfarb, Gertrude. 1983. *The Idea of Poverty.* New York: Knopf.

Hobhouse, L. T. 1911. *Liberalism.* New York: Henry Holt.

Hobson, J. A. 1909. *The Crisis of Liberalism: New Issues of Democracy.* London: P. S. King and Son.

Hodgetts, J. E. 1973. *The Canadian Public Service?: A Physiology of Government.* Toronto: University of Toronto Press.

Hodgetts, J. E., William McCloskey, Reginald Whitaker, and V. Seymour Wilson. 1972. *The Biography of an Institution: The Civil Service Commission of Canada, 1908–1967.* Montreal: McGill-Queen's University Press.

Hoffman, Frederick. 1908. "The Problem of Poverty and Pensions in Old Age." In *Proceedings of the National Conference of Charities and Correction,* 219–32. Thirty-fifth annual session, Richmond, Va. Fort Wayne, Ind.: Fort Wayne Printing Co.

Hofstadter, Richard. 1955. *Social Darwinism in American Thought.* Boston: Beacon Press.

Holli, Melvin. 1969. *Reform in Detroit: Hazen S. Pingree and Urban Politics.* New York: Oxford University Press.

Holt, James. 1975. "The New Deal and the American Anti-Statist Tradition." In *The New Deal: The National Level,* edited by John Braeman, Robert Bremner, and David Brody, 27–49. Columbus: Ohio State University Press.

Holtzman, Abraham. 1963. *The Townsend Movement.* New York: Bookman Associates.

Hoogenboom, Ari. 1968. *Outlawing the Spoils: A History of the Civil Service Reform Movement.* Urbana: University of Illinois Press.

Horowitz, Gad. 1968. *Canadian Labour in Politics.* Toronto: University of Toronto Press.

Horowitz, Ruth. 1978. *Political Ideologies of Organized Labor.* New Brunswick, N.J.: Transaction Books.

Houghton, Walter E. 1957. *The Victorian Frame of Mind, 1830–70.* New Haven: Yale University Press.

Hunt, Lynn. 1984. *Politics, Culture, and Class in the French Revolution.* Berkeley: University of California Press.

Hunt, Lynn. 1989. *The New Cultural History.* Berkeley: University of California Press.

Huntington, Samuel. 1966. "Political Modernization: America and Europe." *World Politics* 18:378–414.

Huntington, Samuel. 1968. *Political Order in Changing Societies.* New Haven: Yale University Press.

Huthmacher, J. Joseph. 1968. *Senator Robert F. Wagner and the Rise of Urban Liberalism.* New York: Athenaeum.

Jackman, Robert W. 1975. *Politics and Social Equality: A Comparative Analysis.* New York: John Wiley.

Jamieson, Stuart. 1973. *Industrial Relations in Canada.* 2d ed. New York: St. Martin's.

Jenkins, J. Craig, and Barbara Brents. 1989. "Social Protest, Hegemonic Competition, and Social Reform: A Political Struggle Interpretation of the Origins of the American Welfare State." *American Sociological Review* 54:891–909.

Jennings, E. T. 1979. "Competition, Constituencies, and Welfare Policies in American States." *American Political Science Review* 73:414–29.

Jenson, Jane. 1986. "Gender and Reproduction; or, Babies and the State." *Studies in Political Economy* 20:9–45.

Jones, Andrew, and Leonard Rutman. 1981. *In the Children's Aid: J. J. Kelso and Child Welfare in Ontario.* Toronto: University of Toronto Press.

Jones, J. R. 1978. *Country and Court: England, 1658–1714.* Cambridge: Harvard University Press.

Jones, Peter D'Alroy. 1968. *The Christian Socialist Revival.* Princeton: Princeton University Press.

Katz, Michael. 1975. *The People of Hamilton, Canada West: Family and Class in a Mid–Nineteenth Century City.* Cambridge: Harvard University Press.

Katz, Michael. 1983. *Poverty and Policy in American History.* New York: Academic Press.

Katz, Michael. 1986. *In the Shadow of the Poor House.* New York: Basic Books.

Katz, Michael, Michael Doucet, and Mark Stern. 1982. *The Social Organization of Early Industrial Capitalism.* Cambridge: Harvard University Press.

Katznelson, Ira. 1981. *City Trenches.* Chicago: University of Chicago Press.

Katznelson, Ira. 1985. "Working-Class Formation and the State: Nineteenth-Century England in American Perspective." In *Bringing the State Back In,* edited by Peter Evans, Dietrich Rueschemeyer, and Theda Skocpol, 257–84. New York: Cambridge University Press.

Kealey, Gregory, and Bryan Palmer. 1982. *Dreaming of What Might Be.* Cambridge: Cambridge University Press.

Keller, John. 1899. "The Public Charities of New York." In *Proceedings of the National Conference of Charities and Correction,* 212–17. Boston: George Ellis.

Keller, Morton. 1977. *Affairs of State: Public Life in Nineteenth Century America.* Cambridge: Harvard University Press.

Keller, Morton. 1980. "Anglo-American Politics, 1900–1930, in Anglo-American Perspective: A Case Study in Comparative History." *Comparative Studies in Society and History* 22:458–77.

Kerr, Clark, John Dunlop, Frederick Harbison, and Charles Myers. 1964. *Industrialism and Industrial Man.* New York: Oxford University Press.

King, W. L. Mackenzie. 1918. *Industry and Humanity.* New York: Houghton Mifflin.

Klebaner, Benjamin. 1964. "Poverty and Relief in American Thought, 1815–1861." *Social Science Review* 38:382–99.

Klein, Ethel. 1940. *Civil Service in Public Welfare.* New York: Russell Sage.

Kleppner, Paul. 1979. *The Third Electoral System, 1853–1892: Parties, Voters and Political Cultures.* Chapel Hill: University of North Carolina Press.

Knott, J. R. 1986. *Popular Opposition to the 1834 Poor Law.* New York: St. Martin's.

Kobrin, Frances. 1983. "The Fall in Household Size and the Rise of the Primary Individual in the United States." In *The American Family in Social-Historical Perspective,* edited by Michael Gordon, 100–111. New York: St. Martin's.

Kohl, J. 1981. "Trends and Problems in Postwar Public Expenditure Development in Western Europe and North America." In *The Development of Welfare States in Europe and America,* edited by Peter Flora and Arnold Heidenheimer, 307–44. New Brunswick, N.J.: Transaction Books.

Korpi, Walter. 1978. *The Working Class in Welfare Capitalism.* London: Routledge.

Korpi, Walter. 1980. "Social Policy and Distributional Conflict in the Capitalist Democracies: A Preliminary Comparative Framework." *Western European Politics* 3:296–316.

Korpi, Walter. 1983. *The Democratic Class Struggle.* London: Routledge.

Korpi, Walter. 1989. "Power, Politics, and State Autonomy in the Development of Social Citizenship." *American Sociological Review* 54:309–28.

Korpi, Walter, and Michael Shalev. 1980. "Strikes, Power and Politics in the Western Nations, 1900–1976." *Political Power and Social Theory* 1:301–34.

Krasner, Stephen. 1978. "United States Commercial and Monetary Policy: Unravelling the Paradox of External Strength and Internal Weakness." In *Between Power and Plenty: Foreign Economic Policies of Advanced Industrial States,* edited by Peter Katzenstein, 51–88. Madison: University of Wisconsin Press.

Kudrle, Robert T., and Theodore R. Marmor. 1981. "The Development of Welfare States in North America." In *The Development of Welfare States in Europe and America,* edited by Peter Flora and Arnold Heidenheimer, 81–121. New Brunswick, N.J.: Transaction Books.

Lachmann, Richard. 1987. *From Manor to Market: Structural Change in England, 1536–1640.* Madison: University of Wisconsin Press.

Lachmann, Richard. 1989. "Elite Conflict and State Formation in 16th- and 17th-Century England and France." *American Sociological Review* 54:141–62.

Ladd, Everett C., and Charles Hadley. 1978. *Transformations of the American Party System.* New York: Norton.

Laslett, Peter. 1971. *The World We Have Lost.* 2d ed. London: Methuen.

Laslett, Peter. 1972. "Introduction: The History of the Family." In *Household and Family in Past Time,* edited by Peter Laslett, 1–90. Cambridge: Cambridge University Press.

Laslett, Peter. 1976. "Societal Development and Aging." In *Handbook of Aging and the Social Sciences,* edited by Robert Binstock and Ethel Shanas, 87–116. New York: Van Nostrand Reinhold.

Latimer, Murray. 1932a. *Industrial Pension Systems in the United States and Canada.* New York: Industrial Relations Counselors.

Latimer, Murray. 1932b. *Trade Union Pension Systems and Other Superannuation and Permanent and Total Disability Benefits in the United States and Canada.* New York: Industrial Relations Counselors.

Laurier, Sir Wilfrid. 1914. "Address of Welcome." In *Report of Addresses and Proceedings,* 8–9. Social Service Congress, Ottawa.

Laxer, Gordon. 1985. "The Political Economy of Aborted Development: The Canadian Case." In *The Structure of the Canadian Capitalist Class,* edited by Robert Brym, 67–102. Toronto: Garamond.

Laxer, Gordon. 1989. *Open for Business: The Roots of Foreign Ownership in Canada.* Toronto: Oxford University Press.

Leacy, F. H. 1983. *Historical Statistics of Canada.* 2d ed. Ottawa: Statistics Canada.

Leff, Mark. 1973. "Consensus for Reform: The Mothers'-Pension Movement in the Progressive Era." *Social Service Review* 47:397–417.

Leff, Mark. 1983. "Taxing the 'Forgotten Man': The Politics of Social Security Financing in the New Deal." *Journal of American History* 70:359–81.

Leman, Christopher. 1977. "Patterns of Policy-Development: Social Security in Canada and the United States." *Public Policy* 25:261–91.

Leman, Christopher. 1980. *The Collapse of Welfare Reform: Political Institutions, Policy, and the Poor in Canada and the United States.* Cambridge: MIT Press.

Lemons, J. Stanley. 1973. *The Woman Citizen: Social Feminism in the 1920's.* Urbana: University of Illinois Press.

Leotta, Louis. 1975. "Abraham Epstein and the Movement for Old Age Security." *Labor History* 16:359–78.

Lescohier, Don, and Elizabeth Brandeis. 1935. *History of Labor in the United States, 1896–1932.* Vol. 3. New York: Macmillan.

Levy, M. J. 1965. "Aspects of the Analysis of Family Structure." In *Aspects of the Analysis of Family Structure,* edited by A. J. Coale, L. A. Fallers, M. J. Levy, D. M. Schneider, and S. S. Tomkins, 1–63. Princeton: Princeton University Press.

Lieberson, Stanley. 1985. *Making It Count.* Berkeley: University of California Press.

Lieby, James. 1960. *Carroll Wright and Labor Reform.* Cambridge: Harvard University Press.

Lijphart, Arend. 1971. "Comparative Politics and the Comparative Method." *American Political Science Review* 65:682–93.

Lijphart, Arend. 1975. "The Comparable–Cases Strategy in Comparative Research." *Comparative Political Studies* 8:158–77.

Lindblom, Charles E. 1978. *Politics and Markets.* New York: Basic Books.

Lindsay, Samuel McCune. 1919. "Next Steps in Social Insurance in the United States." *American Labor Legislation Review* 9:107–14.

Linford, Alton A. 1949. *Old Age Assistance in Massachusetts.* Chicago: University of Chicago Press.

Lipset, Seymour Martin. 1970. *Revolution and Counter-Revolution.* Garden City, N.Y.: Anchor Books.

Lipset, Seymour Martin. 1976. "Radicalism in North America: A Comparative View of the Party Systems in Canada and the United States." *Transactions of the Royal Society of Canada,* 4th series, 14:19–55.

Lipset, Seymour Martin. 1979. *The First New Nation.* New York: Norton.

Lipset, Seymour Martin. 1983. "Socialism in America." In *Sidney Hook: Philosopher of Democracy and Humanism,* edited by Paul Kurtz, 47–63. Buffalo: Prometheus Books.

Lipset, Seymour Martin. 1985. "Canada and the United States: The Cultural Dimension." In *Canada and the United States,* edited by Charles Doran and John Sigler. Englewood Cliffs, N.J.: Prentice-Hall.

Lipton, Charles. 1967. *The Trade Union Movement of Canada, 1827–1959.* Montreal: Canadian Social Publications Limited.

Logan, Harold. 1928. *The History of Trade Union Organization in Canada.* Chicago: University of Chicago Press.

Longman, Phillip. 1987. *Born to Pay: The New Politics of Aging in America.* Boston: Houghton Mifflin.

Low, Seth. 1879. "The Problem of Pauperism in the Cities of Brooklyn and New York." In *Proceedings of the National Conference of Charities and Correction,* 200–210. Sixth annual meeting. Boston: NCCC by A. Williams.

Low, Seth. 1881. "Outdoor Relief in the United States." In *Proceedings of the National Conference of Charities and Correction,* 144–61. Eighth annual meeting. Boston: NCCC by A. Williams.

Lowi, Theodore. 1967. "Party, Policy, and Constitution in America." In *The American Party Systems,* edited by William Chambers and Walter Dean Burnham, 238–76. New York: Oxford University Press.

Lubbock, Gertrude. 1895. *Some Poor Relief Questions.* London: John Murray.

Lubenow, William. 1971. *The Politics of Government Growth: Early Victorian Attitudes toward State Intervention, 1833–1848.* Hamen, Conn.: Archon Books.

Lubove, Roy. 1968. *The Struggle for Social Security, 1900–1935.* Cambridge: Harvard University Press.

Lubove, Roy. [1965] 1973. *The Professional Altruist: The Emergence of Social Work as a Career, 1880–1930.* New York: Athenaeum.

McConnell, W. H. 1969. "The Genesis of the Canadian New Deal." *Journal of Canadian Studies* 4:31–41.

McCormick, Richard. 1966a. *The Second American Party System: Party Formation in the Jacksonian Era.* New York: Norton.

McCormick, Richard. 1966b. "Ethno-Cultural Interpretations of Nineteenth-Century American Voting Behavior." *Political Science Quarterly* 89:351–77.

McCormick, Richard. 1979. "The Party Period and Public Policy: An Exploratory Hypothesis." *Journal of American History* 66:279–98.

McGill, Barry. 1962. "Francis Schnadhorst and the Liberal Party Organization." *Journal of Modern History* 34:19–39.

McGregor, O. R. 1957. "Social Research and Social Policy in the Nineteenth Century." *British Journal of Sociology* 8:146–56.

Machar, Agnes. 1898. "Outdoor Relief in Canada." In *Proceedings of the National Conference of Charities and Correction,* 239–49. Twenty-fourth annual session, Toronto, 1897. Boston: George Ellis.

McInnis, Edgar. 1982. *Canada: A Political and Social History.* Toronto: Holt, Rinehart and Winston of Canada.

Mackenzie, F. 1920. "Old Age Insurance Legislation Now Up to the States." *American Labor Legislation Review* 10:254–55.

Mackenzie, M. A. 1908. "Old Age Pensions." *University of Toronto Monthly* 8:260–65.

MacKinnon, Mary. 1987. "English Poor Law Policy and the Crusade against Outrelief." *Journal of Economic History* 47:603–25.

McLean, Francis. 1901. "The Effects upon Private Charity of the Absence of All Public Relief." In *Proceedings of the National Conference of Charities and Correction,* 139–46. Thirtieth annual session, Washington, D.C. Boston: George Ellis.

McMurry, Donald M. 1922. "The Political Significance of the Pension Question, 1885–1897." *Mississippi Valley Historical Review* 9:19–36.

McNaught, Kenneth. 1959. *A Prophet in Politics: A Biography of James S. Woodsworth.* Toronto: University of Toronto Press.

McNaught, Kenneth. 1982. *The Pelican History of Canada.* Markham, Ont.: Penguin Books of Canada.

McQuaid, Kim. 1978. "Corporate Liberalism in the American Business Community." *Business History Review* 52:342–68.

McQuaid, Kim. 1979. "The Frustration of Corporate Revival during the Early New Deal." *The Historian* 41:682–704.

Magnusson, Warren. 1983. Introduction to *City Politics in Canada,* edited by Warren Magnusson and Andrew Sancton, 3–57. Toronto: University of Toronto Press.

Malloy, James. 1979. *The Politics of Social Security in Brazil.* Pittsburgh: University of Pittsburgh Press.

Mann, Arthur. 1956. "British Social Thought and American Reformers of the Progressive Era." *Mississippi Valley Historical Review* 42:672–92.

Mann, Michael. 1988. *States, War and Capitalism.* New York: Basil Blackwell.

Marsh, Leonard. 1940. *Canadians In and Out of Work.* Toronto: Oxford University Press.

Marshall, T. H. 1950. *Citizenship and Social Class.* Cambridge: Cambridge University Press.

Marshall, T. H. 1975. *Social Policy.* London: Hutchinson and Co.

Martin, Andrew. 1973. *The Politics of Economic Policy in the United States.* Beverly Hills: Sage.

Martin, E. W. 1972. "From Parish to Union: Poor Law Administration, 1601–1865." In *Comparative Development in Social Welfare,* edited by E. W. Martin, 25–56. London: George Allen and Unwin.

Martin, George. 1976. *Madame Secretary: Frances Perkins.* Boston: Houghton Mifflin.

Marwick, Arthur. 1967. "The Labour Party and the Welfare State in Britain, 1900–1948." *American Historical Review* 73:380–403.

Marx, Fritz Morstein. 1957. *The Administrative State.* Chicago: University of Chicago Press.

Mason, Alpheus. 1938. *The Brandeis Way.* Princeton: Princeton University Press.

Massachusetts Bureau of Statistics. 1916. *Report of a Special Inquiry Relating to Aged and Dependent Persons in Massachusetts.* Boston: Wright and Potter.

Massachusetts Commission on Old Age Pensions, Annuities and Insurance. 1910. *Report. Massachusetts House no. 1400.* Boston: Wright and Potter.

Massachusetts Commission on Pensions. 1925. *Report on Old Age Pensions.* Boston: Wright and Potter.

Massachusetts Commission on the Support of Dependent Minor Children of Widowed Mothers. 1913. *Report.* Boston: Wright and Potter.

Massachusetts Special Commission on Social Insurance. 1917. *Report. Massachusetts House no. 1850.* Boston: Wright and Potter.

Mavor, James. 1913. "Old Age Pensions." *University of Toronto Monthly* 14:275–85.

Maxwell, J. A. 1937. *Federal Subsidies to the Provincial Governments in Canada.* Harvard Economic Studies no. 56. Cambridge: Harvard University Press.

Mearns, Andrew. [1883] 1970. *The Bitter Cry of Outcast London,* edited by Anthony S. Wall. New York: Humanities Press.

Meeker, Royal. 1917. "The Relationship of Workmen's Compensation to Old Age, Health and Unemployment Insurance." *Bulletin of the U.S. Bureau of Labor Statistics,* no. 210, pp. 237–51.

Meisel, John. 1967. "Canadian Parties and Politics." In *Contemporary Canada,* edited by Richard Leach, 124–47. Durham, N.C.: Duke University Press.

Melling, J. 1979. "Industrial Strife and Business Welfare Philosophy." *Business History* 231:163–79.

Mencher, Samuel. 1967. *Poor Law to Poverty Program: Economic Security Policy in Britain and the United States.* Pittsburgh: University of Pittsburgh Press.

Mesa-Lago, Carmelo. 1978. *Social Security in Latin America.* Pittsburgh: University of Pittsburgh Press.

Michel, Sonya, and Seth Koven. 1990. "Womanly Duties: Maternalist Politics and the Origins of the Welfare State in France, Germany, Great Britain and the United States, 1880–1920." *American Historical Review* 95:1076–108.

Midwinter, E. C. 1972. "Victorian Social Provision: Central and Local Administration." In *Comparative Development in Social Welfare,* edited by E. W. Martin, 191–218. London: George Allen and Unwin.

Mill, John Stuart. [1881] 1950. *Philosophy of Scientific Method.* New York: Hafner.

Mishra, Ramesh. 1973. "Welfare and Industrial Man: A Study of Welfare in Western Industrial Societies in Relation to a Hypothesis of Convergence." *Sociological Review* 21:535–60.

Mishra, Ramesh. 1976. "Convergence Theory and Social Change: The Development of Welfare in Britain and the Soviet Union." *Comparative Studies in Society and History* 18:28–56.

Mishra, Ramesh. 1984. *The Welfare State in Crisis.* New York: St. Martin's.

Mitchell, B. R., and Phyllis Deane. 1962. *Abstract of British Historical Statistics.* Cambridge: Cambridge University Press.

Mitchell, H. 1928. "What Will Old Age Pensions Cost in Canada?" *Industrial Canada* 28:41–43.

Mitchell, Reid. 1988. *Civil War Soldiers: Their Expectations and Experiences.* New York: Viking.

Modell, John, and Tamara Hareven. 1973. "Urbanization and the Malleable Household: An Examination of Boarding and Lodging in American Families." *Journal of Marriage and the Family* 33:467–78.

Mohl, Raymond. 1973. "Three Centuries of American Public Welfare, 1600–1932." *Current History* 65:6–10, 38–39.

Mohl, Raymond. 1983. "The Abolition of Public Outdoor Relief, 1870–1900: A Critique of the Piven and Cloward Thesis." In *Social Welfare or Social Control?: Some*

Historical Reflections on Regulating the Poor, edited by Walter Trattner, 35–50. Knoxville: University of Tennessee Press.

Moore, Barrington. 1966. *Social Origins of Dictatorship and Democracy.* Boston: Beacon Press.

Morgan, Kenneth O. 1971. *The Age of Lloyd George.* New York: Barnes and Noble.

Morgan, Kenneth O. 1976. "The Future at Work: Anglo-American Progressivism, 1870–1917." In *Contrast and Connection: Bicentennial Essays in Anglo-American History,* edited by H. C. Allen and Roger Thompson, 245–71. Columbus: Ohio State University Press.

Morton, W. L. 1943. "The Extension of the Franchise in Canada." *Canadian Historical Association: Report of the Annual Meeting, with Historical Papers,* pp. 72–81.

Morton, W. L. 1950. *The Progressive Party in Canada.* Toronto: University of Toronto Press.

Morton, W. L. 1972. *The Canadian Identity.* Madison: University of Wisconsin Press.

Moses, Robert. 1914. *The Civil Service in Great Britain.* Studies in History, Economics, and Public Law, vol. 57, no. 1. New York: Columbia University; Longmans, Green and Co., agents.

Mowat, C. L. 1961. *The Charity Organization Society, 1869–1913.* London: Methuen.

Mowat, C. L. 1969. "Social Legislation in Britain and the United States in the Early Twentieth Century: A Problem in the History of Ideas." In *Historical Studies: Papers Read before the Irish Conference of Historians,* vol. 7, edited by J. C. Beckett, 81–96. New York: Barnes and Noble.

Mueller, Dennis. 1979. *Public Choice.* New York: Cambridge University Press.

Mueller, Hans-Eberhard. 1984. *Bureaucracy, Education and Monopoly.* Berkeley: University of California Press.

Munro, William Bennett. 1929. *American Influences on Canadian Government.* Toronto: Macmillan of Canada.

Murrin, J. A. 1980. "The Great Inversion; or, Court versus Country: A Comparison of the Revolution Settlements in England (1688–1721) and America (1776–1816)." In *Three British Revolutions, 1641, 1688, 1776,* edited by J. G. A. Pocock, 368–453. Princeton: Princeton University Press.

Myles, John. 1983. "Comparative Public Policies for the Elderly: Frameworks and Resources for Analysis." In *Old Age and the Welfare State,* edited by Anne-Marie Guillemard, 19–44. Beverly Hills: Sage.

Myles, John. 1984. *Old Age in the Welfare State.* Boston: Little, Brown and Co.

Myles, John. 1988. "Postwar Capitalism and the Extension of Social Security into a Retirement Wage." In *The Politics of Social Policy in the United States,* edited by M. Weir, A. Orloff, and T. Skocpol, 235–64. Princeton: Princeton University Press.

Namier, Sir Lewis. 1961. *The Structure of Politics at the Accession of George III.* 2d ed. New York: Macmillan.

Nash, Gerald. 1960. "The Influence of Labor on State Policy, 1860–1920." *California Historical Society Quarterly* 42:241–57.

Nassau, Mabel. 1915. *Old Age Poverty in Greenwich Village.* New York: Fleming H. Revell Co.

National Civic Federation. 1928. *Extent of Old Age Dependency.* New York: National Civic Federation.

National Civic Federation Industrial Welfare Department. 1929. *State Old Age Pensions: Constructive Proposals for Prevention and Relief of Destitution in Old Age*. New York: National Civic Federation.

National Conference of Charities and Correction. 1896, 1898, 1902, 1912, 1915, 1916. *Proceedings*.

National Conference on Charities and Correction Committee on Standards of Living and Labor. 1912. "Report." In *Proceedings of the National Conference of Charities and Correction*, 376–95. Thirty-ninth annual session, Cleveland. Fort Wayne, Ind.: Fort Wayne Printing Co.

National Industrial Conference Board. 1925. *Industrial Pensions in the United States*. New York: National Industrial Conference Board.

Neatby, H. Blair. 1963. *William Lyon Mackenzie King, 1924–1932: The Lonely Heights*. Toronto: University of Toronto Press.

Nelson, Daniel. 1969. *Unemployment Insurance: The American Experience, 1915–1935*. Madison: University of Wisconsin Press.

Nelson, Barbara. 1984. "Women's Poverty and Women's Citizenship: Some Political Consequences of Economic Marginality." *Signs* 10:209–31.

New York Commission on Old Age Security. 1930. *Old Age Security: Report of the New York Commission on Old Age Security*. Albany: J. B. Lyon.

Niskanen, William A. 1971. *Bureaucracy and Representative Government*. Chicago: Aldine, Atherton.

Nordlinger, Eric. 1981. *On the Autonomy of the Democratic State*. Cambridge: Harvard University Press.

North, Douglass. 1966. *Growth and Welfare in the American Past*. Englewood Cliffs, N.J.: Prentice-Hall.

Numbers, Ronald. 1978. *Almost Persuaded: American Physicians and Compulsory Health Insurance, 1912–1920*. Baltimore: Johns Hopkins University Press.

Numbers, Ronald. 1982. "The Specter of Socialized Medicine: American Physicians and Compulsory Health Insurance." In *Compulsory Health Insurance: The Continuing American Debate*, edited by Ronald Numbers, 3–24. Westport, Conn.: Greenwood Press.

O'Connor, James. 1973. *The Fiscal Crisis of the State*. New York: St. Martin's.

O'Connor, Julia. 1989. "Welfare Expenditure and Policy Orientation in Canada in Comparative Perspective." *Canadian Review of Sociology and Anthropology* 26:127–50.

Odum, Howard W. 1933. "Public Welfare Activities." In *Recent Social Trends in the United States*, edited by the President's Research Committee on Social Trends, 1224–73. New York: McGraw-Hill.

Offe, Claus. 1972. "Advanced Capitalism and the Welfare State." *Politics and Society* 2:479–88.

Offe, Claus. 1984. *The Contradictions of the Welfare State*. Cambridge: MIT Press.

Ogus, A. I. 1982. "Great Britain." In *The Evolution of Social Insurance, 1881–1981*, edited by Peter A. Kohler, Hans F. Zacher, and Martin Partington, 150–264. New York: St. Martin's.

Ohio Health and Old Age Insurance Commission. 1919. *Health, Health Insurance, Old Age Pensions: Report, Recommendations, Dissenting Opinions*. Columbus, Ohio: F. J. Heer Printing Co.

Okin, Susan Moeller. 1989. *Justice, Gender and the Family.* New York: Basic Books.

O'Leary, Cornelus. 1962. *The Elimination of Corrupt Practices in British Elections, 1868–1911.* London: Oxford University Press.

Olson, Laura Katz. 1982. *The Political Economy of Aging.* New York: Columbia University Press.

O'Reilly, J. Fanning. 1904. *The History of the Fraternal Order of Eagles.* New York: Schlesinger.

Orloff, Ann. 1985. "The Politics of Pensions: A Comparative Analysis of the Origins of Pensions and Old Age Insurance in Canada, Great Britain, and the United States, 1880s–1930s." Ph.D. diss., Princeton University.

Orloff, Ann. 1988. "The Political Origins of America's Belated Welfare State." In *The Politics of Social Policy in the United States,* edited by M. Weir, A. Orloff, and T. Skocpol, 37–80. Princeton: Princeton University Press.

Orloff, Ann. 1991. "Gender in Early U.S. Social Policy." *Journal of Policy History* 3:248–81.

Orloff, Ann, and Eric Parker. 1990. "Business and Social Policy in Canada and the United States, 1920–1940." In *Comparative Social Research,* vol. 12, edited by Craig Calhoun, 295–339. Greenwich, Conn.: JAI Press.

Orloff, Ann Shola, and Theda Skocpol. 1984. "Why Not Equal Protection?: Explaining the Politics of Public Social Spending in Britain, 1900–1911, and the United States, 1880s–1920." *American Sociological Review* 49:726–50.

Owram, Doug. 1986. *The Government Generation: Canadian Intellectuals and the State, 1900–1945.* Toronto: University of Toronto Press.

Ozanne, Robert. 1984. *The Labor Movement in Wisconsin: A History.* Madison: State Historical Society of Wisconsin.

Pal, L. A. 1986. "Relative Autonomy Revisited: The Origins of Canadian Unemployment Insurance." *Canadian Journal of Political Science* 19:71–92.

Pal, L. A. 1988. *State, Class, and Bureaucracy: Canadian Unemployment Insurance and Public Policy.* Montreal: McGill-Queen's University Press.

Pampel, Fred C., and John B. Williamson. 1985. "Age Structure, Politics and Cross-National Patterns of Public Pension Expenditures." *American Sociological Review* 50:782–99.

Parris, Henry. 1969. *Constitutional Bureaucracy: The Development of British Central Administration since the Eighteenth Century.* London: George Allen and Unwin.

Pascall, Gillian. 1986. *Social Policy: A Feminist Analysis.* New York: Tavistock.

Pateman, Carole. 1988. "The Patriarchal Welfare State." In *Democracy and the Welfare State,* edited by Amy Gutmann, 231–60. Princeton: Princeton University Press.

Patterson, James. 1981. *America's Struggle against Poverty, 1900–1980.* Cambridge: Harvard University Press.

Patterson, James T. 1969. *The New Deal and the States: Federalism in Transition.* Princeton: Princeton University Press.

Pedersen, Susan. 1989. "The Failure of Feminism in the Making of the British Welfare State." *Radical History Review* 43:86–110.

Pelling, Henry. 1968. "The Working Class and the Welfare State." Chap. 1 in *Popular Politics and Society in Late Victorian Britain.* New York: St. Martin's.

Pennsylvania Commission on Old Age Assistance. 1925. *Report.* Harrisburg, Pa.: L. I. Kuhn.

Pennsylvania Commission on Old Age Pensions. 1919, 1921. *Report.* Harrisburg, Pa.: L. I. Kuhn.

Perkins, Frances. 1962. Foreword to *The Development of the Social Security Act,* by Edwin Witte, v–ix. Madison: University of Wisconsin Press.

Perkins, Frances. [1946] 1964. *The Roosevelt I Knew.* New York: Viking.

Peters, Guy. 1972. "Economic and Political Effects of the Development of Social Expenditures in France, Sweden, and the United Kingdom." *Midwest Journal of Political Science* 16:225–38.

Phelps Brown, Henry, and Sheila V. Hopkins. 1981. *A Perspective of Wages and Prices.* London: Methuen.

Pierce, Lloyd. 1953. "The Activities of the AALL on Behalf of Social Security and Protective Labor Legislation." Ph.D. diss., University of Wisconsin–Madison.

Pietrusza, David. 1978. "New Deal Nemesis. *Reason* 9. 9:29–31.

Pitsula, James. 1979. "The Emergence of Social Work in Toronto." *Journal of Canadian Studies* 14:35–42.

Pitsula, James. 1980. "The Treatment of Tramps in Late Nineteenth-Century Toronto." *Canadian Historical Association, Historical Papers,* pp. 116–32.

Piven, Frances Fox. 1985. "Women and the State: Ideology, Power, and the Welfare State." In *Gender and the Life Course,* edited by Alice Rossi, 265–87. New York: Aldine.

Piven, Frances, and Richard Cloward. 1971. *Regulating the Poor.* New York: Vintage Books.

Piven, Frances, and Richard Cloward. 1979. *Poor People's Movements.* New York: Vintage Books.

Plumb, J. H. 1967. *The Origins of Political Stability: England, 1675–1725.* Boston: Houghton Mifflin.

Polanyi, Karl. 1944. *The Great Transformation.* Boston: Beacon Press.

Polenburg, R. 1966. *Reorganizing Roosevelt's Government: The Controversy over Executive Reorganization, 1936–1939.* Cambridge: Harvard University Press.

Porter, Kirk. 1918. *A History of Suffrage in the United States.* Chicago: University of Chicago Press.

Porter, Kirk H., and Donald B. Johnson, eds. 1970. *National Party Platforms.* 4th ed. Urbana: University of Illinois Press.

Pratt, John W. 1961. "Boss Tweed's Welfare Program." *New York Historical Society Quarterly* 45:396–411.

Preuss, Arthur. [1924] 1966. *A Dictionary of Secret and Other Societies.* Detroit: Gale Research Co.

Pryor, F. L. 1968. *Public Expenditure in Communist and Capitalist Nations.* London: George Allen and Unwin.

Putnam, Jackson. 1970. *Old Age Politics in California.* Stanford: Stanford University Press.

Quadagno, Jill. 1982. *Aging in Early Industrial Society: Work, Family and Social Policy in Nineteenth-Century England.* New York: Academic Press.

Quadagno, Jill. 1984. "Welfare Capitalism and the Social Security Act of 1935." *American Sociological Review* 49:632–47.

Quadagno, Jill. 1988a. *The Transformation of Old Age Security.* Chicago: University of Chicago Press.

Quadagno, Jill. 1988b. "From Old Age Assistance to Supplemental Security Income: The Political Economy of Relief in the South, 1935–1972." In *The Politics of Social Policy in the United States,* edited by M. Weir, A. Orloff, and T. Skocpol, 235–64. Princeton: Princeton University Press.

Quadagno, Jill, and Madonna Harrington Meyer. 1989. "Organized Labor, State Structures, and Social Policy Development: A Case Study of Old Age Assistance in Ohio, 1916–1940." *Social Problems* 36:181–96.

Qualter, Terence. 1970. *The Election Process in Canada.* Toronto: McGraw-Hill of Canada.

Radosh, Ronald, and Murray Rothbard, eds. 1972. *A New History of Leviathan: Essays on the Rise of the American Corporate State.* New York: Dutton.

Ragin, Charles. 1987. *The Comparative Method.* Berkeley: University of California Press.

Reed, Louis. 1930. *The Labor Philosophy of Samuel Gompers.* Columbia University Press.

Richards, Peter G. 1963. *Patronage in British Government.* Toronto: University of Toronto Press.

Richmond, Mary. 1917. *Social Diagnosis.* New York: Russell Sage.

Richmond, Mary. 1922. *What Is Social Case Work?* New York: Russell Sage.

Riis, Jacob. 1890. *How the Other Half Lives.* New York: Charles Scribner's Sons.

Rimlinger, Gaston. 1968. "Social Security and Industrialization: The Western Experience, with Possible Lessons for the Less Developed Nations." In *The Role of Social Security in Economic Development,* edited by Everett Kassalow, 129–53. U.S. Social Security Administration Research Report no. 27. Washington, D.C.: Government Printing Office.

Rimlinger, Gaston. 1971. *Welfare Policy and Industrialization in Europe, America and Russia.* New York: John Wiley.

Rimlinger, Gaston. 1982. "The Historical Analysis of National Welfare Systems." In *Explorations in the New Economic History,* edited by Roger Ransom, Richard Sutch, and Gary Walton, 149–67. New York: Academic Press.

Riordan, William L. 1905. *Plunkett of Tammany Hall.* New York: McClure, Phillips.

Ritter, Gerhard. 1986. *Social Welfare in Germany and Britain.* New York: Berg.

Roberts, David. 1960. *Victorian Origins of the Welfare State.* New Haven: Yale University Press.

Robin, Martin. 1968. *Radical Politics and Canadian Labour, 1880–1930.* Kingston, Ont.: Industrial Relations Centre, Queen's University.

Rogers, Frederick. [1913] 1973. *Labour, Life, and Literature.* Brighton, Eng.: Harvester Press.

Rogers, John. 1929. *The Elder Worker: Restricted Employment, Annuities, and Relief.* Bulletin no. 35, Kentucky Department of Labor.

Rogin, Michael. 1962. "Voluntarism: The Political Functions of an Antipolitical Doctrine." *Industrial and Labor Relations Review* 15:521–35.

Romasco, Albert U. 1965. *The Poverty of Abundance*. New York: Oxford University Press.

Roosevelt, Franklin D. 1938. "Addresses to the Advisory Council on Social Security" (November 14, 1934). In *The Public Papers and Addresses of Franklin D. Roosevelt*, vol. 3, edited by Samuel Rosenman. New York: Random House.

Rose, Michael. 1971. *The English Poor Law, 1780–1930*. New York: Barnes and Noble.

Rose, Michael. 1972. *The Relief of Poverty, 1834–1914*. London: Macmillan.

Rose, Michael. 1976. "Settlement, Removal and the New Poor Law." In *The New Poor Law in the Nineteenth Century*, edited by Derek Fraser, 25–44. London: Macmillan.

Rose, Michael. 1981. "The Crisis of Poor Relief in England, 1860–1890." In *The Emergence of the Welfare State in Britain and Germany, 1850–1950*, edited by W. J. Mommsen, 50–70. London: Croom Helm.

Rowntree, B. S. 1901. *Poverty: A Study of Town Life*. New York: Howard Fertig.

Rubinow, I. M. 1913. *Social Insurance: With Special Reference to American Conditions*. New York: Henry Holt.

Rubinow, I. M. 1934. *The Quest for Security*. New York: Henry Holt.

Rubinstein, David. 1973. Introduction to *Labour, Life, and Literature*, by Frederick Rogers, xi–xxxviii. Brighton, Eng.: Harvester Press.

Rudolf, Frederick. 1950. "The American Liberty League, 1934–1940." *American Historical Review* 56:19–33.

Ruggie, Mary. 1984. *The State and Working Women*. Princeton: Princeton University Press.

Ruggles, Steven. 1987. *Prolonged Connections: The Rise of the Extended Family in Nineteenth-Century England and America*. Madison: University of Wisconsin Press.

Ruggles, Steven, and Ron Goeken. 1990. "Race and Multigenerational Family Structure, 1900–1980: Preliminary Findings." Paper presented at the Albany Conference on Demographic Perspectives on the American Family: Patterns and Prospects.

Russell, A. K. 1973. *Liberal Landslide*. London: Newton Abbot.

Russell, Conrad, ed. 1973. *The Origins of the English Civil War*. New York: Harper and Row.

Rutherford, Paul, ed. 1974. *Saving the Canadian City*. Toronto: University of Toronto Press.

Rutherford, Paul. 1977. " 'Tomorrow's Metropolis': The Urban Reform Movement in Canada, 1880–1920." In *The Canadian City: Essays in Urban History*, edited by Gilbert Stelter and Alan Artibise, 368–92. Toronto: McClelland and Stewart.

Ryan, P. A. 1978. " 'Poplarism,' 1894–1930." In *The Origins of British Social Policy*, edited by Pat Thane, 56–83. Totowa, N.J.: Rowman and Littlefield.

Rys, Vladimir. 1964. "The Sociology of Social Security." *Bulletin of the International Social Security Association* 17:3–34.

Rys, Vladimir. 1966. "Comparative Studies of Social Security: Problems and Perspectives." *Bulletin of the International Social Security Association* 19:242–68.

Sanders, Heywood. 1980. "Paying for the 'Bloody Shirt': The Politics of Civil War Pensions." In *Political Benefits*, edited by Barry Rundquist, 137–59. Lexington, Mass.: Lexington Books.

Schafer, Robert J. 1974. *A Guide to Historical Method*. Homewood, Ill.: Dorsey Press.

Scharansky, Ira, and Richard Hofferbert. 1969. "Dimensions of State Politics, Economics and Public Policy." *American Political Science Review* 63:867–78.

Schiesl, Martin. 1977. *The Politics of Efficiency: Municipal Administration and Reform in America, 1880–1920.* Berkeley: University of California Press.

Schindeler, Fred. 1977. "The Prime Minister and the Cabinet: History and Development." In *Apex of Power: The Prime Minister and Political Leadership in Canada,* edited by Thomas Hockin, 22–47. Scarborough, Ont.: Prentice-Hall of Canada.

Schlabach, Theron. 1969. *Edwin E. Witte: Cautious Reformer.* Madison: State Historical Society of Wisconsin.

Schlesinger, Arthur M. 1957. *The Crisis of the Old Order, 1919–1933.* Boston: Houghton Mifflin.

Schlesinger, Arthur M. 1958. *The Coming of the New Deal.* Boston: Houghton Mifflin.

Schlesinger, Arthur M. 1960. *The Politics of Upheaval.* Boston: Houghton Mifflin.

Schlesselman, James. 1982. *Case Control Studies: Design, Conduct, Analysis.* New York: Oxford University Press.

Schmidt, Alvin. 1980. *Fraternal Organizations.* Westport, Conn.: Greenwood Press.

Schneider, K. S. 1982. "The Sequential Development of Social Programs in Eighteen Welfare States." *Comparative Social Research* 5:195–220.

Seager, Henry. 1910. *Social Insurance.* New York: Macmillan.

Searle, G. R. 1971. *The Quest for Efficiency.* Berkeley: University of California Press.

Sewell, William, Jr. 1985. "Ideologies and Social Revolution: Reflections on the French Case." *Journal of Modern History* 57:57–85.

Shade, William. 1974. " 'Revolutions Can Go Backwards': The American Civil War and the Problem of Political Development." *Social Science Quarterly* 55:753–67.

Shalev, Michael. 1983a. "Class Politics and the Western Welfare State." In *Social Policy Evaluation: Social and Political Perspectives,* edited by Shimon Spiro and E. Yuchtmann-Yaar, 27–50. New York: Academic Press.

Shalev, Michael. 1983b. "The Social Democratic Model and Beyond: Two Generations of Comparative Research on the Welfare State." *Comparative Social Research* 6:315–52.

Shalev, Michael, and Walter Korpi. 1980. "Working Class Mobilization and American Exceptionalism." *Economic and Industrial Democracy* 1:31–62.

Shanas, Ethel. 1979. "Social Myth as Hypothesis: The Case of the Family Relations of Old People." *Gerontologist* 19:1–19.

Shaver, Sheila. 1990. "Gender, Social Policy Regimes and the Welfare State." Paper presented at the annual meeting of the American Sociological Association, Washington, D.C.

Shef'er, Martin. 1977. "Party and Patronage: Germany, England and Italy." *Politics and Society* 7:403–51.

Shefter, Martin. 1978. "Party, Bureaucracy and Political Change in the United States." In *Political Parties: Development and Decay,* edited by Louis Maisel and Joseph Cooper, 211–65. Beverly Hills: Sage.

Shefter, Martin. 1983. "Regional Receptivity to Reform: The Legacy of the Progressive Era." *Political Science Quarterly* 98:459–83.

Shefter, Martin. 1986. "Trade Unions and Political Machines: The Organization and Disorganization of the American Working Class in the Late Nineteenth Century." In *Working-Class Formation: Nineteenth-Century Patterns in Western Europe and the*

United States, edited by Ira Katznelson and Aristide Zolberg, 197–276. Princeton: Princeton University Press.

Sherman, P. Tecumseh. 1923. *Old Age Pensions: Experience in Denmark, New Zealand, Australia, France and Great Britain.* New York: National Civic Federation.

Simey, T. S., and M. B. Simey. 1960. *Charles Booth, Social Scientist.* London: Oxford University Press.

Simpson, James. 1914. "The Extension of Social Justice." In *Report of Addresses and Proceedings,* 39–41. Social Service Congress, Ottawa.

Skelton, O. D. 1915. "Federal Finance." *Queen's Quarterly* 23:60–93.

Skinner, Quentin. 1969. "Meaning and Understanding in the History of Ideas." *History and Theory* 8:3–53.

Skocpol, Theda. 1979. *States and Social Revolutions.* New York: Cambridge University Press.

Skocpol, Theda. 1984. "Emerging Agendas and Recurrent Strategies in Historical Sociology." In *Vision and Method in Historical Sociology,* edited by Theda Skocpol, 356–91. New York: Cambridge University Press.

Skocpol, Theda. 1985a. "Cultural Idioms and Political Ideologies in the Revolutionary Reconstruction of State Power: A Rejoinder to Sewell." *Journal of Modern History* 57:87–96.

Skocpol, Theda. 1985b. "Bringing the State Back In: Strategies of Analysis in Current Research." In *Bringing the State Back In,* edited by P. B. Evans, D. Rueschemeyer, and T. Skocpol, 3–37. New York: Cambridge University Press.

Skocpol, Theda. 1990. "Sustainable Social Policy: Fighting Poverty without Poverty Programs." *American Prospect* (Summer):58–70.

Skocpol, Theda. Forthcoming. *Protecting Soldiers and Mothers.* Cambridge: Harvard University Press.

Skocpol, Theda, and Edwin Amenta. 1985. "Did Capitalists Shape Social Security." *American Sociological Review* 50:572–75.

Skocpol, Theda, and Edwin Amenta. 1986. "States and Social Policies." *Annual Review of Sociology* 12:131–57.

Skocpol, Theda, and John Ikenberry. 1983. "The Political Formation of the American Welfare State in Historical and Comparative Perspective." *Comparative Social Research* 6:87–148.

Skocpol, Theda, and Gretchen Ritter. 1991. "Gender and the Origins of Modern Social Policies in Britain and the United States." *Studies in American Political Development* 5 (Spring):36–93.

Skocpol, Theda, and Margaret Somers. 1980. "The Uses of Comparative History in Macrosocial Research." *Comparative Studies in Society and History* 22:174–97.

Skowronek, Stephen. 1982. *Building a New American State: The Expansion of National Administrative Capacities, 1877–1920.* New York: Cambridge University Press.

Smalley, Eugene. 1884. "The United States Pension Office." *Century Magazine* 28:427.

Smellie, K. B. 1950. *A Hundred Years of English Government.* 2d ed. London: Duckworth and Co.

Smith, Alan. 1967. *The Government of Elizabethan England.* New York: Norton.

Smith, Daniel Scott. 1979. "Life Course, Norms, and the Family System of Older Americans in 1900." *Journal of Family History* 4:285–98.

Smith, Daniel Scott. 1982. "Historical Change in the Household Structure of the Elderly in Economically Developed Societies." In *Old Age in Preindustrial Society*, edited by Peter Stearns, 248–73. New York: Holmes and Meier.

Social Service Council of Canada. 1914. *Report of Addresses and Proceedings*. Social Service Congress, Ottawa. Toronto: Social Service Council of Canada.

Social Welfare. 1919. "Our Principles and Program." 1:120.

Soldo, Beth. 1981. "The Living Arrangements of the Elderly in the Near Future." In *Aging: Social Change*, edited by Sara Kiesler, James Morgan, and Valerie K. Oppenheimer, 491–512. New York: Academic Press.

Sozialgeschichtliches Arbeitsbuch. 1978. Buch II. Munich: Verlag C. H. Beck.

Spiesman, Stephen. 1973. "Munificent Parsons and Municipal Parsimony." *Ontario History* 65:33–49.

Splane, Richard. 1973. *Social Welfare in Ontario, 1791–1893*. Toronto: University of Toronto Press.

Sproat, John. 1982. *"The Best Men": Liberal Reformers in the Guilded Age*. Chicago: University of Chicago Press.

Squier, Lee Welling. 1912. *Old Age Dependency in the United States*. New York: Macmillan.

Starr, Paul. 1982. *The Social Transformation of American Medicine*. New York: Basic Books.

Stead, Francis Herbert. 1910. *How Old Age Pensions Began to Be*. London: n.p.

Stearns, Peter. 1982. Introduction to *Old Age in Preindustrial Society*, edited by Peter Stearns, 1–18. New York: Holmes and Meier.

Steinmetz, George. 1987. "Social Policy and the Local State: A Study of Municipal Public Assistance, Unemployment Relief, and Social Democracy in Germany, 1871–1914." Ph.D. diss., University of Wisconsin–Madison.

Stepan, Alfred. 1985. "State Power and the Strength of Civil Society in the Southern Cone of Latin America." In *Bringing the State Back In*, edited by P. B. Evans, D. Rueschemeyer, and T. Skocpol, 317–46. Cambridge: Cambridge University Press.

Stephens, John D. 1979. *The Transition from Capitalism to Socialism*. London: Macmillan.

Stevens, Alfred. [1907] 1966. *Cyclopedia of Fraternities*. Detroit: Gale Research Co.

Stewart, Gordon. 1986. *The Origins of Canadian Politics*. Vancouver: University of British Columbia Press.

Stone, Lawrence. 1972. *The Causes of the English Revolution, 1529–1642*. New York: Harper and Row.

Stone, Lawrence. 1977. "Walking over Grandma." *New York Review of Books*, May 12, 1977, pp. 10–16.

Stone, Lawrence. 1984. "The New Eighteenth Century." *New York Review of Books*, March 29, 1984, pp. 42–47.

Stone, Lawrence, and Jean F. Stone. 1984. *An Open Elite? England, 1540–1880*. New York: Oxford University Press.

Stone, Robyn. 1989. "The Feminization of Poverty among the Elderly." *Women's Studies Quarterly* 17:20–34.

Strong, Margaret. 1930. *Public Welfare Administration in Canada*. Chicago: University of Chicago Press.

Strong-Boag, Victoria. 1979. " 'Wages for Housework': Mothers' Allowances and the Beginnings of Social Security in Canada." *Journal of Canadian Studies* 14:24–34.
Strong-Boag, Victoria. 1988. *The New Day Recalled*. Toronto: Copp Clark Pittman.
Struthers, James. 1983. *No Fault of Their Own: Unemployment and the Canadian Welfare State, 1914–1941*. Toronto: University of Toronto Press.
Struthers, James. 1987. "A Profession in Crisis: Charlotte Whitton and Canadian Social Work in the 1930's." In *The "Benevolent State": The Growth of Welfare in Canada*, edited by Allan Moscovitch and Jim Albert, 111–25. Toronto: Garamond.
The Survey. 1918. "Labor Getting behind Health Insurance." 39:708–9.
Sutton, John. 1991. "The Political Economy of Madness: The Expansion of the Asylum in Progressive America." *American Sociological Review* 56:665–78.
Sweet, Jim, and Larry Bumpass. 1987. *American Families and Households*. New York: Russell Sage.
Taft, Phillip. 1964. *Organized Labor in American History*. New York: Harper and Row.
Taft, Phillip. 1968. *Labor Politics, American Style: The California State Federation of Labor*. Cambridge: Harvard University Press.
Taira, Koji, and Peter Kilby. 1969. "Differences in Social Security Development in Selected Countries." *International Social Security Review* 22:139–53.
Thane, Patricia, ed. 1978. *The Origins of British Social Policy*. Totowa, N.J.: Rowman and Littlefield.
Thane, Patricia. 1984. "The Working Class and State 'Welfare' in Britain, 1880–1914." *Historical Journal* 27:877–900.
Thompson, E. P. 1978. *The Poverty of Theory*. New York: Monthly Review Press.
Thomson, David. 1983. "Workhouse to Nursing Home: Residential Care of the Elderly People in England since 1840." *Aging and Society* 3:43–69.
Thomson, David. 1984a. "The Decline of Social Welfare: Falling State Support for the Elderly since Early Victorian Times." *Aging and Society* 4:451–82.
Thomson, David. 1984b. " 'I Am Not My Father's Keeper': Families and the Elderly in Nineteenth Century England." *Law and History Review* 2:265–86.
Thomson, David. 1986. "Welfare and Historians." In *The World We Have Gained*, edited by L. Bonfield, R. Smith, and K. Wrightson, 355–78. New York: Basil Blackwell.
Thomson, David. 1990. "Public/Private Relations and the Welfare of the Elderly, 1870–1930: Entering a New Age or Reshuffling Some Old Options?" Paper presented at a meeting: Public/Private Relations in the Shaping of Social Welfare in Great Britain, Germany, and the United States, Bad Homburg, West Germany.
Tilly, Charles. 1975. *The Formation of National States in Western Europe*. Princeton: Princeton University Press.
Tilly, Charles. 1981. *As Sociology Meets History*. New York: Academic Press.
Tilly, Charles. 1984. *Big Structures, Large Processes, and Huge Comparisons*. New York: Russell Sage.
Tilly, Charles. 1985. "War-Making and State-Making as Organized Crime." In *Bringing the State Back In*, edited by P. B. Evans, D. Rueschemeyer, and T. Skocpol, 169–91. Cambridge: Cambridge University Press.
Tilly, Charles. 1990. *Coercion, Capital, and European States*. Cambridge, Mass.: Basil Blackwell.

Tilly, Charles, Louise Tilly, and Richard Tilly. 1975. *The Rebellious Century*. Cambridge: Harvard University Press.

Tishler, H. C. 1971. *Self-Reliance and Social Security, 1870–1917*. Port Washington, N.Y.: Kennikat Press.

Titmuss, R. 1958. "War and Social Policy." In *Essays on the Welfare State*, 75–87. London: George Allen and Unwin.

Trattner, Walter. 1979. *From Poor Law to Welfare State: A History of Social Welfare in America*. 2d ed. New York: Free Press.

Traves, Tom. 1979. *The State and Enterprise*. Toronto: University of Toronto Press.

Treble, James H. 1970. "The Attitudes of Friendly Societies towards the Movement in Great Britain for State Pensions." *International Review of Social History* 15:266–99.

Treble, James H. 1979. *Urban Poverty in Britain, 1830–1914*. London: Batsford Academic.

Tucker, H. J., and E. B. Herzik. 1986. "The Persisting Problem of Region in American State Policy Research." *Social Science Quarterly* 67:84–97.

Uhlenberg, Peter. 1978. "Changing Configurations of the Life Course." In *Transitions: The Family and the Life Course in Historical Perspective*, edited by Tamara Hareven, 65–98. New York: Academic Press.

Underhill, Frank. [1929] 1933. "O Canada." In *Constitutional Issues in Canada*, edited by Robert Dawson, 378–79. London: Oxford University Press.

Underhill, Frank. [1949] 1960. *In Search of Canadian Liberalism*. Toronto: Macmillan of Canada.

United States Bureau of Labor Statistics. 1929. *Handbook of Labor Statistics, 1929*. Washington, D.C.: Government Printing Office.

United States Bureau of Pensions. 1911. *Report, 1910*. Washington, D.C.: Government Printing Office.

United States Bureau of Pensions. 1925. *Synopsis of Pension Laws of the United States*. Washington, D.C.: Government Printing Office.

United States Bureau of Statistics. 1911. *Statistical Abstract of the United States, 1910*. Washington, D.C.: Government Printing Office.

United States Bureau of Statistics. 1912. *Statistical Abstract of the United States, 1911*. Washington, D.C.: Government Printing Office.

United States Bureau of the Census. 1925. *Paupers in Almshouses, 1923*. Washington, D.C.: Government Printing Office.

United States Bureau of the Census. 1960. *Historical Statistics of the United States*. Washington, D.C.: Government Printing Office.

United States Bureau of the Census. 1966. *Long Term Economic Growth, 1860–1965*. Washington, D.C.: Government Printing Office.

United States Bureau of the Census. 1975. *Historical Statistics of the United States*. Washington, D.C.: Government Printing Office.

United States Committee on Economic Security. [1935] 1985. *Report*. Washington, D.C.: National Conference on Social Welfare.

United States Department of Commerce. 1916. *Statistical Abstract of the United States, 1915*. Washington, D.C.: Government Printing Office.

United States Social Security Board. 1937. *Social Security in America: The Factual Background of the Social Security Act as Summarized from Staff Reports to the Com-*

mittee on Economic Security. Washington, D.C.: Government Printing Office.

United States Social Security Board. 1940. *Social Security Yearbook for the Calendar Year 1939.* Washington, D.C.: Social Security Board.

Useem, Michael. 1986. *The Inner Circle.* New York: Oxford University Press.

Van Doren, Durand. 1918. *Workmen's Compensation.* New York: Moffat, Yard and Co.

Van Loon, Richard, and Michael Whittington. 1971. *The Canadian Political System.* Toronto: McGraw-Hill of Canada.

Van Riper, Paul. 1958. *The History of the United States Civil Service.* Evanston, Ill.: Row, Peterson.

Vinovskis, Maris. 1989. "Have Social Historians Lost the Civil War?: Some Preliminary Demographic Speculations." *Journal of American History* 76:34–58.

Walker, Jack. 1969. "The Diffusion of Innovations among the American States." *American Political Science Review* 63:880–99.

Wall, Richard. 1983. "The Household: Demographic and Economic Change in England, 1650–1970." In *Family Forms in Historic Europe,* by Richard Wall, J. Robin, and P. Laslett, 493–512. Cambridge: Cambridge University Press.

Wall, Richard. 1986. "Work, Welfare, and the Family: An Illustration of the Adaptive Family Economy." In *The World We Have Gained,* edited by L. Bonfield, R. Smith, and K. Wrightson, 261–94. New York: Basil Blackwell.

Wallace, Elizabeth. 1950a. "The Changing Canadian State: A Study of the Changing Conception of the State as Revealed in Canadian Social Legislation, 1867–1948." Ph.D. diss., Columbia University.

Wallace, Elizabeth. 1950b. "The Origin of the Social Welfare State in Canada, 1867–1900." *Canadian Journal of Economics and Political Science* 16:383–93.

Wallace, Elizabeth. 1952. "Old Age Security in Canada." *Canadian Journal of Economics and Political Science* 18:125–34.

Ward, Norman. 1950. *The Canadian House of Commons.* Toronto: University of Toronto Press.

Ward, Peter W. 1990. *Courtship, Love and Marriage in Nineteenth-Century English Canada.* Montreal: McGill-Queen's University Press.

Watkins, Susan Cotts, Jane A. Menken, and John Bongaarts. 1987. "Demographic Foundations of Family Change." *American Sociological Review* 52:346–58.

Weaver, Carolyn. 1982. *The Crisis in Social Security: Economic and Political Origins.* Durham, N.C.: Duke University Press.

Weaver, John C. 1977a. "Order and Efficiency: Samuel Morley Wickett and the Urban Progressive Movement in Toronto, 1900–1915." *Ontario History* 69:218–34.

Weaver, John C. 1977b. *Shaping the Canadian City: Essays on Urban Politics and Policy, 1890–1920.* Toronto: Institute of Public Administration.

Webb, R. K. 1974. *Modern England: From the 18th Century to the Present.* New York: Dodd, Mead and Co.

Webb, Sidney, and Beatrice Webb. 1910. *English Poor Law Policy.* London: Longmans, Green and Co.

Weed, Frank J. 1979. "Industrialization and Welfare Systems: A Critical Evaluation of the Convergence Hypothesis." *International Journal of Comparative Sociology* 20:282–92.

Weiler, N. Sue. 1986. "Family Security or Social Security?: The Family and the Elderly in New York State during the 1920's." *Journal of Family History* 11:77–95.

Weinstein, James. 1968. *The Corporate Ideal in the Liberal State*. Boston: Beacon.

Weinstein, James. 1974. "The Problems of the Socialist Party before World War One." In *Failure of a Dream?* edited by John Laslett and Seymour Martin Lipset, 300–340. Garden City, N.Y.: Anchor Books.

Weir, Margaret. 1988. "The Federal Government and Unemployment: The Frustration of Policy Innovation from the New Deal to the Great Society." In *The Politics of Social Policy in the United States,* edited by M. Weir, A. Orloff, and T. Skocpol, 149–90. Princeton: Princeton University Press.

Weir, Margaret, Ann Shola Orloff, and Theda Skocpol, eds. 1988. *The Politics of Social Policy in the United States*. Princeton: Princeton University Press.

Weir, Margaret, and Theda Skocpol. 1985. "State Structures and the Possibilities for 'Keynesian' Responses to the Great Depression in Sweden, Britain, and the United States." In *Bringing the State Back In,* edited by P. B. Evans, D. Rueschemeyer, and T. Skocpol, 107–63. Cambridge: Cambridge University Press.

Weiss, Nancy J. 1983. *Farewell to the Party of Lincoln: Black Politics in the Age of FDR*. Princeton: Princeton University Press.

Wells, Robert. 1982. *Revolutions in Americans' Lives: A Demographic Perspective on the History of Americans, Their Families, and Their Society*. Westport, Conn.: Greenwood Press.

Whitaker, Reginald. 1977a. "The Liberal Corporatist Ideas of Mackenzie King." *Labour/Le Travailleur* 2:137–69.

Whitaker, Reginald. 1977b. "Images of the State in Canada." In *The Canadian State: Political Economy and Political Power,* edited by Leo Panitch, 28–69. Toronto: University of Toronto Press.

Whitaker, Reginald. 1987. "Between Patronage and Bureaucracy: Democratic Politics in Transition." *Journal of Canadian Studies* 22:55–71.

White, Leonard. 1933. "Public Administration." In *Recent Social Trends in the United States,* 2 vols., 1391–429. Report of the President's Research Committee on Social Trends. New York: McGraw-Hill.

White, Leonard. 1935. "The British Civil Service." In *The Civil Service Abroad: Great Britain, Canada, France, Germany,* by Leonard D. White, Charles H. Bland, Walter R. Sharp, and Fritz Morstein Marx, 1–54. New York: McGraw-Hill.

White, Leonard. 1951. *The Jeffersonians: A Study in Administrative History, 1801–1829*. New York: Macmillan.

White, Leonard. 1954. *The Jacksonians: A Study in Administrative History, 1829–1860*. New York: Macmillan.

White, Leonard. 1958. *The Republican Era: A Study in Administrative History, 1869–1901*. New York: Free Press.

Whittlesey, Sarah. 1901. "Massachusetts Labor Legislation: An Historical and Critical Study." *Supplement to the Annals of the Academy of Political and Social Science* 17.

Wiebe, Robert. 1967. *The Search for Order, 1877–1920*. New York: Hill and Wang.

Wilensky, Harold. 1975. *The Welfare State and Equality: Structural and Ideological Roots of Public Expenditures*. Berkeley: University of California Press.

Wilensky, Harold. 1976. *The "New Corporatism": Centralization and the Welfare State*. Beverly Hills: Sage.

Wilensky, Harold. 1981. "Leftism, Catholicism, and Democratic Corporatism: The Role of Political Parties in Recent Welfare State Development." In *The Development of Welfare States in Europe and America,* edited by Peter Flora and Arnold Heidenheimer, 345–82. New Brunswick, N.J.: Transaction Books.

Wilensky, Harold, and Charles Lebeaux. 1965. *Industrial Society and Social Welfare.* Enlarged paperback ed. New York: Free Press.

Williams, Karel. 1981. *From Pauperism to Poverty.* Boston: Routledge.

Williams, Patricia [later Patricia Thane]. 1970. "The Development of Old Age Pensions Policy in Great Britain, 1878–1925." Ph.D. diss., London School of Economics.

Williamson, Chilton. 1960. *American Suffrage from Property to Democracy, 1760–1860.* Princeton: Princeton University Press.

Williamson, John B., Linda Evans, Lawrence Powell, and Sharlene Hesse-Biber. 1982. *The Politics of Aging: Power and Policy.* Springfield, Ill.: Charles C. Thomas.

Williamson, John B., and J. Weiss. 1979. "Egalitarian Political Movements, Social Welfare Effort and Convergence Theory: A Cross-National Analysis." *Comparative Social Research* 2:289–302.

Willoughby, William. 1898. *Workingmen's Insurance.* New York: Thomas Y. Crowell Co.

Wilson, Joan Hoff. 1975. *Herbert Hoover: Forgotten Progressive.* Boston: Little, Brown and Co.

Wisconsin Industrial Commission. 1915. *Report on Old Age Relief.* Madison: n.p.

Wisner, Elisabeth. 1970. *Social Welfare in the South: From Colonial Times to the Present.* Baton Rouge: Louisiana State University Press.

Witte, Edwin E. 1961. "Organized Labor and Social Security." In *Labor and the New Deal,* edited by Milton Derber and Edwin Young, 241–74. Madison: University of Wisconsin Press.

Witte, Edwin E. 1962. *The Development of the Social Security Act.* Madison: University of Wisconsin Press.

Wolfskill, George, and John Hudson. 1969. *All but the People: Franklin D. Roosevelt and His Critics, 1933–39.* London: Macmillan.

Woodward, C. Vann. 1960. "The Age of Reinterpretation." *American Historical Review* 66:1–19.

Wuthnow, Robert. 1987. *Meaning and Moral Order.* Berkeley: University of California Press.

Yellowitz, Irwin. 1965. *Labor and the Progressive Movement in New York State, 1897–1916.* Ithaca, N.Y.: Cornell University Press.

Yeo, S. 1979. "Working-Class Association, Private Capital, Welfare and the State in the Late-Nineteenth and Twentieth Centuries." In *Social Work, Welfare and the State,* 48–71. London: Edward Arnold.

Young, Walter D. 1978. *Democracy and Discontent.* 2d ed. Toronto: McGraw-Hill Ryerson.

Zimmerman, Joseph. 1981. *The Government and Politics of New York State.* New York: New York University Press.

Index

Aberdeen administration, 201
Able-bodied poor: under new poor law, 91–
  92n17, 122–27 passim, 130, 154, 205. See
  also Poor relief
Absolutism, 194, 195, 196, 219, 305
Acadia, 243
Achenbaum, Andrew, 100n2
Adams, Charles Francis: on Civil War Pen-
  sions, 235
Administrative capacities. See State—Capaci-
  ties
Administrative Reform Association (Great
  Britain), 201–2
Afro-Americans: rates of marriage of, 104;
  Civil War pensions and, 137; citizenship
  rights of, 175; excluded from social security
  coverage, 294; isolated in contemporary
  U.S. social provision, 307, 309
Age: considered a disability, 100–102, 135
Aged: as political force, 47, 49–50; redefined
  as "deserving poor," 167, 169, 171–74,
  175–76, 208; high proportion of, voting,
  285. See also Population aging
—Economic situation of: dependence on
  families, 47–49, 103–21 passim, 128–34
  passim, 143, 147–51 passim, 176, 177, 178;
  labor force participation rates of, 97–98; assets and income of, 102–3, 109, 118–19n8,
  147–48
—Institutionalization of: 48, 103–4, 107, 109,
  112–13, 132, 139–40, 145, 146, 149–50;
  proportions institutionalized, U.S., Britain,
  Canada compared, 109, 145, 149–50; emphasized in campaign against outdoor relief,
  130, 131–32, 134; in poorhouses in Great
  Britain, 132, 139–40, 205, 207, 208, 212;

in poorhouses in U.S., 127, 134, 254–55; in
  poorhouses in Canada, 128, 254–55, 262;
  in mental institutions in U.S., 134, 141–
  42, 144, 150; gender differences, 139–40,
  149–50. See also Poor relief; Poorhouses
—Living arrangements: childless, 48, 104,
  106, 111–13, 112n5, 146; never-married,
  48, 104, 108–13 passim; widowed, 48,
  96, 98, 104, 105, 110–11, 115, 123, 128,
  137, 147, 151; described, 96–97, 104–20;
  gender differences in, 109–11, 116; in U.S.,
  Great Britain, Canada, compared, 113–14;
  household headship among, 97, 104–14
  passim; black and white rates of remaining
  single, compared, 104; living alone, 104–5,
  105n3, 107, 108, 117–18; gender differences
  in household headship, 109–11; single aged
  taken in by kin, 116–17, 147
—Poor relief and: 3–4, 7–9, 10, 121–34,
  138–51 passim; proportions receiving,
  127, 139–40, 145, 146; in Great Britain,
  127, 139–40, 193, 208–13 passim; in the
  U.S., 127, 145, 146, 215, 230, 279, 291–
  92; in Canada, 240, 254–55, 259, 262.
  See also Canada; Great Britain; Poor relief;
  Poorhouses; United States
Aged dependency, 138, 170–72, 204, 254,
  258, 273, 278, 284, 290. See also Poor
  relief; Poorhouses
Aged poor: debates on provision for, 14, 152,
  165–66, 167, 181; jailed as vagrants in
  Canada, 133, 254; U.S. and British studies
  of, 138–48 passim, 182, 208; Local Government Board (Britain) circulars on treatment
  of, 139, 208; Royal Commission on the
  Aged Poor (Britain) on, 140; labor politi-

351